Ethical Artificial Intelligence in the Insurance Industry

Balancing Efficiency, Fairness, and Risk

Wasswa Shafik
School of Digital Science
Universiti Brunei Darussalam
Jalan Tungku Link, Brunei Darussalam

CRC Press
Taylor & Francis Group
Boca Raton London New York

CRC Press is an imprint of the
Taylor & Francis Group, an **informa** business
A SCIENCE PUBLISHERS BOOK

First edition published 2027
by CRC Press
2385 NW Executive Center Drive, Suite 320, Boca Raton FL 33431

and by CRC Press
4 Park Square, Milton Park, Abingdon, Oxon, OX14 4RN

CRC Press is an imprint of Taylor & Francis Group, LLC

Library of Congress Cataloging-in-Publication Data (applied for)

ISBN: 978-1-041-23688-7 (hbk)
ISBN: 978-1-041-25647-2 (pbk)
ISBN: 978-1-003-74765-9 (ebk)

DOI: 10.1201/9781003747659

Typeset in Times New Roman
by Prime Publishing Services

Dedication

This book is dedicated to my family, whose unconditional love, sacrifices, and unwavering belief in my potential have been the foundation of all my achievements. Their tireless support and encouragement throughout this book-writing journey have inspired me to strive for excellence and persevere in the face of every challenge.

I also dedicate this work to my friends, whose patience, understanding, and constant motivation have been my anchor through the highs and lows of this book journey. Your presence gave me strength during the most difficult times, and your faith in me kept me going when I doubted myself.

To my mentors, lecturers, and teachers throughout this journey, thank you for shaping my intellectual path and for your invaluable guidance over the years. Your wisdom and dedication to knowledge have not only informed this book but have also profoundly influenced the way I think, work, and aspire.

To all individuals with any form of disability and marginalized groups, the poor people across the globe who fight to earn a living, and who wish to make it in life, but the conditions fail them, and to those who cultivate life with limited recognition but limitless passion, the seed savers and soil stewards the world forgot, but who never forgot the land.

Finally, I would like to thank everyone who contributed to this journey and made this dissertation possible. I dedicate this book to all aspiring researchers who dare to explore, question, and create. May this book serve as a small contribution to the collective pursuit of knowledge and as an encouragement never to stop learning.

Preface

The emergence of artificial intelligence (AI) presents insurance stakeholders with new opportunities for value creation and capture. Yet speed, complexity, and cost advantages are not without peril. An objective, evidence-based analysis reveals that factors influencing efficiency imperatives are driven by AI but understood less thoroughly. These include the automated underwriting of risk and claims processing, personalization at scale, and heightened operational risk. Absent caution, such forces risk harm, injustice, or the compromise of other ethical goals. Moreover, mechanisms for scoring, assessing, and mitigating risk remain underdeveloped. The field's fundamental ethical principles, beneficence, non-maleficence, justice, autonomy, and transparency, can and must be mapped to explore these challenges. Honing in on dimensions of efficiency more directly impacted by AI clarifies the assessment of fairness and nondiscrimination across the technology's social and legal realms. Whereas technical fairness accounts for dimensionally extensive patterns of proxy discrimination, the legal dimension prioritizes fair pricing and access to coverage, with equity across premium schedules and signals serving vulnerable groups as points of concern. Formal transparency, interpretability, and explainability emerge as preconditions for a division of labor that preserves accountability in human-in-the-loop systems.

AI introduces a host of new ethical questions for insurance; these ethical goals and the trade-offs between them must be identified first. Enormous amounts of money, expertise, and effort are being devoted to the development of AI in insurance. Efficiency imperatives driven by this technology have consequences for consumers and society, and a look at these repercussions must follow. The principal ethical issue for AI is fairness, the prospect that these technologies will discriminate against some groups, so fairness and nondiscrimination considerations form the next stage of the analysis. The demand for risk management and accountability comes next, as must privacy and data governance. Thus, the question of augmentation versus automation needs resolution. AI encompasses narrow machine learning, deep learning, imaging analysis, natural language processing, reward-modelling reinforcement learning, and game play; it automates or augments cognitive tasks that typically require intelligence, such as understanding the meaning of text; building predictive models; detecting objects in visual imagery; crunching numbers; creating novel images; producing coherent structured text; and playing games. AI is ethical if it maximizes benefits and minimizes harm. Within the context of fair pricing, AI is fair if it does not discriminate on the basis of irrelevant characteristics. Distinctions can be drawn between technical fairness requirements (applying to the operation of algorithms), legal fairness requirements (in accordance with legislation such as the Equal Credit Opportunity Act), and social fairness requirements (expressing societal values). The analysis encompasses AI applications in underwriting, risk scoring, and claims processing, but not chatbots. These are AI-enabled systems that communicate with customers, typically via social media, email, or text; such communication may indeed affect customer experience, but models deployed behind the scenes determine demand, supply, pricing, and service delivery.

The automation of underwriting, fraud detection, and claims processing is among the areas that are anticipated to be radically transformed. Efficiency gains in these areas can either lower insurance premiums or increase semi-elasticity of premium demand, stabilizing the insurance sector and promoting broader financial stability. Beyond automation, AI has the potential to improve insurance product design and allow for extensive personalization of insurance products and pricing. In such a fast-moving sector, it is critical to identify, consider, and mitigate unwanted side effects of these speed gains. These can include increased operational risk within firms, the possible emergence of new winners and losers among customers, higher volatility in underlying risks, and increased negative externalities in the real economy. Furthermore, the service design and implementation processes can be sped up by using AI technologies, propelling insurers into more user-friendly models that can lead to expected future sales and profitability. The combination of these efficiency and outcome factors offers an exciting area for both AI solution development and general AI performance efficiency.

The ethical use of AI in insurance technology proceeds beyond efficiency considerations. Issues of fairness and nondiscrimination dominate the debate about data-driven technology. AI systems can unintentionally discriminate or disadvantage some individuals or groups. Flagging this risk does not imply that automation will undermine equality and justice within insurance service provision. The central question is whether the employment of AI systems will benefit vulnerable groups, potentially even improving access and service quality, or whether AI deployment will worsen the consequences of disadvantage. Four main aspects demand attention: data, pricing, transparency and explainability, as well as attribution of legal responsibility. First, fairness concerns related to the data that trains AI systems focus on representational bias, proxy discrimination, and inadvertent reinforcement of existing disparities. Fair pricing, access to coverage, premium equity, and the discriminatory effect of pricing signals require scrutiny next. Third, accountability for AI-assessed decisions necessitates clarity about who is responsible for potential incorrect outcomes. Finally, the importance of AI transparency and explainability is examined via the human-factor angle: how model interpretability and explanation can enable user adoption, bolster public trust, and enhance auditability.

Ethical AI in insurance should be analyzed with an objective, evidence-based approach, balancing efficiency, fairness, and risk; formal structure emphasizes definitions, frameworks, and actionable recommendations. Risk management and accountability frameworks are crucial for preserving ethical principles. A first component identifies, assesses, and mitigates impermissible risks, supported by suitable scoring, monitoring, and remediation cycles. A second element specifies decisions, responsibilities, and escalation paths required to maintain alignment with the core principles of beneficence, non-maleficence, justice, autonomy, and transparency during system operation. Insurance is predominantly a risk-pooling mechanism, but AI can create or amplify new risks, such as increased operational risk for individual organizations and the industry as a whole. Careful prioritization of these potential risks helps to focus on the most salient concerns and avoid baseless fearmongering that prevents true innovation. In any case, existing techniques for recognizing, modelling, and mitigating risk can be applied to the ethics of AI in insurance. Impermissible risks must not be ignored, and overall risk must still be managed even when it is not the main focus. The Bible contains many references to predatory lending, social injustice, and price gouging, but no explicit injunction against bank failures. Although the source of all wisdom can clearly see the future, we should be less confident of our ability to foresee the unknowns.

It is essential to establish strong privacy standards in AI-powered systems. In addition to the clear laws regulating the collection, storage, and usage of private data for insurance product pricing, governance should strictly enforce legal bases and consent mechanisms, such as opt-in or opt-out provisions, framed in accessible and understandable language. Moreover, privacy regulations should always be in place to counteract other forms of data misuse, for example, the use of data generated for a particular purpose, a form of secondary data use without user consent. To ensure conformity with the principle of data minimization, insurance companies should strive to require the least amount of personal data necessary to assess products and pricing. Data retention policies must also be implemented: data must be deleted at the end of its useful life. Moreover, data minimization procedures can be further enhanced by anonymization or pseudonymization of personal data through the removal of identifiers. De-identification techniques must rely on clear and explicit guidelines, as poorly managed de-identification processes may lead to significant information loss and threats to the quality of the data analysis performed. In addition to executive procedures for the generation, storage, and use of personal data, procedures for the management of customer rights are also essential. These define how customers can access their stored data, correct any errors, oppose the use of specific data, request the deletion of their data, and manage their consent. Customers must also be informed about the options offered to them regarding transparency notices and control interfaces—the tools that allow them to monitor and manage how their data is treated. Transparency notices must be written in clear and comprehensible language adapted to the business context and the target audience.

Human oversight is essential to mitigate the limitations of AI and the risk of harmful automated decisions. For AI, the core issue concerns the balance between augmentation and automation. The safety and fairness of insurance operations often depend on the intervention of professionals, such as underwriters or claims adjusters. While AI models can enrich human decision-making, eliminate bottlenecks in key processes, or even operate autonomously in standard cases, there are thresholds beyond which human intervention is necessary. In systems designs, the technical decision-making point must therefore be defined for each model or application, specifying whether the operator is an AI solution or a human specialist. Making this distinction requires a good understanding of the model capabilities and translation of these into specific domains, objectives, and decision rules. Human-in-the-loop approaches can further minimize adverse impacts and deepen relationships with customers. These combine AI-powered recommendations with human processing. With such architectures, building nuances are important. AI may suggest what is logical for similar cases, but the final ruling must be left to the human operator. In this context, excessive trust from the operator should also be avoided. The recommendation must not be taken as the definitive answer, even if it is logical and common. The intervention must be understood as an opportunity to debate and customize decision-making, not simply to validate the machine's view. Thus, intervention points must be considered for competitive differentiators where customization matters, offering the chance to deepen relationships and directly address customers' questions and reservations.

Offering ethical guidance and reducing the risk of AI-system impacts are primary motivations for developing formal policies for AI in insurance. Delivering on these aims requires two sets of actions. First, the ethical, operational, data, and governance recommendations emerging from analysis of efficiency, fairness, and risk need to be synthesized into best practices for deploying AI systems in insurance and related sectors. Second, oversight mechanisms that encourage compliance with these best practices and associated redress when they are not followed should be designed. Both aspects are addressed in turn. For ethical AI deployment in insurance, a governance structure that oversees the implementation of ethical AI SDGs, as well as a data governance framework that addresses the demands of the insurance business model, is essential. The various aspects of these recommendations can be grouped into external stakeholder engagement, data-collection and sharing practices, effective mitigation of model bias, and transparency in model explanations and performance. Insurers and their business partners must meaningfully engage with external stakeholders to gather knowledge vital for minimizing adverse impacts on people's life circumstances and of protected characteristics—especially those relating to ethnicity, gender, age, and disability. Moreover, as many AI systems in underwriting are trained or assessed on historical data, appropriately representative training data is critical to reducing the possibility of biased algorithmic outcomes. While these innovations promise significant gains in efficiency and accuracy, they also introduce complex ethical challenges involving bias, transparency, privacy, human oversight, and societal trust. This book responds to these challenges by offering a comprehensive examination of the ethical foundations, practical applications, governance mechanisms, and strategic futures of AI-driven insurance.

Part I establishes the conceptual and regulatory groundwork: Chapter 1 explores the ethical motivations and risks of adopting AI in insurance; Chapter 2 maps the AI value chain and clarifies how data and models shape decisions; and Chapter 3 examines legal, regulatory, and ethical frameworks governing algorithmic insurance practices. Part II shifts to practical applications and emerging dilemmas in real-world insurance operations. Chapter 4 addresses fairness and data equity in algorithmic underwriting, while Chapter 5 evaluates how AI-enabled claims management balances automation with human judgment. Chapter 6 examines fraud detection systems and the ethical limits of predictive analytics, and Chapter 7 interrogates dynamic pricing and behavioral data, focusing on the ethical implications of increasingly personalized premium models. Part III builds on this by offering technical and organizational tools for responsible AI governance: Chapter 8 analyzes bias detection and mitigation, Chapter 9 highlights explainable AI as a foundation for transparency and trust, Chapter 10 outlines privacy-preserving and ethical data governance practices, and Chapter 11 emphasizes the role of accountable human oversight in automated workflows. The book concludes with Part IV, which situates ethical AI within broader strategic and global contexts. Chapter 12 examines how AI can expand insurance access for underserved and marginalized groups, while Chapter 13 presents comparative global case studies revealing regional differences in ethical and regulatory approaches. Chapter 14 provides insurers with a practical blueprint for designing and implementing ethical AI strategies, and Chapter 15 offers a forward-looking roadmap for building sustainable, trustworthy, and human-centric AI ecosystems. Together, these chapters offer a holistic guide for insurers, policymakers, technologists, and researchers seeking to align innovation with fairness, accountability, and long-term societal benefit.

The purpose of this work is to guide practitioners, policymakers, researchers, and educators through the evolving landscape of ethical AI in insurance, clarifying the challenges associated with algorithmic bias, privacy risks, regulatory compliance, and accountability frameworks. By critically examining emerging global standards and real-world industry practices, the book highlights both the opportunities and potential harms that arise when AI systems mediate sensitive decisions affecting individuals, communities, and financial ecosystems. It invites readers to reflect on how ethical design, governance, and risk management can be embedded into every stage of AI development and deployment. Ultimately, this book advocates for an approach to AI that elevates fairness, inclusiveness, and transparency without compromising the sector's drive for precision and speed. It underscores the importance of multi-stakeholder collaboration, engaging insurers, technologists, regulators, ethicists, and consumers in shaping responsible AI ecosystems capable of supporting sustainable, trustworthy, and resilient insurance services. By bridging ethical principles with practical strategies, this preface sets the tone for a comprehensive exploration of how the insurance industry can navigate the delicate balance between innovation and responsibility in an increasingly automated future.

Contents

1

The Ethical Imperative in AI-Driven Insurance: Foundations, Motivations, and Risks

Wasswa Shafik

1.1 Introduction

Insurance is a universal human institution. It has existed in some form or another since the earliest permanence of human settlement into civil societies, where they were confronted by large-scale unexpected catastrophes that the individual could not withstand. Written records demonstrate that in the Sumerian city of Ur, merchants would pay lenders a little more than the loans' worth, which were to be repaid with interest and collateralized for risky voyages. In return, they were promised that if a loss occurred, the loan would not need to be paid back. In Babylon, covering "the ships" was a standard legal clause in maritime loans, providing "insurance" against non-repayment by the ship's captain and owner. The Code of Hammurabi in the 18th century BCE specified maritime regulation of that type. Insurance, as we think of it today, was commercialized and formalized by the Greeks about two millennia later. Families pooled resources to pay out for lawsuits following harm done to a person by another flesh-and-blood person, and then hired an attorney to sue. The very idea of "an act of God"—that insurance covers only bad luck perpetrated by nobody—is relatively new. Insurance has now spread universally, addressing not only property, marine, and liability coverage, but also life, health, and a multitude of different types of miscellaneous life contingencies (Goodell et al., 2023). At bottom, insurance serves a useful purpose: enabling individuals to transform unexpected events from disasters into little more than inconveniences, and enabling communities and nations to rebuild and continue to function as societies.

1.1.1 The Rise of Artificial Intelligence

Artificial intelligence (AI), and its variant machine learning (ML), reached exhilarating heights in the 2020s; its exponential growth in interests and applications making it a core area across many branches of a plethora of different disciplines, as demonstrated in Figure 1.1. Some AI subfields had been around since the mid-sixties but had been at a standstill, as breakthroughs needed for their maturation were not available. AI experienced occasional winter cycles, periods of reduced funding, and application. Nevertheless, other subareas of artificial intelligence, particularly neural networks, had significant growth thanks to extraordinary theoretical advances in the nineties and significant advances in the amount and quality of available data, computational power, and software tools, which allow their training in the tens of millions of parameters. Those advances allowed the generation of speech, voice, text, images, and video indistinguishable from those generated by humans. Other applications allowed better decisions in medicine, transportation, logistics, finance,

DOI: 10.1201/9781003747659-1

and most core areas of the economy, at previously unreachable levels. AI systems were deployed through big tech corporations worldwide, and are heavily relied upon on a daily basis. A plethora of smaller corporations and startups began building their futures by tailoring AI/ML to specific sectors of the economy. The spectacular success of generative pre-trained transformers, and the ensuing strong demand for large-scale foundation models, and most recently ChatGPT, seemed to have created a giant snowball feeding on itself: the larger the dataset, the larger the model, the more memory, energy, and compute needed, the better the service and the profits. The larger and more available the models, the more applications are built around them. The more creative and productive people became using those services, allowing significant and powerful investments in the field, the greater the need for bigger and larger foundational models. At the heart of the phenomenal success of GPT-type models is the concept of filling in the blanks, predicting the next word in a sentence based on the semantic structure of the surrounding words, which today's large language models use as some AI types, as illustrated in Figure 1.1 (Choi et al., 2024).

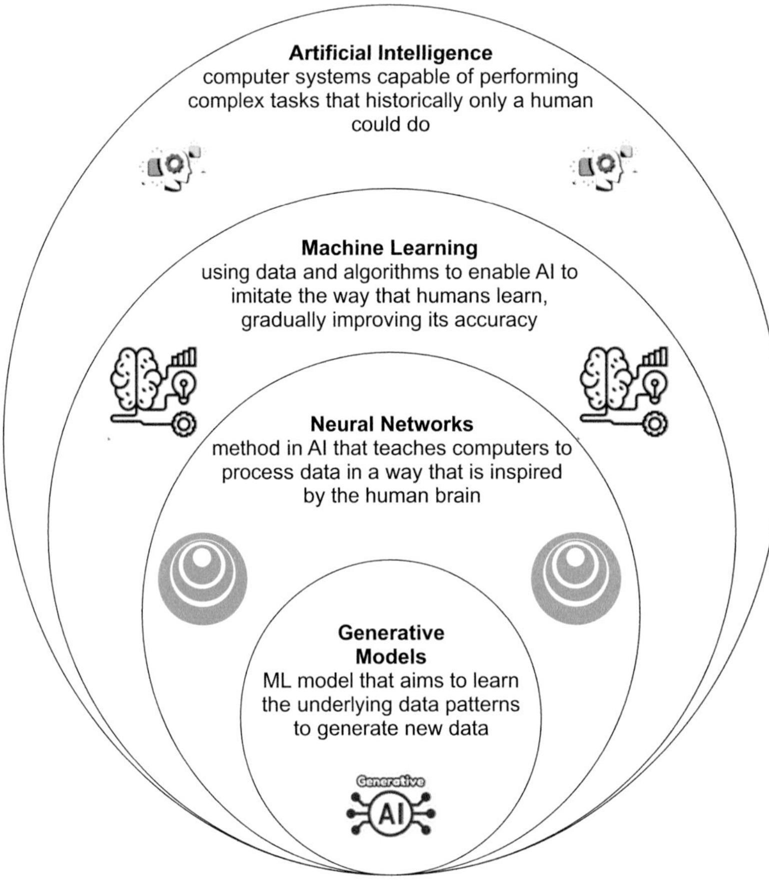

Fig. 1.1 Categories of expert systems.

1.1.2 Understanding Ethics in Technology

The ethical imperative in the decision-automation era addressed in this chapter stems from two essential fields: artificial intelligence and ethics. Although there are many intersections between these distinct fields, artificial intelligence relates to the development of machines capable of performing tasks that require intelligence in human beings; whereas ethics relate to the study of factors guiding human actions pertaining to what is good, right, and just. The intersection between both fields, referred to as AI ethics, is the study of what is good, right, and just when it comes to the creation and use of machines capable of performing tasks that require intelligence in human beings. It addresses different issues and from different perspectives, depending on the goals in question. The growing concerns regarding AI are not exclusively directed to its impact on society, organizations, and individuals, but also to the intentions, decisions, and actions of its developers and deployers. While many AI systems are explicitly directed to decision automation, we are increasingly becoming dependent on AI-enabled tools assisting or augmenting human decision-making. Given their increasing importance and contextualization, being ethical AI-enabled decision support tools, we adopt the perspective of the study of what is correct, right, or just when it comes to the development and deployment of the AI systems instantiating them. This macro perspective aligns with the growing anxieties regarding the legitimacy and moral acceptability of the decisions made by algorithmic tools. For these reasons, we adopt a contextualized view of the ethical imperative in AI-driven decision automation. It refers to the complex decision process regarding the correct, right, or just establishment, instantiation, and use of both the AI and ML tools, making the systems and the decision processes they automatize (Sharma et al., 2023). We apply this macro view of AI ethics to one specific context: the insurance industry.

1.1.3 The Importance of Ethics in Insurance

Insurance is a relevant industry inasmuch as it enables immense financial activities and supports individuals and companies in facing uncertain negative events such as accidents, illnesses, natural disasters, liability arising from damages to third parties, and other incidents that could lead to bankruptcy. The financial activity of insurance is called risk transfer, and it allows for the operational and financial stability of economies because this industry has developed unique skills in economically assessing the probability of negative events occurring and their economic impact. To assess these types of probability and the economic impact for clients and the insurance company, actuary skills are used, and AI is now being invested in. These models, however, must abide by ethical constraints. The insurance industry guarantees not only economic stability for companies or individuals but also well-being for society, and hence it must be based on ethical principles for two reasons. The first is a legal reason. Insurers act for the benefit of people whose assets are detrimentally affected by an uncertain, harmful event. The persons who pay the policy are not always the same ones for whom the loan is granted. Therefore, the payment of benefits is externally imposed on the insurance company. Since law imposes the compensation, life insurance companies cannot have similar interests to those receiving the benefit. For this reason, ethics should play an important role in people's behavior. The second reason is the societal reason. Companies have an impact on their stakeholders. These stakeholders are not only represented by customers, but also investors, employees, suppliers, and the host community. Investors look for ethical companies because bad ethical behavior leads to poor performance in the medium to long term. Consumer choices are also based on a company's behavior from an ethical perspective. Employees prefer to work for firms that operate ethically. The advantage will be in employee retention and lower costs in recruiting new employees. Society remembers companies that are supportive of communities in difficulty (Collaris & Van Wijk, 2023). All this leads to a competitive advantage that translates into economic revenue and value created for the whole community. Indeed, it is the objective of the insurance companies to protect the socio-economic stability of the whole community.

1.2 Foundations of Ethical AI

So, what does a real ethical decision look like, and what does it mean to have a code of ethics as an AI developer or deployer? In this section, we will build on the notion of a shared common good as the foundation of ethical AI and how ethical insights can guide decisions regarding AI systems. We will do this in two steps. First, we will outline principles regarding what ethical AI entails. On this basis, we will conclude with a discussion of ethical frameworks for guiding AI-related decision-making. We thus derive insights from both ethics and the AI ethics definitions. The intent is to arrive at a notion of ethical AI that is useful to those deploying AI systems in practice. While many of the arguments provided in the following text are not exclusive to AI, we believe that they become especially salient in the context of AI applications. We may thus not only derive insights regarding the ethical development of AI systems, but also about how they are deployed in a specific sector. We argue that the particularities of the AI systems, however, should have implications for the principles and frameworks. In doing so, we draw mainly from work in the areas of tech ethics around the "Ethics of Things" agenda, as well as AI ethics and critical AI ethics.

1.2.1 Principles of Ethical AI

Should human stakeholders be deemed integral to AI systems? AI may either exceed humans' capacity or relieve them of performing specific tasks, allowing them to engage in more fruitful and meaningful activities. Ideally, by being laser-focused on serving humans, the very objective of its being, AI will create numerous opportunities and enhance people's welfare. Therefore, the guiding principles underlying the design, development, and management of AI technologies should ensure that their deployment ultimately serves human goals and ethics. Nonetheless, even among the academic community, there is no uniformity on which principles should govern ethical AI systems. The high-level principles relatable to the ethical use of AI in established reports and policy guidelines broadly aim at strengthening the trustworthiness of AI systems, in effect, presenting an ethical direction toward an idealized technological outcome. The key ethical principles can be grouped into transparency, fairness and nondiscrimination, accountability, safety and security, and the protecting of human rights and freedoms. Each of those sets of principles speaks to human flourishing and refers to specific human capabilities and interventions that need to be conceptually aligned for the construction of AI systems. Human stakeholders can't be removed or replaced with purely symbolic objects; their welfare needs to be at the center of ethical consideration (Lozano-Murcia et al., 2024). But more often than not, an AI system cannot operate properly or produce desirable outcomes, or cannot be created without the support of its technical designers, builders, and deployers. Therefore, the various people shaping the technology are directly involved in the ethical outcomes of their systems.

1.2.2 Frameworks for Ethical Decision-Making

Recent years have seen the emergence of an increasing number of tools, frameworks, and ethical checklists to help organizations implement ethics in AI. Here, we outline a few of them, more or less in chronological order. The principles were proposed as a result of a conference in 2017, attended by renowned experts in AI from different fields. The conference aimed at encouraging discussions about AI safety and governance. The resulting principles were nine in number: research transparency, driverless cars, research collaboration, communicating research, safety, AI for the benefit of humanity, avoiding an arms race, multi-stakeholder cooperation, and long-term research. A set of ethics guidelines for trustworthy AI was prescribed on 8th April 2019. The guidelines prescribe firstly that the stakeholders should be adequately informed about the AI system and be included in its design, development, and implementation to the extent possible. Second, the AI systems should be designed to minimize risk and a margin of error commensurate with the risk of the intended purpose. And third, the systems should be pursued for a purpose that is lawful and that is in the service of the common good and the public interest. The fourth and fifth guidelines ensure a human in command along with technical robustness and safety (Fritz-Morgenthal et al., 2022). The sixth guideline is about nondiscrimination, the seventh about privacy, data governance, and accountability, the eighth about transparency, and the ninth is about environmental and societal well-being. Some of the ethical aspects are presented in Table 1.1.

Table 1.1 Ethical foundations and motivations for AI in insurance.

Aspect	*Definition*	*Importance of Insurance*	*Real-World Example*	*Ethical Concern*
Transparency	Clear visibility into AI models and decision logic	Builds trust with policyholders	Explainable underwriting systems	Opaque algorithms leading to distrust
Fairness	Equal treatment across demographics	Prevents discriminatory practices	Bias audits in claims handling	Disparate impact on minority groups
Accountability	Assigning responsibility for AI decisions	Ensures stakeholders can respond to failures	Auditable AI pipelines in fraud detection	Lack of clear accountability in automated decisions
Privacy Preservation	Respecting data rights and confidentiality	Safeguards sensitive personal and medical data	General Data Protection Regulation (GDPR)-compliant data practices	Overcollection and misuse of personal data
Human Oversight	Involving humans in critical decisions	Adds a layer of judgment beyond automation	Manual review for AI-denied claims	Fully automated decisions causing harm
Consent and Autonomy	User awareness and agreement to data use	Enhances user control and trust	Informed consent in the use of health data	Implicit consent practices
Non-maleficence	Not to harm AI deployment	Prevents systemic risk in insurance coverage	Stress testing AI models before launch	Harmful predictions impacting livelihoods
Justice and Inclusion	Equitable access and treatment across populations	Ensures that underserved communities aren't excluded	Inclusive pricing algorithms	Exclusion of low-income policyholders
Proportionality	Matching AI complexity to the task's ethical stakes	Avoids overengineering decisions with high human impact	Simpler AI in basic coverage inquiries	Overreliance on complex black-box models
Sustainability	Long-term ethical use of data and technology	Aligns AI practices with societal values	Ethical AI procurement and use policies	Short-term focus compromises long-term ethics

1.3 Motivations for Implementing Ethical AI

Implementing ethical AI systems can yield positive results for insurers in three major areas: enhancing consumer trust and system transparency, ensuring and demonstrating compliance with emerging regulations, and a long-term profitability increase due to reduced brand risk and reputation damage. The creation of society's trust in AI-driven insurance systems, particularly in underwriting and claims assessment, is a necessary step in providing AI-driven insurance services, with transparency being a key pillar of this trust. Insurers, driven by competitive influence or by demand from select consumer segments, may decide to offer products that include the use of ethical AI. Ethical AI presumes, among others, clear communication with consumers regarding the workings of an AI system. Providing accurate information while addressing consumers' concerns in a digestible manner may contribute to their trust in an insurance company. This would aim to help insurers address concerns regarding the level of control and autonomy consumers may lose, and their worries around data security and the integrity of their data. Furthermore, society's trust in AI systems may result from their understanding that the AI systems will provide unbiased and nondiscriminatory assistance for their unique needs. This understanding will only be reached by the insurance company's clear communication regarding ethical AI requirements, such as fairness, accountability, and explainability, during the development and use of an AI system. Governments worldwide are pushing forward to develop regulations on AI use, and insurance is not exempt. The primary aim of the regulations will be to mitigate the potential harms of AI systems. Insurers need to proactively comply with these regulations, which may include certain aspects of ethical AI implementation, to avoid hefty fines and brand damage (Zhdanov et al., 2022). Ethical AI, being an approach to developing AI systems, could help insurance companies in their endeavor to comply with potential reform regulations, utilizing models, guidelines, and risk management.

1.3.1 Consumer Trust and Transparency

Trust is a vital component of any business relationship. Consumers are more likely to remain loyal and to continue to engage with companies whose services they trust. This fundamental business principle has been a driving force behind the rise of ethical consumerism, whereby consumers use purchasing decisions as a way of signalling approval or disapproval of how a business operates based on their own internal beliefs about broader issues. Ethical consumerism has the potential to elicit an important signal of confidence in a company, either by what they choose to invest in or by what they choose to eschew. The combination of a transparency-driven approach to developing AI models that provide regulatory compliance, such as decreased discrimination, can have important implications for the insurance industry's corporate social responsibility initiatives. AI models, especially the advanced and sophisticated deep learning algorithms, are often described as black boxes that cannot easily be explained. But for an AI model to serve the needs of the insurance industry, it must be able to be constructed in such a manner that it can be easily explained or audited so that all parties can understand how the final decision is reached (Guo et al., 2024). And this audit ability must extend throughout the life of the model to allow for retraining in order to guard against discrimination, unfair razor-thin pricing, or any other consequences that would erode consumer trust. Such AI model auditability translates into increased corporate social responsibility through building a foundation of trust with potential and current policyholders.

1.3.2 Regulatory Compliance

Insurance is one of the world's oldest regulated professions. Historically, professional regulations served mainly for market behavior control and consumer protection reasons. Given the technological advances of the previous centuries, AI represents yet another important area in need of appropriate political and legal measures at all levels: local, national, and international. To a large extent, policies are required not because AI cannot be used responsibly. Rather, the ethical dimension of any action taken within the AI-driven insurance context results from the sad history of us taking shortcuts in the absence of appropriate obligations and incentives. Unfortunately, at the time of writing, the regulatory framework concerning AI is still very much in its infancy, and often insurance professionals have a hard time complying with it in the AI context. The source of the problem is mainly that most of the existing requirements were written for pre-AI times, and numerous new frameworks are still being developed. The pre-AI landscape consists of numerous acts, rules, regulations, directives, and recommendations: a patchwork of explicit and implicit obligations concerning anti money laundering and countering the financing of terrorism; discrimination; general data protection regulation; misleading and aggressive marketing rules; non-life-insurance contract directive; prospectuses regulation; prohibition of credit for vulnerable consumers; product oversight and governance rule; risk measurement and transparency rules; and others (Bermúdez et al., 2023). Keeping up with these existing and forthcoming frameworks pertaining to AI will certainly increase the cost of compliance and product development, which may result in increasing entry barriers for smaller and younger insurance companies.

1.3.3 Long-Term Profitability

Andrew Chen offered a punning joke about why insurance companies go broke: "It's good to be an insurance company until it's not." But no matter how broken it may be, short-term profit must always drag the offer of the entity's public managers. Insurance companies should be strictly careful with the way they are assessing risk since they cannot develop predictive models the same way a delivery app is developing theirs, for example. A delivery company can charge more in the winter with more snow than it charges driver partners during the summer with more demand. An insurance company is stuck with heavy contractual duties protected by regulation, so their only way in and out is through the care of the predictive models, time, and accuracy behind fairness. An insurance company loses money every time an unexpected event happens, such as a boat sinking or a catastrophe natural event happens with a conflict of interest. The way an insurance company maintains profitability is by charging the right price every time, seasonally, and where predictive models are unable to get in and out. If these predictive models fail, the economic forecast dissipates and the effect is multiplied for a publicly held company the same way as it happened with the shares during the 1990s. Offer prices were set too low compared to the risk transfer provided. Other companies writing homeowners insurance were incapable of withstanding the adversity, leaving the market (Braun & Matthes, 2018). In moral hazard, there isn't an ethical solution for the timing–naive–deceit until regulatory supervisors find perfect cut-off screening equation in general and when activity generates poor models.

1.4 Risks Associated with AI in Insurance

The application of AI in the insurance industry enables several benefits, but it also comes with inherent risks. In this section, we identify and discuss three particular risks: bias and discrimination, data privacy concerns, and automation and job displacement. The first two present ethical dilemmas, constraints, and risks that insurance companies should consider before adopting AI solutions in their business processes. The last one is a general concern driven by the fast-paced growth of AI in different industries and its perceived potential to generate mass unemployment if large numbers of human jobs are eliminated or replaced through automation. While such radical change is not expected in the insurance industry in the short term and jobs are likely to be redesigned rather than disappear, it is not unreasonable to think that within a few years, the continuation of rapid AI growth could lead to significant change in the work carried out by experts in insurance firms. A valid concern for insurance companies is ensuring that the AI solutions generated and implemented treat individuals equally and do not favor a certain group of people or penalize others with specific characteristics. In this sense, fairness is a broad concept, and it is not always feasible to ensure that an algorithm is neutral with respect to all sensitive attributes, such as education, gender, religion, and race, among others. It is not possible to build an AI model that is equally accurate for all groups of individuals in the population. Such limitations derive from the fact that groups of people can differ in significant aspects unrelated to the sensitive attributes that need to be neutralized. In fact, a lack of discrimination is not always desirable as designing gambles that ensure individuals from different classes get the same expected utility may not always align with social morals (Sachan & Muwanga, 2023). For instance, allowing a healthy person to pay the same as an unhealthy person for health insurance may go against their sense of justice.

1.4.1 Bias and Discrimination

Since its inception, the insurance industry has relied on data-driven technologies. These systems are crucially designed and implemented to assess risk and ultimately inform decision-making. However, the relevance of these technologies in making ethical decisions regarding customer treatment in relation to individual risk has been scrutinized. Especially because in using a digital ecosystem to inform sensitive decisions, unintended consequences could impose disproportionately harmful effects on certain communities. Bias may be introduced into these systems in many ways, including but not limited to: the selection and weighting of particular risk assessment criteria considered to be overvalued or undervalued; biased decisions by underqualified human analysts interpreting the model outcomes; biased sampling or exclusion of particular subgroups during the training phase; and allowing the AI system to operate without checks on its real-world performance. Evolving AI capabilities enable the processing of extremely large reserves of individual-level data containing potentially sensitive information or hidden patterns relevant to insurance decisions regarding underwriting, pricing, accrual of benefits, and payout conditions. The inclusion of AI in this domain has raised the stakes especially since these algorithms often produce complex and opaque decision paths or hidden patterns. Algorithms have been shown to replicate and even amplify societal inequities, as well as racial and socioeconomic discrimination. The potential for such effects could arise from biased model development or the retention of biased input data. The latter is an especially sensitive issue because of abundant historical data capturing societal inequities, some of which may be relevant for optimizing risk assessment (Van Nguyen et al., 2023). Hence, entirely permissible criteria incorporated to price a risk can yield suboptimal adjustments, such as pricing an insurance product for individuals or members of other minority groups at rates departing from underlying costs for the risk exposure while reinforcing historical societal bias, among other several applications as presented in Figure 1.2.

1.4.2 Data Privacy Concerns

The use of AI in insurance results in increased gathering and utilization of personal data. Insurance companies already collect a wide variety of information when issuing new policies, including personally identifiable information, property standards, health and pharmacy history, and employment background. But with the advent of AI and connected devices, a vast amount of otherwise private information is now being tracked, determined, and stored without the knowledge of the consumer. This includes global positioning system (GPS) data about day-to-day movements and remote biometric monitoring of physiological characteristics, such as how often individuals engage in physical activity, their weight, their sleep patterns, and a range of other physical signs. Such tracking may appear necessary for certain coverages, such as from travelers for trip interruption or medical assistance, and event cancellation due to the pandemic and associated quarantines. Still, tracking may also be seen as an overreach for less likely future losses, such as pre-pandemic underwriting

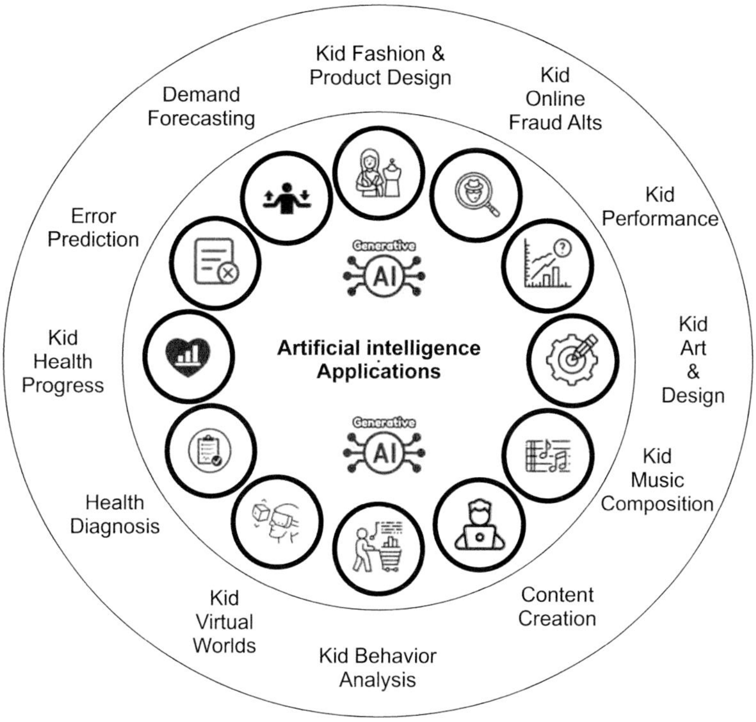

Fig. 1.2 Application of artificial intelligence.

of key person life insurance for executives who had more than one area of travel. More than this, because certain underwriting AI tools rely on nontraditional or “alternative” data—such as social media profiles, smartphone histories, or credit-related information, all of which may themselves be based on biased algorithms—there is also the risk of privacy invasion. This includes determining whether individuals have legal documents or whether they may be associated with people who have admitted to criminal or unethical conduct. In general, it has seemed appropriate to provide transparency regarding the data utilized for algorithm training, including for monitoring such nontraditional data-type risks (Bork et al., 2023). Individuals must have the opportunity to select or delete their profiles, as well as object to an algorithmic decision they disagree with or feel was made improperly.

1.4.3 Automation and Job Displacement

The prospect of AI exceeding the capabilities of humans in a broad number of cognitive domains has sparked fears of mass job loss through automation. AI has begun to disrupt labor markets and is expected to contribute to displacing several million jobs over the next several decades. However, the full scope of future automation is uncertain and will likely vary depending on different variables, including the nature of tasks, skills required by different occupations, labor market institutions, and regional policies. Furthermore, the job impact of AI is likely not zero-sum since AI offers the potential to eliminate menial work and enhance productivity, thereby allowing workers to free their time for more satisfying activities and find jobs that make better use of their more creative and productive capacities. Nonetheless, some researchers have raised concerns that, while the total number of jobs may not change substantially, workers will find it increasingly difficult to find a job that matches their skills and education level. Research into the impact of AI models in the areas of predictive analytics, computer vision, and natural language processing suggests that occupations dealing primarily with data entry, data analysis, or logistics will see the greatest threat of job automation. Moreover, early movers in AI adoption may have a critical share of the rents, exacerbating inequality (Collecchia, 2021). Various studies suggest that the adoption of AI may increase income inequality as it enhances the capabilities and productivity profile of higher-skilled workers and reduces demand for lower-skilled workers in jobs that can easily be automated. AI may substitute for low tasks in some occupations and complement high tasks in other occupations, as illustrated in Table 1.2.

Table 1.2 Risk landscape of AI in insurance and mitigation strategies.

AI-Driven Risk	*Description*	*Impact Area*	*Real-World Case/ Scenario*	*Mitigation Strategy*
Data Bias	Historical data reflecting social inequities	Underwriting, pricing	AI is charging higher premiums to minority groups	Bias audits, representative datasets
Model Overfitting	AI was trained too specifically on past data	Risk prediction	AI misclassifies rare but high-cost illnesses	Regular model validation and retraining
Black-Box Decisions	Lack of interpretability in algorithm outcomes	Claims decisions	Denied claims with no explanations	Implement explainable AI (XAI)
Cybersecurity Threats	Unauthorized access to sensitive personal and actuarial data	Data privacy	Hacking into policyholder databases	Encryption, threat modeling, and firewalls
Regulatory Noncompliance	AI violating data use or discrimination laws	Legal and ethical compliance	Use of noncompliant biometric data	Compliance audits, legal reviews
Moral Disengagement	Delegating too much responsibility to machines	Corporate ethics	Employees deferring ethical judgment to AI	Training and ethical accountability protocols
Automation Overreach	Excessive automation replacing human judgment	Customer service and resolution	Delays in resolving appeals of rejected claims	Human-in-the-loop (HITL) systems
Discrimination	Indirect exclusion or penalization of protected groups	Access and affordability	Gender-based premium differentials due to outdated proxies	Use of fairness constraints in ML models
Lack of Consent	Data used without informed consent	User rights	Behavioral data scraped without user knowledge	Transparent consent mechanisms
Feedback Loops	Biased outcomes reinforce and amplify systemic issues	Pricing, risk pools	Higher rates in marginalized communities → worse scores over time	Model calibration and continuous monitoring
Data Incompleteness	Inaccurate or missing data affecting decisions	Risk assessment	Underwriting errors due to incomplete credit histories	Data enrichment and cross-verification

Contd.

Table 1.2 *Contd.*

AI-Driven Risk	*Description*	*Impact Area*	*Real-World Case/ Scenario*	*Mitigation Strategy*
Liability Ambiguity	Unclear responsibility for AI-driven mistakes	Legal disputes	Lawsuits over wrongful claim denial	Defined liability frameworks and documentation
Unequal Digital Literacy	Users are unable to understand AI-driven processes	Accessibility and justice	Elderly customers are confused by AI-generated quotes	Multi-format communication and education
Environmental Cost	Resource-intensive AI models consume energy	Operational sustainability	Energy-hungry data centers for predictive analytics	Green AI practices, cloud optimization

1.5 Case Studies of Ethical AI in Insurance

Throughout the nascent AI cycle of insurance, it is not surprising that there exist some case studies of success and failures. Successes illustrate the process of human involvement to which we outlined as necessary in the initial training layers that handed the baton to AI, confirming that these are initiatives we can celebrate as ethical implementations of AI. We also have AI efforts in insurance that have missed the ethical injunction—the industry and the public should use these to avoid excesses. These are companies that released systems without first proving that their models would not fail. Both ends of case studies on implementation provide relevant lessons for the ethical future of AI in insurance. Existing implementations of ethical AI in insurance are largely inside the regulations relevant to insurance, as the focus of ethical AI developments is on minimizing risk. Although there are private and non-private sector initiatives being proposed for many products and policies outside of those that traditional insurance regulates, these are due front and center on ethical AI implementation in traditional insurance (El Qadi et al., 2023). The moral obligations of these firms are still not established principally; for example, the duty to regularly disclose data transparency and accountability defaults from any agency in relation to these institutions. Audit rules, even for AI systems, are also already part of the regulations these firms abide by.

1.5.1 Successful Implementations

Increasing concern about the social impacts of AI and calls for strict regulation that will hinder the development of AI and block the deployment of innovation have prompted some insurance executives to ask what their companies can do to increase public faith in AI, expand its societal benefits, and improve the quality of decisions made by algorithms. To this end, a number of insurance companies are trying out, and some are already implementing what they call ethical AI principles. Thus, data preparation around bias detection, bias correction, and disparate impact constraint enforcement is an essential factor of automatic model development, selection, and monitoring processes for high-risk screening. Of course, simply proclaiming a set of ethical principles is not enough. Some insurance companies are actively implementing specific measures to put their ethical AI principles into practice. For example, some are performing premortem analysis with diverse stakeholders before starting new projects and a postmortem analysis of every AI project after development. Along similar lines, insurers are undertaking complementary measures to develop and deploy ethical AI systems and good data for them by creating AI project monitoring committees, hiring or training data ethicists, developing data labeling and monitoring standards, introducing IT explanation and algorithm testing tools, and cultivating partnerships with universities and research centers to work on accountability and auditability technologies (Tronchin et al., 2024). It is noteworthy that these companies are not only acquiring the ethical principles of AI that they consider necessary, but are also explicitly training and monitoring the people responsible for developing and using AI systems to implement them.

1.5.2 Lessons Learned from Failures

However, before we present the two cases of ethical failures in AI implementations in insurance, we note that just because a diversity-sensitive software architecture could have produced better results in these cases, it is not necessarily practical or economic to implement. The cost of bad ethics could vastly exceed any additional burden posed by ethical technology; otherwise, there would be little incentive to adopt better models. That is what happened with a company that had implemented a diversity-sensitive software strategy and eventually had to abandon it because of how expensive it was. The company's goal was to deliver customized ads to different people in the same geographic area; yet, custom ads eliminate the market, which, anyhow, delivers no revenue. Without good management practices at all levels, nobody knows who is trying to provide a good product or a bad product, and how many commodities are on the marketplace. Because there is no one at the head of the company monitoring the whole ad design process, the creative people doing the work have no particular incentive to suggest models. Management wants results. So, diversity-sensitive policies would probably only be viable in an insurance company at the insistence of upper management, which has the right incentives in place to achieve excellence in marketing. In that case, such policies really would help deliver revenue results that are in everyone's economic interest. And so, by extension, we believe it is worth at least looking into (Braun & Matthes, 2018). Suppose there is a diversity-plus-values compliance marketing strategy that can be shown to be economically feasible. Why not try to adopt it, whether or not the incentives are in place to reward the attempt.

1.6 Regulatory Landscape for AI in Insurance

AI technologies are rapidly changing how insurance companies develop their products, actuaries create their predictive models, underwriters assess prospective clients, and claim adjusters evaluate the validity of claims and process insurance payments. The growth of ubiquitous AI systems in the insurance industry brings with it new risks of harm to consumers and society alike. While insurance is an industry that has long been and is heavily regulated, the regulation of underwriting and evaluating claims has tended to lag behind broad anti-discrimination laws and the surveillance questions related to privacy concerns. The introduction of AI systems in these areas has raised the risks of bias and surveillance to new levels and triggered a reconsideration by regulators and legislators of the adequacy of existing regulations. The challenge, as in many aspects of economic life, is getting the regulations right to balance economic needs and innovation with the need to prevent antisocial outcomes. This chapter surveys the current regulatory landscape globally and at the national level. The chapter then looks at the questions regarding fair AI as a foundation of consumer protection, future proofing for computational evolution, submission of computational models, and risk models underlying disparate impact. The chapter discusses the penalties and private enforcement, the split between data protection agencies and anti-discrimination agencies, the private action question, as well as remedies and individual versus collective action (Choi et al., 2024).

1.6.1 Current Regulations

Insurance is one of the most regulated sectors across economies, with the goal of safeguarding vulnerable customers from potential harm, irrespective of whether they are individuals or corporations. Historically, insurance contracts were written as adhesion contracts, heavily favoring the insurer. For this reason, there have been calls for improving consumer literacy and understanding with regard to insurance contracts. Insurers are obliged to disclose extensive information about policy features. At the same time, nondisclosure clauses are strictly regulated by contract law. The regulation of insurers' use of AI and algorithms is also evolving. Here, we focus on algorithms used for pricing, underwriting, and claims processing. Algorithms are used in many aspects of insurance. However, most current regulations govern specific applications of algorithms. One area of growing concern is the reliance on attributes that are associated with prohibited discrimination on the basis of nationality, gender, ethnic origin, belief, sexual orientation, handicap, or age that may be used indirectly, such as making inferences about the risk characteristics of individuals who do not belong to the main demographic group. Another concern is relying on non-insurance-related attributes to make inferences about risky behavior or noncompliance based on available financial information (Sachan & Muwanga, 2023). This is exacerbated in markets with high information asymmetries, which also characterizes reinsurers' markets, against the backdrop of design rules that insurers must comply with when offering insurance contracts.

1.6.2 Future Trends in Regulation

Insurance regulation is a slowly evolving discipline, as compared to AI's rapid advancements. The initial AI regulation trends in insurance focus on preexisting principles, such as transparency, nondiscrimination, and certain AI-specific regulations that could be adopted in insurance. Regulation is best implemented when it is based on established ethical principles. Versions of the following fundamental principles are considered in the wide range of disciplines writing on ethical AI. Regulations focusing on transparency have been included in privacy laws. The transparency principle mandates that explanatory information be provided for every impactful insurance decision. Such transparency and enlightenment would help a prospect or policyholder understand why an AI model rejected them for coverage, whether a quote was incorrect, or whether their claim is being denied or the payout is being halted. This is without overstretching transparency's limits or by being over-bureaucratic, as in certain AI regulations, where an overly bureaucratic explanation for a classified AI system is requested.

1.7 The Role of Stakeholders in Ethical AI

AI and insurance are interdependent within a larger ecosystem of stakeholders that include insurers and consumers, and this ecosystem interdependence affects the ethical imperative. An insurer is, of course, a company that provides insurance—the business that uses AI to optimize processes and services, such as pricing and claims assessment, and mitigate risk. Consumers are individuals and businesses that obtain insurance, that is, purchase policies to transfer risk. Regulators are governmental authorities that impose rules and guidelines, including standards for accident compensation, consumer protection, financial probity, and many others. Each stakeholder plays an important role in creating and maintaining the ecosystem. Insurers are responsible for the ethical design and implementation of AI. ML has proven transformative for the insurance industry, greatly enhancing operational efficiency and profitability, and allowing for enhanced predictive power vis-à-vis both underwriting and claims assessment. However, AI should not only deliver profit; insurers are also responsible for protecting consumer welfare, observing both deontological principles and consequentialist social justice in their use of AI. These responsibilities impose limits on risk prediction models. Insurers should take input factors identified by individuals into account, allowing consumers to revise their policies in consideration of data-driven algorithmic assessments consciously. But insurers should be aware of the bias consequences of the input factors used. For example, in automobile insurance, the input factor "average distance traveled per week" necessarily correlates with "income level." But, using the second factor as a model input—that "minority nationality" correlates with "low income level"—could have discriminatory consequences (Van Nguyen et al., 2023). The use of an input factor that might correlate with a discriminatory variable could put the insurance company at risk of public backlash and possibly regulatory fines.

1.7.1 Insurers

Because of their unique position in the commerce ecosystem, insurers are a vital stakeholder in ethical AI. First, because of efficiency gains compared to traditional means, these AI systems are creatively applied in various phases of the insurance business, not just underwriting and pricing, such as AI systems for managing fraud, claims processing, and, more recently, customer engagement. Second, disparate impact, even absent suspicion of unfairness in insurance pricing, has, for some fair value advocates and regulators, gone too far, killing the business model and presaging erosion of the industry. Insurers must avoid or reduce bias in their AI systems; whether as users or developers, they also have a business interest in doing so. Not only do deceptive and predatory practices lead to more rigorous regulation on the practice, but they can also drive out longer-term profitability if sophisticated consumers buy insurance from nonethical competitors. At the same time, as a core competency of the industry, efficacy in marketing responsible practices is an incentive for controlling the appropriate business policies and practices throughout the insurance value chain, from product ideation to sale to renewal. Third, as guardians of society and the judiciary against breaches of the social contract that are impertinent to the spirit and textual core of insurance, insurers also must safeguard against the unjust uses of AI technologies (Sharma et al., 2023). To avoid the adverse societal consequences of deploying AI, they should work together with developers and governments to help predict destructive as opposed to constructive deployments of AI technology, setting in advance the rules of the game.

1.7.2 Consumers

The complete potential misalignment of values, interests, and motivations between AI developers and insurers also exists to a degree for consumers. After all, consumers are also the only stakeholder group that is limited solely to the adoption of AI-driven insurance initiatives. We can think of consumers as taking on the role of either insurance customers or policyholders. Yet their perspectives on the use of AI in insurance are not the same. Naturally, customers are more impacted by the use of AI in the design and development of insurance products. Policyholders, on the other hand, are also more affected by the use of AI in the delivery of insurance products, and are therefore potentially more exposed to misalignments due to any bias arising from data imbalance within the AI products. The main concern of consumers revolves around how biased or unethical AI products can negatively impact their lives. There has been less research on the contrast between consumers' dual roles as both customers and policyholders. Since positive consumer experiences during the testing phase would be immensely helpful in determining the long-term success of insurers' AI-based insurance products, customer experience variables must be carefully examined and understood (Shafik, 2025b). It opens avenues for additional research stemming from the importance of how consumer perceptions could be investigated in the context of varying differences between customers and policyholders.

1.7.3 Regulators

AI rules are excellent tools, but do not cover every scenario. It is impossible to detect individuals behind an AI application, so these laws do not prevent treating individuals and businesses in a discriminatory manner. It is not feasible to ban every unfathomable technology, as not all technology is bad. There is no state entity with the necessary skills to propose or oversee a sector-wide ethical AI strategy, and the idea of AI commissions relies on limited iteration.

(i) Regulation through approval of AI applications could inspire new ethical guidelines, and incentives to use and generate ethical data could also be provided to other stakeholders. Regulators could start addressing the issue of AI ethical deployment in insurance markets by prohibiting or disincentivizing the use of bias-increasing algorithms and putting safeguards that limit the risk of excessive use of algorithms and dimensionality on data. It could also facilitate consumer empowerment through education and encourage the pricing of ethical benevolence.

(ii) Some laws could facilitate ethical choices for consumers, unleashing "ethical consumerism." They could lead the generalized ecosystem toward ethical behavior. Laws could promote clear labeling of firms and consumer groups or non-profit institutions controlling the destinations of investment funds, emphasizing their pattern of investment.

(iii) Regulators could also support insurance firms in the use of ethical AI strategies, such as promoting the funding, insurance, or granting of tax benefits for AI development plans that sustainably consider their ethical implications, or the tax deductibility for companies liable for misbehavior of the costs of non-repetitive disincentives, such as going through negative reputational tourist cycles.

1.8 Future Directions for Ethical AI in Insurance

While we anticipate rapid advances in the use of AI technologies, we also encourage an ethical scaffolding, an ethical implementation reflective of the realities of the industry and the challenges we have outlined. We hope that this would lead not only to a positive outcome from an industry perspective but also that it would provide the elevation, acceptance, adoption, sustainability, and success of these advanced technologies. In no particular order of priority, we note several directions and opportunities that are surfacing in these discussions. Based on our observations as well as emerging narratives from differing industry players, here are some directions to consider. Advanced generative models have shown prospects for surfacing novel ideas and innovations. In insurance and adjacent industries, we can benefit from innovations in products, new approaches to pricing, policy structuring and conditions, considerations for underwriting, including the socio-economic impact on vulnerability, and faster settlement of claims. In a world where time to market is reduced, continued diversification of coverage options and conditions and hyper-personalization of pricing based on predictive risk segmentation can be of value. More opportunities will include areas of growing interest—cyber insurance, usage-based insurance, especially for personal and commercial vehicle insurance, insurance programs focusing on credit and loans, issues around gig economy workers, etc. Similar innovations and problems can also be expected in insurance-related verticals (Shafik, 2024a). The personalization in machine learning models to product, customer, risk, pricing, and underwriting challenges opened up by AI advances can create new possibilities in those areas.

1.8.1 Innovations on the Horizon

There are many exciting practical opportunities for applying ethical AI in insurance. With dynamic real-time pricing insurance, earlier innovations in insurance pricing and underwriting associated with predictive modelling will evolve beyond hazard identification. It will allow real-time detection and pricing of moral hazard. This opens new paths to improving the ethics and efficiency of personalized insurance by integrating insurance price changes as a direct function of changes in underlying risk and risk behavior. The challenge is to innovate this capacity in a way that recognizes the potential for wrongdoing in a self-promoting feedback loop, recognized in a dynamic insurance marketplace that favors subscription by low-risk insured groups and disruptive failures and exits by high-risk insured groups sensitive to price changes based on escalatory moral hazard. Predictive modelling, driving creative product development in insurance, seems at first sight still mired in its historic past—that risk selection, risk segmentation, capacity development, insurance product enhancement, and retention incentives are all at least indirectly directed by high predictive models focused on loss prediction. A very exciting area for innovation is insurance products driven by algorithms that radically broaden the use of AI beyond management to direct relationships between consumers and the covered objects or people (Shafik, 2024c). This product space has opened as a result of technological advances in AI-related tools that enable cost-effective collection and analysis of consumer exposure data. Embedded insurance is leading the way here, using collaborative data-sharing arrangements among corporates to enrich the consumer experience.

1.8.2 Potential Challenges Ahead

Despite these numerous advantages and investments in ethical AI for insurance, the challenges ahead need to be discussed. We need to work on understanding the terms and acknowledging the tension between innovation regarding the auto-adaptation of models and ethical principles of accountability or efficiency-equality trade-offs. Since machine learning is mostly data-driven, and algorithms are aiming at optimizing the predictive power through constant improvements, we should always ask ourselves whether some issues could show up with regard to fairness or discrimination, privacy or transparency, security, safety and reliability, human dignity or emotional responses, or diversity. Reinforcement learning is still facing the problem of exploding and vanishing rewards. In principle, theoretical solutions exist to prevent this issue, but empirical results are still rare, especially when it comes to applying to life insurance problems. We should also ask ourselves how far we really went when talking about processes or decision-making transparency, and what about the human control factor? Methods without structured and human-understandable output might work for short-term decision-making processes in property-casualty, but how far will we go in observing fundamental ethical principles, such as safety, stability, or reliability? Also, the insurance sector needs to be adequately educated to understand how AI really works. For example, even when machine learning techniques are technically explainable, without previous knowledge, understanding them might be very exhausting (Shafik, 2024b). Therefore, the insurance sector should take into account the public's perception of the implications of AI-driven decisions, because of possible backlashes.

1.9 Best Practices for Ethical AI Implementation

While this chapter briefly describes a number of best practices gathered through various surveys of executives, team leaders, researchers, consultants, and vendors, a prescriptive roadmap is not realistic at this early stage of development. Each organization, including each insurance company, has its own goals, visions, and values, and as such, its own culture. Likewise, every AI implementation is unique in its way. There cannot be a one-size-fits-all implementation plan. However, we believe following the guidelines provided in the following text will increase the chances of success.

(i) Creating an ethical culture determining which AI implementation best fosters achievement of your company's stated objectives, selecting AI solutions that can be relied upon, and engaging in appropriate monitoring throughout the life cycle of an enterprise's use of AI, whether in your implementations or product offerings dependent on third party solutions, are keys to building a sustainable AI-driven future for your enterprise. While this undertaking requires short- and long-term commitments of resources, ultimately the success of an AI implementation will be determined by the extent to which various stakeholders—such as customers, investors, and regulators—trust the organization, and your ability to leverage the value of that trust in support of the stated company mission. Accordingly, every AI project must demonstrate, first and foremost, why it is ethical in the sense of contributing long-term to the realization of the goals you espouse.

(ii) Continuous monitoring and evaluation is mandatory. Your efforts should not stop at a particular point. The ethical challenge is not addressed and accomplished merely by the ex-ante process of preparing the AI for rollout. You should continuously monitor and evaluate your AI implementations throughout their entire life cycles. Just as the AI space is in a constant state of evolution, so too are both the internal and external operating environments for every enterprise.

1.9.1 Creating an Ethical Culture

This chapter is focused on providing a roadmap for organizations seeking to adopt ethical principles in the implementation of AI proactively. It focuses on these issues from an internal rather than external perspective, providing advice from those who have studied the implementation of ethical practices regarding AI. Building an ethical culture around AI implementation is as important as developing ethical guidelines regarding bias, accuracy, privacy, and security. Without the right focus, other efforts at developing ethical AI may fall flat. Organizations need to reinforce a common understanding to help individuals confront difficult dilemmas. No single effect will create and sustain an ethical culture, but it requires a range of actions (Shafik, 2025a). Organizations will want to establish a solid foundation, which includes adopting aspirational values and engaging in stakeholder dialogue, to shape their culture further. The next level of structure requires training and internal stakeholder dialogue to encourage individuals to think carefully about the ethical implications of their actions. Organizational structure serves as the next level of foundation. Importantly, this includes establishing internal accountability mechanisms that can help deter unethical behavior as well as reporting and enforcement policies that can assure that individuals will be held accountable for their actions. The final components are reward and recognition systems. While organizations do not need to reward ethical action, they need to avoid throwing consistency aside (Shafik, 2024d). In summary, organizations need to ensure that their people in their AI unit understand and embrace the company's values and ethical culture. To do so, organizations need to make ethical guidelines a central part of their AI implementation processes and reinforce them through all aspects of their human resource management. Doing so will help individuals confront the ethical dilemmas that arise and avoid using AI unethically.

1.9.2 Continuous Monitoring and Evaluation

As the insurance practice matures, more insurance products will be created and more processes will be automated with AI technology; however, monitoring for ethical standards needs to remain in effect. Furthermore, no matter how careful and responsible the design and release of AI-driven systems are, these technological systems are highly complex and will experience phenomena that never occurred within the training data. Therefore, these systems need to be constantly evaluated for ethical violations and updated to mitigate ethical breaches. If the unforeseen conditions within which the system is operating lead to an actual ethics breach, then the business must be responsive enough to reclaim its commitment to ethical guiding principles promptly. Organizations need to assess a few particular high-risk areas constantly, including decision quality and fairness, accidental discrimination, slack work response, denial of service, threat or violence detection, and epistemic closure. Due to the small ratio of deep learning data compared to the actual size of the AI systems deployed in practice, ground truth labeling of these key goal variables is bound to be a small fraction of what deep learning systems typically use for performance predictions. The problem is exacerbated by the social implications of how to judge ethical or unethical behavior. A method by which sufficiently large AI models can be tested and criteria for ethical and unethical behavior can be defined, and data labeled for at least some of the use cases, at some point in time, allowing for establishing and tracking key ethical behavior variable trends over time (Braun & Matthes, 2018). The system run is referred to as supervised black blob audits, meaning oversight by teams of PhDs, data scientists, and engineers using various techniques, including prompt engineering, to audit the ethical behavior of the AI model.

1.10 Conclusion

We present the foundations and motivations for an ethical imperative in society generally, and, more specifically, in AI-driven insurance. In addressing the ethical imperatives, we weave together hurdles and solutions relevant to a multitude of issues facing AI-driven insurance. A key hurdle is the insurance not being endowed with empathy for the insurers as humans, and losses due to a lack of empathy. Solutions to this and other hurdles include value-sensitivity design, nudges, regulation, and supervision. Using the solutions that overcome hurdles facilitates embedding understanding, consideration, honesty, cooperation, and respect, leading to insurers being inclined to give trust to the insurance as an institution, cyber as well as physical. Risks persist in the capabilities and operation of algorithms, resulting in adverse outcomes and insurers seeking redress. Addressing negative outcomes can turn people into adversaries of AI in their lives and business, damaging the insurance as an institution, even when unintended. Events leading to the reduction in trust in AI-driven insurance exist at micro, meso, and macro levels, and hurt insurers and insurance alike. The chapter shows that empathetic and ethical insurance can contribute to and begin to solve pressing ethical dilemmas and questions. We illustrate how ethical, empathetic AI-driven insurance can accelerate progress in solving major societal challenges. We close with a myriad of ethical dilemmas surrounding rapid AI development, use, and impact by triggering open questions directly supporting an ethical imperative. We hope that the stages to ethical, empathetic AI-driven insurance will contribute to other industries, triggering a comprehensive rethinking of fast-paced AI as an enabling industry. The profound desire to spur the ethical foundations of AI is a matter of critical importance for relatively small fish in the bigger pond of business.

References

Bermúdez, L., Anaya, D. and Belles-Sampera, J. (2023). Explainable AI for Paid-Up Risk Management in Life Insurance Products. *Finance Research Letters*, *57*. https://doi.org/10.1016/j.frl.2023.104242

Bork, D., Ali, S.J. and Dinev, G.M. (2023). AI-Enhanced Hybrid Decision Management. *Business and Information Systems Engineering*, *65*(2). https://doi.org/10.1007/s12599-023-00790-2

Braun, D. and Matthes, F. (2018). Generating Explanations for Algorithmic Decisions of Usage-Based Insurances Using Natural Language Generation. *Lecture Notes in Informatics (LNI)*, *P-279*.

Choi, J.H., Choi, Y., Lee, K.S., Ahn, K.H. and Jang, W.Y. (2024). Explainable Model Using Shapley Additive Explanations Approach on Wound Infection after Wide Soft Tissue Sarcoma Resection: "Big Data" Analysis Based on Health Insurance Review and Assessment Service Hub. *Medicina (Lithuania)*, *60*(2). https://doi.org/10.3390/medicina60020327

Collaris, D. and Van Wijk, J.J. (2023). StrategyAtlas: Strategy Analysis for Machine Learning Interpretability. *IEEE Transactions on Visualization and Computer Graphics*, *29*(6). https://doi.org/10.1109/TVCG.2022.3146806

Collecchia, G. (2021). Let's Open the Black Box: eXplainable Artificial Intelligence (XAI). *Recenti Progressi in Medicina*, *112*(11). https://doi.org/10.1701/3696.36848

El Qadi, A., Trocan, M., Díaz-Rodríguez, N. and Frossard, T. (2023). Feature Contribution Alignment with Expert Knowledge for Artificial Intelligence Credit Scoring. *Signal, Image and Video Processing*, *17*(2). https://doi.org/10.1007/s11760-022-02239-7

Fritz-Morgenthal, S., Hein, B. and Papenbrock, J. (2022). Financial Risk Management and Explainable, Trustworthy, Responsible AI. *Frontiers in Artificial Intelligence*, *5*. https://doi.org/10.3389/frai.2022.779799

Goodell, J.W., Ben Jabeur, S., Saâdaoui, F. and Nasir, M.A. (2023). Explainable artificial intelligence modeling to forecast bitcoin prices. *International Review of Financial Analysis*, *88*. https://doi.org/10.1016/j.irfa.2023.102702

Guo, Y., Li, Y., Liu, D. and Xu, S.X. (2024). Measuring Service Quality Based on Customer Emotion: An Explainable AI Approach. *Decision Support Systems*, *176*. https://doi.org/10.1016/j.dss.2023.114051

Lozano-Murcia, C., Romero, F.P., Serrano-Guerrero, J., Peralta, A. and Olivas, J.A. (2024). Potential Applications of Explainable Artificial Intelligence to Actuarial Problems. *Mathematics*, *12*(5). https://doi.org/10.3390/math12050635

Sachan, S. and Muwanga, J. (2023). Integration of Explainable Deep Neural Network with Blockchain Technology: Medical Indemnity Insurance. *CEUR Workshop Proceedings*, *3554*.

Shafik, W. (2024a). *Consumer Behaviour Analysis* (pp. 75–108). https://doi.org/10.4018/979-8-3693-9122-8.ch004

Shafik, W. (2024b). Generative AI for Social Good and Sustainable Development. In *Generative AI: Current Trends and Applications* (pp. 185–217). Springer.

Shafik, W. (2024c). Science of Emotional Intelligence. In *Enhancing and Predicting Digital Consumer Behavior with AI* (pp. 284–310). IGI Global. https://doi.org/10.4018/979-8-3693-4453-8.ch015

Shafik, W. (2024d). Toward a More Ethical Future of Artificial Intelligence and Data Science. In *The Ethical Frontier of AI and Data Analysis* (pp. 362–388). IGI Global. https://doi.org/10.4018/979-8-3693-2964-1.ch022

Shafik, W. (2025a). Ethical and Legal Considerations in Artificial Intelligence. *AI-Enabled Threat Intelligence and Cyber Risk Assessment*, 90.

Shafik, W. (2025b). Security, 15 Privacy, and Trust in Fintech. *FinTech and Financial Inclusion: Leveraging Digital Finance for Economic Empowerment and Sustainable Growth*, 216.

Sharma, M., Goel, A.K. and Singhal, P. (2023). Explainable AI Driven Applications for Patient Care and Treatment. In *Intelligent Systems Reference Library* (Vol. 232). https://doi.org/10.1007/978-3-031-12807-3_7

Tronchin, L., Cordelli, E., Celsi, L.R., MacCagnola, D., Natale, M., Soda, P. and Sicilia, R. (2024). Translating Image XAI to Multivariate Time Series. *IEEE Access*, *12*. https://doi.org/10.1109/ACCESS.2024.3366994

Van Nguyen, K., Islam, M.R., Huo, H., Tilocca, P. and Xu, G. (2023). Explainable Exclusion in the Life Insurance Using Multi-Label Classifier. *Proceedings of the International Joint Conference on Neural Networks*, *2023-June*. https://doi.org/10.1109/IJCNN54540.2023.10191171

Zhdanov, D., Bhattacharjee, S. and Bragin, M. A. (2022). Incorporating FAT and Privacy Aware AI Modeling Approaches into Business Decision Making Frameworks. *Decision Support Systems*, *155*. https://doi.org/10.1016/j.dss.2021.113715

2

Architecting Intelligence: Understanding the AI Value Chain in the Insurance Ecosystem

Wasswa Shafik

2.1 Introduction

Various terms colloquially describe the life cycle of AI within an organization, including the "AI value chain," the "AI development life cycle," or the "AI development toolkit." The AI value chain is a set of key elements needed to integrate AI into business strategy successfully. They include data exploration and validation, model training and testing, production and deployment, and production monitoring and troubleshooting. Each step in the value chain requires a series of specific tools, products, services, and resources for successful deployment. Companies often integrate multiple tools and services from multiple vendors to create their own unique AI development stack. Across every industry and business function, one primary requirement for successfully deploying AI is data. AI Applications cannot succeed without a well-executed data strategy. Alongside this data strategy, investing in the best tools available and creating synergies across these tools from vendor to vendor to suit unique business needs are vital. This text details how insurance organizations can successfully employ AI by creating the right data development strategy and selecting the best tools and resources for each component of the AI value chain. The components of the AI value chain represent the major subfunctions of the value chain. Companies often integrate products across multiple stages of the AI development life cycle and from multiple vendors to create an AI development stack that suits their specific needs. The AI value chain includes product offerings that allow companies to move quickly through these development steps to get insights on specific business problems (Sharma et al., 2023). The AI value chain comprises three major components. These groups can be further categorized into services or tasks or tools, or products. The three major components are:

(i) Low-code and no-code tools that bypass technical debt.
(ii) Professional services and outsourcing to augment or replace internal teams.
(iii) Sourcing advanced data science talent for bespoke solutions.

2.1.1 Definition of AI Value Chain

We are way beyond the initial stage of exploration, where AI was treated as a niche technology by a few tech firms. AI is rapidly moving to mainstream as organizations have started deploying various AI applications at scale. Over time, these organizations have accumulated considerable expertise in creating and deploying diverse AI applications across their respective organizations. One issue that they all continuously grapple with is the creation of a compelling question of how to create

DOI: 10.1201/9781003747659-2

diverse AI applications. Working on AI systems does require dedication and expertise, and AI is not without its challenges. The speed, volume, and variety of data inputs, even months or weeks into the deployment of an AI application, may expose errors in the design or execution that require a complete rethink of the AI application itself. Each type of AI has varying levels of complexity and expertise required to develop and deploy at an organizational level. These features shape the level of commitment, level of diversity, and domain of focus for those actively pursuing the creation of AI applications. Unfortunately, there isn't a recognized concise definition or lexicon on the topic. This has deep implications in how AI applications get created with commonalities and divergences in approach, dependent on the organizational depth of experience. Many of these diverse adoptions either tap into an existing industry or organizational stack or emerge into a new space with its own set of regulations and operating norms. In this essay, we present the AI value chain and its various components as a definitive guide to organizations looking to pursue AI as a product and technology focus for generative and continuous intelligence (Ahmed et al., 2024). This value chain maps existing industry AI capabilities and finds solutions as well as focus areas for becoming an industry leader or pursuing a focus on generative and continuous intelligence.

2.1.2 Components of the AI Value Chain

The AI value chain encompasses an array of stages, components, and players that enable different use cases of artificial intelligence. It involves three core components: the products and services offered, the data foundations powering these capabilities, and enabling the generation, processing, analysis, decision-making, orchestration, and infrastructure. There are five segments involved in four auxiliary components comprising the AI value chain and key players at various parts and assets across each segment. While enterprise-facing segments develop different AI-related offerings, upstream technology providers develop the fundamental elements while also supporting the phases dependent on their technology. The hierarchy of AI capabilities supporting the AI value chain focus on the product and service outcome. The outcome-oriented vision has well-defined business applications, user-driven interaction frameworks, and specific cognitive supporting attributes for the end objectives. Emerging is also an enabling approach to complement cognitive and experience-related capabilities, especially in orchestrating services and partly substituting human capabilities with intelligent automation. It provides a greater input-driven mix of the components across the AI infrastructure stack from analytics capabilities layering across visualization, business for decision-making, data prep for informing models, machine learning (ML) for use case development and performance monitoring, tracking/detecting for deployment, and integration for operations and enabling a stack escalation approach through the hybrid cloud (Lozano-Murcia et al., 2024).

2.2 Data Acquisition in Insurance

Data acquisition is the first step in machine learning or artificial intelligence deployment in the insurance ecosystem. There are three building blocks in the AI value chain, namely data, algorithms, and computation.

Data is a very important ingredient of the AI value chain. Properly designed and trained machine learning models could lead to increased efficiencies and transfer significant value to the insurance ecosystem. That said, the use of AI can provide limited value without unbiased, noncorporate-sourced data and a realistic control for biases built into a model via well-conceived and proven algorithms. AI models based on garbage data will produce garbage results. Company-generated internal data used to build models for sensitivity score computations or to augment models to compute loss amounts is often biased. Smart players look to use third-party external data sources in tandem with internal company data and a proven algorithm that is unbiased and tested for accuracy against a gold standard.

The two main sources of data in the insurance domain are internal data from corporate repositories and external third-party data. Internal data set generated from company activities provides the most cost-effective source of company information, as detailed transactions are available, which could include information that would be nonpublic for a competitor. Additionally, companies generate vast amounts of internal data during their daily activities, ranging from sales to claims prevention to claims handling and settlement, including all interactions with policyholders, agents, and third-party claim experts (Tronchin et al., 2024). Though painstaking to collate, sanitized internal data has the advantages of being exciting as it tells the story for a company in relation to its policies and policyholders, using its own profitable and unprofitable books as the first driver to develop AI models, and also for being the most current available set.

2.2.1 Sources of Insurance Data

Data is the basis of knowledge. Just as knowledge is the basis of insurance industry decision-making, business processes, and productivity, data is the basis of decision-making, business processes, and productivity across all industries. Data accumulation throughout the entire life cycle of customer, insurance policy, and risk will allow insurers to increase their predictive capabilities significantly and ultimately unlock the next generation of market value and business opportunities. The data acquired from the insurance ecosystem by insurers falls into one of the two categories. First, there are the historical data collected by insurers during interactions with customers: acquiring a customer, marketing, underwriting, claims handling, customer service, and managing the customer relationship. The historical data is unique to the insurer; no other company has access to it, and designing the appropriate insurance product and properly underwriting the risk and pricing the premium require analyzing unique insurer historical data. Second, there are the external data that any company can purchase, license, or otherwise access: consumer and business attributes, credit, claims, risk characteristics, social media, third-party transactions, and more. There are many suppliers of external data, but some value-added service providers specialize within the insurance industry. Historical data from customer interactions and external data from suppliers are combined and integrated to create insights about the current and future risk of customers, insurance products, and policies. Insurers use data and statistical methods to answer the question (Masello et al., 2023): what are the expected losses associated with a customer? Insurers with a closed-loop feedback model can gain insights from analyzing results and apply these learnings to improve underwriting, pricing, risk control, claims management, and technology investments.

2.2.2 Data Quality and Reliability

Insurance continues to be an industry mired in legacy processes, driven mainly in hopes of de-risking their business operations, given the fiduciary responsibilities that they need to fulfill. Risk analytics has always had a prominent role when it comes to loss control, mitigation, and postmortem reviews. This risk coverage role is also key in the understanding and development of AI solutions. Any data-centric solution will rely on the underlying risk evaluation model used, and it becomes a closed loop with a feedback mechanism once automated. This section will explore the issues around data quality and data-quality metrics, as well as the reliability of the sources used in the AI solutions.

Data quality is about the degree to which data objects address the intended data use in a specific context. Data quality is application dependent, defined in relation to the AI use case; it is neither absolute nor universal: what is good for one application may be of little use for another. Data quality is a generalization of the traditional dimensions: accuracy, completeness, consistency, and timeliness. To support an AI use case, on top of those dimensions, one must also consider the various quality aspects that are specific to different types of data: images, video, text, tabular data, and specialized scientific data. The importance of solid, well-curated data sets is essential for the success of complex AI-based models.

One of the most common challenges of descriptive models, and now AI-based predictive models, is the lack of verification and validation of the source data (Guo et al., 2024). The insurance industry has relied on traditional processes to curate internal data sources for years, and now must expand them to include verification and validation steps for external data sources, as they are being integrated into the AI-based models depending on the big data and its associated approaches, as illustrated in Figure 2.1.

Fig. 2.1 Big data and the merits of the artificial intelligence value chain.

2.3 Data Processing Techniques

Data processing is often considered the most critical and arduous step in data science and machine learning pipelines. This is because of the various technicalities, tediousness, and intricacies involved in data cleaning, enrichment, and transformation, all of which are often domain-specific. Not only do insurance domains have very strict and rigid regulations surrounding the usage of certain data sources, but insurance data also comes from different entities that contribute to a massive volume and number of unique underwriting data formats for various types of insurance. For instance, regarding a property insurance, involvement of corporations and organizations often contributes massive amounts of social media and ground-level property data, whereas a personal or health insurance, typically with just individuals attached, handles very minute and limited information. Furthermore, insurance documents such as policy documents, claim documents, medical records, or even customer service chat or interaction logs are often a mixture of structured data and unstructured documents containing mixed formats. Due to the unique characteristics of insurance documents, additional data processing steps may be required, such as document-specific extraction techniques as well as postprocessing to enforce certain rules. These include, but are not limited to, rule-based transformation methods in order to reshape or coerce a certain column's characteristic and data types, coupling or splitting of the data between columns, etc. In this work, we provide some of these document-specific techniques to generate ready-to-use datasets for building downstream applications or training of machine learning models (Bermúdez et al., 2023). These techniques can be flexibly used for certain data types that we have used across multiple datasets and projects.

2.3.1 Data Cleaning and Preparation

In AI, data cleaning (or data cleansing) and data preparation (or data preprocessing) refer to a wide variety of tasks or strategies involved in transforming raw data into a clean dataset. Data preprocessing is oftentimes the most crucial part of the entire AI value chain, and it is described as "the tedious task of selecting, combining, cleaning, and transforming the input data before the act of modeling." These key actions are also summarized: "data are combined from a few different sources into a single table, combined data need to be prepped further, with missing and erroneous values filled in or removed, categorical features one-hot encoded, and text transformed into numerical features." In the context of the AI development life cycle, data preparation is one of the steps occurring before the data is fed into the AI algorithm to extract "information" from the data in the form of a model or any other representation. Data cleaning and preparation are parts of a multistep pipeline through which data flows before it becomes ready for further downstream processing and use. Data cleaning checks for and removes duplicates, repairs errors, fills in missing values, and standardizes the data. Data preparation makes the data more appropriate for use and processing by performing transformations, restructuring for integration with other datasets, and generating new variables based on specific algorithms or conditions. In business applications, much of the work involved in data preparation is a manual process, but using data preparation tools allows for at least partial automation of many of the tasks (Koster et al., 2021). While this data preparation processing pipeline description is generic, specific business-use cases of data preparation may rely on the implementation of specific tasks performed through methodologies relevant to the given domain, depending on the type of data, as illustrated in Figure 2.2.

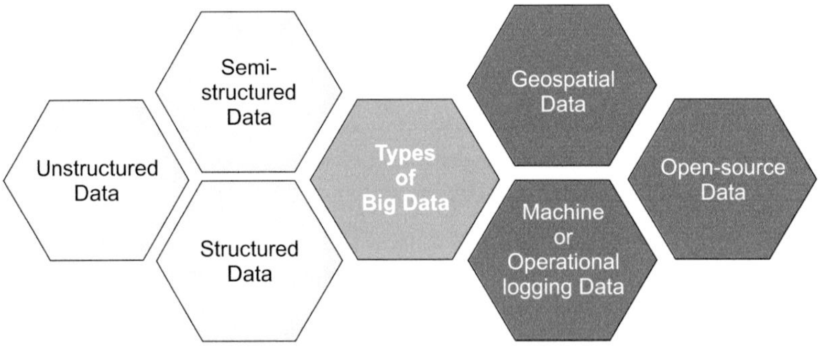

Fig. 2.2 Types of big data as applied in the insurance industry.

2.3.2 Data Transformation Methods

The transformation of data is an essential aspect of data processing that involves changing the form or structure of raw data to facilitate its further use. There are various methods for data transformation. Data discretization creates discrete data ranges from continuous data to facilitate analysis. Data aggregation condenses data to generate summary reports for further analysis. Data generalization abstracts data from lower levels or finer granularity. Data selection extracts appropriate data subsets according to user-defined requirements. Data cleaning addresses missing or incorrect values by imputing, filling, or removing them. Data construction derives new attributes from existing ones. Data reduction decreases the amount of data to be analyzed, while data combination integrates data from different sources. Data transformation is an essential part of the data preparation stage of knowledge discovery in databases. The goal is to prepare various subsets of the whole data set with transformed variables and points relevant for analysis by a variety of specific modeling technologies. It is important to note that transformation methods may include singular value decomposition, but not other ways of combining variables, because they are not allowed to transform the original dataset design. Transformations are often selected for possibilities to visualize aspects of model results. Correspondence analysis applies a specific transformation to the deltas of the variability criteria for the linear mixed models, which are primarily used for the construction and analysis of cross-sectional time series data (Shafik, 2025b). This allows visualizing inter-block relations, but not the actual modeling relations, which are specific for each block of the designs, as some AI value chains are presented in Table 2.1.

Table 2.1 AI value chain in the insurance ecosystem.

Stage	*Core Functions*	*Technologies Involved*	*Business Impact*	*Use Cases*
Data Acquisition	Collecting structured and unstructured data	Internet of Things (IoT), wearables, mobile apps, APIs-Application Programming Interfaces	Informs decision-making, feeds predictive models	Telematics for auto insurance, wearables for health monitoring
Data Processing	Cleaning, structuring, and storing data for model readiness	ETL pipelines, cloud storage, data lakes	Improves data quality and consistency	Data lakes integrating customer relationship management (CRM), claims, and risk data
Analytics & Modeling	Risk scoring, behavior analysis, forecasting	Machine learning, statistical models	Drives risk assessment, pricing, and personalization	Dynamic underwriting models, churn prediction
Decision Automation	Automating tasks such as underwriting, pricing, and claims adjudication	Rule-based systems, AI decision engines	Increases efficiency, reduces human error	Automated quote generation, real-time policy adjustment
Customer Interaction	Enhancing communication, personalization, and service	Natural language processing (NLP) chatbots, recommender systems	Improves user experience and engagement	Virtual agents for claims support, AI-powered recommendation tools
Fraud Detection	Identifying anomalies and suspicious behavior in claims	Anomaly detection, Graph AI	Reduces financial losses and increases trust	Pattern-based claims investigation
Compliance & Reporting	Ensuring legal, regulatory, and ethical standards are met	Regulatory tech, explainable AI	Mitigates legal risks and builds transparency	Anti-Money Laundering (AML) compliance automation, GDPR-aligned data usage
Feedback & Learning	Continuous model retraining and improvement	Active learning, model monitoring, A/B testing	Keeps systems adaptive and accurate	Real-time fraud patterns retraining
Partner Integration	Interfacing with external providers (e.g., reinsurers, brokers)	APIs, blockchain, smart contracts	Enables ecosystem-wide collaboration	Smart contract execution with reinsurers
Strategic Insights	Data-driven decision-making for innovation and growth	Business Intelligence (BI) tools, dashboarding, AI forecasting	Supports long-term planning and market differentiation	AI-enhanced product development roadmaps

2.4 AI Algorithms in Insurance

Machine learning, a subfield of artificial intelligence with its roots in statistics and computer science, is about endowing algorithms with the ability to learn patterns and relationships in electronic data via training on large data samples. What makes an ML algorithm special is its self-improvement over traditional statistical modeling in terms of prediction power as more data becomes available; the algorithms adjust their internal parameters on a regular basis via a process of continuous optimization. Algorithms such as regression analysis, decision trees, support vector machines, and random forests are among the most common techniques used predominantly in insurance. ML is not about model explainability but predictive power by any means. ML algorithms are more likely to be adopted in areas with abundant data. That is the case of many traditional insurance use cases such as risk selection, claim management, and customer relationship management (CRM). Use of ML in these areas has seen exponential growth lately since vast amounts of technical, customer, and market data are flowing on the market. And more interestingly, the trade-off between explainability and prediction power of algorithms is beginning to be rebalanced via an array of ML technique developments relating to interpretable ML and explainable AI.

Deep learning (DL), an even more specialized subfield of ML, is based on deep neural network (DNN) model architectures. Neural networks, originally developed to simulate human brain processes, try to perform automatic feature engineering without requiring domain expertise to convert data from its original representation to the features that can be effectively used for the prediction of the target outcome. The greater self-learning capacity of neural networks, and, in particular, of deep neural networks, is made feasible by massively available storage capabilities and processing speed, especially in terms of graphics processor units. These networks have layers that transform the representation of the data at each layer using a different set of features and mapping functions (Shafik, 2024b). In this way, the early layers are able to detect low-level features such as edges in images, while the higher layers combine these low-level features to extract higher-level features such as objects. DL has surged in adoption in the last decade. While these algorithms will never completely displace traditional ML algorithms, they are likely to be used increasingly.

2.4.1 Machine Learning Techniques

Most ML algorithms fall within one of the following categories of supervised, unsupervised, self-supervised or reinforcement learning, and others may be simply derivative or hybrid models utilizing ensemble techniques. In either case, the earliest primitive forms of ML techniques are already deployed in combination with traditional analytics methods at their branches and head offices. These models are typically first steps into the ML realm and are simple to deploy, quick to detect outliers, easy to interpret, and transparent, as they allow examination of the model's decision criteria and underlying assumptions in ways that more complex derivative or hybrid ML and DL models cannot easily offer. These traditional ML techniques typically include t-distributed stochastic neighbor embedding, support vector machines, genetic algorithms, lazy learning, hidden Markov models, Bayesian networks, Gaussian mixture model, naive Bayes, dimensionality reduction with principal component analysis or matrix factorization, nearest neighbors or K-means, basic regression models, and ensemble methods such as boosting, bagging, among others. For instance, random forest is capable of handling sparse datasets very efficiently, and simple regression models are often combined with penalization that helps form sparse and interpretable models. However, correlation is not causation. ML usually attempts to find correlations and relationships within the data and encodes this reliance in the model's parameters (Shafik, 2024a). ML techniques are inherently limited by the features used, in terms of what commonalities they can find in the datasets they are trained on, as well as the distance metric used for quantifying similarities among items in a dataset.

2.4.2 Deep Learning Applications

Deep learning is a machine learning technique currently generating significant interest in academia and industry. It is recognized as being ideally suited for addressing problems involving large volumes of unstructured data or high-dimensional problems. DL models are architectures inspired by biology, self-learning capabilities, and can automatically extract features from data in multiple layers. Feature selection, which is a major challenge in ML, is performed automatically by DL. By training specialized architectures on sufficient data, DL is able, in some cases, to outperform even traditional expert-designed approaches by significant margins. Traditional ML algorithms, in comparison with DL, are more reliant on handcrafted features and expert domain knowledge to succeed. In this section, we will focus our discussion of DL architectures on the supervised learning paradigm within the insurance domain using the deep neural networks architectures, which have become the DL algorithm of choice. Other formulations of DL are beyond the scope of this chapter. Supervised classification and regression tasks are at the core of many of the applications of intelligent systems to insurance. DL continues to come up with results for both supervised image classification and regression tasks that exceed the accuracy of all previous algorithms. It has also been cited as the only algorithm used to win a number of recent challenges in these areas (Recki et al., 2023; Shafik, 2024c). The use of DNNs for natural language processing tasks has also shown similar results in terms of accuracy and has been argued to be the workhorse of modern baselines for state-of-the-art systems. Hence, these areas should look to DL for guidance in the construction of intelligent systems that deal with nonstructured data.

2.5 Model Development and Validation

The model development and validation subsystem is focused on the actual model implementation and periodization aspects of Line of Business (LOB) impact. These processes take place according to the different time forms in which the variables considered in the loss component—explanatory, risk, and severity variables, and the technologies applied to their processing and combination change—are considered. Therefore, we can differentiate within the periodization phase: the temporal Periodization, which captures the changes operated periodically on the model inputs; the flash-factor periodization, focused on sudden events that can dramatically modify the input variables and that usually do not have defined periodicity; and the continuous periodization, which accounts for continuous but periodic changes in the explanatory variables that affect frequency and severity. This procedure allows us to simplify the LOB-impact loss component, reducing it to two different models: one focused on the mean of the expected loss ratio conditional on the relevant explanatory variables of the loss component; and another that analyzes the residuals of penalties and deductibles of the LOB-impact framework through a quantile regression approach. The average conditional model describes how the companies' market share—the basic LOB-impact assumption—is affected by the continuous time/technology/trend during the temporal periodization phase. Developing a predictive model in insurance is certainly a challenging task, especially when using statistics and ML methods. On the other hand, developing an AI-assisted predictive model is a further increase in complexity, since it adds additional degrees of freedom to this kind of model development. Indeed, the question arises of whether all of these degrees of freedom are consistent and coherent with human common sense. In other words, does a combination of statistical and ML models and an AI-assisted predictive model make sense? How do we validate a parametric, AI-assisted, and predictive model that lacks some of the assumptions underlying validity criteria (Sharma et al., 2023)? However, placing our proposal in the framework of model fusion, we could state that implementing an AI-based model within the model fusion framework offers an opportunity to overcome the limitations.

2.5.1 *Training AI Models*

The training of AI models can have a few different interpretations based on the context. In particular subject areas such as computer vision or natural language processing, the phrase implies the tuning of model weights such that the model recognizes specific attributes in the data. In areas such as reinforcement learning, it implies applying an algorithm to learn the model's policy for choosing actions. In other areas, it may imply the learning of conditional probability distributions such as the distribution of y given x in the case of supervised learning. When developing a generative AI model, these multiple interpretations may exist across the different methods used. For most of the popular generative AI models today, the "training" activity centers around adjusting model parameters and is formulated as a maximum likelihood problem over a certain time horizon. It essentially involves learning the probability of data at a certain time step conditioned on the data at a subsequent time step. This is done using variational inference. Denoising diffusion models approximate the probability by defining a Markov chain that mirrors the diffusion process and training it to reverse the diffusion process. Generative AI models trained in this fashion are known to have several advantages, including the ability to produce high-fidelity, high-resolution generated data. Similar observations hold for other "training" pipelines as well, including diffusion models, autoregressive models, and normalizing flow models. For the specific task of reinforcement learning, the training involves choosing an optimal policy that outlines a distribution over possible future actions and corresponds to the distribution of returns. Guidelines have been proposed for making the training process more efficient as well as for alleviating unwanted behaviors such as getting stuck in local optima (Ahmed et al., 2024). There are also settings such as imitation learning that alleviate inefficiencies of self-play by learning from human feedback.

2.5.2 *Model Testing and Evaluation*

Machine learning algorithms are typically evaluated against standard performance metrics from different model categories. Based on the business problem at hand, evaluative metrics such as those for regression, classification, clustering, and ranking are selected. A good performance on the selected metrics is not sufficient to deploy machine learning models into production use cases in risky business domains such as insurance, finance, and healthcare. Poor performance on high-risk cases, such as estimated incorrect probabilities of insurance loss, financial credit default, and patient disease risk, would have disastrous consequences. Hence, model evaluation must go beyond predefined performance metrics on test data. Model testing and validation start with the selection of the right test and hold-out data. The evaluation must consider the demographics, seasonality, etc., so that those attributes representing high-risk scenarios are measured with the right intensity. Concept drift is another issue. It can be caused by classification algorithms as the comparative relationship between predictor attributes and the target label changes over time. This could imply that the model is no longer representative at the time of testing. Thus, these algorithms need to be validated against changing evaluation standards as algorithms go through drift (Lozano-Murcia et al., 2024). A bad performance can lead to retesting, retraining, or retraining under partially observed data. Model validation and testing can help avoid blind trust in machine learning workflows, which can incur losses for the business.

2.6 Deployment of AI Solutions

In the AI value chain depicted in the earlier text and illustrated with multilayered color-coded sections, we have immediately identified the critical overarching AI strategy that requires multiple inputs and tightly integrates both technology and business aspects in every decision made. However, a successful approach must encompass the last-mile deployment of the Performance Development Plan (PDP) modular system while recognizing its integration into existing systems and continuing performance evaluation. This is necessary because any business changes made first require broad-based organizational motivation and learning. Consequently, investment budgets must first be allocated for supporting the integration and monitoring expenses required for business performance enhancement. National policy decisions and goals directly impact the objectives that insurance companies communicate both internally and externally. Change is difficult, as the limits experienced by each employee must be challenged if performance is to be improved. The correct use of predictive models can allow companies to write more insurance with a smaller number of employees and lower loss adjustment expenses. Complex external factors such as the supply and demand in the regional economies must thus also be influenced by data transparency controls and the incentives offered to specialists to manage these variables. Challenges of company scale impair the use of advanced technical models and may eclipse the responsibility of business units for performance improvement if external consultants focus only on the implementation aspects of AI tool solutions (Tronchin et al., 2024). Taking full advantage of this insight requires the involvement of both business and technical specialists not simply for strategic model selection, but also for all critical aspects of AI development: data collection, data preparation, predictive model building, deployment, and performance monitoring.

2.6.1 Integration with Existing Systems

As a consideration behind the architectural principle of composability outlined, available AI tools, solutions, and services may be integrated within the current insurer's ecosystem, guided by the limitations of each system and the workflows driving the insurer's value creation. Assessment should aim to drive the delivery of specific use-case objectives, considering all dependencies with existing systems required for the desired level of automation to take place. At the same time, instances providing similar functions may be available. For instance, regarding exploration and recommendation engines, pricing differences between AI capabilities explored by domain knowledge will mostly derive from underlying data, features used, and models implemented, thus considering available pretrained models.

(i) AI-generated recommendations may also be cross-considered with traditional analytical systems, for example, predictive analytics that use statistical modeling or machine learning to derive future expected behavior based on past behaviors. It is also possible to leverage what-if questioning and exploratory modeling with frameworks that specialize in allowing risk analyzers to dynamically model risk behavior and analyze subsequent results while controlling for certain variables; query systems or data agnostic engines connecting with the various underlying engines, systems, and models available, or rules that codify the expert decision frameworks and knowledge behind the role played by decision-makers (Masello et al., 2023).

(ii) The depth of reasoning and insight regarding how much to deploy and what native architectural considerations should also leverage existing legacy systems in place, which codify the insurers' historical decisions and assistance in controlling specificity in the decision-making process that would take automation from initial recommendation algorithms to fully fledged deployment of intelligent advisors. Therefore, the choice of layerizes between automation of the journey, safeguarding adherence and company analytics on the touchpoints applied, firm internal insights, product solutions, and capability and expertise underlying the journey application (Guo et al., 2024).

2.6.2 Monitoring AI Performance

The academy has proposed several responsible approaches to deploying—and monitoring—AI systems. For instance, reflection, audit, and accountability approaches are suggested. Reflection requires organizations to spend time thinking about the possible impact of deployment of the AI system on users, while audit suggests independent monitoring of the AI system's user impact, trend tracking, and why the policy has changed. Accountability suggests appointing a person or a group of people within the organization to monitor the effect of the AI system on users. Such monitoring is particularly important if the AI predictions can result in certain harms to the users. Additionally, the organization should be held accountable for decision-making based on potentially wrong AI predictions. This idea is reflected in the framework of an "artificial intelligence officer," who is expected to be legally accountable to the stakeholders during the entire life cycle of an AI system, especially AI development and deployment. Over time, users can stop being influenced by a certain AI bias corrective action and user behaviors can become similar to the predicted patterns for the unprotected groups, especially if the user groups are dynamic. That is why monitoring the possible negative impact of the biased user behavior on predictions of decisions for the protected groups of users should be tracked. Such a monitoring system can be established automatically. External validation is more formal and is expected to provide formal monitoring standards (Bermúdez et al., 2023). For instance, expert panels can be formed to validate the fairness and performance results of the AI system. Additionally, experts can be embedded within organizations using the AI systems to provide dual checks of both the fairness and performance of the AI systems, as presented in Table 2.2.

Table 2.2 Roles, benefits, and challenges of AI in insurance departments.

Department	*AI Applications*	*Benefits*	*Challenges*	*Examples*
Underwriting	Automated risk assessment, dynamic pricing	Faster decisions, personalized premiums	Data bias, explainability	AI models pricing home insurance based on location and risk
Claims Management	Automated triage, image/video claim analysis	Reduced fraud, faster settlement	Data integrity, model drift	Drone imagery for property damage claims
Customer Service	Chatbots, sentiment analysis, voice recognition	24/7 service, reduced support costs	Lack of human touch, multilingual complexity	Virtual assistants answering policy queries
Product Development	Market segmentation, usage-based insurance modeling	Hyper-personalization, innovation acceleration	Overfitting to historical trends	AI-based wellness incentive programs in health insurance
Marketing & Sales	Customer profiling, lead scoring	Improved conversion, targeted campaigns	Privacy concerns, model interpretability	Predictive targeting for policy renewals
Risk Management	Scenario simulation, catastrophe modeling	Proactive risk mitigation, capital optimization	Model accuracy, lack of historical extreme-event data	AI modeling hurricane risk for coastal areas
Compliance & Legal	Monitoring transactions, ensuring policy compliance	Automated audits, regulation alignment	Regulatory ambiguity, data sovereignty issues	Automated audit trail for policy changes

Contd.

Table 2.2 *Contd.*

Department	*AI Applications*	*Benefits*	*Challenges*	*Examples*
Actuarial Science	Predictive analytics, survival models	Greater precision in projections	Resistance to model transparency	AI for life expectancy modeling
IT & Infrastructure	Model deployment, cloud orchestration	Scalable AI solutions, centralized systems	Security vulnerabilities, system integration	Hybrid cloud architecture for AI pipelines
Executive Strategy	Portfolio optimization, market intelligence	Data-informed governance and future-readiness	Misaligned metrics, AI risk ignorance	AI scenario planning for new markets
Partner/Third-Party Ops	Reinsurance analytics, API-based data sharing	Enhanced coordination, shared risk pools	Integration challenges, differing AI standards	Real-time data exchange with global reinsurers
Training & Change in Management	Upskilling workforce, AI ethics workshops	Organizational adaptability	Resistance to change, lack of expertise	Employee training on AI-supported decision systems
Innovation & R&D	New use-case testing, AI pilot projects	Competitive advantage, faster iteration cycles	Cost of experimentation, unclear return on investment (ROI)	AI incubators within insurance innovation hubs
Data Governance	Data lineage tracking, ethics boards	Better data quality and accountability	Data fragmentation, cross-border regulations	Blockchain for immutable data trail

2.7 Ethical Considerations in AI

The ubiquity of AI over the past years has also drawn some ire and concern—for good reason. More and more entities leverage AI decision tools that impact the lives of others—from predicting recidivism and parole eligibility, to making credit and insurance eligibility decisions, to determining release and detention decisions for minors, to curbing online hate speech, to deciding which job applicants should receive a callback—leading to concerns and scrutiny over algorithmic fairness, decision transparency, and procedural accountability. While these concerns are not new, recent pushes toward expansion of the AI toolkit—in both breadth and scope—have led to a renewed discourse on the ethics and responsibility of AI deployment. The data-driven nature of designing and deploying AI systems raises concerns about bias and fairness. There are two types of bias: bias during data collection, and bias during data cleaning, model building and testing, and model deployment (such as algorithmic discrimination, disparate impact, overcorrection). Concerns with these biases center on the selection of features and labels within decision tools—what attributes do AI systems use to make decisions, and how do the AI decisions differ across "protected classes"? Such decisions raise fairness concerns, as they may embed biases and propagate inequality. The nature of bias within an AI product often depends on the usage context (Braun & Matthes, 2018). Debiasing tools and techniques may help alleviate some of the fairness concerns, especially as they relate to algorithmic discrimination and disparate impact.

2.7.1 Bias and Fairness

The insurance ecosystem is traversed by social networks and user-generated content, and large tech companies are able to deploy and monitor AI systems at extreme performance with relatively few ethical implications. However, insurance players must navigate a complex set of ethical considerations while emerging AI value chains unlock unprecedented value. In this light, within the ecosystem, two main considerations become essential: Are we operating in a possible bias and unfairness dimension with the production of our AI-governed services or solutions? And if bias and unfairness are detected, how can we further disclose our AI strategies or algorithms beyond the current legal requirements? Once again, the efficiency and the ability of modern supervision systems will define the tactical response of midplay participants. Companies may choose blind approaches and broker customer data, and allow bias and unfairness processes to automatically delete specialized advertisers, but for insurance players, who have a fiduciary responsibility with their customers, societies and markets are not in the same position. Companies deploy AI-created customer experiences through custom-built infrastructures in the public cloud. Both companies would perhaps prefer to have a lack of data and plan for data scarcity, but the reality suggests otherwise. They will be forced to deploy and monitor their algorithms, looking for tweaks or shifts in outcomes or valuations that regulators and shareholders could find unsatisfying (Sharma et al., 2023). In this light, new business models will emerge from these approaches, and a second wave of customer-centric insurance players will come to life, benefitting from policies and ethical considerations within the playing field.

2.7.2 Transparency and Accountability

The opacity of many AI systems is of growing concern. Powerful systems, especially those based on deep learning, often use large numbers of parameters trained on large data sets, the operations of which internally remain obscure, known as the black-box problem. Regulators have taken note. The EU GDPR requires an explanation when "an individual is subject to a decision based solely on automated processing, including profiling, that produces legal effects concerning him or her, or similarly significantly affects him or her." Many regulators want to be able to interrogate AI systems. Proposed AI regulations would create requirements for management of high-impact AI systems including logging input data, parameters, and predictions or decisions. The case for transparency is not based solely on regulatory requirements. AI has a long responsibility gap. Traditional liability frameworks are based on a person or organization being responsible for a decision, and having the knowledge necessary to take responsibility for its consequences. Accountability requires explanation. If a complex algorithm is simply churning out results, how can liability ever be established? Over time, increasingly complex algorithms have produced increasing numbers of decisions that impact many aspects of society (Ahmed et al., 2024). Deciding when someone else's liability may be actionable, and adequate levels of insurance coverage, will need to be determined as algorithms take on bigger decision-making roles.

2.8 Regulatory Landscape for AI in Insurance

The regulatory landscape for AI in insurance is evolving. Laws and regulations are being introduced that will impact how AI is deployed in the insurance ecosystem. However, the AI ecosystem is in its infancy, and its future trajectory is difficult to predict. Some trends such as the current movement toward rules-based regulation may be augmented by principles-based regulatory guidance. AI regulation is also further complicated by the cross-jurisdictional nature of many technology companies and the global nature of the internet economy, which are calling for harmonized AI regulatory oversight.

(i) Currently, there are no explicit laws that directly regulate specific aspects of AI in insurance. However, for the general AI solutions as well as for some specific AI use cases, there are existing indirect regulations that may impact how AI is used. These indirect regulations either govern the insurance industry itself or govern subdomains that AI overlaps with, such as privacy, consumer protection, anti-discrimination, intellectual property, or data protection. For example, at the insurance industry level, there are efforts to set standards for domestic and foreign companies. Furthermore, at a more domain-specific level, there are currently new risk assessment tools that help monitor changes across the insurance market.

(ii) At a more general level, there are legal restrictions on data, privacy, and consumer protection that may have an impact on the implementation and use of AI solutions in insurance. For instance, there are stricter regulations governing consent, data processing, data sharing, data protection, and cross-border transfer of personal data with a more significant penalty structure for violations when compared to existing regulations. This has rulings around privacy that could have far-reaching ramifications on the use of AI technology.

2.8.1 Current Regulations

The development of AI applications in the insurance industry, such as predictive algorithms for underwriting and fraud detection, process automation through chatbots and virtual assistants, robotic process automation, and image analysis, has opened up new possibilities to enhance business processes and improve existing services. However, the rapid expansion of AI tools has raised important ethical, regulatory, and design issues. The use of nondiscriminatory underwriting algorithms is not a new problem for actuarial science, as insurers have spent years developing algorithms to forecast the future risk insurance applicants represent for the company. Currently, the best example of regulation in insurance is the business regulations issued by various state authorities. These industry-critical states regulate mortality data, morbidity data, and disability reports, among others, which recognized agents must audit. Regulations also fit the function of marketing automation (pricing). An algorithm capable of estimating the future cost of hiring a service, be it a car insurance contract or the renewal of a life insurance policy, is part of the competitive forces of businesses. For this task, business environments elaborate laws, rules, or best practices to guarantee that such models avoid racial, ethnic, economic, disability, or gender discrimination (Lozano-Murcia et al., 2024; Shafik, 2024d). The existing guidelines are based on auditing and oversight for the construction and use of algorithms capable of regulating a business environment of insurance sector actors.

2.8.2 Future Trends in Regulation

The insurance industry is undergoing tremendous development regarding how regulations will be created specifically for AI. These changing expectations may have more impact on current business practices than the AI systems being used. Furthermore, any industry using AI and AI applications will be affected as insurance products in the US are often created by more than one company, with a premium being placed with a different entity from the one issuing the policy. Insurers were required to reserve enough capital for anticipated losses. Other regulations include the safeguarding rule which covers the protection of consumer information by requiring the implementation of safeguards to protect the confidentiality, integrity, and security of customer records and information, though data aggregation and warehousing are not yet considered specifically by any official in the US. Similarly, anti money laundering laws require diligence when determining if part of the insurance purchase is being used to launder money. So far, nothing has specifically addressed requirements for insurance policy generation processes such as potential bias in these policies being issued or how algorithms might influence risk determination decisions by underwriters. What is clear is that regulations will continue to develop. Political entities—from counties to states to the federal government—are very active in creating laws and rules regarding how AI is applied in many aspects of consumer life, and it is anticipated that insurance applications will be reviewed closely to determine that they abide by consumer protection guidelines. With various departments in each location requiring information based on the insurance application, scan and aggregate capabilities for AI models need to be auditable in order to support official requests (Shafik, 2025a). As methods for response speed change, AI-based systems will need to design for audit solutions that will support different tools used to scan for confirmatory select disclosure request processes.

2.9 Case Studies of AI in Insurance

In this section, to illustrate core aspects of AI value chain in action, we present a few case studies around real-life applications of several technologies enabling Insurance 4.0. As demonstrated in the following text, by relying on AI models with high prediction power and business partners with distinct types of expertise, insurance organizations can anticipate an observable impact in their core metrics.

(i) In insurance, claims processing has high operational costs, leading to a need for insurance organizations to solve business pain points. To illustrate this, we highlight the case of a health and wellness specialized insurance company, requiring immediate loan payout to replace loss caused by equipment downtime. The company sought to identify potential auto claims to be affected, from around 60% to over 90% of these claims yearly. To achieve that, it partnered with a specialist in AI applied to claims, responsible for developing models focused on optimizing load shed automation within insurance organizations, and then verified these models using historical data.

(ii) To solve the problem of classifying and prioritizing auto claims, the models obtained both structured and unstructured data from insurance organizations, including policy documents, claim reports, and interview transcriptions. Doing so allowed for improved accuracy. After quality assurance and system integration from the service provider, the customer increased volumes from the tool by over 200% in quarterly releases. Results were achieved in six months: with 75 test classifications, model predictions achieved over 95% accuracy. Through the tool, the customer reduced reliance on manual review. The project highlighted the opportunity for developing native ML model operations applications to accelerate enterprise-wide AI adoption.

2.9.1 Claims Processing Automation

Intelligent automation of damage assessment in claims processing has the potential to boost efficiency and improve the customer experience. Since claims can account for as much as 70% of the workflow in insurers, deploying AI in this area can create substantial efficiencies. The effort to assess damage is tedious, for all classes of claims. In the process of damage assessment, claims personnel review underwriting terms and conditions, policy endorsements, loss details, applicable laws, industry standards, prior decisions and settlements, and state average loss costs. The overall process can take up to several weeks, resulting in lost customer goodwill. Applying AI can boost transparency and speed in this area, and improve loss outcome accuracy. Furthermore, AI-based solutions in this space can extract loss description documents, automate and analyze loss report details, extract key information at scale, classify complex loss cases into a loss type category, and recommend a severity level. AI also has the potential to automate risk assessment and litigation prediction for different lines of insurance, surface insights leveraging third-party data, and benchmark against available market-level data. The AI-based solution can score for the likelihood of subrogating the claim, and get back options for different claim scenarios. Sounds simple, but deployment in this case is not without its challenges (Braun & Matthes, 2018). It is a complex task, as there are different lines of damage visible in pictures and videos at different angles, and damage assessment at fine granularity levels is particularly complicated.

2.9.2 Fraud Detection Systems

Fraud detection is another area where AI and machine learning are showing impact. Fraud in insurance can happen at multiple stages—across quote, application, policy, and claims. And data exists for all these interactions. As with other functions, the regulations for insurance create a perverse incentive for insurance companies to manually inspect high-office claims. Fraud operation is therefore a joint probabilistic problem. Fraud detection is sometimes done at the individual claim level but many techniques are better applied in aggregate on a segment such as policies or claims. Anomalies in the use of the policy, clusters of activity, or other features are more powerful indicators of links to a larger organized crime activity than any standalone claim. Many cases of fraud, or at least attempted fraud, are discovered by journalists or government investigators rather than by insurance companies. The ramifications are more significant for travel insurance than for other categories. Assisting agents and brokers to detect fraud on the frontlines or in the policy writing and renewal stages takes a lot of the burden off and help customers. Additionally, counterintuitively, the ability to identify and rank policies that are most likely to be fraudulent enables companies to offer faster claims processing assistance and serves to further enhance customer experience (Recki et al., 2023). What is needed though is the lack of sufficient data, limiting the effectiveness of supervised learning techniques.

2.10 Customer Experience Enhancement

AI is helping insurers around the world respond to their customers faster and in a more personalized way. Systems are now able to analyze how customers—whether prospects or policyholders—interact with them in the digital world, how they feel about those interactions, and what qualities are driving those sentiments.

(i) AI-Powered Client Data Lakes: Traditionally, insurers maintained separate repositories of client data across various parts of their organization including product manufacturing, distribution, underwriting, and claims. Companies built digital engagement systems in order to create a prospect-to-purchase-to-claim client journey, but without the ability to capture, store, and analyze all engagement data from those various points, the systems lacked intelligence and did not work together well.

(ii) New capabilities in data lakehouses enable insurers to cleanse, visualize, and analyze vast quantities of structured and unstructured client data. This data includes demographic and transaction information, as well as interaction data captured from social networks and websites. Machine-learning-driven insights from these data lakehouses can help insurers—once ready—identify profitable market segments, tailor their message to prospects and policyholders, and promote their full range of relevant services.

(iii) Personalized Virtual Assistants: In addition to creating more personalized experiences across various customer engagement channels, AI is helping insurers enhance their customer interactions through virtual assistants that anticipate clients' needs, offer expert level advice, and provide 24 × 7 service. Such assistants decrease policyholder workload and frustration while increasing the insurer's efficiency and boost customer satisfaction with immediate responses.

(iv) Insurers are employing virtual assistants for many tasks including client onboarding, claims status updates, and call deflection. Some insurers started using AI-powered chatbots several years ago, but others are just deploying them today. Insurers are currently using chatbots for high-volume transactions that require little human interaction, such as premium payments and policy issuance.

2.11 Challenges in Implementing AI

Despite the challenges in the larger adoption of AI and its techniques in the insurance sector, it is also important to highlight and understand some of the specific hindrances that the insurance space is experiencing that could be tailored to specific companies. The challenge for any insurance company is to understand why mostly their experiments on AI are failing. It emerges that there are some common challenges for AI at scale, which often have similar patterns within the sector. One of the foremost challenges has been the technical complexity of AI itself. Most often the very techniques which are expected to work for data-heavy verticals like insurance are the hardest to work with. Most insurance organizations are not organizing their team structures and the business processes required for an ideal AI framework, where the large success cases can drive a continuous process improvement and through that AI be accessible to both skilled as well as unskilled employees. The second common and a critical challenge has been the expected cultural resistance and inertia, which would invariably come in the way of large-scale implementations of the required solutions. It is a well-known fact in the industry that change is hard, and that at the same time with AI solutions the changes in business process workflows are often very intensive. Because of this, the follow-through of the business along with the central AI teams and tech platforms becomes critical, especially in the early stages, to deliver and manage the right kind of business outcomes (Sharma et al., 2023). It may take time, but organizations do adapt, and, at times, move away from the more traditional data-driven analytical techniques toward the more advanced use of AI models.

2.11.1 Technical Challenges

AI encompasses the technological and scientific developments that enable machines to perform cognitive tasks. In particular, the term is generally used to refer to applications of machine learning, an area of statistics that developed its own identity through the availability of larger datasets and the computational capacity to analyze them, but also through a renewed interest in artificial neural networks and their successive enhancements. The term AI has thus become synonymous of supervised learning and more recently also of unsupervised learning, through generative adversarial networks. In supervised learning, human developers define features of the datasets that will enable the algorithm to link input with results from which it learns to classify. In generative adversarial networks, the task is not to classify, but to generate realistic-looking synthetic data which is similar to real data fed into it. Beyond supervised, unsupervised, and assisted learning, AI is also associated with reinforcement learning, where algorithms are given a particular goal with a set of performance measures and learn to take actions that will enhance their chances of success through trial and error. The technical challenges of implementing AI are firstly the availability of the data, in sufficient quantity and quality to train the ML models, then how to organize that data in order to train existing models or create new ones, thirdly how to store that data in a way that is accessible when needed, fourthly how to develop models in a cost-effective and timely way, who to involve in the actual production of the models, how to integrate the AI models in current business processes, and finally how to keep the models up to date. In the case of supervised ML, challenges relate to how to define the features you need, and how to label the data. For supervised models, extra challenges arise at the moment of deploying the ML engine in the operational application (Guo et al., 2024). The efficient execution of AI models can either be real-time inference or batch inference, and cost-effectively addressing the two requires different architectural designs.

2.11.2 Cultural Resistance

The same holds for the current atmosphere of anxiety regarding current AI systems that contribute to an avalanche of job losses. ChatGPT and the other GPTs demolish marketing copy and warehouse workers lose their jobs. This is no time for loss of jobs in the insurance industry. Investment in AI for underwriting, claims, customer service, risk modeling, and premium optimization may find many experts within the company who may see it as a threat and not a platform for leveraging specialized knowledge. The finance sector has walked this road before with the introduction of major algorithmic systems modeling risk for the financial industry, channeling collateralized debt obligations and options. Making sure that the major stakeholders and industry experts see AI as a partnership and not as a takeover is important. The essential, specialized knowledge in risk modeling, customer behavior, claim estimates, and the entire insurance ecosystem must be made into a partnership with AI, or the desired flow and partnerships will not happen. The investment in the AI ecosystem is going to take a major part of the corporate budget for several years. As with any new platform for the undertaking of work, time and patience are required while the infrastructure is put in place to monitor the major investment in AI and the best use of AI is implemented. The tendency in AI called transfer learning will be one answer to those on the engineering side who seek to tie in as many systems as possible and move on (Shneiderman, 2020). This is a tough sale as the engineering ethos is to make cutting-edge native models everywhere, but acquiring a major asset of a model that is the market's best of breed can enhance investment flows to create other platforms while cutting down costly investment in AI.

2.12 Future of AI in the Insurance Sector

AI is a constantly evolving technology, and managing its integration into any industry ecosystem is no easy task. It changes the work that employees do and how efficiently they can perform these functions at higher levels of quality. The overall effect creates a new set of opportunities and challenges for the various participants involved. Over the next decade, we expect the pace of change and integration of AI into the insurance ecosystem to grow thanks in part to advances in new technologies, the maturation of the adoption of AI led by companies in industries adjacent to the insurance ecosystem, demographic changes in the workforce creating an AI-native population, capital markets desiring higher returns on equity, and other technological developments that we will likely discover. At its core, insurance is a data-driven business, aiming to price risk fairly and use the collected premiums to cover insured losses efficiently. Digital transformation is enhancing the capabilities of insurance organizations to offer digitized, customer-centric experiences, and AI-led processes will help accomplish this goal at a faster rate and higher quality level than is presently possible. As a part of the drive for better user experiences, insurance organizations will require AI to enable simpler processes while working seamlessly with other related processes (Guo et al., 2024). Not only will AI be required to enhance the frontline user-centered ecosystems, but also the back-office support capabilities to deliver financial and operational benefits.

2.12.1 Emerging Technologies

The emerging technologies on the horizon include open AI, human-augmented AI, brain–computer interfaces, and autonomous AI. The development of these technologies is not rocket science or heavy engineering. Instead, these technologies are all a part of continual innovation, adding ingredients for self-learning, including human feedback, additional training data, acting in the real world, and providing some level of autonomy. They are also part of the same technological evolution in the way people use utilities. The utility model existed for electricity. The latest development is being implemented with cloud services. The next logical frontier is to do this with cognition. Autonomous AI does this by enabling AI to manage cognition as a service. The other frontier is in utilizing human value in the loop instead of avoiding it, leading to human-augmented AI. An obvious challenge for all AI systems is to learn faster and in less expensive ways than just using large amounts of training data and epochs, which increases the requirement for building explanation and interpretability features into AI systems. Instead, there is an inherent impatience with traditional ways of product development, and AI is evolving differently. When scaling, it pulled the AI research community behind it, but avoided the additional requirements for being enterprise-ready. Inflation in training data has pushed the charter for every cognizant organization to take big leaps in training data, but also in contending with language models to understand and build solutions, particularly in the niche areas that require domain expertise (Sharma et al., 2023). The other aspect was that after the initial explosion on several consumer-centric tasks, such as content creation, it lives more in the background, with the enterprise-specific task being addressed by more customized embedding and model loading features.

2.12.2 Predictions for AI Integration

There is a great deal of noise around the AI hype cycle at the moment. The fortune that is at stake to the good/bad use of AI is vast and so everybody wants to show they are at the forefront of AI; be it government, industry titans, world religions, or technology start-ups. Who can blame them? AI has the potential to effectively change the face of our planet by creating a predictive algorithm that delivers personalized recommendations to everyone ahead of schedule. In the insurance world, personalized insurance products are driven by AI that is triggered by massive amounts of internal and external data being fed back to the AI systems in real time. So, what lies ahead for AI (Tronchin et al., 2024)? The first prediction is that the entire life of AI will change in three phases.

(i) Phase 1: Experiment
(ii) Phase 2: Integrate
(iii) Phase 3: Transform

These three phases will shape the way AI is integrated into the insurance ecosystem. The second stage will dominate the years ahead. Industry players will seek to integrate AI into the existing conditions and paradigm of their businesses, peeling off the obvious layers of costs and risk in their existing structures. What will not happen is a radical transformation. The business conditions that will bear out over the next five years will not be comfortable, but they will be sufficient for core insurance businesses, and the technology and the people will be there to support a sensible AI investment strategy. There will be little incentive to invest in radically new business models: the players in the best position to capitalize on these profiles are small innovators such as Insurtech and global technology companies (Braun & Matthes, 2018). The corporatization of insurance is still limited to those who are exploiting commoditization all through. Even insurance distribution is far from fully corporatized. Insurance cannot afford to be complacent.

2.13 Conclusion

The pace of growth of AI in the insurance industry is tremendous; hence, there are inherent risks that may impede progress. Existing players need to collaborate and partner across the AI value chain to understand the best use cases, the underlying technology, and the workings of data processing and model training. Insurance companies need to keep pace with start-ups that are effectively leveraging the AI capability across these three critical tenets. New players need to familiarize themselves with the insurance industry to build solutions that are likely to get adopted. Lastly, there needs to be a certain willingness to experiment, invest, and test the solutions for them to get integrated into the operating models. We hope the framework presented becomes the standard industry reference that can enable a strategic and structured discussion on AI integration among all stakeholders involved. As we move toward an increasingly digital world with rapidly evolving customer expectations and needs, insurance companies find themselves at a crucial juncture: adapt to continue to flourish or stagnate. AI has the potential to reshape the insurance landscape dramatically, in many ways changing how the players in its ecosystem interact. As we gear up toward this impending wave, a slingshot cannot be averse to the stone that enables momentum.

References

Ahmed, A., Topuz, K., Moqbel, M. and Abdulrashid, I. (2024). What Makes Accidents Severe! Explainable Analytics Framework with Parameter Optimization. *European Journal of Operational Research, 317*(2). https://doi.org/10.1016/j.ejor.2023.11.013

Bermúdez, L., Anaya, D. and Belles-Sampera, J. (2023). Explainable AI for Paid-Up Risk Management in Life Insurance Products. *Finance Research Letters, 57*. https://doi.org/10.1016/j.frl.2023.104242

Braun, D. and Matthes, F. (2018). Generating Explanations for Algorithmic Decisions of Usage-Based Insurances Using Natural Language Generation. *Lecture Notes in Informatics (LNI), P-279.*

Guo, Y., Li, Y., Liu, D. and Xu, S.X. (2024). Measuring Service Quality Based on Customer Emotion: An Explainable AI Approach. *Decision Support Systems, 176*. https://doi.org/10.1016/j.dss.2023.114051

Koster, O., Kosman, R. and Visser, J. (2021). A Checklist for Explainable AI in the Insurance Domain. *Communications in Computer and Information Science, 1439.* https://doi.org/10.1007/978-3-030-85347-1_32

Lozano-Murcia, C., Romero, F.P., Serrano-Guerrero, J., Peralta, A. and Olivas, J.A. (2024). Potential Applications of Explainable Artificial Intelligence to Actuarial Problems. *Mathematics, 12*(5). https://doi.org/10.3390/math12050635

Masello, L., Castignani, G., Sheehan, B., Guillen, M. and Murphy, F. (2023). Using Contextual Data to Predict Risky Driving Events: A Novel Methodology from Explainable Artificial Intelligence. *Accident Analysis and Prevention, 184*. https://doi.org/10.1016/j.aap.2023.106997

Recki, L., Esau-Held, M., Lawo, D. and Stevens, G. (2023). AI Said, She Said – How Users Perceive Consumer Scoring in Practice. *ACM International Conference Proceeding Series*. https://doi.org/10.1145/3603555.3603562

Shafik, W. (2024a). *Consumer Behaviour Analysis* (pp. 75–108). https://doi.org/10.4018/979-8-3693-9122-8.ch004

Shafik, W. (2024b). Generative AI for Social Good and Sustainable Development. In *Generative AI: Current Trends and Applications* (pp. 185–217). Springer.

Shafik, W. (2024c). Science of Emotional Intelligence. In *Enhancing and Predicting Digital Consumer Behavior with AI* (pp. 284–310). IGI Global. https://doi.org/10.4018/979-8-3693-4453-8.ch015

Shafik, W. (2024d). Toward a More Ethical Future of Artificial Intelligence and Data Science. In *The Ethical Frontier of AI and Data Analysis* (pp. 362–388). IGI Global. https://doi.org/10.4018/979-8-3693-2964-1.ch022

Shafik, W. (2025a). Ethical and Legal Considerations in Artificial Intelligence. *AI-Enabled Threat Intelligence and Cyber Risk Assessment*, 90.

Shafik, W. (2025b). Security, Privacy, and Trust in Fintech. *FinTech and Financial Inclusion: Leveraging Digital Finance for Economic Empowerment and Sustainable Growth*, 216.

Sharma, M., Goel, A. K. and Singhal, P. (2023). Explainable AI Driven Applications for Patient Care and Treatment. *Intelligent Systems Reference Library, 232*. https://doi.org/10.1007/978-3-031-12807-3_7

Shneiderman, B. (2020). Bridging the Gap between Ethics and Practice: Guidelines for Reliable, Safe, and Trustworthy Human-Centered AI Systems. *ACM Transactions on Interactive Intelligent Systems, 10*(4). https://doi.org/10.1145/3419764

Tronchin, L., Cordelli, E., Celsi, L.R., MacCagnola, D., Natale, M., Soda, P. and Sicilia, R. (2024). Translating Image XAI to Multivariate Time Series. *IEEE Access, 12*. https://doi.org/10.1109/ACCESS.2024.3366994

3

Navigating Legal, Regulatory, and Ethical Frameworks in Algorithmic Insurance Practices

Wasswa Shafik

3.1 Introduction

To address the issue of excessive insurance algorithm pricing, we first need to unpack how algorithms are defined and used in the insurance sector. This involves critically discussing how algorithms fit into the broad pecking order of technological interfaces and how we can build a taxonomy of algorithms relevant to insurance. This allows us to elaborate on the role of algorithms as decision-making grounds and how different algorithms with differently calibrated levels of autonomy, from advice-driven interfaces to ones that operate autonomously and bifurcate entire businesses, dictate the allocation of responsibility in the decision-making loop (Margan, 2021). It is common to use the term algorithm colloquially to refer to a wide array of digital systems, including websites, software solutions, and technology interfaces that fulfil a range of functions, from quantizing and automating decisions to administrating processes more efficiently and saving resources.

But underlying the harsh interplay between insurance's quest for uniformity and its need for precision, it is precisely the allegedly impenetrable and objective nature of algorithms that entails the promise and peril of their deployment in the insurance context. They are envisioned as miracle cures that hold the potential of result-perfect decision-making. But insurance is also increasingly haunted by the perilous shadow of insurance algorithm concoction. Incorrectly calibrated or poorly understood algorithms that become the basis for underwriting day-to-day business can put entire business models under threat, for example, in the context of price discrimination. Algorithms determine policyholder selection for profit and loss purposes, premium levels, product design, and in what situations the policyholder will be compensated. In this critical function, algorithms hold insurance business hostage (Townsend et al., 2018). And the stories of those affected abound: algorithmic discrimination in health insurance, motor insurance for Proof of Concept (POC), and the hijab aversion of algorithmically calibrated business travel models.

3.1.1 Definition of Algorithms

While the use of algorithms predates computers, the term algorithm in the contemporary sense refers to a precise rule specifying how to solve a problem by following certain steps. In practical terms, algorithms specify how to get from the start to the end of a certain process, such as ranking different signers for good risk. Algorithms can be described both conceivably and operationally.

DOI: 10.1201/9781003747659-3

The former means that an algorithm may be conceived as involving the separation of enclosed sets of instructions specifying why, not how, to do what. The latter implies that an algorithm is written out in actual computer code that does what digital coders say it does. It follows that an algorithm in its operational sense is a description of the way a computer, more specifically a digital computer for algorithmic processing, performs a certain activity. This activity may be achieved either sequentially or, more contemporarily, massively in parallel (Philip & Suresh, 2024). In addition, algorithms can be classified as being deterministic, randomized, or heuristic. The notion of algorithms is thus fundamentally tied to computation and computer code, although other forms of algorithms do not fit neatly into this definition. Evaluation algorithms, that go by this name, typically use tables to associate specific values with the possible outcomes from a specific type of event subject to uncertainty, such as loss amount or frequency. Given that computational resources are finite, programs that apply such algorithms cannot account for all possible outcomes in an insurance process and may not fully consider any actuarial opinion regarding the specific distribution of this process. However, different outcomes may share certain characteristics that render their handling by an evaluation algorithm reasonable and efficient (Golden et al., 2016). Indeed, algorithms can be thought of as tables, scanning a predefined script for instructions about what should happen next, when applied to the institutionalized rules in the current insurance market.

3.1.2 Types of Algorithms Used in Insurance

Insurance companies are increasingly relying on algorithms for a variety of tasks, ranging from processing customer claims to underwriting and fraud detection. Algorithms help insurers enhance their existing offerings and create new products, reduce costs, and improve the efficiency of their operations. The motley assortment of algorithms available today can be categorized in various ways. However, a very useful approach is to classify algorithms in terms of their relative complexity and ability to handle structured or unstructured datasets.

(i) Based on this classification, algorithms can be grouped into fifteen. Those at the lowest end of the complexity spectrum are automated task scripts. These apply straightforward if-then-else rules to pre-coded situations and are often useful in helping customers customize straightforward product offerings of do-it-yourself (DIY) insurance portfolios. The next level of sophistication is Bayesian or logic-based models, which develop simple models connecting inputs and outputs. Most commercial algorithms used for insurance underwriting fall into this category. The third category is signal processing algorithms, which make sense of encrypted data such as a vehicle's tire pressure signal or GPS signal (Choi et al., 2024). However, these are often designed for a very specific offering.

(ii) The next is cluster analysis, where similar data points/entities are grouped into clusters. The K-means algorithm is a popular example and is often used to identify customer segments with distinct risk levels. The fifth type is decision trees, which analyze all the inputs and create a tree-like model determining the possibilities of various outcomes based on the various input values processed. These types of models can tackle a broader variety of datasets better than Bayesian or logic models, and can provide significantly more accurate predictions as well. The next algorithm type is neural networks using multilayer perceptrons, which are a slightly more complicated subset of decision trees that learn mappings of input to output values from the input patterns and output patterns seen during training (Aina et al., 2024).

3.2 Legal Frameworks Governing Algorithmic Insurance

Algorithmic insurance is a rapidly growing sector of the industry, not least in the area of private sector, peer-to-peer, and social insurance. These latter markets are both global and local in scope and national and transnational in regulation. In terms of public sector insurance, the goals of blockchain-based systems related to insurance services are complementary to existing conditional cash transfers for disaster mitigation. Such technology-based insurance systems in both the private and the public sector are partly facilitated by the fact that disaster risk (especially for people with low incomes) is increasingly being systemized through natural hazard risk models, using publicly available online big data, which are available for re-insurance evaluation and pricing (McDonnell et al., 2023). Nevertheless, these nascent insurance systems are running into both local struggles and wider restructuring of the insurance industry and the relationships among its stakeholders internationally, especially when it comes to the cross-border insurance rules. Insurance systems are, however, composed primarily of rules and regulations, using processes demonstrated in Figure 3.1. Existing insurance rules are flexible and dynamic in order to be able to evolve along with changing risks and any new management or engineering solutions in managing and mitigating these risks. An important challenge in establishing decentralized finance systems is therefore to develop an additional tech creation layer, responsibly and ethically leverage Distributed Ledger Technology (DLT), and contract smart technology to support the existing insurance system, within the broader network that is composed of our formal and informal private and public multilevel governing institutions, rather than dismantling these institutions, which in the case of developing countries are often fragile (Gramegna & Giudici, 2020; Shafik, 2025b).

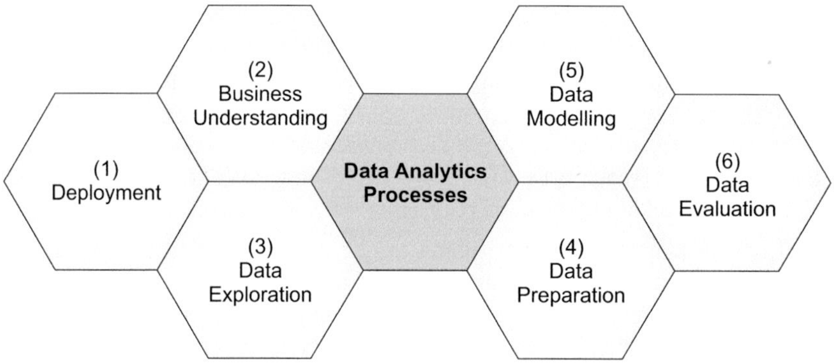

Fig. 3.1 Data analytics processes.

3.2.1 Key Legislation

Algorithmic insurance practices carry novel and significant risk, which is, per current legislation, at times inadequately mitigated for individuals and society. For the insurance contract and core fairness principles concerning parties to that contract (including "utmost good faith," "cooperation," "small print," "imbalance of power," and "insurer as expert"), certain additional data and algorithmic and systemic fairness principles are relevant in the context of external, especially societal, impacts of (non-)insurance decisions. These add to existing insurance legal contracts, which themselves must be executed correctly and not distorted or discriminatory against by any automated tools. This regulatory discussion is reconsidering what constitutes a violation of ordinary insurance laws. Certain federal statutes apply in a range of ways to algorithmic insurance, though these, especially concerning the treatment of data and algorithms by insurance companies, are siloed and thus inconsistent and not appropriately comprehensive (Shafik, 2025a). Additionally, data-fishing for unjust reasons could fall under the tort of "intentional infliction of emotional distress," other torts, or mean actions under some laws, defeating the business purpose of executing lawful contracts.

3.2.1 International Regulations

Several international documents inform the ethical use of algorithms in all industries, including the insurance sector. They include policy recommendations, principles, and guidelines that relate either directly to algorithmic use or broadly to the use of artificial intelligence (AI) technologies. Functions performed by algorithms in the insurance industry raise significant ethical concerns, mainly regarding risk assessment and customer profiling (cover or deny insurance), but also automation and microtargeting (target advertising about insurance products without discrimination), claims management (fraud detection and claims settlements), product design (option of not offering insurance products), pricing and underwriting (exclusionary pricing or denial of service), and product distribution (unaccountable decision-making about insuring or not insuring) (Gramegna & Giudici, 2020). An organization that fosters policy dialogue and economic cooperation internationally has created an established algorithmic ethics model. In 2019, it published a report that provides ten principles: innovation that is robust, safe, and trustworthy; human-centered values and fairness; transparency and explainability; robustness, security, and safety; accountability; collaboration of multiple stakeholders and multilateral agreements; respecting sovereignty, democracy, and the rule of law; ensuring a pursuit of the common good for all; justice and inclusiveness; and propelling and evolving a sustainable economic and employment development. These principles can serve as tools to assess the ethical use of algorithms as a foundational basis for the development of specific legislative, regulatory, and accountability instruments. Building on this work, in 2021, an organization dedicated to upholding human rights and the rule of law in Europe and promoting European culture published a document that emphasizes the need to develop artificial intelligence in a human-rights-compliant manner (Koster et al., 2021). More specifically, it exhorts states to ensure trustworthy and human-rights-respecting artificial intelligence systems and emphasizes the need to develop standards that take into account the protection of legal, ethical, and human rights.

3.3 Regulatory Bodies and Their Roles

Multiple regulatory bodies have the power to review and approve algorithmic models in insurance as well as other business practices. In contrast to most other business sectors, regulations in insurance have evolved over many centuries to protect policyholders from being exploited by insurance companies. This was largely accomplished by creating strict and detailed regulations and then establishing specialized agencies responsible for regulating the sector. The intended role of the regulatory agencies is to protect the policyholders, as most insurance companies are very sophisticated with large lobbying budgets that enable them to exert powerful influence over the politicians in government (Margan, 2021). The powers of insurance regulatory agencies can include the requirement for companies to obtain approval for rate filings before a policy is issued and to establish standards for techniques that may be used to develop predictive models that are used for underwriting and pricing products. Data protection authorities (DPAs) are the government entities that oversee the data governance policies in society and impose the largest share of regulatory burdens associated with algorithmic insurance. In particular, DPAs are responsible for protecting the privacy and security of consumer data that is required by law to be safeguarded. DPA has emerged over the last thirty years with the rise of the data economy and associated awareness of the importance of data protection (Poshtiri et al., 2024). Most developed nations, and many developing ones, have enacted comprehensive data protection laws that have established DPAs.

3.3.1 Insurance Regulatory Authorities

Traditionally, regulatory authorities in the field of insurance have mostly focused on consumer protection. This is evident in regulations that ensure the prompt payment of claims and protect against company insolvency and fraud. Consumer-facing algorithms have the potential to affect aspects of a consumer's experience with insurance, and by extension the company's general policies and procedures, such as how information relevant to underwriting and premiums is collected and analyzed; how third-party service providers use these algorithms to provide services that impact consumers; how claims decisions are made; and how fraudulent activity is detected. Consequently, we are concerned that regulators may be ill-equipped to address more upstream issues in insurance and technologies that affect the business practices of the insurers themselves (Van Nguyen et al., 2023). Nevertheless, to the extent that consumer-facing algorithms in insurance do have a consumer protection angle, this has implications—both for how these algorithms should be regulated and by whom. A significant consumer protection perspective in insurance regulation is that of achieving fairness in underwriting and claims decisions, and ensuring that decisions are made on the proper bases (for underwriting, the basis that reasonably predicts a claimant's risk of loss; for claims, that the insured event really happened). The associations of insurance company executives are focused on what they see as the consumers' right to a fair and equitable marketplace for insurance. Their statement of principles includes the commitment that no individual in Canada would be refused insurance or charged a higher premium than the individual would otherwise be charged solely by virtue of being a member of a specific group (Sachan & Muwanga, 2023). Supposedly discriminatory practices arising from the use of models for underwriting and claims adjustment with negative outcomes for certain groups of consumers may attract the attention of insurance regulators, including through the use of guidelines urging insurance companies to act in a certain way.

3.3.2 Data Protection Agencies

In the European Union, the General Data Protection Regulation (GDPR) is "an important landmark in the creation of a multidisciplinary regulatory framework related to the use of algorithmic procedures with personal data." The GDPR lays down the principles applicable to all data processing, including, inter alia, fairness, accuracy, purpose limitation, transparent and informed consent, data protection by design and by default, rights of data subjects including rights to data access, rectification, erasure, and objection, as well as rules on authorizations, the appointing of data protection officers, and on the transfer of personal data. The GDPR aims to ensure the protection of individuals and acts as a roadblock against the most dangerous types of data processing for society and individuals at large. Each European Union (EU) state has to set up at least one independent authority responsible for monitoring the application of the GDPR, and acting as a "watchdog" on potentially abusive data processing by private actors, but also by governmental authorities and public administration on the basis of ulterior legislative acts (Butterworth, 2018; Daudén-Esmel et al., 2024).

Once the GDPR defines the basic principles and rules on the implementation of those principles, individual countries are free to set further regulations related to the collection and processing of personal data within an insurance context. Countries have the choice to complement them with stricter measures that can define, in more detail, the specificities of the insurance market. Such specific regulations should always be coherent with the principles and rules laid down in the GDPR. In EU countries, however, "DPAs do not have the power to modify the principles or rules laid down in the GDPR." According to EU law, data protection authorities have powers of administrative sanctions as well as investigative powers. They also have the power to act in judicial procedures in case of noncompliance with GDPR, or in case compulsory orders were not complied with (Dorfleitner et al., 2023). Therefore, in case of serious noncompliance with the rules set forth by the GDPR, DPAs have the power to impose sanctions on insurance companies involved in algorithmic practices that involve personal data for either unlawful processing or unauthorized use, as presented in Table 3.1.

Table 3.1 Legal and regulatory frameworks in algorithmic insurance.

Jurisdiction/ Region	*Relevant Laws & Regulations*	*Focus Areas*	*Implications for Insurers*	*Challenges*
United States	Fair Credit Reporting Act (FCRA), Americans with Disabilities Act (ADA), AI Bill of Rights (proposed)	Credit-based pricing, disability access, and fairness	Limits use of credit scores, mandates inclusive practices	Regulatory fragmentation at the state and federal levels
European Union	GDPR, AI Act (draft), Solvency II	Data privacy, explainability, and risk management	Requires data minimization, algorithm transparency	High compliance costs, ambiguous guidelines
Canada	Personal Information Protection and Electronic Documents Act (PIPEDA)	Consent, accountability	Requires transparent consent practices	Lags behind in AI-specific legislation
UK	Data Protection Act 2018, FCA AI Guidelines	Fairness, explainability, and consumer protection	Encourages ethical audits and algorithm explainability	Compliance complexity with EU divergence
Singapore	Model AI Governance Framework	Transparency, human oversight	Promotes sector-specific ethical toolkits	Voluntary adoption may lead to inconsistent practices
Australia	Privacy Act, AI Ethics Principles	Data integrity, fairness	Insurers must conduct impact assessments	Poor enforcement of AI-specific provisions
South Africa	POPIA-Protection of Personal Information Act, Treating Customers Fairly (TCF) principles	Data security, nondiscrimination	Ensures data accuracy and consumer redress	Legal literacy and enforcement gaps
Brazil	General Data Protection Law (LGPD)	Consent, lawful processing	Similar to GDPR, but with less stringent enforcement	Regulatory uncertainty in AI use
China	Personal Information Protection Law (PIPL), AI-specific guidance	Algorithmic accountability, fairness	Mandatory algorithm review and filing	Limited appeal mechanisms for algorithmic decisions
Global Initiatives	OECD-Organisation for Economic Co-operation and Development AI Principles, ISO/IEC 42001	International AI governance, technical standards	Encourages harmonization and AI risk classification	Voluntary adoption, nonbinding
Insurance Regulators	EIOPA-European Insurance and Occupational Pensions Authority (US), EIOPA (EU), Insurance Regulatory and Development Authority of India (IRDAI) (India)	Supervision of AI use in underwriting/ claims	Push for fairness, transparency in automated systems	Capacity to audit black-box algorithms

Contd.

Table 3.1 *Contd.*

Jurisdiction/ Region	*Relevant Laws & Regulations*	*Focus Areas*	*Implications for Insurers*	*Challenges*
Consumer Protection Laws	General consumer rights laws and anti-discrimination statutes	Unfair practices, algorithmic bias	Can trigger legal challenges in AI-based denial of claims	Difficulty in proving algorithmic bias
Cybersecurity Laws	Sectoral cybersecurity standards (NIST-National Institute of Standards and Technology, ISO-International Organization for Standardization, etc.)	Data breaches, cyber resilience	AI systems must integrate cybersecurity by design	Rapidly evolving threat landscape
Taxonomy & Risk Grading	EU AI Risk Categories, NIST AI Risk Management Framework	Classifying AI use by risk level	Enables differentiated oversight by AI impact	Ambiguity in risk definitions

3.4 Ethical Considerations in Algorithmic Insurance

The moral issues associated with insurance rely on specific ethical values embodied in the social contract that insurance has with the insured. Ethical values such as fairness, equity, empathy, and fiduciary responsibility form the backbone of traditional insurance. Traditionally, mutuality is not only the foundation of cooperative insurance, but it states the need for insurance companies to take care of the insured after a loss occurred. As such, authorities enacted laws preventing adverse selection and moral hazard, and obliged insurance companies to treat all insureds in a fair and just manner, that is, to disclose all important facts, especially concerning their own risk, allow for payment delays, and prudently bear risks. Transparency, reciprocity, and a process-oriented view of justice play an important role in shaping an insurer's social reputation. With the introduction of algorithmic insurance, new tools that insurers apply to upend these requirements and subvert the moral principle of human ecology suddenly gain traction (Dorfleitner et al., 2021). Some of the reasons that drive this shift include monetary appetite, as insurers are allowed to develop "innovative" products based on a focus on profitability. Such products may provide monetary rewards for good behavior and present increased premiums as punitive measures for bad behavior. Algorithms lend themselves well for this as they continuously monitor behavior, but they do not necessarily respect the ethical requirements that traditional insurance caters to. We argue that negligent behavior on the part of the insurer will corrupt the contract and thus make insurance redundant. Rather, empathy and altruism demand that algorithms increase, rather than decrease, the level of cooperation among insureds on the one hand and between the insurers and insureds on the other (Mohammad Amini et al., 2023).

3.4.1 Bias and Fairness

The core objective of insurance as a risk-sharing mechanism, compensating losses while maintaining equity among parties, forms the foundation for wider discussions about fairness in algorithmic insurance decision-making processes. In addition to presenting concerns that emerge from the general use of algorithmic decision-making systems in society, enabling discussions about ethical considerations of fairness in data-driven decisions in insurance also needs a look into questions that drive the insurance business. Broadly, why do customers buy insurance? What value does insurance provide to customers? The connection between the purpose of insurance and ethical considerations of fairness in algorithmic insurance is also a common thread through the discussion and controversies about algorithms driving insurance business models (Shafik et al., 2025). Such consideration should also serve as a motivation for healthy skepticism toward bias and fairness problems in general. Analytically, bias and fairness need to be understood in the context of those gradients driving decision-making. Unreasonable bias in an insurance algorithm deflects customers from the fact that the purpose of insurance needs to counterbalance everyday drivers. Furthermore, unfair insurance processes create roots of distrust not only toward the algorithmic process but also impact the company and brand, counterbalancing the value of computational methods that insurers believe in general. This creates a problem of distrust that goes beyond algorithmic insurance practice and touches all aspects of how insurers operate (Shafik, 2025d). Distrust toward decisions not only hurts companies, but it can also go beyond a commercial perspective and erode trust in the social contract aspect of what insurance means.

3.4.2 Transparency and Accountability

Transparency in AI policy can concern who gets to make AI choices, how much information is provided about those choices, how the information is communicated, and the degree that there are other incentives that require transparency. We are concerned with transparency in regard to how information is revealed itself. Specifically, the concept of transparency and what we mean by it in our research. While constructing and utilizing algorithmic decision-making systems should be transparent, different stakeholders in society have differing levels of technical expertise, information-gathering capacity, and incentive structure to investigate whether a system is operating fairly. As such, a system could be transparent to the company employing it, but not to outside researchers or even the impacted communities (Shafik et al., 2025). Therefore, we argue that while companies should reveal the processes they use to build AI systems, full transparency isn't feasible or necessary. Accountability relates to the question of not only who gets to make choices but also the consequences of those choices. Situating a decision in a larger information ecosystem may help alleviate many of the concerns about AI. Rather, decisions should not be placed solely on the algorithm. The grounds for providing answers should be made into intuitive visual interfaces, allowing the person providing answers to have a good sense of the reasoning behind their conclusions. Research and policy must also consider how reporting works in practice. Making algorithms accountable to these metrics could encourage equitable treatment without requiring them to be unbiased on any single metric (Singh et al., 2024). Diverse users will build better algorithms, meaning all users should have the opportunity to contribute to industry standards and share the rewards, depending on the sources, as illustrated in Figure 3.2.

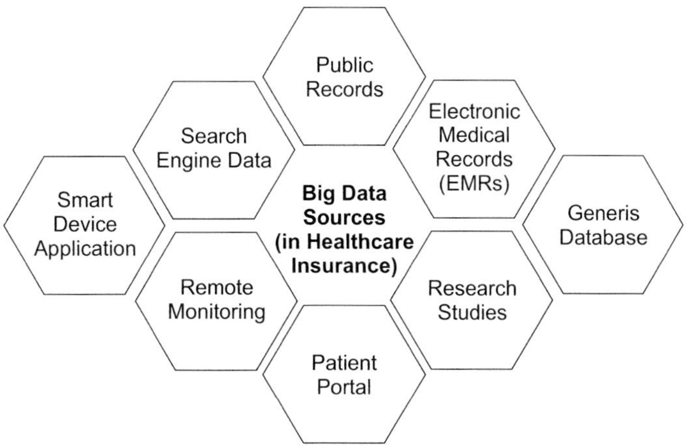

Fig. 3.2 The big data sources in healthcare insurance.

3.5 Risk Management in Algorithmic Insurance

Algorithmic decision-making is not risk-neutral: some decisions produce better outcomes than others, and algorithms differ in terms of their effectiveness and efficiency. In principle, algorithms can outperform human experts: they are less likely to fall prey to cognitive bias or emotional overheating, they can store and process vast amounts of information, and they may be able to learn from experience through various machine learning (ML) methods. Yet, this is not always the case. In some contexts, automation bias sets in, with potentially catastrophic consequences. Bots give bad advice, produce false negatives and false positives, and misjudge the confidence levels of results that have equal statistical weight. Great caution is mandated when deploying algorithms for high stakes decisions in very specific contexts. An algorithm is not a talisman against error, inefficiency, or bias (Margan, 2021). Intersubjective judgment, common sense, experience, and a sensibility for the particularities of the case at hand are needed to temper the machine. Judges, juries, and adjusters must not only decide whether something happened, but who did it and why; they must decide on intentions, motivations, and meaning through empathetic understanding. Algorithmic decision-making may be less costly, faster, more consistent, error-prone, and free of bias than human decision-making. It is especially effective in high stakes decision-making domains. Risk management strategies are thus crucially important. First, insurers can deploy algorithms across the entire value chain, from frontline to back-office operations. Bots may fill in the gaps for adjusters who are physically shut out or socially distanced from the scene. Analysis of social media, surveillance footage, and sensor data can be used to provide timely and accurate evidence of losses, whereas human intervention may take weeks (Choi et al., 2024).

3.5.1 *Identifying Risks*

Risk management ensures the safety of stakeholders and is thus crucial to align algorithmic insurance with hosts of legal, regulatory, and ethical frameworks. For traditional insurance, this relies on both real-world expertise as well as the integration of specialist knowledge into algorithms. In algorithmic insurance, however, there tend to be at least two distinctions with regard to what constitutes risk: the move away from traditional concepts of actuarial science to build prediction models to be managed by non-actuaries, and that insurance is likely to take place in a more validated way than traditional risk models (Wall, 2022). As these developed both in parallel to the creation of financial risk for the insurance company as well as the modeling of adverse selection, moral hazard, and systemic risk through the efforts of economists, they rather served to define the workings of markets and address internal risks for the insurance company than map the various risks associated with the outsourcing of remorse and decisions to automated algorithmic processes. Whereas loss prediction mapping can thus be seen as external risks but also as risks of the model or the algorithms if they lead to decisions based on unsuitable features and data. In addition to this, the choice of the algorithm itself seems to have mostly internally focused risk implications, while validation typically serves as a remediating measure. Besides the ethical and the security risks that pervade algorithmic decision-making in general, other external risks are also on top of mind as they typically move upfront in rethinking insurance and its claim processes (Oben et al., 2024). However, the decisions on when to move to algorithmic insurance, which are rather business process simulation or design decisions in traditional insurance, are now into move design decisions heavily impacting pricing, growth, and complexity.

3.5.2 *Mitigation Strategies*

While a straight-up banning of algorithms in insurance seems impractical, so-called "high touch, high data" approach to underwriting (aided by technology) is both feasible and attractive for some insurers. It's also reasonable to set up some type of policies that help in dealing the worst cases or unintended consequences of potentially detrimental algorithms. In this section, we introduce a few risk management strategies for the use of algorithms in insurance. They include:

(i) Adverse reaction strategies, which are concerned with addressing algorithm models per say.
(ii) Risk-based strategies occasionally resort to tools that typically belong with investment theory and general issues of value.
(iii) Straightforward ethical and working practice principles.
(iv) Alternative approaches to machine learning that we think are aligned with the concerns presented and that we hope will have wider applications in the insurance business—fair, sparse, and honest approaches to algorithmic models.

Adverse reaction strategies are sophisticated tools designed to address concerns about the potential disparity and unfairness consequences of algorithm models. They include: additional testing, auditing, and in-workplace consultancy by outside experts; pre-use-disparities-related testing of model design; post-use-effects-related testing of models; persuasion strategies used on model designers to convince them of the importance of fairness in training and testing their models; mandated minimum disparity standards in model sign-off and approval processes; mandated second sourcing and public commenting on commercial models; and post-use sanctioning of undesirably disparate effects of model and model-driven decisions (Choi et al., 2024). One of the core tenets of these and all other adverse reaction strategies is that they generate additional work that the decision-makers and their organizations need to do, which might be in the form of additional testing, transparency and justification, auditing and consultancy by outside experts, or the generation and constant measurement of monitoring metrics.

3.6 Consumer Protection Laws

Regulation of insurance pricing and coverage has hermetically protected policyholders and potential customers from deceptive behavior by insurers. Federal and state consumer protection statutes and rules generally prohibit false or misleading advertising about insurance but rarely challenge the basic terms of the bargain—pricing and coverage. Although the authority of certain agencies has been curtailed, and enforcement efforts directed exclusively toward problem areas such as misleading endorsements and failure to disclose material facts, both pricing and coverage can be challenged under consumer protection laws. Class action suits for cost increases or deficient coverage may also thrive, particularly those using a state consumer protection statute (Shafik, 2024a, 2024d). Consumer protection statutes also embrace the concept of informed consent. Certain laws give borrowers the right of access to information concerning their credit accounts. Without such access, a consumer cannot fairly confront the insurance company's reasons for not extending coverage. Such a statute, however, applies only to credit transactions, not those involving other types of insurance. Borrowers of life insurance and annuity products are most likely to be protected by this concept of informed consent. In the case of life insurance, however, the actual issuance of a policy on an unqualified basis can be fraudulently obtained in the same manner as a loan in order to effectuate the scheme. Because of the lifelong nature of such insurance, however, a policyholder will be subject to the same potential damages as a deceptive billing under a credit transaction for the life of the policy, regardless of amount (Shafik, 2024c).

3.6.1 Rights of Policyholders

Consumers have the right to have in-depth technical and fully disclosed assistance contracts. This means that an insurer offering a product must fully disclose the terms and technicalities of that product, ensuring that the person receiving the information also has sufficient technical knowledge to understand the information. Furthermore, certain legal obligations help minimize the typical imbalance in a contract of adhesion. Contracting asymmetry is partly overcome by the fact that certain recourse channels are in favor of the insured party: if the insurer interprets contract clauses in order to decline coverage or reduce the insured amount, this interpretation must be made in the most favorable way for the settlement of the claim, that is, in favor of the insured (Tan et al., 2022). Furthermore, if the insurer establishes doubts concerning the coverage of the insurance, it must resolve those doubts in favor of the insured. In case the coverage of the policy is not specific and clear, or if it contains exceptions to it, that which is not specifically excluded therein shall be understood as included. Moreover, if the characteristics of the insured risk have not been the subject of a previous evaluation by the insurer, any damage must be compensated without regard to any excess of this value. In order to protect the public interest more, policies regulated by the Public Credit Law must comply with the general requirements for insurance contracts, especially those that undermine the rights of the policyholder or related third parties. On the other hand, an act that is part of the exercise of the prerogative of discretional autonomy of the administration when carrying out contracts for public credit is the determination of the duration, modalities, and terms of operation of different insurance policies (Călin & Izvoranu, 2018). The reasonableness principle applies; the administrator, in the framework of the public interest, must guarantee control of risks, of their coverage, of the interest with which they are contracted, and of the analytical technique on which they are based.

3.6.2 Dispute Resolution Mechanisms

Just as policyholders have a right to the insurance their insurers offer truthfully, they also have a stake in practices of insurance that directly affect them as consumers. This is part of the rationale for consumer protection laws, which specify and regulate the basic conditions of consumer experience through insurance products. Disputes relating to algorithmically driven insurance practices will arise inevitably, leading to claims of misrepresentation or breach of contract by aggrieved policyholders. Policyholders may even claim that unfair, deceptive, or abusive acts or practices and regulatory violations irreparably harm them, warranting compensation through monetary damages. More fundamentally, policyholders may allege that the behaviors or practices fired up by algorithmic insurance, which most negatively affect their consumer experience, such as denial of claim, failure to pay upon proper claim, or poor service by the insurance promisee, are disruptive enough to qualify as violations of law (Shi & Gan, 2023). The law specifies established mechanisms for the redress of such disputes by policyholders against their insurers. These mechanisms include litigation, mediation, arbitration, and settlement. Litigation is the most familiar and conventional of these mechanisms, forming essentially an adversarial effort where policyholders rely on an impartial third party to protect their rights and provide a legal remedy. In international trade disputes, trade agreements and treaties often provide specific procedures and timing for resolution. Whether private or public authority, the impartial third party typically issues a legally enforceable decision laying out the rights and obligations of the parties. There have been calls to accelerate litigation processes to accommodate the technology industry and its product cycles where possible (Koster et al., 2021). Such processes involve judicial guidelines for cases involving rapidly developing technologies.

3.7 Data Privacy and Security in Insurance Algorithms

Insurance companies have always depended on data to assess the risk level and potential liabilities of their clients. Recently there has been an explosion in the volume of data that insurers have access to, and it is not always clear how that data is gathered and accessed, from the standpoint of both consumers and regulatory bodies. The form of de-identified data that is often used for training algorithms is also used for many other services in the insurance space with no clear consumer-consent norms or framework. Privacy and data retention considerations are crucial because they influence the scope of services that can be delivered. The mere fact that complex algorithms are being used for policy decisions beyond initial underwriting is not in itself a reason for data retention challenges (Margan, 2021). For simplicity, we refer to the use of alternative data for algorithmic decision-making as being applied in underwriting and claims, though clearly there are many other activities, such as mid-term adjustments and pricing, that are also affected by data requirements, availability, and consent. The European Union General Data Protection Regulation came into effect in 2018, and is likely to act as a template for privacy regulation worldwide. It says companies need consent from customers to process their data. The regulation focuses on privacy by design, and raises key questions about algorithmic transparency, fairness, and accountability, as well as data retention limitations. The notion of data minimization is particularly challenging for deeply embedded artificial intelligence systems that depend on a variety of customer data inputs, which may be cached. These systems also face the challenge of algorithmic regulation, with provisions governing profiling, monitoring, and decision-making of the implementation of algorithms (Braun & Matthes, 2018). Clearly, providing transparency to consumers about how their data is used, and obtaining explicit consent for data use, will be key responsibilities of insurance companies, if they are to offer a broad range of algorithmic services in the future.

3.7.1 Data Collection Practices

Insurance is a data-driven industry; it depends on data to detect and establish risks, set premiums, and pay claims. By and large, this raises no insurmountable data-protection concerns. However, in an increasingly digital society accentuated by the acceleration of the digital transformation, data collection is undergoing a transformation. Policy proposal reports, guidelines, and papers have pointed out that insurance companies are gearing up to leverage a plethora of digital footprint data and data from Internet of Things devices in order to optimize their business models. These developments present a data-protection conundrum. There are few horizontal or sectoral laws that specifically focus on privacy and data protection in the context of data privacy. The GDPR may be the only major regulation that applies in this regard, but its application is limited to specific data, meaning insurers can collect vast troves of other data about their customers without having to worry about privacy laws albeit other regulations may have something to say about the collection of some of this data (Abdulkadir Isa & Fernando, 2023). This means that it is of the utmost importance to consider how privacy law applies and what ways we can act within the regulatory framework in order to ensure that the use of these data to optimize insurance underwriting improves customer welfare while guaranteeing a minimum of privacy protection. This lack of privacy regulation means that participants and advocates may be exposed to insecure practices when it comes to informed consent; that is, they may not be fully aware and informed about what data are being collected, how they are being collected, and how such data are being used in terms of profiling, segmentation, analysis, and marketing with the ultimate aim of risk assessment and premium pricing. This is true for both traditional data collection practices such as underwriting questionnaires used for formalizing applications for medical and travel insurance and profiling and analysis of digital footprint data on social networks for risk assessment and premium setting with regard to home insurance, as well as new data collection practices related to the analyzing of customer behavior through telematics data related to their driving (Koster et al., 2021).

3.7.2 Compliance with GDPR

The European Union's General Data Protection Regulation is a comprehensive data protection law that directly affects insurers and reinsurers and other entities that act as controllers or processors of personal data. The following principles lay the groundwork for ensuring compliance with the regulation. Personal data must be collected only for specified, clear, and legitimate purposes. Information collected from an insured should not be excessive in relation to the purposes for which it is processed and should also be accurate and, where necessary, kept up to date. Generally, personal data must be stored no longer than necessary, and it can only be transferred to third parties or a country outside the European Economic Area if certain conditions are met. Encrypting personal data helps protect its confidentiality, but this alone does not suffice as a safeguard to ensure compliance with the regulation (Bermúdez et al., 2023). Furthermore, insurance companies must explain to their customers both verbally and in writing their rights, including the right to access, the right to erasure, and the right to make a complaint to a supervisory authority. Companies should assess their adherence to these principles before making automated decisions affecting customers and should conduct a "data protection impact assessment" in cases where a high risk is likely to be presented. Such an assessment requires consulting with relevant stakeholders, including customers, to evaluate the specific risks and disadvantages while considering issues such as the volume, variety, and sensitivity of the data being processed, in addition to the complexity and degree of invasiveness of the profiling or special category processing. Repairing the potential damage to individuals covered from a breach by an insurer or reinsurer can pose all sorts of practical and legal issues (Settipalli & Gangadharan, 2023). These potential difficulties give rise to the strong recommendation that entities avoid scenarios of possible disproportionate harm.

3.8 Case Studies of Algorithmic Insurance Practices

Because many of the themes in this book are still exploratory, it may be useful to see some concrete examples of applications of algorithms in insurance. While we do not intend to provide a comprehensive survey, there are a few examples that share many of the concerns of the themes in the book. We can generally divide them between successful implementations and some that were poorly thought out and are considered failures. The latter group usually teaches us valuable lessons on what to avoid in future implementations. Because of the wealth of data generated by usage-based insurance, telematics' applications have the potential to incorporate algorithms in discovery, modeling, and validation (Arockiam & Pushpanathan, 2023). In brief, telematics monitors how much someone drives and how they drive (hard braking/acceleration, sharp cornering, speed, etc.). It entails a lower data quality issue than a traditional risk survey, thanks to constant data capture. Based on the gathered data, the insurance company identifies how risky each driver is and charges the drivers with the biggest risk the most, thereby aligning their incentives and allowing good drivers to pay a lower premium. Implementations capitalize on the predictive strength of such data over loss when it comes to certain perils, and allow the insurance company to assess better the risk associated with a specific driver, reward effortlessly with discounts those who display good behavior, and improve loss control (Murphy & Moosa, 2021).

A few insurers have boldly gone into telematics, and it seems to work for the careful drivers as well. Insurers usually use their algorithms when awarding discounts. One insurer held around 78% of the telematics market and developed its proprietary algorithms. There is still some level of external verification with audits carried out by regulators or consulting firms, but overall, it seems that a lack of due diligence is usually not an issue. Many other implementations have, however, been inadequate for several reasons, including data accuracy problems and formative years, especially worry in Europe because of its defense of civil liberties paired with a strong regulatory apparatus. At first, the algorithms that insurers used relied heavily on the past to forecast future accidents, which was fine when talking about high-frequency events, for which the statistical methods insurers used were developed long ago (Parlak, 2023). The late 2010s saw a few companies being formed with the will to market solutions based on new high-dimensional algorithms able to predict low-frequency events accurately and perform real-time detection of high-severity catastrophes based on external events.

3.8.1 Successful Implementations

While past actions have resulted in negative consequences for companies implementing algorithmic systems, these detrimental circumstances can be avoided. In furtherance of this, there are numerous real-world use cases that provide proof of successful algorithmic practices within insurance. For instance, predictive "shedding claims model" algorithms reduce fraud and enable more efficient claims reviews. Through data partnerships, the model implements a wide variety of sources, revealing external factors influencing individual claim decisions. Further, "contextual decision intelligence" platforms allow insurance companies to reduce exposure to fraud and credit risk. Their clients, being major insurers, use the AI platform to screen for false positives by revealing true identity networks through visualizations that overturn false assumptions on business affiliations and links (McDonnell et al., 2023). Insurers are using this multidimensional approach to automate data collection that performs entity resolution, business affiliation discovery, address verification, and more. Then, there is a legacy company that has developed the first commercial third-party Administrative Services Organization. The company accomplishes the digitization dream by using cloud technology to replace legacy insurer core systems that have become existential threats to the entire industry. In this regard, the company helps dozens of carriers and service providers to execute fully automated underwriting with straight-through processing. Moreover, another company uses big data information analysis to determine unique insurable risks, thereby meeting market demand for consumer-friendly insurance (Braun & Matthes, 2018). Furthermore, they provide dental insurance coverage—an area that has witnessed a significant turnaround due to the product development stages taken by their team focused on insurance for the purchasing of preventive services.

3.8.2 Failures and Lessons Learned

As a sector that relies on decision-making in the face of extreme uncertainty, insurance presents itself as a promising domain for algorithmic practices. While there have been some successful implementations of algorithmically assisted decision-making in insurance, especially related to pricing, more detailed work reveals that the promise of algorithms in insurance decision-making goes hand-in-hand with several important risks. Algorithmic processes can support and strengthen established discrimination practices, even in the case of designs that have used fairness constraints to limit biases substantively. Other decisions relate to the availability and role of specific data. In predictive policing, for instance, the question of whether to gather data or what data to integrate into a wider index of risk depends on the interest at play. Increasingly detailed, seemingly hyper-localized models that score specific micro-areas and individuals can have destructive effects if they steer policing practices in biased and discriminatory directions (Yang et al., 2023). In other instances, the particular concerns of citizens and insurance customers are not prioritized. This outcome is evident in the case of dynamic pricing of car insurance, where usage-based algorithms calculate individualized policies based on in-car communication about driving performance. More generally, the complex decision chains involved in many algorithmic implementations also multiply the points at which things can go badly wrong. It is often not the algorithm itself that fails that leads to an unsatisfactory decision outcome, but rather the wider chain of events, actions, and decisions that is fastened and mediated by the algorithm. In this regard, the construction of algorithms is important, but it can never be a self-contained solution. Algorithmically driven decision-making needs to be embedded into wider social practices and tailored to particular use contexts (Abdulkadir Isa & Fernando, 2023). It is with attention to this ecosystem of deliberation, monitoring, social accountability, and checks and balances that the greatest promise lies, when it comes to delivering satisfactory, just, and fair insurance practice, as presented in Table 3.2.

Table 3.2 Ethical principles and risk mitigation strategies in algorithmic insurance.

Ethical Principle	*Application in Insurance*	*Associated Risk*	*Risk Mitigation Strategy*	*Implementation Approach*
Fairness & Non-bias	Pricing, underwriting, and claims evaluation	Discriminatory premiums or denials	Bias testing, fairness constraints in ML models	Fairness-aware insurance scoring algorithms
Transparency	Algorithm explanation, customer understanding	Black-box decisions, trust erosion	Explainable AI (XAI), user-facing decision summaries	Providing rationale for claim rejection
Privacy & Consent	Use of personal and behavioral data	Unauthorized access or misuse	Consent dashboards, granular opt-ins	Opt-in models for wearable data in health insurance
Accountability	Assigning responsibility for outcomes	Lack of clear recourse for errors	Human-in-the-loop systems, audit logs	Appeals process involving an AI oversight panel
Human Autonomy	Avoid overreliance on algorithmic outputs	Deskilling or lack of human intervention	Decision-support rather than full automation	Manual override in automated claim settlement systems
Proportionality	Matching AI complexity to task significance	Overengineering low-risk decisions	Use of rule-based systems where appropriate	Rules for small claims, ML for high-impact cases
Sustainability	Long-term trust, ethical AI life cycle management	Short-term optimization undermining fairness	Periodic algorithm reviews and life cycle management	Biannual ethical performance audits
Equity & Inclusion	Addressing underrepresentation in datasets	Bias due to incomplete or unbalanced data	Data diversification, inclusion-focused audits	Incorporating socio-economic and regional factors in training
Trust & Confidence	Public perception of algorithmic fairness	Lack of adoption, reputational damage	Ethical branding, public disclosure of AI policies	Transparency reports for AI use in pricing
Safety & Robustness	AI reliability in dynamic environments	Model collapse, adversarial manipulation	Adversarial testing, robustness checks	Simulated stress testing of risk prediction algorithms
Consent Revocation	Allowing users to revoke data-sharing agreements	Data use beyond user expectations	Consent management interfaces	Revocation option for driving behavior data
Ethical Use of Big Data	Managing the use of massive behavioral and third-party data	Profiling, surveillance concerns	Limitations on inference granularity	Restricting micro-segmentation to avoid exploitative pricing
Moral Responsibility	Aligning algorithm outcomes with societal good	Value misalignment	Establishing AI ethics review boards	Internal ethics committees in large insurance firms
Continuous Improvement	Learning from feedback and mistakes	Ethical stagnation, loss of relevance	AI performance dashboards with ethical Key Performance Indicators (KPIs)	Ongoing user feedback loop in claims handling AI

3.9 Future Trends in Algorithmic Insurance

While algorithmic innovations may continue to lead to new types of insurance products, we note that all the products will still have to be designed to meet existing legal requirements. Therefore, we think the products and services will follow, and not lead, legal concerns in the coming decade. Further, there are a number of fronts on which regulatory change may come quickly. If the past is any guide, many regulators worldwide may wait for a strong, unexpected negative outcome at scale to act. Introducing regulatory changes that are new and untested for insurance may not be an optimal policy due to insurance's special role as a preparatory tool, unless an insurable actor is not acting in good faith. This is because night guard and harm principle justifications for regulation here may not alone carry sufficient weight to require regulatory changes (Jouini & Sethom, 2023). However, this is not to say that innovative regulation that requires clear, measurable benefits, rather than merely adverse impacts, is not desirable. As insurance markets evolve, we provide a prediction as to which areas are most likely to be approached by regulators in the coming decade. We may see significant regulatory focus on the new risks created for insured parties and other stakeholders, such as through unintended consequences of foregone decisions such as moral hazard, halo effects from a noncompetitive digital economy, data access and portability considerations that weigh too heavily on the user, and insurance fraud. We may also see similar regulation in the form of general purpose regulation gamed or applied to insurance, such as antitrust law and rules relating to essential facilities and digital platforms. However, although certain concentration levels in insurance markets have created secondary impacts on local economies in the past, these kinds of unintended consequences will not be experienced everywhere at the same trajectory (Alam et al., 2020). Therefore, we would expect regulatory deterrence action ahead of scaling in underserved insurance markets before action for sanctions, joint investigations, and penalties is taken by regulators in the remaining markets.

3.9.1 Emerging Technologies

In this section, we briefly discuss and identify various emerging technologies that may further change consumers' and insurers' expectations of algorithmic insurance. However, we do not attempt to encompass predictions about future developments or to describe the technology in its intricate execution. Recently, much public attention has come to insurance algorithms from generative AI developments. New language models allow efficient and convincing rewriting of policy contracts, insurance applications, and other insurance documents. Other generative AI models can synthesize realistic yet fictitious datasets about insurance events, although critics focus on their potential to perpetuate historical biases. Such models might allow small and new-market entrants to enter the insurance market, offering custom-tailored pockets of algorithms while lowering the costs of developing tools, methods, or policies. However, these same models might also contribute to serious prediction failures and a price war by major existing incumbents seeking to gain commodity price status and widen margins with low-cost algorithmic products. Data availability constraints might also fluctuate with the evolution of new technologies such as sensor networks, autonomous drones, and the Internet of Things (Van Nguyen et al., 2023). The insurance gig economy model enabled by drone technologies for home and commercial property insurance—on-demand scheduled loss control posts, inspection, and evaluation based on high-definition aerial imaging, using data for model building and peak fragility mitigation testing—could magnify algorithmic informational advantages while allowing speedier and more accurate loss mitigation services.

3.9.2 Predictions for Regulatory Changes

Many in the insurance industry view regulation as a hindrance to innovation, favoring lax governmental influence. Intermediary firms such as Managing General Agents (MGAs) or data brokers may favor self-regulating structures. Yet, these parties may also alternatively favor a strong regulatory environment, especially with regard to controlling customers' data access from technology providers. They may feel that strict regulation, especially by consumer protection entities, best ensures that products unleashed onto the market have been sufficiently tested and are safe and equitable. It would suggest that technologists and firms, after scrutiny, should ensure their products are ethical, compliant with current anti-discrimination and other relevant laws, and accurately understandable by insurers and consumers alike. Only then would public–private partnership models enable rapid approval in a post-launch, real-world validation phase. To do otherwise would risk governmental overregulation, limiting the innovation capability of technologists (Pnevmatikakis et al., 2021). For example, technologists could increase regulatory understanding and trust by openly publishing their tools' guidelines and datasets, enabling validation by outside experts. More generally, the primary ethos that allowed the internet to become freely available, open source, and mostly free from regulation has begun to decline in favor of more and more regulation in various domains. Areas of concern include interoperability and openness, privacy, competition, content responsibility, tracking, industry responsibility, the need for safety and quality cornerstones, and a better connection and balance to society at large. Special interests by industry sector exploit decision-making deliberation, ability, and balance to have it go their way, often with unfortunate consequences. Wherever possible, we advocate for a principle-centered approach to regulation, while relevant law jurisdictions overrule regulations proposed, outlined, and enacted (Sachan & Muwanga, 2023).

3.10 The Role of Artificial Intelligence in Insurance

AI, and in particular machine learning algorithms, have recently gained traction in the insurance industry. In particular, the insurance underwriting and claims management functions at insurance companies have widely adopted AI, driven primarily by the efficiency and profitability goals of the insurance industry. Examples of AI adoption in insurance include the use of telematics data for more granular auto insurance pricing, facial recognition technology to automate and make more reliable life insurance underwriting, and computer vision and natural language processing tools to process images, video, and text for mobile insurance claims. The industry advocates argue that the use of AI in these applications can increasingly lead to lowered costs for underwriting insurance and managing claims, and added convenience for insurance consumers in their business interactions (Arockiam & Pushpanathan, 2023). In addition, advancements in AI are seen as providing insurance companies and insurance technology firms with competitive advantages, particularly the speed, scalability, and efficiency benefits associated with the use of AI versus traditional statistical methods of prediction. The abovementioned positive developments associated with AI deployment coexist with the well-documented potential risks associated with AI and machine learning technology that must be confronted in order to maximize stakeholder benefit. These risks are often discussed in the context of the "trustworthiness issues" that must be addressed if industry actors are to develop, deploy, and use AI systems that include, among others, fairness, accountability, and transparency concerns. These issues include the risk that algorithms may be used to discriminate among people based on protected class characteristics; accountability—or, more accurately, a lack of accountability for the decisions made by AI systems; and transparency—the challenge of establishing a degree of understanding of how algorithms arrive at their decisions among stakeholders as well as a degree of algorithm "explainability" (Philip & Suresh, 2024). The importance of addressing these risks in insurance is amplified by the fact that insurance operates in a framework of regulation premised on consumer protection and risk pooling within a trusting social contract.

3.10.1 AI versus Traditional Methods

One of the main drives for AI—and especially for machine learning—is its promise of superior performance: along several metrics, AI is superior to traditional methods. Not only can it generate better predictions, it can also task resources in a better way; for example, by better allocating agents answering a help line to minimize support flow waiting times. AI methods can also execute specific tasks better than specialists. For example, it can incorporate many more variables into a prediction of customer behavior or account assessment. When assessing loan applications, algorithmic systems are also capable of deciding more rapidly and at lower costs. In addition, AI methods can analyze data patterns unseen by humans. Last but not least, it can infer preferences without asking customers: as long as a behavior is tracked through time, the AI might be able to generate better recommendations than traditional recommendation systems based on direct queries (Shafik, 2024b, 2025c). Most insurance products are characterized by a low frequency and a high cost per claim, resulting in a high cost and loss rate. This increased ratio of loss to revenue places a great deal of pressure on the insurer's services, from underwriting the risk to pricing and settlement of claims. Given the relatively limited data that undergirds the decisions made by insurance companies, the costs of AI deployment might, at least, seem to outweigh the benefits. For example, compared to traditional methods, AI requires larger amounts of internal data in addition to external data and a process to collect that external data. Furthermore, former methods are often based on the mediocre performance of rules-of-thumb optimized during previous experiences. However, when such external databases of customers are available, such as credit bureaus, their use can radically reduce the cost of AI. Experts suggest algorithms can reduce these costs by as much as 20 times, potentially entailing annual savings of between $200 billion and $360 billion per year. (McDonnell et al., 2023). In light of these potential benefits, it is unsurprising that AI adoption within insurance has reached feverish levels.

3.10.2 Ethical AI in Insurance

Insurance, by its very nature, is deeply concerned with the plights of the most vulnerable segments of the entire insurable population. A deeply indebted society does denial of coverage by insurance for things we cannot preemptively define. More people walk away from insurance payouts unfulfilled than there are people insured for risks like premiums that can pay an available reward for claim submissions. An overreliance on algorithmic means for determining insurability is nothing short of a modern con woman scam of admiring the very people trying to give her a handout. Especially when many of the people driving the insurance enter that realm to shield themselves from life's inevitable worst events, scaled to a life. With that background, we take the ethical lens to the algorithmic fitness function definition within insurance. A resolution of "capturing more and paying out less," duly confronted with the decision opt-in or opt-out, of the entire population of clients. We work to suggest an approach for stopping the over-parameterization of algorithms and creating a better fitness-defining beam scan of the necessity of coverage for the people needing it (Owens et al., 2022; Shi & Gan, 2023). If a pervasive lack of proper rewards triggered bad behavior, we also would hope to change the AI definition of optimal behavior, leading to different and hopefully more ethical situations where niche and bad behavior of insurance company denialism is abdicated.

3.11 Global Perspectives on Algorithmic Insurance

Algorithmic insurance is developing as a global phenomenon, with distinctive applications emerging in settings as diverse as social insurance systems, international reinsurance, and agriculture. Nevertheless, regions differ widely in their regulatory objectives, flows of investment and talent, and degree of popular knowledge or concern regarding algorithmic determinants of risk or claim eligibility, as well as the understanding of those designs among regulators. Governments are more often watchdogs than midwives, revising legal and regulatory frameworks reactively as socially harmful insurance design practices gain publicity. This topology also varies across product lines, with private health and life underwriting being scrutinized most intensely, but legal standards are still under-crafted (Van Nguyen et al., 2023). So far, aside from certain regions, the resolution of challenges is primarily a matter of national law and regulation. Incorporation of global norms or mutual recognition of sanctions against tortious insurers seems unlikely for some time, but organically emergent or governmentally led collaboration among innovators in practice and purpose would seem likely to iterate diverse strategy solutions to both design and implementation in a form of reverse-adaptive learning. Investors and insurers warrant scrutiny both pre-launch as voices to be consulted in product definition, as early adopters whose experiences might shape a domestic market, and knowledgeable early defectors whose negative evaluations might scare off any further expansion. The text proceeds in three sections. The first considers algorithmic underwriting and claims handling of specific lines of business (Pnevmatikakis et al., 2021). The second paints topical pictures of practices and policies. The third concludes. These regions are treated in alphabetical order.

3.11.1 Regional Differences

Algorithmic risk assessment has moved quickly from niche applications in specialized markets into the mainstream marketplace. With a slew of promotional statements about a long list of new types of risk and growing accusations of algorithmic redlining, however, these new technologies and their advanced techniques of exclusion have also faced pushback—even censorship. In this chapter, we examine the global algorithmic insurance landscape. Insurance across borders and domains is not standing still or proceeding in parallel. National norms and regulations differ greatly, as do their enforcement across countries, states, and provinces. Accordingly, we describe what political economy, ethics, insurance, privacy, civil rights, and consumer protection advocates are saying about the regulation of algorithmic insurance (Aina et al., 2024). Discussion of algorithmic insurance has been brisk in the United States, the United Kingdom, and the EU. For the most part, critiques have tended toward a wait-and-see position and pointed to certain regulations. Still, sensitive information could trigger additional scrutiny, given the heightened awareness around behavioral credit scoring and the need for balance and fairness. Outside the West, however, discussions of algorithmic insurance are tentative. In the United States and the United Kingdom, anti-redlining laws have stemmed the worst abuses, to the point that these floral bouquets of excesses may be loath to risk losing the whole garden. In countries such as Singapore and India—even China—politicians still heap praises on the new information-driven economy built on technologies such as big data, virtual currencies, and the Internet of Things.

3.11.2 International Collaboration

International collaboration will be essential to create effective international regulatory policies for algorithmic insurance. Irreplaceable lessons on algorithms and insurance practices can be learned from cyberethics, international human rights law, and cooperation frameworks and programs established in the spheres of trade and commerce. The business and human rights movement recognized the power of companies to cause and mitigate harm. The significant political and economic influence that large technology companies exert makes it logical that they be incorporated into discussions about algorithmic insurance. Discourse on the necessity of human rights' due diligence helps to establish how algorithms impact the dissemination of information and creation of economic opportunity and, subsequently, how this interplay affects both underwriting and claims practices (Sachan & Muwanga, 2023). Computer scientists, machine learning specialists, economists, actuaries, financial compliance specialists, and business people will need to speak openly about the capability of insurance and algorithms to cause or mitigate harm. Trade and commerce can be greatly impacted by algorithmic bias. The adoption of liberalized free-trade commitments can lead to economic losses in vulnerable, marginalized communities. Adopting set lobbying criteria and seeking the adoption of international regulatory policy on algorithms that influence trade practices, such as lobbying for the adoption of the Corporate Transparency Act, determine the impact of algorithms on supply chains for trade with regions impacted by systemic labor and social equity issues in tech infrastructure. Finding mutual ground in how algorithms are used by small businesses and trade-committed economic actors in order to reduce harm is another possible collaborative step. Establishing impact criteria for algorithms utilized in trade finance, supply chains, and customs compliance that guide the algorithm and machine learning specialists is a necessary part of developing international regulatory policy (Jouini & Sethom, 2023).

3.12 Challenges in Implementing Algorithmic Insurance

Over the last decade, numerous startups have ventured into algorithmic insurance, also referred to as insurtech. However, they do not allocate any expenses to capital reserves. In fact, they frequently turn to reinsurance to cover at least a portion of the reserves. Additionally, a few insurance companies, offering the logic of insurtech without the technology stack and differentiation, have also incorporated machine-learning techniques into their processes. Despite all the excitement, investment, and breakthroughs, the majority of these companies exhibit losses, and, in some cases, deeply negative equity reserves. Reinsurance is not viable for the long term, and insurtech should ideally be in the black after some years of operation (Bermúdez et al., 2023). Before assessing the legal and compliance risks surrounding algorithmic insurance and the adoption of a regulatory lens on algorithmic agency, it is critical to understand some of the practical constraints and challenges faced by both the startup attempts and the legacy actors in the insurance value chain. The arena for developing algorithmic insurance is fraught with challenges and hurdles. Insurtech is an amalgamation of insurance and technology. Starting with the technology piece, creating an algorithm for a problem has become easier with more data and experience on the part of data scientists, in the sense that data collection and cleaning, model tuning, and training may be simpler than before. However, from deployment to monitoring long after the original team involved has moved on, significant difficulties remain. Insurance companies harbor vast troves of data, and insurtech initiatives often mine this data to create algorithms that help price and organize the various risks involved (Margan, 2021).

3.12.1 Technical Barriers

Algorithmic decision systems are evolving tools that can promote the rapid implementation of automated decisions across various sectors, including insurance. However, not all algorithmic decisions achieve the promised results without significant challenges and obstacles. In the case of algorithmic insurance, technical drivers may pose major barriers to the establishment of accountability and legal certainty around technologically enabled insurance practices. Algorithmic decision systems are often described as "black boxes" whose internal workings, data inputs, and predicted outcomes are shrouded in secrecy or complexity. This is mainly because mathematical techniques or combinations of techniques capable of generating model results are increasingly too sophisticated for humans, including domain experts, to evaluate reliably. The technical barriers for implementation of algorithmic practices are particularly acute in insurance, where imperfect data on an infrequent event is combined with the need to promote the interests of diverse stakeholders legitimately (McDonnell et al., 2023). Modeling the future occurrence of low-frequency, high-impact events, such as hurricanes and floods, crime, or particular health outcomes, is both complex and uncertain. In addition, insurance algorithms must balance performance metrics that do not necessarily align. For commercial insurance, profit-centric insurers must satisfy shareholders while minimizing risks for policyholders through risk-transfer tools designed to assure risk payers are compensated for losses. At the same time, with all stakeholders from policyholders to third-party service providers affected by the risks posed by low-frequency, high-impact events, the need for algorithms that promote equity and avoid regulatory scrutiny is amplified in the context of insurance as a risk transfer tool (Jouini & Sethom, 2023). These competing priorities raise questions about how accountability will be met in practice when low-frequency, high-impact events simultaneously affect the diverse interests of insureds and society at large.

3.12.2 Regulatory Hurdles

The development of nontraditional insurance services brings with it great challenges from the point of view of the regulatory frameworks that supervise other social and commercial activities derived from the use of information technology and algorithms. In fact, the already established regulatory frameworks are not an adequate solution to the compliance challenge posed by algorithmic insurance. For the vast majority of jurisdictions, several legislative paths are involved in limiting the use of algorithms in a wide array of sectors, such as anti-discrimination laws, insurance contracts, unequal bargains, unfair competition, market conduct, pricing and rates, companies' practices, product development, litigation and consumer protection, data collection, tax, privacy, financial restitution and cybersecurity, financial market regulations, through their respective regulatory agents. However, in civilian countries, the challenges that algorithmic insurance poses, such as wrongful discrimination in the determination of risks and opportunities or in the elaboration of rates and prices, even strangling competition in the sector, are already addressed (Gramegna & Giudici, 2020). The case of the United States, with its lack of a federal data regulatory entity capable of providing a unified regulatory framework, is particular. Since 2019, eight states have considered state legislation concerning algorithms in the insurance sector, with California and Illinois attempting to establish the strictest regulation teams. It is noteworthy that, within the rules already in force, within the United States, twenty states force the use of manual techniques for underwriting subprime drivers for the activity of auto insurers, notwithstanding the unconstitutionality of such prohibitions (Braun & Matthes, 2018). Moreover, within the European Union, the proposals on AI regulation or data fund regulation are not yet in force and don't reach the insurance sector. Thus, even for the US and EU, compliance with algorithms in insurance is still an unresolved challenge.

3.13 Conclusion

Algorithmic insurance practices are emerging as a natural consequence of the continued use of advanced data analytics across diverse business sectors. The insurance sector is among those fields in which data-driven decision-making processes have been traditionally crucial and have progressively been upgraded with algorithmic tools that are increasingly embedding a central role in all business functions. These practices can generate important enhancements in efficiency, productivity, profitability, stability, and customer service. At the same time, despite their alleged potential to reshape the insurance market for the better, they raise severe concerns about the different legal, regulatory, and other ethical challenges associated with such practices, which appear as potential traps for the unwary. Navigating the legal, regulatory, and ethical frameworks within which algorithmic insurance practices are established and developed is made more complex by important idiosyncrasies of the insurance sector. These challenges deserve careful assessment because algorithmic insurance practices represent a double-edged sword for the industry. It is hoped that the guidelines presented will contribute to a greater awareness of the issues arising from algorithmic practices in insurance and help practitioners think in a structured way about how to mitigate risks when performing tasks that entail ethically sound behavior complying with existing laws and regulations. Ultimately, all stakeholders in the insurance sector can work together to design and allow for algorithmic tools that affect their business positively by also monitoring the insurance practice's societal impact.

References

Abdulkadir Isa, U. and Fernando, A. (2023). Explainable AI and Interpretable Model for Insurance Premium Prediction. *Journal on Artificial Intelligence*, *5*(0). https://doi.org/10.32604/jai.2023.040213

Aina, I., Ayinde, O., Thiam, D. and Miranda, M. (2024). Crop Index Insurance as a Tool for Climate Resilience: Lessons from Smallholder Farmers in Nigeria. *Natural Hazards*, *120*(5). https://doi.org/10.1007/s11069-023-06388-x

Alam, A.S.A.F., Begum, H., Masud, M.M., Al-Amin, A.Q. and Filho, W.L. (2020). Agriculture Insurance for Disaster Risk Reduction: A Case Study of Malaysia. *International Journal of Disaster Risk Reduction*, *47*. https://doi.org/10.1016/j.ijdrr.2020.101626

Arockiam, J.M. and Pushpanathan, A.C.S. (2023). MapReduce-Iterative Support Vector Machine Classifier: Novel Fraud Detection Systems in Healthcare Insurance Industry. *International Journal of Electrical and Computer Engineering*, *13*(1). https://doi.org/10.11591/ijece.v13i1.pp756-769

Bermúdez, L., Anaya, D. and Belles-Sampera, J. (2023). Explainable AI for Paid-Up Risk Management in Life Insurance Products. *Finance Research Letters*, *57*. https://doi.org/10.1016/j.frl.2023.104242

Braun, D. and Matthes, F. (2018). Generating Explanations for Algorithmic Decisions of Usage-Based Insurances using Natural Language Generation. *Lecture Notes in Informatics (LNI)*, *P-279*.

Butterworth, M. (2018). The ICO and Artificial Intelligence: The Role of Fairness in the GDPR Framework. *Computer Law and Security Review*, *34*(2). https://doi.org/10.1016/j.clsr.2018.01.004

Călin, H.C. and Izvoranu, A.M. (2018). Public–private Partnership and Its Influence on Agricultural Insurances. *Quality – Access to Success*, *19*(S1).

Choi, J.H., Choi, Y., Lee, K.S., Ahn, K.H. and Jang, W.Y. (2024). Explainable Model Using Shapley Additive Explanations Approach on Wound Infection after Wide Soft Tissue Sarcoma Resection: "Big Data" Analysis Based on Health Insurance Review and Assessment Service Hub. *Medicina (Lithuania)*, *60*(2). https://doi.org/10.3390/medicina60020327

Daudén-Esmel, C., Castellà-Roca, J. and Viejo, A. (2024). Blockchain-Based Access Control System for Efficient and GDPR-Compliant Personal Data Management. *Computer Communications*, *214*. https://doi.org/10.1016/j.comcom.2023.11.017

Dorfleitner, G., Hornuf, L. and Kreppmeier, J. (2021). Promise Not Fulfilled: Fintech Data Privacy, and the GDPR. *SSRN Electronic Journal*. https://doi.org/10.2139/ssrn.3950094

Dorfleitner, G., Hornuf, L. and Kreppmeier, J. (2023). Promise Not fulfilled: FinTech, Data Privacy, and the GDPR. *Electronic Markets*, *33*(1). https://doi.org/10.1007/s12525-023-00622-x

Golden, L.L., Brockett, P.L., Ai, J. and Kellison, B. (2016). Empirical Evidence on the Use of Credit Scoring for Predicting Insurance Losses with Psycho-social and Biochemical Explanations. *North American Actuarial Journal*, *20*(3). https://doi.org/10.1080/10920277.2016.1209118

Gramegna, A. and Giudici, P. (2020). Why to Buy Insurance? An Explainable Artificial Intelligence Approach. *Risks*, *8*(4). https://doi.org/10.3390/risks8040137

Jouini, O. and Sethom, K. (2023). AgriBIoT: A Blockchain-Based IoT Architecture for Crop Insurance. *Lecture Notes in Networks and Systems*, *655*. https://doi.org/10.1007/978-3-031-28694-0_32

Koster, O., Kosman, R. and Visser, J. (2021). A Checklist for Explainable AI in the Insurance Domain. *Communications in Computer and Information Science*, *1439*. https://doi.org/10.1007/978-3-030-85347-1_32

Margan, S.K. (2021). Drifting into Algocratic Insurance? In *The AI Book: The Artificial Intelligence Handbook for Investors, Entrepreneurs and FinTech Visionaries*. https://doi.org/10.1002/9781119551966.ch20

McDonnell, K., Murphy, F., Sheehan, B., Masello, L. and Castignani, G. (2023). Deep Learning in Insurance: Accuracy and Model Interpretability Using TabNet. *Expert Systems with Applications*, *217*. https://doi.org/10.1016/j.eswa.2023.119543

Mohammad Amini, M., Jesus, M., Fanaei Sheikholeslami, D., Alves, P., Hassanzadeh Benam, A. and Hariri, F. (2023). Artificial Intelligence Ethics and Challenges in Healthcare Applications: A Comprehensive Review in the Context of the European GDPR Mandate. *Machine Learning and Knowledge Extraction*. *5*(3). https://doi.org/10.3390/make5030053

Murphy, S.D. and Moosa, S. (2021). The Views of Public Service Managers on the Implementation of National Health Insurance in Primary Care: A Case of Johannesburg Health District, Gauteng Province, Republic of South Africa. *BMC Health Services Research*, *21*(1). https://doi.org/10.1186/s12913-021-06990-4

Oben, E.E.E., Ndi, H.N. and Tchuikoua, L.B. (2024). Livestock Farmers' Willingness to Pay for Farming Insurance in Four Divisions of the West Region of Cameroon. *Asian Journal of Geographical Research, 7*(1). https://doi.org/10.9734/ajgr/2024/v7i1211

Owens, E., Sheehan, B., Mullins, M., Cunneen, M., Ressel, J. and Castignani, G. (2022). Explainable Artificial Intelligence (XAI) in Insurance. *Risks. 10*(12). https://doi.org/10.3390/risks10120230

Parlak, M. (2023). Blockchain-Based Immutable Evidence and Decentralized Loss Adjustment for Autonomous Vehicle Accidents in Insurance. *ArXiv*.

Philip, B. and Suresh, G. (2024). Cultivating Resilience: An In-depth Exploration of Agricultural Insurance Initiatives and Their Transformative Role in India's Farming Landscape. *Universal Journal of Agricultural Research, 12*(1). https://doi.org/10.13189/ujar.2024.120109

Pnevmatikakis, A., Kanavos, S., Matikas, G., Kostopoulou, K., Cesario, A. and Kyriazakos, S. (2021). Risk Assessment for Personalized Health Insurance Based on Real-World Data. *Risks, 9*(3). https://doi.org/10.3390/risks9030046

Poshtiri, Z.P., Soleimani, A.G., Delafrooz, N. and Shahroudi, K. (2024). Designing the Insurance Coverage Model for FinTech Startups: A Novel Approach to the Necessity of Digital Transformation Track of in Insurance. *Interdisciplinary Journal of Management Studies, 17*(1). https://doi.org/10.22059/ijms.2023.345002.675187

Sachan, S. and Muwanga, J. (2023). Integration of Explainable Deep Neural Network with Blockchain Technology: Medical Indemnity Insurance. *CEUR Workshop Proceedings, 3554*.

Settipalli, L. and Gangadharan, G.R. (2023). WMTDBC: An Unsupervised Multivariate Analysis Model for Fraud Detection in Health Insurance Claims. *Expert Systems with Applications, 215*. https://doi.org/10.1016/j.eswa.2022.119259

Shafik, W. (2024a). *Consumer Behaviour Analysis* (pp. 75–108). https://doi.org/10.4018/979-8-3693-9122-8.ch004

Shafik, W. (2024b). Generative AI for Social Good and Sustainable Development. In *Generative AI: Current Trends and Applications* (pp. 185–217). Springer.

Shafik, W. (2024c). Science of Emotional Intelligence. In *Enhancing and Predicting Digital Consumer Behavior with AI* (pp. 284–310). IGI Global. https://doi.org/10.4018/979-8-3693-4453-8.ch015

Shafik, W. (2024d). Social Media Insights into Consumer Behavior. In *Intersection of AI and Business Intelligence in Data-Driven Decision-Making* (pp. 283–308). IGI Global. https://doi.org/10.4018/979-8-3693-5288-5.ch010

Shafik, W. (2025a). Ethical and Legal Considerations in Artificial Intelligence. *AI-Enabled Threat Intelligence and Cyber Risk Assessment*, 90.

Shafik, W. (2025b). Generative Adversarial Networks: Security, Privacy, and Ethical Considerations. In *Generative Artificial Intelligence (AI) Approaches for Industrial Applications* (pp. 93–117). Springer.

Shafik, W. (2025c). Generative Artificial Intelligence for Social Good and Sustainable Development. *Generative AI: Disruptive Technologies for Innovative Applications*, 153–185.

Shafik, W. (2025d). *SDG 12: Responsible Consumption and Production—The Circular Economy* (pp. 365–390). https://doi.org/10.1007/978-981-96-7299-8_13

Shafik, W., Singh, R. and Kumar, V. (2025). Artificial Intelligence Transparency and Explainability in Sustainable Healthcare. In *Transforming Healthcare Sector Through Artificial Intelligence and Environmental Sustainability* (pp. 165–191). Springer.

Shafik, W., Zakari, R.Y. and Kalinaki, K. (2025). Ethical and Privacy Concerns in Bioinformatics and Cyber-Physical Systems Integration in Healthcare. In *AI-Driven Personalized Healthcare Solutions* (pp. 333–364). IGI Global Scientific Publishing.

Shi, X. and Gan, L. (2023). Equilibrium in Competitive Insurance Markets with Medical Tourism. *Studies in Microeconomics, 11*(2). https://doi.org/10.1177/23210222211051439

Singh, R., Shafik, W., Crowther, D. and Kumar, V. (Eds.). (2024). *Transforming Healthcare Sector Through Artificial Intelligence and Environmental Sustainability* (1st ed., Vol. 1). Springer Nature Singapore. https://doi.org/10.1007/978-981-97-9555-0

Tan, T.M., Makkonen, H., Kaur, P. and Salo, J. (2022). How Do Ethical Consumers Utilize Sharing Economy Platforms as Part of Their Sustainable Resale Behavior? The Role of Consumers' Green Consumption Values. *Technological Forecasting and Social Change, 176*. https://doi.org/10.1016/j.techfore.2021.121432

Townsend, C., McIntyre, M., Lakhani, A., Wright, C., White, P., Bishara, J. and Cullen, J. (2018). Inclusion of Marginalised Aboriginal and Torres Strait Islander Peoples with Neurocognitive Disability in the National Disability Insurance Scheme (NDIS). *Open Access, 5*(2).

Van Nguyen, K., Islam, M.R., Huo, H., Tilocca, P. and Xu, G. (2023). Explainable Exclusion in the Life Insurance Using Multi-Label Classifier. *Proceedings of the International Joint Conference on Neural Networks, 2023-June*. https://doi.org/10.1109/IJCNN54540.2023.10191171

Wall, J. (2022). *Keynote Speech 4: A Conversational AI Approach to Detecting Deception and Tackling Insurance Fraud.* https://doi.org/10.1109/icicis52592.2021.9694118

Yang, J., Chen, K., Ding, K., Na, C. and Wang, M. (2023). Auto Insurance Fraud Detection with Multimodal Learning. *Data Intelligence*. https://doi.org/10.1162/dint_a_00191

4

Algorithmic Underwriting: Addressing Bias, Transparency, and Data Equity in Risk Assessment

Wasswa Shafik

4.1 Introduction

The rapid infusion of digital innovation into the risk assessment domain, enabled in large part by vast amounts of available private or public data, both structured and unstructured, has sparked a new business model called algorithmic underwriting. Algorithmic underwriting typically refers to processes in which artificial intelligence or machine learning models are trained on huge datasets to produce accurate risk predictions. In essence, algorithmic underwriting leverages data in novel ways to make decisions about specific risks and target the best customers for financial products. The business case behind algorithmic underwriting rests largely on the premise that with enough data and the ability to interpret it accurately, the consumer credit market could be reevaluated and reignited. For lenders, this could mean reduced time in collecting and processing data, reduced losses from credit risk, and greater ability to rely on analytical models; for consumers, it could mean vastly broadened and simpler access to credit. Some niche lenders have already begun experimenting with toolkits built on new, expansive data sources that allow them to expand their portfolios, especially in developing markets: social network data, wearable data derived from smartwatches, and financial transaction data mined from mobile wallets (Choi et al., 2024). Others have forged new partnerships with FinTechs, buying their data-stacked credit models to better screen applicants.

As risk assessment moves to a more data- and algorithm-centric reality in the pursuit of efficiency, risk data becomes an increasingly important and powerful tool. Using data to streamline risk assessment can make solvable problems more actionable, but could also exacerbate existing inequities and create additional barriers for marginalized groups in obtaining insurance. Data that is drawn from a narrow range of observations tends to reinforce existing patterns of behavior found in previous similar groups of people. This focus on the past leads to what is present, existing composition of data, not what will be in the future, and thus does not hold the promise of moving toward the efficiency gains envisioned by those promoting big data. Further, risk models based on historical claims data can threaten availability in underserved markets in the event of an unpredicted catastrophic occurrence. And claim data alone cannot drive the insurance ecosystem to a place of equity and fairness. This could lead to not just a lack of availability of insurance products targeting a particular class of consumers, but could also create real solvency issues in the case of an unexpected catastrophic event (Murphy & Moosa, 2021). Insurers, consumers, and regulators need to work together to find a solution.

DOI: 10.1201/9781003747659-4

It is increasingly recognized that the current practice of using historical data alone to create risk equity measures for the future puts an unfair burden on consumers who may be part of a specific group. Its role is not only crucial in predicting what the future risk outcomes for an individual may be, but is also a crucial input into the creation of fair and equitable risk assessment, evaluation, and monitoring rules by regulators. Data can manifest bias if the input and output data are chosen in a way that entrenches advantages—the "right" consumers are charged less because they are deemed at lower risk according to historical loss experience, whereas the "wrong" consumers are forced to pay more because they are deemed at higher risk according to some data-driven algorithm-informed analysis from prior years (Golden et al., 2016).

4.2 Types of Data Used in Algorithmic Underwriting

The type and quality of variables used in algorithmic scoring models drive their performance. A variable refers to data about an insured risk, event, or individual that has been processed to be used in an algorithm or model. In a correlational underwriting algorithm, the inputs are variables of the insurance policy, and the value to predict is the expected loss for its underwriting period. Variables can incorporate any underlying characteristics of the risk that predict its riskiness with statistical significance. The parameters of the algorithm reflect the risk disparity as a function of those input variables over the insured population of the insurer and its insurance products. In algorithmic underwriting, variables can be structured or unstructured, traditional or alternative, generated by an insurer or collected from third-party sources, and hyperlocal or at consensus or national levels (Philip & Suresh, 2024). Structured, traditional data would be standardized policy-level variables generated by an insurer about past claims history. Unstructured and alternative data would be non-standardized attribute-level information collected on unique incidents of risks sourced externally. Moreover, algorithms generally utilize multiple variables simultaneously. The interplay of multiple inputs can also drive and shape the output of a model, potentially amplifying or mitigating the impact of the individual variables. Traditionally, suggestions of what to include or exclude in parameters of algorithmic scoring models are often informed by the so-called "common sense" rules about logical connections between risk factors and the events being predicted. Accountants have used reasonable estimates of loss reserves based on historic claims information as an initial marker of adequate solvency for evaluating the financial condition of an insurance entity, while outperforming their models in experience (Townsend et al., 2018).

4.2.1 Structured Data

Machine learning models process large collections of predefined variables or features. In traditional underwriting, these features are primarily derived from closed-form questionnaires, policy applications, and legacy credit and insurance scoring systems. The variables used by algorithms in prediction vary widely, fueled in part by new AI-based scoring systems. Many new AI models are "black boxes" for which understanding is difficult. However, it has been possible for decades to create more understandable "glass box" models that can use industry-standard insurance scoring models, or well-validated proxies, to estimate rates of insurance loss and calculate premiums. Such systems combine solid science with a straightforward interactive user interface, minimizing liability exposure. The most common structured features used in underwriting have been key demographic variables suggested by policies to avoid subtle redlining. These demographic variables are search variables, which insurance actuaries have known how to use for analogy-based risk sourcing and predictive modeling, sensitivity analysis, and claiming demand estimation for decades. Actuaries in the 1960s proposed comparison-based estimates based on the relative original premium with a standard adjustment for the insured amount (Philip & Suresh, 2024). Digital algorithms have now made automated comparison, estimates, and corrections possible.

4.2.2 Unstructured Data

In addition to traditional structured data such as demographic and credit history information, recent algorithmic underwriting solutions also increasingly use so-called unstructured data, which is not generally collected or readily available in underwriting contexts. This unstructured data often comprises image or audiovisual information (ranging from still images, e.g., of a person's face to video-recorded medical examinations; from photographs of property to aerial footage taken by drones, etc.) or text data specific to social media interactions or email communication. Examining unstructured data likely enables developers and users of these technology-based systems to predict a wider set of attributes and assess the eligibility for risk coverage across additional risk pools than would be possible using only structured data, especially within emerging applications of AI in niche underwriting areas (Golden et al., 2016). For example, among other potential advantages, image data and facial recognition processes have been explored to expand risk prediction and available insurance coverage for unattractive risk segments such as underinsured drivers and road users (e.g., to enable the underwriting of vehicle-related risks in the absence of digital fingerprints such as digital accounts verifying positive commitment to pay insurance premiums), and to facilitate the provision of parametric or other coverages for property damage in developing countries with limited underwriting expertise and based on models with constrained evidence bases. However, the algorithmic analysis of unstructured data also raises serious biographical and ethical challenges. First, the use of unstructured data feeds into various conversations around issues of big data. These discussions focus on whether unstructured data entails specific privacy or data protection challenges compared to structured data (Murphy & Moosa, 2021). In addition to categorizations along the dimensions of novelty, quantity, and the absence of social norms about secondary uses, there have been developments over the years of blockchain, as presented in Figure 4.1.

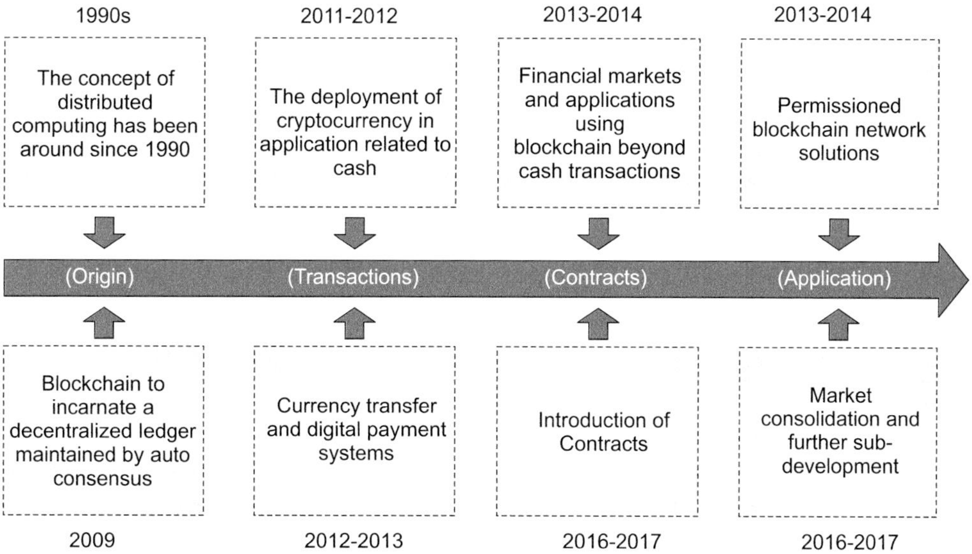

Fig. 4.1 Introduction of blockchain in insurance.

4.2.3 Alternative Data

Insurance and lending organizations have deployed mathematical models to automate risk and pricing decisions for a number of years. Understanding how datasets induce model decisions, what influences those decisions, and how to quality-check those decisions presents an array of challenges. Industry regulations require various checks and measures to be constructed prior to deploying a model, including model approval and possibly model description, model design disclosure, and consumer compliance evaluations. These procedures can help alleviate concerns about the adverse impact experienced by the consumption of these algorithmic decision-making systems. However, these procedures are incompletely capturing deeper and more subtle structural problems underlying data issues, data deficiencies, and data unpredictability. With the emergence of a variety of alternative assets, some of the data used to create algorithmic models is novel, unconventional, and a departure from actuarial pedigree. These nontraditional datasets, labeled "alternative data," are often utilized by growing segments of the insurance and lending sectors to create and calibrate algorithmic models. Examples of alternative data include resume search engines, customer relations management systems, psychometric, economic, and social media data, and new business enterprise data (Choi et al., 2024). This assortment of datasets often drives and shapes novel underwriting classes, part of the diverse push for a greater number of shared homogeneous risk classes.

These alternative, unconventional, fast-moving data provide not only greater data precision but also greater data volatility, dimensionality, leaked features, intercorrelations, incompleteness, transience, and data privacy. The algorithmic decision-making systems built using alternative data can be more capable, yielding a larger set of accurate, non-expensive, available features, reducing the cost of inaccurate, nonavailable, expensive, missing features typically found in contractual data. Higher model performance, public-facing bots, and companies and markets with a deeper understanding of their algorithmic models—model explainability—give customers of these services and products an upper hand in advancing profitability goals. But with high model performance comes greater responsibility due to the potential unpredictability of the decisions derived from algorithmic models developed using alternative data (Philip & Suresh, 2024). Quantifying the risks underlying new insurance or loan decision products becomes nearly insurmountable and implies the reverse is also true—that new dataset availability enables new models to inform available goods.

4.3 Bias in Algorithmic Models

Algorithmic models are not value-free; only value-transparent. By reflecting, amplifying, extending, and producing the biases of their developers and the societies that surround them, models encode worldviews and visions of the future, expressed mostly implicitly. When developers do not recognize or confront the values implicit in their models, they can perpetuate inequities based on immutable traits such as race and gender or remove access to crucial services, such as medical and educational assistance. In many places, the government is shifting away from the delivery of services and oversight of how they are provided toward direct assignment of resources made with risk assessment algorithms, such as risk scores for individuals, but also risk assessments for large populations (Townsend et al., 2018). This shift means that how algorithms express values can make the difference between the success or failure of program objectives, such as delivering medical assistance to those who need it most. In algorithmic underwriting, bias is a nonrandom difference in predictions across populations that concurrently have a difference in an outcome. Bias strongly influences how well a model's predictions will perform at the infinite horizon; specifically, the predictions for groups and individuals with maximal empirical risk according to the model are maximal. In fact, bias is an ideal basis for establishing whether or not a propensity score will be a determining factor in a specific model. A description of bias is not a description of error. Bias can be that which optimizes many forms of surplus, such as total, dynamic, or equity surplus. Bias, either alone or combined with other criteria such as inertia, explainable insight, or handleability, or some balance of these factors, will deterministically construct the social graph, which surfaces selections and social consequences (Oben et al., 2024).

4.3.1 Types of Bias

Bias can take many forms, the most prominent of which are statistical discrimination and statistical parity. General descriptions of these two categories are usually presented as an introduction to more specific sub-variations. Rule-based bias describes biased behavior by an algorithm that employs a discriminatory rule. Discriminatory rules are explicit algorithmic rules that declare someone disfavored based on reference to an individual or socially protected characteristic, or based on membership in a group defined based on these characteristics. For example, a discriminatory rule may assign conditions to a particular group disproportionately compared to others, leading to the denial of benefits or the allocation of burdens to that group (Aina et al., 2024). Normatively, this is fair or unfair depending on whether the rule uses information of membership in the class of protected characteristics, or makes assignments harmful to that group when the statistical information favoring the group is contrary to the assignment. Filtered bias affects predictive accuracy for the disfavored group, although the algorithm designer is not explicitly using membership in that group as a criterion. In lending, for example, the model may set very low requirements for obtaining credit for certain groups after adjusting for other predictive characteristics, be it on the grounds of nationality or sex, while setting the requirements for other groups higher. Although the algorithm based its decision completely on other criteria, thus seemingly unbiased, a test with members of the different groups shows discriminatory performances for by far not the same class of people in the different groups. This demonstrates prediction accuracy that is lower for one group and, in this example, the privileged group than for the other and, in this example, the non-privileged group (Oben et al., 2024).

4.3.2 Sources of Bias

Bias in predictive models can arise from several sources and can often be difficult to escape. The data used to train risk models, and indeed the model outputs, are often a reflection of existing and historical societal norms and structures. It is perhaps unavoidable that current predictive models reflect these same norms. For example, modern applicant screening models used to assess the creditworthiness of new customers often reflect historical patterns of user acceptance and delinquency. Because economic disadvantages can be correlated with race and geography, these data can inadvertently lead to distrust in algorithmic assessments coming from those communities (Philip & Suresh, 2024). In addition to existing societal bias, there are several other locations where bias can arise in risk models. The input datasets to the models can also be intrinsically biased. Indeed, if the input features supplied for model training also reflect demographic disparities, the model outputs would also, to some degree, be biased. Because these models predict economic behaviors that can vary significantly by demographics, it might also be natural that these model inputs be correlated with race. For example, homeownership or credit usage might reflect subtle variations over geography, which can be correlated with the presence of communities that are predominantly one race. Further, credit usage itself can have demographic variances (Murphy & Moosa, 2021). Prior races that have been generally remiss at credit delinquency might lead to the predictive features for a new credit customer being associated with their race, as summarized in Table 4.1.

Table 4.1 Common bias sources and mitigation strategies in algorithmic underwriting.

Bias Source	*Description*	*Impact on Underwriting*	*Mitigation Technique*	*Implementation Approach*
Historical Bias	Bias is embedded in past data due to social inequalities	Discriminatory risk predictions	Debiasing historical datasets	Reweighting past claims by socio-demographic fairness metrics

Contd.

Table 4.1 *Contd.*

Bias Source	*Description*	*Impact on Underwriting*	*Mitigation Technique*	*Implementation Approach*
Representation Bias	Underrepresentation of minority groups in training data	Inaccurate risk estimation for marginalized populations	Inclusive sampling and synthetic data augmentation	Adding synthetic profiles for underrepresented applicants
Measurement Bias	Inaccurate or inconsistent data collection practices	Skewed model predictions	Standardized data input protocols	Harmonizing data collection for income and health attributes
Label Bias	Subjective or biased outcome labeling in training data	Reinforcement of discriminatory practices	Third-party validation of labels	Human review of claim denial reasons
Proxy Bias	Use of correlated but unethical features (e.g., zip codes)	Redlining or indirect discrimination	Feature sensitivity analysis	Removing zip code as a predictor for premium decisions
Sample Size Bias	Small datasets for niche or new insurance markets	Overfitting or unstable predictions	Data pooling, federated learning	Collaborating across insurers for rare event modeling
Algorithmic Bias	Model architecture favoring the majority data	Lower accuracy for edge cases	Fairness-aware ML algorithms	Applying adversarial debiasing techniques
Economic Bias	Overreliance on income or occupation	Penalizes low-income applicants	Socio-economic normalization	Adjusting for cost of living and employment types
Feedback Loop Bias	Self-reinforcing predictions from previous underwriting outcomes	Perpetuation of prior decisions	Intervention audits and reset points	Retraining the model on post-adjusted data after policy changes
Data Drift	Change in population behavior or data quality over time	Model degradation and fairness erosion	Ongoing monitoring and revalidation	Recalibration of risk models quarterly
Label Leakage	Use of future information in the training phase	Over-optimistic model leading to real-world errors	Strict feature auditing and timeline enforcement	Removing post-claim variables from training
Regulatory Noncompliance	Misalignment with antidiscrimination laws	Legal and reputational risks	Legal risk scanning during model design	Automated compliance validation with data protection laws
Automation Bias	Excessive trust in algorithmic decisions	Lack of human oversight and correction	Human-in-the-loop systems	A hybrid underwriting model with mandatory final human review
Geographic Bias	Disproportionate impact on rural or low-access regions	Unfair premium or denial patterns	Geo-demographic normalization	Calibrating models for urban–rural feature balance

4.4 Impact of Bias on Risk Assessment

Bias that results in discrimination and disparities in socio-economic risk assessment impacts society as a whole. This effect is most evident in the context of criminal risk assessment, an area where many of the current algorithmic techniques are utilized. Several of these tools have come under severe criticism, to the extent that calls for caution have been made, that such products should be outlawed altogether. A notable contribution is the study, which uncovered that the use of risk assessment in criminal justice caused significant bias, as it resulted in Black defendants being wrongly singled out as likely to commit future crimes at almost twice the rate of White defendants. Furthermore, a quarter of White defendants identified as being at high risk actually posed no such risk (Choi et al., 2024). The analysis does suggest, however, that an important condition for those disparities is the choice of ground truth for validating the algorithmic risk assessment; they chose a rather short time window of two years to identify recidivism, while increasing this interval would mitigate against the described systematic differences. It should be mentioned that these findings have been criticized, making the issue a controversial talking point. More recently, an additional study has been published investigating a larger time horizon for the predicted recidivism. In this analysis, the authors confirm the disparities reported but also emphasize the consequences of documenting such disparate outcomes and warn against practices of using proxy variables such as race. Thereby, providing a rather complex picture of the actual performance of the risk assessment. The detected disparities should serve as a motivation for researchers working in this area to delve deeper into this topic (Golden et al., 2016). A critical point raised by many studies is that such positive bias could be a reflection of different underlying base rates for different demographics, making the discussion on whether the biases found in these studies are problematic or not a rather nuanced and critical process.

4.4.1 Case Studies

The closest parallels to algorithmic underwriting may come from the existing literature on algorithmic discrimination, which includes numerous accounts of actual harm attributable to algorithmic systems. However, almost all of this literature revolves around machine learning systems that make decisions on behalf of private firms in domains that antidiscrimination rules have historically governed. In contrast, such rules will not directly govern algorithmic underwriting systems; rather, they will focus on the outsourced assessment of risk in a domain where decisions are allowed to be informed by discriminatory factors. The case studies we present in this part of the study are inspired by historical instances of disparate impact and discrimination described in the existing literature, but will not focus exclusively or directly on algorithmic systems or the algorithmic underwriting space (Philip & Suresh, 2024). The case studies touch upon disparate impacts and direct harms associated with models used by government agencies unable to pay for advanced proprietary models.

4.4.2 Statistical Analysis

This section offers a more statistical point of view on bias. In this section, we will not delve into mathematical details and empirical models, but describe the potential direction and types of disagreement among the population in order to quantify bias in future research work better. A recasting of a Venn sphere in a 2D format to show that the scope of disagreement, once we define exactly what we mean by risk (the actual, or predictive, or ex-ante default probability associated with the classifier's decision) as well as by which classification is of societal concern, can be defined using a combination of the terms encircled. Risk measure, risk society, classification choice, and directions of more versus less bias are represented in different colors, while the classification category of interest (default versus non-default) is in dashed. Following this, we can specify which circles to encircle and how, in order to characterize the two-dimensional bias aspect of algorithmic underwriting in the reader's mind, possibly including data subsets, and reflecting preferences regarding unfair advantage versus unfair disadvantage scenarios. There are many candidates for specifying the risk measure in the outer layer (Murphy & Moosa, 2021). The most popular today is probably the classifier's classifier probability, with the threshold specified by the classifier control grid search, employed to optimize the area under the Receiver Operating Characteristic (ROC) curve or to minimize the risk of the choice of action associated with the classifier's relative cost and benefit, as illustrated in Figure 4.2.

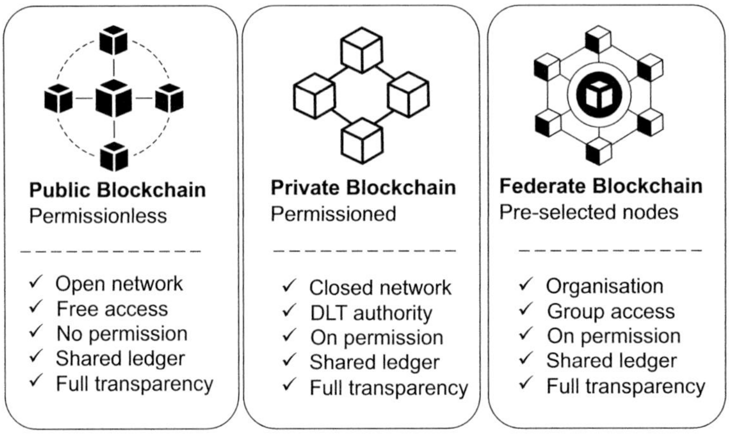

Fig. 4.2 Types of blockchain networks adoptable in insurance.

4.5 Transparency in Algorithmic Underwriting

The use of proprietary algorithms in decision-making processes that have a substantial effect on people's lives raises potentially serious issues of accountability and due process, particularly in highly automated environments where most judgments come from algorithms, rather than people. Mechanical judgment can be exceedingly harsh in many risk-related sectors, for example, insurance, credit, lending, and law enforcement. With the decision-making located at a distant company site, consumers are deprived of a local and relational mechanism for dispute resolution. These companies have thus been pressed to ensure that sufficient transparency exists throughout the decision-making processes to allow sufficient analysis to establish whether the outputs are systematic violations of civil rights (Sachan & Muwanga, 2023). Because of this trend, it is critical to design algorithms that limit the damage caused by the company–individual relationship imbalance. This chapter introduces the topic of transparency in algorithmic risk assessment, including some of the basic methods for enhancing transparency that can be deployed at various data science life cycle steps. Given that using algorithms for risk assessment can lead to significantly adverse consequences for individuals, it is essential that algorithmic outputs are predictable and any decisions made using these outputs are explainable in some meaningful way. Because of some inherent characteristics of algorithmic systems, such as the execution of data-driven procedures, the usage of heuristics that highly simplify underlying mechanisms, or global optimization for problem-solving constrained by utility and efficiency, any generated output is normally incomprehensible to end users. Therefore, in designing algorithms for commercial practices related to people, adequate investment must be made to maintain the algorithm design principles of transparency and interpretability so that potential violators of civil rights can be held accountable for their actions (Wall, 2022). The solution to this issue may take various forms, ranging from model-agnostic interpretability methods and algorithmic design principles to algorithm requirements imposed by regulatory systems.

4.5.1 Importance of Transparency

Algorithms are a part of our daily life. They have been incorporated in many different applications, including search engines, social media, artificial intelligence assistants, data mining, security systems, recommendation systems, and many others. Algorithms are also being increasingly used to make important decisions, such as granting loans, hiring employees, approving health insurance requests, and more. Today, many companies around the world are employing algorithmic, automated decision-making, especially when it comes to sensitive social and financial decisions, such as financial credit decisions, employment screening, insurance coverage, and law enforcement. Algorithmic underwriting, for example, utilizes artificial intelligence and machine learning to automate lending decisions (Settipalli & Gangadharan, 2023). Algorithmic underwriting particularly attracted the interest of many investors, who started pouring large sums of money into promoting the business models of many FinTech companies that offer to replace traditional banking with automated services. However, the recent and ongoing financial crisis in the United States, as well as lessons learned from previous financial crises, urge us to assess the algorithms being used to write underwriting carefully. Critics point to the severe social problems produced by the poor oversight of lending practices in the years leading to the housing market crash in 2008, and warn that algorithmic underwriting may repeat the very same mistakes that were made during the human-based traditional underwriting procedures. Unfortunately, most of the categorical prohibitions on discriminatory conduct that have guided traditional underwriting cannot be transferred to the new method. This interrogation of the conduct bears relevance to a wider context than underwriting alone and may not even be enforceable with regard to other common algorithmic practices (Arockiam & Pushpanathan, 2023). Any assessment of how to translate the principles into practice inevitably raises the critical question of the explanatory demands set on algorithms: how transparent must the decision-making of an algorithm be?

4.5.2 Methods for Enhancing Transparency

A model can be considered transparent for a number of reasons. Some of these reasons are properties of the model itself: it may be simple and interpretable. Alternatively, the model could use data we are intimately familiar with. A data model can be considered transparent, even if the model is a complex black box. If the model creates a clear path from the data to the outcome and explains how changes in the data affect changes in the outcome, we can interpret the outcome. Some of these properties can be further enhanced by selecting a specific combination of training method, pretraining and fine-tuning, distillation, and post-hoc explanation. Choosing simple and off-the-shelf algorithms, such as linear logistic regression with a small number of selected features, can enhance interpretability, but may come at the cost of accuracy. However, we shouldn't always worry too much about the accuracy–interpretability trade-off (Shafik, 2025). Often, even highly complex models yield little or no gain from models we can easily interpret, as presented in Table 4.2.

4.6 Data Equity in Risk Assessment

Human decisions have always involved a certain degree of randomness. In general, broader access to relevant information improves decision-making. However, algorithmic decision systems operating on synthetic data cannot overcome the limitations inherent to the available training data. Without unbiased, sufficiently large datasets, algorithms cannot improve upon the entrenched stereotypes and assumptions of human experts, particularly when the candidates face novel challenges that differ from their peers. We have already identified the risks of failing to account for specific data equity lapses on a case-by-case basis when discussing diagnostic tools and identity and dialect

Table 4.2 Key principles of transparency and data equity in algorithmic risk assessment.

Principle	*Role in Underwriting*	*Associated Risk*	*Operational Strategy*	*Example Tool/Practice*
Explainability	Clarity on how decisions are made	Trust erosion, dispute difficulty	Use of Explainable AI (XAI) tools	LIME–Local Interpretable Model-agnostic Explanations, SHAP–SHapley Additive exPlanations for model interpretability
Data Transparency	Knowing what data is used and how	Hidden features leading to bias	Data provenance logs and disclosures	Transparency statements with underwriting decisions
Equity in Data Access	Ensuring data fairness across groups	Disadvantage to groups with less digital footprint	Inclusive data sourcing policies	Outreach to underserved communities for data inclusion
Algorithmic Accountability	Clear accountability in model outcomes	Denial of responsibility for discriminatory outcomes	Establishing clear responsibility tiers	AI governance charter defining model ownership
Data Minimization	Only using necessary data for decision-making	Privacy intrusion and overfitting	Feature selection and minimization audits	Removing nonessential personal traits from input data
Model Auditability	Ability to inspect and evaluate model decisions	Unregulated black-box models	Periodic fairness and accuracy audits	Independent audits using bias-detection frameworks
Stakeholder Inclusion	Engaging stakeholders in model design	Misalignment with user needs and values	Codesign workshops with legal, actuarial, and consumer reps	Participatory model development sessions
Risk Communication	Articulating uncertainty in AI outputs	Misinterpretation of scores as facts	Probability bands and confidence intervals	Risk score with 95% prediction interval
Feedback Integration	Learning from user/claimant input	Static models that ignore evolving trends	Human-in-the-loop feedback mechanisms	Customer appeal system feeding into model adjustments
Ethical Data Governance	Managing data use with fairness and oversight	Data misuse and surveillance concerns	Ethical review boards and consent-based governance	Internal review committees for new data source approval
Feature Fairness	Ensuring features contribute equally across groups	Indirect discrimination	Disparate impact testing	Feature contribution analysis segmented by demographics
Temporal Fairness	Equitable treatment across time	Bias amplification over time	Longitudinal fairness audits	Tracking fairness metrics over multiple underwriting periods
Accessibility	Ensuring people understand automated decisions	Exclusion of low-literacy or differently-abled applicants	Plain language summaries and multilingual support	Decision letters with visual risk explanations
Ethical Oversight	Embedding values into design and operation	Unethical optimization for profit	Ethics-centered KPIs–Key Performance Indicators and model constraints	Embedding fairness as a performance metric in model deployment

classifiers (Singh et al., 2024). To fortify automated risk assessment against such risks, insurers must consider data equity during the model development process itself. Automated underwriting systems that learn from algorithms optimize for overall accuracy. Some applicant features, such as ethnicity, may produce a model that improves point estimates of electrocardiogram readings for the majority population while creating significant error bands for minority populations. This bias may be further compounded when this model is used on small cohorts from minority populations. Understanding the limitations and risks associated with the model on dialect, accent, or identity might have increased sensitivity toward its negative effects. Insurers would not want their students denied entry due to an artifact created by a model. Ultimately, data equity requires careful consideration of the model's performance with respect to various minority and at-risk subsets, not just the overall performance. We should implement mechanisms to identify segment-specific model failure modes, guide additional data-collection efforts, and hold third parties increasingly accountable for the models they deliver (Margan, 2021).

4.6.1 Definition and Importance

Data equity refers to the idea that data used in algorithmic and statistical models should be complete, representative, and accurate. It speaks to concerns regarding whether underrepresented groups, especially those that are historically disadvantaged and marginalized, have the same access to credit and insurance products as other groups. It considers whether the data used to assess risk is qualitatively the same for those making decisions about whether to give access to products and services, the terms associated with the products, and privileged status in underwriting models. And it speaks to potential optimization processes used that incentivize the omission of groups from sampling and data collection procedures. Without addressing the principles of data equity, many of the best practices guiding responsible AI will have limited effect. There is simply no way to achieve fairness in algorithmic assessments of decision-making without using the right data that sufficiently captures all potential groups. Achieving data equity also introduces other demands for proper risk assessment. It calls for a more ethical view of data as a social creation—a product of social processes, not engagements with technology. It recognizes that the choice of what is measured for any group, and how measurement occurs, is a reflection of the priorities and practices of a trusted social institution (McDonnell et al., 2023). It also implies a need for quantitative methodologies, technical tools, and strategies that are participant-friendly and can guide the creation of trustworthy databases that underpin informed decisions by trusted institutions.

4.6.2 Strategies for Achieving Data Equity

Data equity formulates certain demands on how data is used. Understanding these demands is essential for assessing and evaluating existing algorithmic underwriting models. But what are concrete strategies for achieving data equity? Efforts to reduce the amount of existing inequitable data probably do not qualify as a solution. While one may not want to inhibit conversation and research about the existence of missing groups in datasets, nor about the implications for risk assessment, it seems problematic to suggest that insurers could respond to this gap by trying to remove this gap. The idea of simply removing the underrepresented market segments from the data seems problematic from a broader point of view (Gramegna & Giudici, 2020). These underrepresented segments are likely particularly in need. While risk pooling would presume that they could profit from the provision of hedging possibilities such types of insurance would provide, it is also likely that the provision would lead to dissimilar costs. Focusing on strategies of data sufficiency can incorporate principles of risk equity or data equity and strives to contribute to the original purpose of insurance in the first place: enabling a community to reduce financial burdens caused by exceptional situations. Strategies for achieving algorithmic risk equity may include the construction of safety net models in collaboration with governmental actors and initiatives. These safety net models can help to reduce particular risk factors in specified market segments. Or they can provide additional compensation when risk factors materialize (Călin & Izvoranu, 2018). These strategies can help to ameliorate the adverse effects of predictively inequitable pricing by insurance companies.

4.7 Regulatory Frameworks and Guidelines

This chapter provides an overview of current regulations applicable to risk assessment, as well as proposed guidelines for the future. Next, we provide a detailed treatment of how these regulations mitigate biases and ensure transparency. Such discussion is partly prescriptive and partly descriptive as we aim to elucidate regulatory responses that can help address present and future mathematical and algorithmic concerns. The fact that risk transfer, with its core product of insurance, may not be characterized by universal altruistic motives makes it particularly compelling to discuss asymmetric information regulatory responses in this field. The following question appears particularly adept to be answered in our context: Which or what kind of rules can guarantee the correct development of the algorithm, or the correct utilization of the algorithm? There is a long history of regulations governing algorithmic decision-making in high-risk areas such as credit analysis or predictive policing, with major rules being in force for decades. These regulations primarily concern two aspects of the potential harmful consequences of algorithmic decision-making: fairness, especially the prohibition of certain discriminatory grounds, and transparency, or more widely, the obligation of explainability and the comprehensibility of an algorithm's predictions (Poshtiri et al., 2024). The rationale for these regulations is based on clear ethical and moral grounds: mandatory fairness and transparency are economically desirable in these areas, as otherwise society would suffer from the adverse impacts of unequal risk assessment and discriminatory overprediction or rather underprediction of certain sections of society.

4.7.1 Current Regulations

Individual insurance and lending markets in the USA are regulated at both the federal and state levels to ensure consumer protection, financial stability, and fair competition. At the federal level, the primary financial services regulators apply just a few existing laws to prevent and address consumer discrimination in the markets they regulate. Those laws prohibit unfair discrimination based on race, color, religion, national origin, sex, disability, or familial status. The laws are more comprehensive in scope, specifically prohibiting discrimination in a wide range of housing-related transactions. However, only one expressly prohibits discriminatory effects in these transactions (Van Nguyen et al., 2023). While one law states that credit reporting agencies cannot discriminate based on race, color, religion, sex, marital status, national origin, and age, it does not prohibit the affected lenders from doing so, nor does it extend to all lenders. State laws mirror or expand upon these federal rules; the most comprehensive approach generally being found in the corresponding state fair housing laws. While there are some differences in interpretation across jurisdictions that affect particular applications of these laws, they all focus on determining whether groups have been treated differently within a discriminatory "protected class." Thus, they operate largely as disparate treatment laws, not explicitly prohibiting data-driven algorithmic discrimination or disparate impact on the basis of other factors that do not appear in those lists (Sachan & Muwanga, 2023). That lack of express prohibitions creates a large regulatory gap for algorithmic underwriting, which explores these issues.

4.7.2 Proposed Changes

A wide variety of stakeholders offer policy debates in order to suggest new or modified guidelines for how models should be evaluated and how insurers should account for models in business processes. One proposal requires that algorithms be "fair" by not providing systematic advantages or disadvantages to certain groups in society. These determinations can be made using model performance criteria, and ever larger datasets with more cross-sectional information on customers might allow for the standard evaluation of fairness criteria in large model classes (Aina et al., 2024). Responsive reports to such proposed changes to insurance regulation would require large datasets that describe what consumers will buy and how responsive they are to different insurance offerings. In addition to the technical requirements regarding what data to keep for model monitoring and to inform updates, reports would also require transparent procedures and best practices for how companies would approach these challenges. Neoliberalism suggests that society must rely on private actors in different roles, and that these actors motivate and shape society both through the costs and savings they generate and through the roles they occupy. Some consider that it is the responsibility of actuaries to ensure that models show credible performance on fairness criteria and to communicate those results to regulators. Others suggest that insurers have hypothesized how access can differ among races and genders. In that case, the onus is on the regulators to determine what fairness standard should be applied and what performance criteria should be reported (Townsend et al., 2018). In that case, some policymakers suggest that regulators should assess what performance metrics ensure.

4.8 Ethical Considerations in Algorithmic Underwriting

Societies create rules and ethical norms designed to promote fairness, justice, and well-being. When using algorithms to make economic, political, or social decisions, these norms can be broken down into the more detailed technical notions associated with "fairness" or "justice" in theoretical discussions of AI ethics. However, whether an algorithm is fair or unfair cannot always be expressed in a source code algorithm. Not all ethical concerns can be resolved completely in advance. Computer code exists in an environment defined and surrounded by a social context in which the consequences of a decision will be enacted. Ultimately, ethics is not about codes; it is about sensitivity and wisdom. Such wisdom operates not just with the guidance of rules, but by being able to know when applying or interpreting a rule produces something unjust or disastrous (Golden et al., 2016). Recognition of a higher principle invokes a duty to correct for the sake of moral goodness. The goal of this chapter is to explore ethical perspectives on algorithms that raise questions about fairness and potential use as a social decision-making technology. We wish to explore how algorithm decision-making has consequences for different stakeholders, especially those stakeholders on the short end of the power and privilege sticks. These stakeholder perspectives do not need to be at war with disciplines such as statistics and data science. Indeed, data science can deepen or elaborate the scholarship that the stakeholder perspective draws upon, and ethnic studies and critique can expand and enrich the interpretive frames that drive data science (Choi et al., 2024). Data science methods can be useful in mapping power differentials or various other forms of group suffering, but such operationalizations should at least take heed of the stakeholder research that has long processed the social suffering described in the frame.

4.8.1 Ethical Frameworks

In a report, a group of scholars articulates that "the dominant discussion of fairness is problematic in important ways. It may obscure important and relevant elements of algorithmic decision-making important to stakeholders, and the goals of stakeholders that are not captured by standard fairness metrics." The report calls for a new approach to understanding fairness in decision systems, saying that "policymakers, the public, and stakeholders of all kinds must have clarity on a number of important questions: Fair to whom? Fair with respect to what attributes? Fair relative to what outcomes? With respect to which algorithmic systems use which data? With respect to whose values?" There are ample reasons for making algorithmic risk assessments transparent. Transparency allows adjudicators and those being adjudicated to understand better how decisions explicated in algorithms are made, increasing accountability and trust. Moreover, a lack of transparency can render fundamental distinctiveness standards impossible to assess. Adverse decision outcomes from opaque algorithms cannot be traced back for correction when humans themselves may not understand the decision logic of such systems (Murphy & Moosa, 2021). In financial services, when certain types of data are available only from third-party vendors who are not required to disclose their data use or algorithms used to process it, transparency is made exceedingly difficult.

4.8.2 Stakeholder Perspectives

Algorithmic underwriting raises a range of ethical questions and concerns that go beyond the formal functions of individual stakeholders. The volume and complexity of data today enable the creation of powerful algorithmic solutions. However, creating models that perform well and operate without overt bias is neither an easy nor a trivial task. Many stakeholders, besides the model sponsors asking for an automated solution, are involved in the data collection and model development process. Different stakeholders perceive algorithmic risk assessment differently, being concerned about different risks and requiring different protections. Some stakeholders may consider it a useful tool that adds valuable insights, while for others, it can be a source of discrimination or exclusion. Additionally, algorithms can also impact different stakeholders differently. When viewed through the lens of different stakeholder groups, algorithmic solutions can be problematic for some and protective for others (Choi et al., 2024). Decision transparency, fairness, accountability, and, ultimately, trust in algorithmic products revolve around these differing stakeholder perspectives on algorithmic risk assessment. Some stakeholders may feel that the decision-making process embedded in an algorithm is useful because it explicates the connections between input variables and provides insights into that relationship. However, this is not the view of all stakeholders. Data subjects may want a decision-making process that relies on only objective criteria that are clear and understandable to a layperson. Data sponsors are concerned about an algorithm that may not yield an appropriate predictive model. Model sponsors are likely to care about algorithm performance from a different perspective depending on the implementation context: whether it is during development, after implementation, or toward model retirement (Golden et al., 2016). Such distinctions also signify the technical orientation and expertise of stakeholders in relation to the relevant issue.

4.9 Technological Innovations and Solutions

Countering the risks that come from algorithmic underwriting, fairness-aware algorithms approach the issue in a variety of ways. The most common technique is modifying the learning algorithms by adding knowledge fairness constraints to the optimization objective. Others go further than fairness constraints to consider the data for disparate impact proactively. There are several existing software solutions for auditing commercial algorithms. There are also some fairness-aware classifiers available as software packages in Python. These packages typically share the limitation of not being designed or pretrained with a specific industry sector in mind. Each of these libraries of fairness-aware package implementations abstracts fairness into a single notion via a fairness measure. Auditors would be at the mercy of the meanings and measuring of fairness defined by the package designers. Software engineer teams that develop these packages tend to have a computer science background, and business analysts would probably not be experts in machine learning, either (Choi et al., 2024). Because of this limitation, as more algorithmic new features and innovations, the heavier the financial tolls. Reducing bias and rebutting inequity complaints will take a time shift, a focus from establishing a top-down fairness notion to adopting a bottom-up stance and allowing users to define their fairness.

4.9.1 Machine Learning Techniques

When discussing innovative technology developments, solutions utilizing machine-learning techniques come to the forefront, as they have the potential for widespread implementation in contemporary risk assessment systems. These solutions utilize more advanced algorithms in recognition of the fact that improved predictive performance has been observed in these algorithms compared to classical statistical techniques. However, in addition to increased operational performance, companies desire these predictive solutions for decreased internal development costs and shorter time-to-market cycles. Innovations from the technology sector, such as assembled modeling, externally developed tools and technologies, and cloud-based services, have resulted in a burgeoning technology development ecosystem. The advanced, off-the-shelf solutions and services, as well as the work product of established consulting firms, provide auditing companies with the ability to realize highly innovative predictive solutions quickly (Van Nguyen et al., 2023). Machine learning is a subset or family of techniques within the broader field of artificial intelligence and is defined as a method by which systems develop a behavior based on data rather than according to explicit programming. It is distinguished from classical statistical solutions in that the emphasis is placed upon prediction rather than on inference, and that immense scale is possible. Utilizing the hardware and software capabilities of the big-data ecosystem, the input data to the risk score development process can incorporate a more varied, deeper, and wider range of predictive information than has been traditionally considered together. The resulting predictive scores can be used, adjusted, and interpreted within the broader enterprise framework according to the particular business context in which they are being employed (Philip & Suresh, 2024).

4.9.2 Fairness-Aware Algorithms

Human decisions are filled with biases for many reasons, from the way humans learn and make choices to the lack of structured data, stated judgments, and explainable and optimal decisions. Algorithmic decisions, made by machine learning and other models, can help improve the quality of these decisions. These algorithms are, however, vulnerable to bias as well. Such constraints on algorithmic fairness arise from the type of data used, the manner in which it is handled, and how the algorithm learns and generates actions and these decisions. A dataset that reflects past discrimination will not only preserve that bias in training the model but also exacerbate that effect. In addition, models use mathematical correlation or association to learn relationships between variable sets to better predict or classify and rely on hidden variable sets to derive these results (Choi et al., 2024). These hidden variables, educated on biased input data, may use correlations reflecting bias as shortcuts in building the prediction mechanism, leading to racially imbalanced or skewed predictions when optimized on the proportion of misclassified groups. Much potential exists to mitigate protection and fairness lessons from experience and responsible and ethical learning using a wide range of data computation and sentiment analysis. The development of fairness-aware algorithms, which can guarantee certain fairness constraints while making decisions, should continue on all fronts. For example, in data, the fairness-open workers should help curate fair and representative datasets against the commercial platform constraints based on optimality, capturing rich alternatives for algorithms based on unintended correlation and group fairness. In tools, more integrated data spaces and data repositories that have self-learning capabilities regarding their contents should be explored, which can help data ethics managers, with built-in logics to address social constraints using historical machine learning guidelines, do appropriate equity assessments with automated quality and algorithm rules (Arockiam & Pushpanathan, 2023).

4.10 Case Studies of Algorithmic Underwriting

Algorithmic underwriting is usually employed in insurance. In the insurance industry, risk models are used by underwriters to assess the level of risk a potential client or insured represents. Based on the result of the risk assessment, the underwriter decides whether the insurer wants to assume the risk and, if so, sets the correct premium. Risk models are derived based on risk factors that assume a discernable correlation with the likelihood of the onset of a future insured event. Risk factors can be physical characteristics of the insured or factors relating to the insured object or action. Yet, risk models can incentivize shortsighted decisions of individuals, discrimination against marginalized communities, or impacts related to climate change throughout time horizons relevant to a government. In general, these models are affected by adverse selection (Van Nguyen et al., 2023). Without a just solution, AI will ultimately perpetuate the inequitable treatment of racial minorities established by traditional underwriting models.

In recent years, there have been some conservative pushes to allow transparent AI risk models in the auto and property market segments. There are implementations of algorithmic underwriting in the property market segment in addition to risk assessments of toxicity. Health experts and physicians advocate against algorithmic underwriting altogether, claiming that algorithmic risk selections are essentially in conflict with the social motives of a welfare state. An example of this worrying trend is the growing popularity of diabetes monitoring as a new risk factor among clinicians in the discussion of health tech. A case study in algorithmic underwriting highlights some of the critical ethical issues around algorithmic risk assessments (Bermúdez et al., 2023). In the Netherlands, access to healthcare services for vulnerable populations is governed by specific regulations. These groups are defined by income, illness, disability, or dependency. The algorithm used to allocate budgets was based on demographic risk factors such as gender, age, and degree of urbanization. The outcome of the algorithmic assessment resulted in the municipality being charged for the services rendered for adverse selection. Algorithm designers recommended cutbacks of service. However, such recommendations could not replace the human discussions that took place between assessors and applicants, which had some merit. The example shows that people with societal goals must implement risk models. Algorithmic underwriting could help in making decision-making transparent, too (Wall, 2022).

4.10.1 Successful Implementations

There is a sizeable gap between the ambitious visions outlined at the outset of the part and the reality of the major financial institutions. Some also argue that lessons learned from particular successful implementations can be of even greater practical use in the current period. This section investigates some of the standout case studies, including data-driven lending models for microfinance and risk-based insurance pricing models, programs implemented to explore and assess potential creditworthiness in noncredit consumers. Each of these models arguably shows pathways to help solve the credit access gaps, or unfavorable terms, for consumers with limited or no existing credit files, typically classified as thin-file or no-file consumers (Aina et al., 2024). Among specific use cases, perhaps the best example of a successful and scalable implementation of data-driven risk assessment comes from the microfinance sector, which has pioneered a new strategy for data-driven assessment of creditworthiness with the introduction of a marketplace system. In particular, the marketplace illustrates how innovative lending models can leverage microentrepreneurial activities to address poverty challenges across the globe. More than a lending platform, the mission is to connect people through lending to alleviate poverty. It was founded as a nonprofit organization and was the first online microlending platform connecting lenders to borrowers for donation-based lending (Oben et al., 2024). On the marketplace, anyone can browse the website and choose from a selection of entrepreneurial micro-entrepreneurs (typically in developing countries) who are looking for funds to help grow or start their small business.

4.10.2 Failures and Lessons Learned

Two notable case studies of automated underwriting systems come from the domain of insurance. In 1993, the National Association of Insurance Commissioners set out to standardize the initial collection of life-insurance underwriting data in order to facilitate the retrospective analysis of insurance functions. A research effort and consensus statements issued over several years resulted in the Designated Data Elements for Life Insurance guidelines published in December 1999. The primary intention of the guidelines is to ensure that the categories of life insurance risk characterizing distinct purchasing events are consistently and completely specified across totally disparate life insurers.

(i) In July 2001, the Prudential Regulation Authority placed a ban on various activities by the insurance company, Prudential, whose underwriting went substantially automated in order to avoid the added costs of hiring experienced underwriters. The ban was dissolved four years later after Prudential agreed to employ human review of exceptions during the screening process, with quality audits of flagged cases. While the claimed advantage of the novel prudential system was its efficiency, the company intended to use artificial intelligence software for detailed database analytics of remnant screening due to apparent system overload (Murphy & Moosa, 2021). The aim was to reduce the large number of misleading false positives generated.

(ii) The abovementioned examples illustrate considerable variability in how insurance firms approached the automation of underwriting and the impact this had on quality control and corrective measures. We can learn in particular from the Prudential case that an insurance company with a mass market business cannot afford to deploy an entirely algorithmic process with no human intervention. The model of human-free incorporation is to embed analytic databases to flag exceptions for human underwriting reviews that guarantee the required quality controls (Choi et al., 2024).

4.11 Future Directions in Algorithmic Underwriting

Critics of the insurance industry argue that the economic interests of firms, executives, and shareholders dominate over stakeholder interests. One clear example is the use of underwriting algorithm features detrimental to specific groups, just because those features correlate positively with high risk. These harms caused by biased and discriminatory algorithms can lead to a number of important requests and outcomes: they can motivate states to pass laws banning the use of certain variables in underwriting as discrimination safeguards; provide grounds for federal civil rights litigation alleging violation of disparate impact or disparate treatment; or expose the firms to significant amounts of reputational damages. For these and other reasons, civil society groups have been demanding greater transparency and accountability from insurance companies (Golden et al., 2016). Recent trends show that insurance companies have to comply with these requests for transparency and embrace the principles of algorithmic fairness more than in the early days of algorithmic underwriting. A growing number of actuaries are committed to emerging empirical research on algorithmic justice and on their application domains, while insurance regulators have created scores of committees focused on issues of transparency and accountability in the use of algorithmic decision-making systems. All in all, a consensus is forming around the adoption of "responsible AI" principles. Yet, the shift to algorithmic transparency will come with challenges. First, risk scoring models are complex, and using measures such as normalization, stripping, or hidden layer visualization is not always effective. Second, there are few agreed-upon standards on how to share underlying data and model codes for future validation and challenge. Algorithm audits also create liability and confidentiality issues (Philip & Suresh, 2024). Algorithms undergo continuous learning, creating additional questions on their status as regulated objects. Testing data for discrimination, for instance, may become outdated with time or invalid if discriminatory practices are changed.

4.11.1 Emerging Trends

In recent years, we have seen a new focus on the potential for unfair discrimination and lack of transparency in algorithmic decision systems. It could be that doing the same thing that has been previously done, but at scale, is really the best that can be done. However, there is movement in regulation, standardization, civil society organizations focused on algorithmic equity, and many researchers who are taking on the difficult problems of how to ensure that algorithms are developed, tested, and deployed in a way that does not harm the use of such systems by society. It will take some time before there is a consensus as to whether algorithmic systems that serve to identify underlying risk in use for any one classification purpose should follow the same standards, requirements, and other categorical limits that have been established for the use of classical statistical models developed over the past 60 or more years by the fields of statistics, economics, and social science (Murphy & Moosa, 2021). It is our opinion that the statistical and data considerations that have guided traditional retainers of such methods should not be ignored. Use of any increased data and statistical or algorithmic capabilities to classify risk for any purpose, be it risk underwriting, hiring, lending, e-crime, or how to act or not act upon any of these classifications, should hold equal risk of producing unfair discrimination and other social harms. We may be able to use more design, but not at the expense of the importance of the "how" to do such evaluation and validation before use. As we reflect and then look ahead toward how to adapt and improve algorithmic models for risk assessment to address the many concerns we have listed throughout the book, we will start by addressing what we see as more immediate emerging capabilities in the evaluation of such models (Townsend et al., 2018).

4.11.2 Potential Challenges

To our knowledge, no published algorithmic underwriting models are currently being employed in the wild. This may reflect the myriad challenges that need to be reconciled before evaluating algorithmic underwriting in practice. The United States has been an especially high-profile locus of recent discourse and research on fairness in algorithmic decision-making. Federal agencies and civil rights advocates, particularly for housing and employment, have articulated a clarion call for enhanced civil rights protections against algorithmic bias. These considerations imply that for underwriting to be successful with machine learning, it would have to more broadly meet the social role of radically improving credit access among historically excluded populations, while protecting consumers with superior underwriting predictive performance and transparency (Settipalli & Gangadharan, 2023). At the same time, significant components of the commercial insurance markets, such as auto and commercial property, have been guided historically by underwriters who built highly idiosyncratic rules around idiosyncratic knowledge of local conditions. These underwriters built their experience with long supervisory contracts with insurance companies, which would transfer their risk onto reinsurance companies. Consequently, in the face of a widespread rash of data-driven discriminatory actions in parallel sectors such as employment and housing, any tendency to recapitulate discriminatory practices in commercial insurance might well motivate regulatory responses against smaller underwriting firms who lack such posse and hard-won reputation and scale advantages (Abdulkadir Isa & Fernando, 2023). Such actions might arise in part out of a sense that broader lender and borrower relationships would be recast as a condition for economic access and social license to operate.

4.12 Conclusion

Algorithmic underwriting, a rapid development in the insurance, credit, and lending industries, refers to the utilization of algorithmic risk assessment systems to evaluate the insurability, creditworthiness, and capacity to pay premiums and repay debts. Risk assessment systems have been the subject of increasing scrutiny due to concerns with various forms of bias, opacity, and unequal impact. These issues are particularly glaring in algorithmic underwriting because risk assessment systems are often the sole decision-making mechanism, without modification or review, in significant transactions affecting long-term risk in both the risks being assessed and the opportunities to reduce those risks. The work explores issues of bias, transparency, data inclusiveness, and impact. Data equity in insurance and finance extends beyond the factors considered in risk assessments to the factors omitted from risk assessment inputs. If the purpose of risk assessment is to predict future events, the assessment's data must be relevant to future risk. More broadly, data equity encompasses data selection and preparation, including the use of proxies in algorithmic underwriting. Algorithmic risk assessments may also be inconsistent with fairness concepts if they fail to comply with industry standards, rebuttable presumptions, or stakeholder rules, recommendations, or norms. The disparities in performance or effect due to algorithmic underwriting, the greater automated features of algorithmic underscoring systems, and the greater potential for disparate impact and disadvantageous effects on groups sharing a protected characteristic, all suggest a need for particular care in algorithmic underwriting decision-making. In conclusion, algorithmic underwriting combines elements of both the general issues of algorithmic risk assessment and the specifics of underwriting. Moreover, the concerns of policymakers with algorithmic underwriting decisions and oversight, and the potential impact on wide sectors of economies and societies, warrant particular attention. Consequently, it is essential to approach these systems with a sense of urgency combined with deliberation as their use expands and becomes normative.

References

Abdulkadir Isa, U. and Fernando, A. (2023). Explainable AI and Interpretable Model for Insurance Premium Prediction. *Journal on Artificial Intelligence*, *5*(0). https://doi.org/10.32604/jai.2023.040213

Aina, I., Ayinde, O., Thiam, D. and Miranda, M. (2024). Crop Index Insurance as a Tool for Climate Resilience: Lessons from Smallholder Farmers in Nigeria. *Natural Hazards*, *120*(5). https://doi.org/10.1007/s11069-023-06388-x

Arockiam, J.M. and Pushpanathan, A.C.S. (2023). MapReduce-Iterative Support Vector Machine Classifier: Novel Fraud Detection Systems in Healthcare Insurance Industry. *International Journal of Electrical and Computer Engineering*, *13*(1). https://doi.org/10.11591/ijece.v13i1. pp756–769

Bermúdez, L., Anaya, D. and Belles-Sampera, J. (2023). Explainable AI for Paid-Up Risk Management in Life Insurance Products. *Finance Research Letters*, *57*. https://doi.org/10.1016/j.frl.2023.104242

Călin, H.C. and Izvoranu, A.M. (2018). Public–Private Partnership and Its Influence on Agricultural Insurances. *Quality – Access to Success*, *19*(S1).

Choi, J.H., Choi, Y., Lee, K.S., Ahn, K.H. and Jang, W.Y. (2024). Explainable Model Using Shapley Additive Explanations Approach on Wound Infection after Wide Soft Tissue Sarcoma Resection: "Big Data" Analysis Based on Health Insurance Review and Assessment Service Hub. *Medicina (Lithuania)*, *60*(2). https://doi.org/10.3390/medicina60020327

Golden, L.L., Brockett, P.L., Ai, J. and Kellison, B. (2016). Empirical Evidence on the Use of Credit Scoring for Predicting Insurance Losses with Psycho-Social and Biochemical Explanations. *North American Actuarial Journal*, *20*(3). https://doi.org/10.1080/10920277.2016.1209118

Gramegna, A. and Giudici, P. (2020). Why to Buy Insurance? An Explainable Artificial Intelligence Approach. *Risks*, *8*(4). https://doi.org/10.3390/risks8040137

Margan, S.K. (2021). Drifting into Algocratic Insurance? In *The AI Book: The Artificial Intelligence Handbook for Investors, Entrepreneurs and FinTech Visionaries*. https://doi.org/10.1002/9781119551966.ch20

McDonnell, K., Murphy, F., Sheehan, B., Masello, L. and Castignani, G. (2023). Deep Learning in Insurance: Accuracy and Model Interpretability Using TabNet. *Expert Systems with Applications*, *217*. https://doi.org/10.1016/j.eswa.2023.119543

Murphy, S.D. and Moosa, S. (2021). The Views of Public Service Managers on the Implementation of National Health Insurance in Primary Care: A Case of Johannesburg Health District, Gauteng Province, Republic of South Africa. *BMC Health Services Research*, *21*(1). https://doi.org/10.1186/s12913-021-06990-4

Oben, E.E.E., Ndi, H.N. and Tchuikoua, L.B. (2024). Livestock Farmers' Willingness to Pay for Farming Insurance in Four Divisions of the West Region of Cameroon. *Asian Journal of Geographical Research*, *7*(1). https://doi.org/10.9734/ajgr/2024/v7i1211

Philip, B. and Suresh, G. (2024). Cultivating Resilience: An In-depth Exploration of Agricultural Insurance Initiatives and Their Transformative Role in India's Farming Landscape. *Universal Journal of Agricultural Research*, *12*(1). https://doi.org/10.13189/ujar.2024.120109

Poshtiri, Z.P., Soleimani, A.G., Delafrooz, N. and Shahroudi, K. (2024). Designing the Insurance Coverage Model for FinTech Startups: A Novel Approach to the Necessity of Digital Transformation Track of in Insurance. *Interdisciplinary Journal of Management Studies*, *17*(1). https://doi.org/10.22059/ijms.2023.345002.675187

Sachan, S. and Muwanga, J. (2023). Integration of Explainable Deep Neural Network with Blockchain Technology: Medical Indemnity Insurance. *CEUR Workshop Proceedings*, *3554*.

Settipalli, L. and Gangadharan, G.R. (2023). WMTDBC: An Unsupervised Multivariate Analysis Model for Fraud Detection in Health Insurance Claims. *Expert Systems with Applications*, *215*. https://doi.org/10.1016/j.eswa.2022.119259

Shafik, W. (2025). *SDG 12: Responsible Consumption and Production—The Circular Economy* (pp. 365–390). https://doi.org/10.1007/978-981-96-7299-8_13

Singh, R., Shafik, W., Crowther, D. and Kumar, V. (Eds.). (2024). *Transforming Healthcare Sector Through Artificial Intelligence and Environmental Sustainability* (1st ed., Vol. 1). Springer Nature Singapore. https://doi.org/10.1007/978-981-97-9555-0

Townsend, C., McIntyre, M., Lakhani, A., Wright, C., White, P., Bishara, J. and Cullen, J. (2018). Inclusion of Marginalised Aboriginal and Torres Strait Islander Peoples with Neurocognitive Disability in the National Disability Insurance Scheme (NDIS). *OPEN ACCESS*, *5*(2).

Van Nguyen, K., Islam, M.R., Huo, H., Tilocca, P. and Xu, G. (2023). Explainable Exclusion in the Life Insurance Using Multi-Label Classifier. *Proceedings of the International Joint Conference on Neural Networks*, *2023-June*. https://doi.org/10.1109/IJCNN54540.2023.10191171

Wall, J. (2022). *Keynote Speech 4: A Conversational AI Approach to Detecting Deception and Tackling Insurance Fraud.* https://doi.org/10.1109/icicis52592.2021.9694118

5

AI-Enabled Claims Management: Automation, Fairness, and Human–AI Collaboration

Wasswa Shafik

5.1 Introduction

Claims management refers to the processes that handle requests for compensation after loss events. While the concept of claims may evoke considerations of insurance, it is also widely applicable to many different areas, including logistic service fulfillment, warranty, consumer protection, and recovery from financial crime. Across different domains, claims management can be defined as the combination of tasks that are necessary for the execution of claims processing and resolution, as well as communication and coordination. Claims management is more than just automatically deciding if a claim is valid, which was the main focus of prior work. Instead, it also entails trust building, case resolution, data collection, communication, human involvement, coordination, and claim verification. Trust impacts claims management because the parties building claims will have motives to misrepresent their loss (Wang et al., 2019). Agents of organizations that are responsible for a claim-requesting party's experience will have to synchronize the interests and motivations of the two parties.

A trust resource model has been proposed that enhances conventional decision theory by incorporating the notion of trust. Therefore, trust enhances or mitigates the standard decision-making approach by its role as a variable mode for interrelationship restructuring. Involvement of compensators leads to ongoing interaction with claimants and thus possible adjustments to trust levels for both parties. Furthermore, trust can be built during the claims management process or provided through the organizational and societal context mechanisms. This aspect of trust building makes claims management radically different from the traditional claims processing function. It is also multi-issue and multidisciplinary. Claims management is multi-issue because multiple objectives, such as conflict resolution, service delivery, and compliance, must be satisfied. It is multidisciplinary because disparate areas such as marketing, finance, operations, and law are involved in the design, realization, and evaluation of the claims management system (Jarrahi, 2018). Due to the interdependencies among various aspects, resolving one issue in one area may negatively influence other issues in other areas, making design and resolution challenging.

5.1.1 Overview of Claims Management Processes

Claims management entails the inside-out operations established by providers in their insurance and reinsurance against third parties' claims related to financial and economic loss associated with

DOI: 10.1201/9781003747659-5

unforeseen risks, detours, and adverse events. The overarching objective of claims management is to safeguard the organizational resources by ensuring fast and fair settlement of claims while managing the financial expenses and potential quantitative overpayments associated with misuse and fraud. In any insurance or reinsurance, there is an uncertainty concerning the timing and amount of the claims that third parties would lodge during the term of the contract. For instance, in property or health insurance, individuals subscribe for protection against financial or economic loss linked to property damage, or personal malady, or injury caused by accidents (Morrison et al., 2023). Accordingly, individuals pay contractual premiums to insurance providers to obtain restoration, or reimbursement of the incurred costs, during the term of the insurance. These restoration payments, at an average incidence calculated using historical data and predetermined combinatorial methods, constitute the primary financial burden of insurance companies. Reinsurers then cover excess claims by guaranteeing payment of claims lodged beyond a prescribed higher limit, in return for contractually established periodic premiums. Through this capability to mitigate the losses from risk claims enabled by establishing insurance and reinsurance contracts, both entities are alleviated from the uncertainty of financial loss arising in the event of adverse contingencies of humans and the business of third parties (Sundar, 2020).

5.1.2 Challenges in Traditional Claims Handling

Artificial intelligence (AI)-enabled claims management systems face one major challenge for their successful implementation—the claims handling performed by human claims handlers is filled with biases and errors, and it is really difficult to obtain correct or, at least, deducible information about those biases and errors. The most important factors influencing the current state of the art of claims management are: a low level of automation of the claims processes; an inherent need for a human-centric approach; the lack of industry-specific development of AI-based tools; structural issues related to both claims management organizations and claims systems; and differing motivations between insurers and customers. The level of automation in claims processes is relatively low. Some simple tasks such as loss reporting, payments, and initial assessment can be performed quickly and without any human intervention (Qian & Wexler, 2024). Almost all other tasks are still being performed manually, using different systems, databases, or tools. This means that claims handlers must deal with various systems and tools and access multiple data sources. The majority of the remaining tasks are made up of group decision-making processes involving several stakeholders, such as a case director or a settlement manager leading the workflow. These people become the bottlenecks of the process, especially if case discussions and decisions are delayed or postponed. The overall effectiveness of the claims process can therefore be negatively affected. The need to include multiple people at different stages of the process requires an ever-increasing dedication of human resources to ensure the timely processing of claims. Traditional claims management cannot rely on complicated automation procedures based on natural language processing (NLP) or machine learning (ML) algorithms aimed at minimizing the need for human intervention, or enabling a whole new level of human–AI collaboration, which would allow for higher productivity (Rezwana & Maher, 2023).

5.2 The Role of AI in Claims Management

Advancing AI technologies are streamlining and augmenting various claims management tasks. These technologies allow claims managers to unlock previously untapped efficiency and quality indices while relieving them of repetitive tasks. It is crucial to mention here that the responsibility of a claim manager is shifting toward an orchestrator role, working with a team composed of systems and humans. By augmenting the capabilities of the claim's handlers, serious well-being effects at work can be created. Encouragingly, both continued technological progress and the evolution of regulatory norms seem to be headed in that direction, with almost global standards for transparency and accountability already being worked on. The proposed AI standards are currently focused on trustworthy AI. On an operational level, reports note that key drivers are generating momentum for AI investment decisions: COVID-19, speed of migration to the cloud, availability of data, and the need for automation. These investments are, in fact, begetting not only faster basis-AI development but also the mainstreaming of more complex AI techniques involving deep learning and reinforcement learning (Su et al., 2022). This novel markup of technology adoption follows the basic dynamics of the technology life cycle: innovation, takeoff, maturity, and decline.

The opportunities and challenges presented by the use of AI in the work environment have not gone unexamined. Reports point to growing interest in creating the conditions for a fair development and deployment of AI systems. These merit special relevance in safety-critical quadrants such as health, judicial, social welfare, and claims management. However, some may argue that eye-popping operational improvements justify a wide, unchecked rollout of technology. But technological and organizational solutions can guarantee highly defended service levels while preventing some of the unattended drawbacks of AI systems. In fact, rollout support may not only be preferred but also necessary and even possible with existing technology enabling a high degree of human–AI collaboration. Thus, we see AI not as an automatic replacement for human claims managers but as a powerful collaborator enabling human claims managers (Berretta et al., 2023). This support involves transferring low-complexity productivity tasks to AI algorithms for basic productivity input work, allowing claims managers to focus on higher-complexity cognitive tasks for value-added output work using blockchain, as illustrated in Figure 5.1.

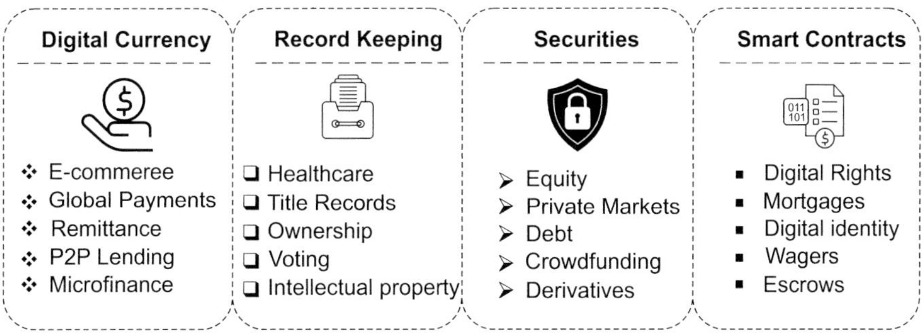

Fig. 5.1 Insurance blockchain approaches.

5.2.1 AI Technologies in Use

Numerous companies and research efforts are currently working on applying existing AI technologies to insurance claims management, as we will discuss in this section. We provide examples but only briefly mention the organization names behind the applications. Specifically, we utilize scholarly papers for research efforts and detail any noteworthy developments in the work of specialized publications. For brevity reasons, we also do not review the general work on application fields, or the potential dangers in applying technology; instead, we key into what is currently being used. Furthermore, we do not touch on the technology development or risk mitigation aspects of the research mentioned in the earlier text, but rather, simply summarize the usages. Three important areas of technological application work are in automation, advancing the quantitative aspects, and managing the qualitative aspects of claims processing (El-Assady & Moruzzi, 2022). Within these areas, we identify seven technology categories under automation, quantitative aspects, and qualitative aspects. With any applied AI, whether to claims management or any other task, there is a risk of pitfalls and repercussions, and so, it is useful to categorize the approved technology work, as no specialized review is available, to understand and identify these work aspects and possible outcomes more clearly, in our opinion. These categories will also later help inform an overview of the kind of benefits or drawbacks these types of work bring about. We next briefly describe the category areas and their related technologies now, with an example-based summary table at the end for brevity (Mahmud et al., 2023).

5.2.2 Benefits of AI Integration

A substantial body of empirical work has demonstrated that autonomy increases worker satisfaction, and several reports have shown positive effects of AI automation. Consequently, we believe that in a claims environment, a well-designed AI system could reduce burnout, lead to greater job satisfaction, and ultimately foster a stronger bond between employees and their employer. The unique aspect of the present application is to build both an effective automated system—freeing adjusters from mundane tasks—while continuing to employ (and helping to grow) a large number of adjusters by giving them more interesting decision-making challenges. The system is further designed to promote a collaborative relationship between the adjusters and the AI system (Wan et al., 2024). We foresee a world where adjusters have access to the AI system for advice as well as for information gathering and structuring, allowing them to offer faster, more informed insurance decisions to customers. The overall aim of the joint work between AI and adjusters is to ensure the fair and proper treatment of every claim. Automated prescreening of claims for reasons to further investigate can catch errors in fraudulent claims, where adjusters may not be sufficiently proficient or armed with the time to investigate. AI claims processing can further allow for selective automated processing of claims that exhibit clear-cut obviousness, so that reduced staffing would not lead to customer dissatisfaction due to slow response times. Claims that have been flagged for further review may be efficiently routed to adjusters who possess deep expertise on the issue or fairness determination, thus expediting resolution and overall promoting fairness in the claims processing system (Svensson & Keller, 2024).

5.3 Automation in Claims Processing

Claims processing generates huge volumes of claims. In order to maintain profitability and value to stakeholders, claims functions must control and reduce costs while maintaining timely and fair handling of claims. The result is widespread interest in automating various aspects of the claims process through the inclusion of robotics, machine learning, and other AI techniques. Automated decision-making has been the subject of substantial analysis. Automation has also been implemented in the adjacent areas of insurance underwriting and fraud detection, with data-processed decision-making replacing traditional manual processes and enabling high-volume operations and processing-cost reduction (Xu et al., 2021). Fully automated processes and decision engines are in active use in many settings, particularly within low-complexity claims where the "accident profile" of the claim closely matches large historical pools of affordable and realistic compensation settlements. The automation of claims processing can yield significant cost savings, improve customer experience through faster processing, as well as enable the reserves and payout histories of simple types of claims to be leveraged and audited using procedures. Other advantages also accrue through maintaining a heavy back-office focus on the simple sort of repeat claims processing that these techniques facilitate. Processing decisions for low-cost and high-volume claim types would constitute highly usable templates for hard-to-quantify high-volume claims on a corporate-wide basis, with implications. Technical capabilities also exist to employ neural networks seeded with training data generated from historical databases in a fully automated fashion (Lee et al., 2023).

5.3.1 Automated Decision-Making

A brief examination of prior use of automation in the claims domain indicates that the deployment of technology prior to the current wave of machine learning systems was to follow and enforce rules for decision-making that insurance administrators and other decision-makers articulated. In this prior use, the cases for which technology provided a recommendation without direct input from the official had low-value resolutions that rarely raised the money at stake, raised novel questions of interpretation that were unlikely to recur, or relied on parameters that officials could not efficiently inspect for all cases. Today, we hear assurances of AI systems that can do far more than rule-based systems, including analyzing thousands of parameters relevant to any given claim, learning rules from all prior cases that are known to a system, and applying such rules to make automated decisions regarding classification, investigation, and resource allocation for the majority of claims in a manner that would leave few trackable queries for highly targeted fraud officials. Such systems would thus permit such officials to focus their scarce time on the most vague or contentious high-value claims, directly ruling upon those or at least helping their clients optimize their behavior. Automated decision-making systems are increasingly piloted, fine-tuned, and rolled out in industries and applications where outcomes have previously been decided primarily by humans, or where technology has only been applied to shallow aspects of different correlations with novel data (Wienrich & Latoschik, 2021). Automated decision-making has been tested in public sector applications such as risk-based prioritization of candidates for federal prosecution by a single office, allocation of customs screenings to different country ports, decisions to suspend access to public pension security, and identification of patients using state-controlled substances.

5.3.2 Efficiency Gains through Automation

The insurance and financial services industries have been truly transformed by advances in AI, particularly in the area of claims processing. In any marketplace, the speed, quantity, and quality of claims processing will come to define the success of the insurance company, as they link insurance carriers, agents, and policyholders and facilitate the transfer of information and resources. In recent years, claims management has been a fertile ground for innovation, offering insurers the opportunity to engage customers more fully, differentiate their brand, and lower their costs. As a key part of the industry value chain, AI has the potential to reduce cycle times, improve quality, and increase the number of products and services transacted in real time. Claims management activities requiring a degree of judgment—verifying the policy details, assessing the need for further investigation, estimating the accident damage—are already utilizing AI tools such as chatbots, social media analysis, predictive mapping, and image recognition. These initiatives aim not only to lower processing time and operating cost, but also to improve the service experience. In less than five years, billions of dollars will be spent annually on AI and platform capabilities. AI investors are optimistic, expecting much of the hoped-for efficiency gains to happen within a short timescale. But many stakeholders remain skeptical that such savings will materialize (Jarrahi, 2018). Specifically, there's uncertainty in the degree of true decision automation that can be achieved, whether that is a desirable direction, and at what cost. But it is widely accepted that, at least in the near term, we should expect an increased level of human–machine collaboration, as presented in Table 5.1.

5.4 Ensuring Fairness in AI Systems

As human beings, we often unconsciously rely on our own experiences to determine if a scenario is fair or not. However, in the case of AI systems, the challenge lies in our inability to correlate their decisions with our past experiences or any other logic that would allow us to determine the fairness of their decisions personally. This lack of experience has underlined the importance of examining

Table 5.1 Automation stages in AI-driven claims management and their ethical implications.

Claims Process Stage	*AI Functionality*	*Automation Benefit*	*Ethical Challenge*	*Mitigation Strategy*
First Notice of Loss (FNOL)	Natural language processing (NLP) for intake	24/7 accessibility, faster reporting	Misinterpretation of input	Human verification layer, multilingual NLP models
Fraud Detection	Anomaly detection, pattern recognition	Early detection of fraudulent claims	False positives impacting honest claimants	Use of hybrid rule-based + ML with manual review
Document Triage	Computer vision to classify and verify documents	Faster document processing	Discrimination from poor image recognition	Regular dataset audits, inclusive training data
Claims Segmentation	Predictive analytics to prioritize claims	Resource optimization	Unfair prioritization based on biased features	Disparate impact testing; explainability checks
Damage Estimation	AI-based image and video assessment	Real-time assessment, cost efficiency	Inaccurate assessments due to model generalization	Region-specific retraining and quality assurance layers
Decision Recommendation	Machine learning scoring models	Consistent decision support	Black-box decisioning	Integration of explainable AI (XAI, e.g., SHAP–SHapley Additive exPlanations, LIME–Local Interpretable Model-agnostic Explanations)
Automated Settlement Offers	Rule-based and predictive modeling	Speed and reduced administrative burden	Over-automation without claimant consent	Hybrid decision pipeline with opt-out provisions
Customer Communication	Chatbots and automated updates	Real-time communication, user engagement	Insufficient empathy and personalization	Human fallback protocol in sensitive cases
Human-in-the-Loop Oversight	Human review of flagged or complex cases	Ethical accountability	Overreliance on automation	Clearly defined review thresholds and escalation policies
Appeals & Disputes Handling	AI-supported analysis of disputes	Quicker resolutions	Lack of transparency in decision trails	Maintain detailed logs for auditability
Data Integration	Real-time APIs–Application Programming Interfaces and data pipelines	Holistic view of claims data	Risk of data leakage and misuse	End-to-end encryption and privacy-first design
Continuous Learning	Feedback loops from resolved claims	Model improvement over time	Reinforcement of biased patterns	Periodic fairness revalidation
Workflow Orchestration	AI-managed task assignment and tracking	Efficiency and traceability	Job deskilling and autonomy reduction	Augmented task design with human judgment valued
Final Settlement	Coordinated payout execution via smart systems	Timely and accurate settlements	Potential lack of human empathy in decisions	Final checkpoint by human claim specialists

fairness-bias and discussing its implications. Without question, the need for fairness should not be exploited to push the overall debate to the side, given the numerous unresolved problems of machine learning deployment and usage, such as privacy and security. Presented in the following text are several definitions of the term "fairness" that are interchangeable within specific applications. We unveil a number of potential sources of bias embedded in AI systems involving unfair decision-making processes and subsequent recommendations in the form of algorithms. We also enrich the discussion regarding the requirements for fair AI systems by applying these principles in practice. Novel artificial intelligence techniques are increasingly being developed to improve the accuracy and automation of operations in rich and complex data (Morrison et al., 2023). Improved predictive analytics solutions promise to help management in key operational areas such as claims management by eliminating or redistributing a portion of the repetitive data capturing and keystroke processes performed by adjusters in evaluating and approving insurance claims.

5.4.1 Bias in AI Algorithms

Bias can take several different forms in AI algorithms. First is sampling bias, which occurs when a sample of the population is not representative of the distribution of the population. This can happen, for instance, if we collect data from a certain location, such as a state or city, and then model the entirety of a country. Or if we are modeling men's productivity, estimating a model fitted only with data from women. Using this model would lead to wrong conclusions about men's productivity. However, this is not a bias of the algorithm itself, but rather the availability of that data sample, which is related to the data generation process. The second type of bias is labeling bias, which happens when the data used to train the algorithm is labeled by humans in a biased way. For instance, if a training dataset of job applicants is labeled based on hiring decisions made by the company in question, and those hiring decisions were influenced by implicit or explicit bias at that company, then the training data will reflect that bias. As a result, fairness would be compromised by labeling bias even if no sampling bias exists. The third type of bias is algorithmic bias and refers to the way that AI algorithms may unintentionally lead to discrimination. For instance, in three different locations of a city, the possibility of a person being sent to jail while waiting for a trial can be estimated. It happens that in location one, the estimated probability is 4%, in location two, 7%, but in location three, 45%. Should a person whose estimated probability is 45% be treated the same way as a subject with an estimated probability of 4% (Rezwana & Maher, 2023)? The dataset does not take into consideration the specific context of a person's estimated risk; however, there are no defined "protected groups," and the outcome is shown to be different based on geographical location alone.

5.4.2 Strategies for Fairness

In consequence, learning representations such that the training data displays little correlation with these sensitive attributes already allow models to perform better in terms of Corporate Social Responsibility (CSR). Other fairness- and interpretability-enhancing interventions at inference time include example weighting, rejection options, or result adjustment and postprocessing. Important fairness strategies throughout the AI pipeline, because they mainly address the ethical principles' applicability, responsibility, and auditability, are to apply human-in-the-loop supervision, educate users about model limitations and biases, and explain and provide interpretability for model outputs. Fairness, accountability, and interpretability should be at the core of every AI-sponsored task performance support design. Finally, for assisting users and promoting decision support, we suggest heuristics through which unfair AI model predictions can be identified (Su et al., 2022). The core idea behind the proposed heuristics lies in the logic that unfair AI model predictions are not just likely to happen in case model enrichment leads to the model being trained on the same samples for which it is later used to infer the decisions supported through the model's predictions, but also that domain informed hypothesized examples, meaning examples for which domain experts could provide and agree upon an inferred output are available. Moreover, the hypotheses apply independently of whether the Corporate Income Tax (CIT) here is claim handling or another IT-embedded Continuous Improvement (CI). However, measuring bias during both the model training and later prediction rainy seasons, as proposed by the present work, is a nice-to-have in the majority of cases. In the end, a comprehensive set of heuristics is needed to promote end-user awareness of model weaknesses as much as possible. In the end, the degree to which bias-sensitive model weaknesses can be identified and addressed by utilizing data on biasing attributes is restricted to the domain knowledge behind them (Mahmud et al., 2023).

5.5 The Human Role in AI-Driven Processes

Gaps in AI capabilities make the human role in claims processing essential, but also at risk. We first summarize roles fulfilled by claims adjusters and model the impact of AI on their responsibilities and tasks. Traditionally, adjusters' work consists of collecting, reviewing, and analyzing information, making recommendations, and supporting customers. In cases where fraudulent claims are suspected, they also supervise investigations. With the help of AI systems, we expect changes in the responsibility distribution: adjusters remain responsible for decisions with impact on customers, such as payouts, but AI will take over the recommendations of how to act, as well as information collection and review tasks. Thus, the two key changes with AI adoption occur in responsibility transfer for the process step with the highest decision impact and a significant additional support in information handling. This responsibility shift may at first seem appealing; however, our earlier discussion about AI-assistance capability shows that AI systems still struggle with complex, multifaceted, and subjectively ambiguous decisions (Lee et al., 2023).

Consequently, the adjustment of human responsibility may have implications for decision fairness. In such cases, fairness requires that the human adjuster reviews the claim file in detail, reflects on possible customer impact as well as biases related to claims with similar circumstances, and actively challenges themselves about the rationale of the AI recommendation. In a learning system scenario with the transfer of additional responsibility to the AI, interaction bias emerges: the human adjuster might implicitly weight the AI recommendation more strongly. In this section, we investigate how AI can serve as an enabler and enhance claims adjusters' decision-making. With an informative and collaborative user experience, AI can provide claims adjusters with valuable insights when handling claims. With its capabilities to process large amounts of data, identify complex patterns, and learn from past decisions, we argue that AI could further enhance the adjusters' decision-making for cases in which financial payout recommendations are trivial. Therefore, AI can recommend actions based on identified patterns and rely on the adjusters' domain knowledge only for verification, transferring most of the decision responsibility to the AI. Also, in cases where the difficulties with AI handling are the highest, AI can assist during the sensemaking process by providing an adequate user experience (Wang et al., 2019). In this scenario, the adjuster remains responsible for the decision based on experiential and tacit knowledge and utilizes the AI during the information processing stage.

5.5.1 The Human Role in AI-Driven Processes

It is commonly assumed that AI can decide, process, and deliver results in complex tasks like claims management processes. We believe in the ability of AI to change the nature and scope of enabled processes, because of positive or negative events. The events bring context and meaning to the process results, and the human effort is indispensable to evaluating events. It is also impractical for a human to intervene in each enabled task. We view any claim management process as a continuous human–AI collaboration task. With that perspective, we discuss in this section the human role in enabling AI-driven claims management processes. There are many factors in AI successfully augmenting human skills in driving value in human–AI collaboration. Two basic structures of augmenting humans in tasks are the antecedents of decision-making and the consequences of decisions. In AI systems, the models predict the decision-making process or the result of the process (Wang et al., 2019). The models with high-quality predictions support the human decision-making process by reducing the time or effort needed to reach a decision, or support the best decision through content-based recommendation, or provide an explanation to help human understanding. Predicting event outcomes that humans then evaluate is important for a number of application domains, such as those with high inference and decision cost. In some claims management processes, it is very inconvenient to have humans in the decision-making process flow. For example, need for moderation of decisions without major bias and delay, until the detection of a major claim. Obviously, it is impractical to involve humans in the moderation of each enabled task phase. Humans know a great deal of domain-specific information that is not possible to capture, structure, and consolidate into a machine-learned process (Wienrich & Latoschik, 2021). Thus, successful automation of processes needs to integrate the human role in continual high-leverage task allocation of decision training, definition, and refining, amid several positives and negatives of blockchain technology as illustrated in Figure 5.2.

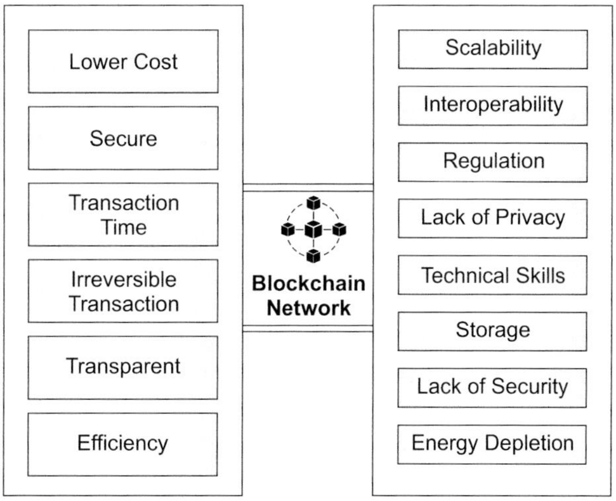

Fig. 5.2 The blockchain networks.

5.5.2 Enhancing Decision-Making with AI

AI technology is not meant to replace humans, but rather assist them in their work. In fact, we are definitively moving toward a future where human capabilities can be augmented by AI technology, creating a symbiotic effect that works for both humans and machines. Humans are naturally skilled at common-sense reasoning, while AI-assisted tools can perform routine tasks with speed, precision, and consistency. In particular, if applied correctly, AI supports a continuum-based view of decision-making. When technology is used as the only input in the claims process, it is efficient but prone to automated bias. Moving up the ladder to augmented intelligence, the AI-assisted view provides a safety net for humans and is less costly than human-intensive processes, while allowing organizations to check and mitigate the risk of human bias. In the embedded AI approach, pretrained models and established rules guide claims decision-making (Sundar, 2020). Decision automation allows claims processing organizations to achieve important cost and efficiency gains. Embedded and augmented human intelligence allow claims personnel to work on higher-complexity cases and reduce the risk of negative outcomes from biased, incorrect, or unduly harsh decisions by humans. In the most collaborative approach to human–AI decision-making, the decisions made by AI directly inspire human responses in a loop that continuously improves the underlying model to the more complex claims. AI technology augments human intelligence by identifying complex, edge cases for priority and insistent attention. Technology has the ability, through predictive, descriptive, and prescriptive analytics, to add to the quality of AI-first intelligence processes, working as a leading indicator or explanation, insight generator, and helper in human selection (El-Assady & Moruzzi, 2022).

5.6 Case Studies of AI in Claims Management

Claims management is a considerable focus area for automation and innovation efforts by both incumbent and InsurTech companies. Given its core business function, an understanding of the early successes and failures bearing the development and deployment of AI systems in claims management processes is an invaluable resource for the roadmap for future research work in this area. In this section, we provide a brief overview of successes and failures in case studies for automation solutions in claims management. We draw from two streams of claims management literature: empirical reviews of implementation successes or failures in evidence, and documented industry implementations for process digitization and automation use cases, which have considerable novelty and innovative potential (Wan et al., 2024). Our findings highlight the importance of stakeholder-centered design solutions, with success depending on user and external stakeholder buy-in, promoting desired technology use motivation. As explained in earlier sections, the potential transformative benefits of AI systems for reducing processing costs by major reductions in time and human resources are often bogged down by nontechnical issues that refine design elements or even belie the appropriateness of automation for a specific stage in claims management. While a large volume of to-date evidence has focused predominantly on organizations and their customer interactions as key users in the delivery of technology-enabled claims service, we find a key gap in addressing the roles of intermediaries. This is reflected in a growing volume of earlier evidence identifying potential downsides of a lack of customer-expert engagement, such as false engagement and detection of ambiguity in policy terms, resulting in information overload, reducing expertise utility value to customers, thereby negating cost-efficiency benefits (Svensson & Keller, 2024).

5.6.1 Successful Implementations

AI has successfully been put to use at scale to solve specific problems in claims management, especially in property and casualty insurance. A raft of vendors have built and deployed tools used by insurers or as modules in other vendor-supplied solutions. Insurers themselves have also implemented solutions, both offering them to partners and using them internally. These include large incumbents deploying complex and varied capabilities with multiple solutions and newer entrants deploying more focused capabilities at speed and scale of operations, often featuring personalized user experiences and rapid time to market. Seasoned insurers such as Liberty Mutual and Allstate compete to assist third-party claims handlers with the greatest speed, quality, and cost-efficiency. These large incumbents utilize solutions offered by companies having fully integrated capabilities to assist with claims requests through the entire process and maximize payer experience. Focusing primarily on the personal lines, Liberty Mutual's Express Managed Repair solves claims related to repairs for its insured. Allstate has a similar program to reduce claim cycle time and adjust loss costs on repairable vehicle damage. Both are either using or issuing policies on tech-enabled collision repair, whereby nearly all repairs are handled and tracked through apps and backend systems (Lee et al., 2023). By collaborating closely with network parts suppliers and repairers, Liberty Mutual and Allstate claim that the costs of repairs conducted under their supervision are lower than those of other insurers.

5.6.2 *Lessons Learned from Failures*

The purpose of this section is not to demonize these case studies but instead to explore some of the failures surrounding resulting AI implementations. This way, we can analyze not just what went well with systems that have been deployed into production, but also learn how to understand and avoid pitfalls when deploying an AI system in a sensitive field as claims management. With that, we want to bridge the gap between research by providing insight from the field, and also give a real-world perspective to researchers in the field by showing some difficult choices that need to be made. The first example is the Nameay case, a notable failure in claims assignment and prioritization using AI. In addition to the failures surrounding this deployment, we also analyze the difficulties with algorithmic fairness in real-world deployments in similar tasks by analyzing the attempts to lessen the algorithm's bias (Wang et al., 2019). We provide insight into some of the difficulties of collaboration and the risk of disuse of AI systems by highlighting the Aviva Fraud Finder case study. Claim assignment and prioritization using an AI algorithm is depicted in the Nameay case. An insurance company chose the company to implement a computer AI-assisted set of algorithms to be integrated with other rules for claims assignment and prioritization. The goal was to solve the technical and organizational difficulties that impeded the fast and fair processing of claims. Its system, however, led to a lack of trust from claims handlers and was abandoned quickly after its deployment. The deployment revealed a reluctance to cede agency and responsibility to an AI algorithm and increased mistrust and conflict between departments responsible for claims handling and security management. These two departments had potentially contradictory tasks, and the implementation of the algorithm was the responsibility of the security department. The AI algorithm was intended solely to assist the claims handler, but the security management department wanted the recommendation to be the final decision, thus increasing tension between both departments (Sundar, 2020).

5.7 Regulatory and Ethical Considerations

Developing AI systems in a manner that conforms to regulation and ethical standards is expected to be a primary design consideration throughout the work, and thus embedded in the technical content. In this section, we investigate this question and discuss its implications. Different countries have established a regulatory framework for handling AI technology that includes its use in automation for insurance claims processing. Outside of compliance with such regulation, there are additional ethical considerations for stakeholders developing this technology and building tools for it that go beyond those that apply to traditional technology and system design principles, including user-centered design, design fairness, the ethics of automating socially responsible work, and paternalism without consent. Although in the longer term, ethical design will become part of regulatory requirements, for the short- and medium-term futures, the range of ethical principles, frameworks, and goals that appropriate design will flow from is much wider than for regulation. The core design requirements that will shape this work are as follows: To what extent will these AI-enabled systems operate with autonomy, and to what extent are they tools for humans? What is the nature of the collaboration? What will these systems be able to accomplish, and how will their use affect the outcomes, and their ethical dimensions including fairness, transparency, and social purposes? How can industry and technology creators convince stakeholders that their systems can be trusted? Accompanying the use of AI that supports the process of claims management and its decisions are duties that the stakeholder has a social responsibility to fulfill (Berretta et al., 2023). There are a variety of potential ethical lapses associated with the use of AI in this function: enabling tooling that could be capable of following either a path that welcomes human rejection of its decisions, or the other that forcibly imposes those decisions.

5.7.1 Compliance with Regulations

Artificial intelligence is being widely deployed across all industries, including insurance, to increase efficiency, productivity, and lower costs. However, AI systems also raise a number of legal compliance concerns, including the potential for algorithmic bias, privacy violations, and a lack of proper oversight. Developers and companies deploying AI technology should take care to address industry-specific regulations and ensure compliance with relevant laws. Other chapters outline some ethical issues: implications of AI technology, including developing algorithms that do not discriminate or introduce bias, and the required level of oversight of AI systems, interactions with customers, and mixed networks of human and AI agents. Insurance companies are heavily regulated (Mahmud et al., 2023). Insurance is a risk-sharing contract, and as individuals and businesses transfer their risk of financial loss to their insurer by paying a premium, the insurer must stay solvent so it remains able to cover any legitimate claims. Insurance companies are required to hold reserves in case of major adverse events, and regulatory bodies carefully monitor financial reports from insurance companies to make sure they are well capitalized and solvent. At the same time, insurance companies are also responsible for adhering to local, state, and federal regulations when accepting applications for insurance coverage, determining rates, paying claims, and having a general duty to act in good faith. The basis of the insurance business model is trust—the policyholders have trust that the insurance company will honor its commitments in the event of an insured adverse event (Xu et al., 2021).

5.7.2 Ethical Implications of AI Use

Questions about the ethics of using AI applications in insurance claims management abound. Although some people may be reluctant to view AI as a neutral tool, the concerns specific to its use in claims processing are qualitatively no different than those specific to any other kind of claim's adjustment. Traditional ethical obligations that apply to insurance claim professionals, and to negligence tort law that applies to all of us, do not in themselves offer sufficient guidance about what it means to act fairly during the process that generates the output of AI predictions (Wienrich & Latoschik, 2021). In this section, we code the ethical implications of AI use that require consideration beyond compliance with antidiscrimination laws and industry-specific adjustment protocols into four categories, and within each category, we present issues that may arise and complications that consideration of AI use may create. Rule-based input and output requirements are within-discipline particulars of generally recognized ethical duties that apply in both implicit and explicit forms to all professionals. In the case of insurance claims adjustment, one of the critical ethical tensions is between the duty of care that claim adjusters have to individual claimants and their fair treatment and the broader goal of system efficiency, which privacy legislation and other considerations have increasingly constrained to a lesser injustice, not to zero or minimize injustice. What makes AI-enabled claims management different is the pressure on adjusters to comply with recommendations relative to traditional adjustment practice, and the fact that if they don't comply, litigation may result (Wan et al., 2024). Other ethical issues arise when adjusters depend upon the output of AI predictions as rules for their conduct of adjusting decisions, particularly in the complex and subtle process of determining claims subrogation, as presented in Table 5.2.

Table 5.2 Human–AI collaboration roles and fairness considerations in claims processing.

Collaborative Element	*AI Role*	*Human Role*	*Fairness Benefit*	*Example/Tool*
Claims Intake	NLP classifies and parses the initial input	Assist customers, ensure accuracy	Reduces language bias	Google Bidirectional Encoder Representations from Transformers (BERT) for multilingual text input
Evidence Evaluation	Image/video analysis	Validate physical context, correct misinterpretation	Balances model overfitting	Tractable, CCC Intelligent Solutions
Risk Profiling	Predictive modeling identifies claim severity	Evaluate nonquantitative aspects	Reduces proxy discrimination	IBM Watson for insurance risk
Decision Explanation	XAI generates rationale	Interpret and translate for the claimant	Increases transparency and contestability	SHAP visualizations provided to claimants
Ethical Auditing	Logs every AI decision path	Audit and evaluate edge cases	Supports fairness through oversight	Fairlearn, Aequitas
Policy Interpretation	Text summarization of policy terms	Cross-check for context and exceptions	Avoids overgeneralized denials	GPT–Generative Pre-trained Transformer-powered document intelligence
Escalation Management	AI flags anomalies and ambiguities	Investigate and make the final call	Preserves due process	AI triage with rules-based escalation triggers
Process Optimization	Workflow analytics suggest process changes	Strategize implementation and communication	Ensures ethical improvements are actioned	UiPath + human process re-engineering
Model Feedback Loop	Captures user disputes and appeals	Qualitative feedback on user experience	Reduces cumulative unfairness	Real-time customer sentiment analysis pipelines
Human-Centered Design	AI suggests user interaction flows	Design empathetic interfaces	Avoids the exclusion of digitally disadvantaged	Co-design workshops with UX-User Experience designers and claims officers

5.8 Future Trends in Claims Management

Because the claims management field is destined for major transformations, traditional claims operation models will change in the future. Disruptive technologies are enabling alternative workflows with remarkable potential to create value. Emerging digital ecosystems and newly available data sources will be of major importance for the future of claims management. After more than five hundred billion dollars have been invested in InsurTech startups since 2005, the future is likely to be disrupted by emerging technologies such as AI and blockchain, which at present are seen as promising tech undercurrents. Artificial intelligence will hardly require a decade to empower a new generation of intelligent business support systems, chatbots, and hyper-automation systems, achieving 15% to 20% productivity improvements in knowledge work processes (Wang et al., 2019). By allowing customer self-service and automating end-to-end claims processes based on AI-powered bots, and enabling hyper-automation of most claims management processes, business process efficiency can be significantly increased. Embedded insurance will acquire additional importance due to the potential for the distribution costs of brokers or agents to be replaced by lower-cost lead generation from other digital service providers. By using a combination of AI assessments of all available data about the event, a satisfying customer experience is established through immediate reimbursement in low-value claim cases, such as for minor damages caused by storm or hail. Increased flexibility is the next step. Especially small value claims may force insurers to consider ways to provide claims service without users having to file any claims at all. This means that insurers need to adopt emerging new forms of risk management (Wan et al., 2024). Blockchain applications will play a more important role in claims management, enabling direct interaction with the insurance contracts during the claims management process.

5.8.1 Emerging Technologies

In this chapter, we take a longer look into the future to see what new technologies will be used to support claims management in the next decade. This timeline is ambitious, but we attempt it since many of the current emerging technologies have the potential to transform claims management in the near-term future. More long-term trends may be too far removed from practical relevance or even unrealizable. For example, there are visions where all insurance processes are automated and insurance companies need to care for their bottom line, and competition is even less than it is today. These visions are interesting, but not likely to materialize. Crucially, we acknowledge that on-par investments of all actors in claims management have not been made and could very well never be the case. Insurance is a big market, and the administrative cost of whatever form the future claims management will take will be staggering (Lee et al., 2023). Hence, every actor in this ecosystem must be careful about any imbalance of power considerations that could lead to crises of confidence, threatening the very foundation of life policies, for example, distrust vis-à-vis insurance companies leading to increased lapse rates. Our predictions guide us by noticing which technologies are already developing or commercially available, since the technological innovations associated with claims management are motivated by the capabilities of these technologies and how they are offered in digital ecosystems. Thus, many of the changes in the claims management of the next decade will be based upon libraries of existing components being combined creatively and with a suited business model. These libraries themselves may derive from the creative and suited combination of fundamental technologies (Wang et al., 2019).

5.8.2 Predictions for the Next Decade

While the transformation of the insurance domain has already begun, its next phase may well start to materialize in the mirror of the growing thrust and strength of the insurance digital transition wave. Several factors are at play as enablers of such a cruise acceleration: the increasing expectancy of consumers for seamless and personalized digital services, not just in insurance but in general for all sectors such as banking and car renting; the consolidation of new companies shaking up the market; the merging of digital and video gaming natives with the insurance domain experience; the insurance domain crystallization and consolidation, that freeing up capitals for investing in the new frontier; the research carried out in collaboration with startups, and the lessons learnt from proof of concepts; and the entrance of Asian players who are innovating using artificial intelligence, big data, digital platforms, and digital client relationship management to optimize customer experience and service (Wan et al., 2024). The next decade will be crucial for the insurance world. The insurance market will optimize customer experience by extending the offering communicated through digital platforms operated by high-skilled operators. They will, in their own area of activity, prepare claims advice and insurance fraud detection. The actuary will use their historical and predictive skills to analyze consumer behavior, to improve the prediction models of claims frequency and severity. Data sources will be extended to social networks, car drives, meteorological sources, satellite images, and data from IoT, for all insurances, from automobile digital boards to fire building protection (Jarrahi, 2018). Risk transfer, for all actors of the market, will remain with the insurance companies, with compensation guaranteed.

5.9 Conclusion

Signals of improvements to claims management are everywhere: lower costs for payers; reduced delays, better outcomes, and fewer disputes for patients; automation relieving the administrative burden for claims administrators; more equitable treatment for riskier classes of insurance coverage; and a diverse work environment combining the very best of human talent with sophisticated AI agents. Our exploration leads us to conclude that with prudence, planning, experiment, and review, significant improvements are possible, and accelerating them merits the time and resources required. In summary, AI-enabled automation is rapidly transforming—and can help to transform—claims management in the direction of higher efficiency, lower costs, and faster resolution of legitimate claims. But advances depend on designing and deploying well-planned projects that address bias and fairness, avoid consequences that are accidentally negative or mostly ameliorate them with careful policy features, and address human collaboration actively, so that teams of human agents and AI agents can achieve superior results. Despite their recognition of potential biases, the focus of trend studies has been primarily on the potential promised benefits of automation, rather than whether organizations are actually managing the process of designing systems to result in those benefits. Similarly, there is a danger that in the focus on generative AI, many organizations are tempted to lose a robust understanding of how to ensure that systems learn securely, effectively, and appropriately, and how to ensure that humans and AI truly collaborate effectively, rather than turning into dislocated workers or conflictual adversaries. Neglecting either could impose steep costs on insurance systems, and on us, partially or completely funding their design, ownership, and operation. Further, while these opportunities are not yet inevitable, the insurance industry is taking its role as the driver and catalyst of the evolution of the insurance value chain. It's time for training and research to step up to help them and society as a whole.

References

Berretta, S., Tausch, A., Ontrup, G., Gilles, B., Peifer, C. and Kluge, A. (2023). Defining Human–AI Teaming the Human-Centered Way: A Scoping Review and Network Analysis. In *Frontiers in Artificial Intelligence* (Vol. 6). https://doi.org/10.3389/frai.2023.1250725

El-Assady, M. and Moruzzi, C. (2022). Which Biases and Reasoning Pitfalls Do Explanations Trigger Decomposing Communication Processes in Human–AI Interaction. *IEEE Computer Graphics and Applications*, *42*(6). https://doi.org/10.1109/MCG.2022.3200328

Jarrahi, M.H. (2018). Artificial Intelligence and the Future of Work: Human–AI Symbiosis in Organizational Decision-Making. *Business Horizons*, *61*(4). https://doi.org/10.1016/j.bushor.2018.03.007

Lee, S., Lee, M. and Lee, S. (2023). What If Artificial Intelligence Become Completely Ambient in Our Daily Lives? Exploring Future Human–AI Interaction through High Fidelity Illustrations. *International Journal of Human–Computer Interaction*, *39*(7). https://doi.org/10.1080/10447318.2022.2080155

Mahmud, B., Hong, G. and Fong, B. (2023). A Study of Human–AI Symbiosis for Creative Work: Recent Developments and Future Directions in Deep Learning. *ACM Transactions on Multimedia Computing, Communications and Applications*, *20*(2). https://doi.org/10.1145/3542698

Morrison, K., Shin, D., Holstein, K. and Perer, A. (2023). Evaluating the Impact of Human Explanation Strategies on Human–AI Visual Decision-Making. *Proceedings of the ACM on Human–Computer Interaction*, *7*(CSCW1). https://doi.org/10.1145/3579481

Qian, C. and Wexler, J. (2024). Take It, Leave It, or Fix It: Measuring Productivity and Trust in Human–AI Collaboration. *ACM International Conference Proceeding Series*. https://doi.org/10.1145/3640543.3645198

Rezwana, J. and Maher, M. Lou. (2023). User Perspectives on Ethical Challenges in Human–AI Co-Creativity: A Design Fiction Study. *ACM International Conference Proceeding Series*. https://doi.org/10.1145/3591196.3593364

Su, Z., He, L., Jariwala, S.P., Zheng, K. and Chen, Y. (2022). "What is Your Envisioned Future?": Toward Human–AI Enrichment in Data Work of Asthma Care. *Proceedings of the ACM on Human–Computer Interaction*, *6*(CSCW2). https://doi.org/10.1145/3555157

Sundar, S.S. (2020). Rise of Machine Agency: A Framework for Studying the Psychology of Human–AI Interaction (HAII). *Journal of Computer-Mediated Communication*, *25*(1). https://doi.org/10.1093/jcmc/zmz026

Svensson, B. and Keller, C. (2024). Agentic Relationship Dynamics in Human–AI Collaboration: A Study of Interactions with GPT-Based Agentic Information Systems Artifacts. *Proceedings of the Annual Hawaii International Conference on System Sciences*.

Wan, Q., Hu, S., Zhang, Y., Wang, P., Wen, B. and Lu, Z. (2024). "It Felt Like Having a Second Mind": Investigating Human–AI Co-Creativity in Prewriting with Large Language Models. *Proceedings of the ACM on Human–Computer Interaction*, *8*(CSCW1). https://doi.org/10.1145/3637361

Wang, D., Weisz, J.D., Muller, M., Ram, P., Geyer, W., Dugan, C., Tausczik, Y., Samulowitz, H. and Gray, A. (2019). Human–AI Collaboration in Data Science: Exploring Data Scientists' Perceptions of Automated AI. *Proceedings of the ACM on Human–Computer Interaction*, *3*(CSCW). https://doi.org/10.1145/3359313

Wienrich, C. and Latoschik, M.E. (2021). eXtended Artificial Intelligence: New Prospects of Human–AI Interaction Research. *Frontiers in Virtual Reality*, *2*. https://doi.org/10.3389/frvir.2021.686783

Xu, W., Dainoff, M.J., Ge, L. and Gao, Z. (2021). From Human–Computer Interaction to Human–AI Interaction: New Challenges and Opportunities for Enabling Human-Centered AI. *International Journal of Human–Computer Interaction*, *39*(3).

6

Combating Insurance Fraud with AI: Balancing Predictive Power and Ethical Constraints

Wasswa Shafik

6.1 Introduction

While losses from fire, crime, auto accidents, and other perils affect all businesses, insurance companies face an additional burden: a certain amount of these losses will be fraudulent, falsified, or exaggerated. Insurance fraud is defined broadly as the act of intentionally deceiving an insurance company to collect a payout that is not legitimately owed. In other words, an insured does not have the genuine loss they claim. Insurance fraud can take place before a policy is purchased, or after the event. Any insured may attempt to gain an unjust advantage by committing fraud against an insurer. Schemes range from an insured pretending to experience confessed loss in demand for reimbursement of fraudulently induced losses, to conspiracies involving claims that were designed to induce loss. Such schemes are pervasive across different lines of business. An individual application for insurance may skip a material fact, eventually leading to excess exposure of the insurance company without any premiums commensurate with that exposure (Alam et al., 2020). Substantial and consistent losses attributed to one cause, or a series of similar claims, may indicate the existence of fraud.

Phony medical reports or services not delivered, and exaggerated claims for hysterectomies without necessary justification, may be the vehicle for committing fraud in health and disability insurance. Deliberate falsification of information at the inception of a contract, false statements to claim examiners, misrepresentation intended to deceive or mislead, failure to disclose prior statements and material facts, and seeking recovery from a nonexistent insurance contract are some of the areas where fraud is committed in general liability insurance. Insurance fraud pervades the entire operations of an insurance company, including market conduct violations, premium fraud—including premium overcharging and over-requiring and unnecessary data request refund—claims fraud, life agent fraud via unsuitability and pretext interviews, and medical fraud in life insurance and disability insurance. The operation of any line of business and the products offered are affected (Philip & Suresh, 2024). The pyramid of fraud is so varied and diverse that realistic detection and elimination should be the goal of any insurance company utilizing the tools of its trade.

6.1.1 Types of Insurance Fraud

Fraud costs insurance companies more than $40 billion per year, which puts a burden on severely profiting insurers and insured parties alike. Insurance fraud perpetrated by insurance consumers,

DOI: 10.1201/9781003747659-6

insurance companies, healthcare parties, and insurance producers comprises two main types: hard fraud, where the insured purposely creates a loss; and soft fraud, where the insured inflates a legitimate claim. Some industry sectors are more liable to perpetrate fraud. For example, automobile insurance fraud can take different forms, which include exaggerating an accident's severity, submitting a claim for a nonexistent injury, or staging a crash. More generally, property insurance can also suffer from fraudulent claims that exaggerate the genuine value of damaged property, storm claim fraud, mold claim fraud, etc. Yet, healthcare fraud can be even more costly by involving providers such as physicians, hospitals, nurses, and pharmacists billing an insurer for services that were never provided, altered, or unnecessary services, or upcoding diagnosis codes or procedure codes. In this case, provider-side fraud might occur along with the patient-side soft fraud. The resulting crime can also involve elements of wire fraud and money laundering. Other fraud types include workers' compensation fraud and life insurance fraud (Murphy & Moosa, 2021). Regardless of their type, fraudulent claims are each made up of a small number of similar patterns that signal suspicious behavior or are caught together with violations of patterns that are known to be innocent, and insurance companies thus need methods advantageous to their needs for discovering which patterns indicate risks of malicious behavior.

6.1.2 Impact of Insurance Fraud on the Industry

Insurance fraud is recognized as a pervasive white collar crime, often occurring when the insured suffers a loss covered by their policy, declaring it or attempting to inflate the loss to receive payment from the insurer. Such behavior has led to high costs for the insurance industry and disrepute for the insurance business. In addition to premium increases needed to cover costs related to insurance frauds and create profits, the insurance industry also is associated with fraud at its inception, as stories come forward of an insured's staging an accident solely to collect on a premium for a policy taken out a few days earlier, which is another contribution to an increase in premiums. Such acts also lead to dissatisfaction with the industry as a whole. From the perspective of the consumer, insurance premiums are at a historically high level, especially for those in high-risk states. The insurance industry has seen failures of some of the most prominent names throughout the past recession, with one of the biggest casualties. Society has become focused on profits and the stock price. This has resulted in carriers looking at cutting expenses wherever they can, including their efforts to fight fraud (Choi et al., 2024). The establishment of insurance fraud bureaus, anti-fraud statutes, and training programs has taken the industry down one avenue. On the other hand, fraud detection and data analysis companies have focused their products on attempting to solve the fraud detection problem.

6.2 The Role of AI in Fraud Detection

Structure and Overall Summary: Artificial intelligence (AI) is a collection of very powerful, quite general, and applicable tools that automate task completion through the realization of any cognitive function. AI encompasses three mechanisms for the realization of intelligent behavior. These three mechanisms are:

(1) reactive rule-based expert systems,
(2) cognitive behavioral simulation models, and
(3) learning or self-organizing models, specialized in the automation of supervised learning, associative functions, and relational function approximation.

AI technologies have become an essential tool in solving the information overload problem nowadays in many business areas. One of these areas is fraud detection in the financial sector, where AI is rapidly being adopted. The main AI technologies applied in fraud detection are:

(i) rule-based systems,
(ii) knowledge-based systems,
(iii) analogy-based systems,
(iv) expert systems,
(v) genetic algorithms,
(vi) fuzzy logic systems,
(vii) artificial neural networks, and
(viii) intelligent agents.

There are several machine learning (ML) algorithms applied in fraud detection. The most common machine learning algorithms used in fraud detection applications are:

(i) supervised learning algorithms,
(ii) unsupervised learning algorithms, and
(iii) reinforcement learning algorithms.

As more data becomes available in the insurance sector, and training data archives grow in size and diversity, ML techniques gain importance in tackling complexity and scale and improving prediction performance. For example, one attraction of deep learning (DL) methods for classifying images or texts or automating tasks like speech recognition is their ability to learn directly from raw data without expert-created features. Data scientists agree that the key factors in the success of an ML application are:

(i) data size and quality,
(ii) research and previous experiments of other practitioners,
(iii) the right ML technique coupled with the right training data, and
(iv) ML toolkits and their Application Programming Interfaces (APIs).

Existing classical statistical techniques do not scale to today's data sizes and dimensions. Moreover, they do not take into consideration the structural properties of the type of data found in applications such as insurance fraud detection.

6.2.1 Overview of AI Technologies

"AI" is one of the terms used to describe the still early stage of developing what some have called the "fourth industrial revolution." This revolution combines advances in computing power and storage, algorithmic development, vast amounts of data, and the creation of digital services. The focus of this paper is on how much of the excitement being generated by AI now comes from the application of algorithms to the field of insurance fraud detection. The term "predictive analytics" is commonly used to refer to the new business applications of AI technology. These terms embrace various algorithms for pattern detection, classification, regression, clustering, embedding spaces, potential causal relationship investigations, and data cleansing that, when applied intelligently, powerfully, and in innovative ways, extract signals from noise in big data (Shafik, 2024). Perhaps belated by bursts of excitement followed by periods of skepticism and disillusionment, the technology now in the hands of user companies integrates and streamlines specific algorithms and earlier applied statistical approaches to data analysis. This technology has expanded beyond its roots in statistical pattern recognition, information theory, and inferential statistics; includes new kinds of algorithmic approaches; draws upon greater amounts of cleaner, more accessible, and more complex data; and is more user-friendly. Advanced predictive algorithms trained and implemented by both data scientists and non-data scientists alike can now analyze diverse unstructured textual data, image/video data, and complex graph data, as well as more traditional structured numerical data. Numerous companies offer software platforms enabling user companies to automate predictive modeling, which can also be trained more effectively by data scientists (Shafik et al., 2024). Some software platforms focus specifically on the preparation of large datasets for analysis, CIAPSR (Collaboration, Innovation, Automation, Performance, Security, Reliability) drivers, as illustrated in Figure 6.1.

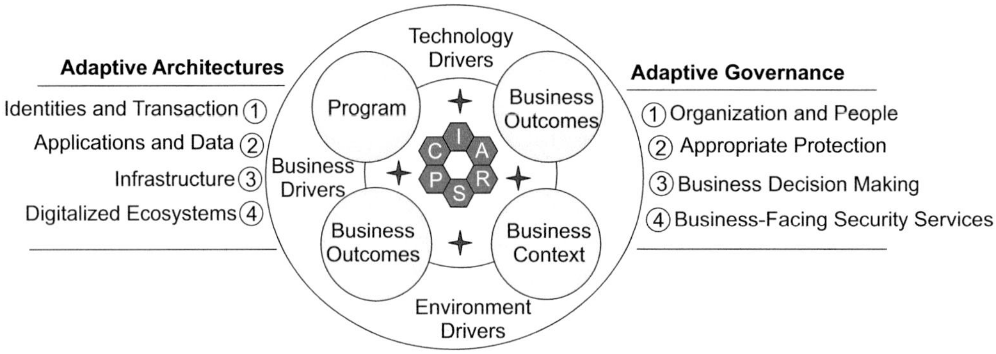

Fig. 6.1 CIAPSR drivers.

6.2.2 Machine Learning Algorithms Used in Fraud Detection

Fraud detection is a classification task where the goal is to classify each transaction or customer as "fraudulent" or "legitimate," according to a number of descriptive features. The classification is generally performed from labeled past data by supervised learning, which consists of training the algorithm to optimize a classification measure, which is often weighted to take the imbalanced nature of the problem into account, since fraudulent instances represent only a minuscule fraction of the dataset. After the model is built, it is then applied to future data to predict the fraudulent and legitimate instances.

(i) **Traditional Machine Learning Algorithms:** Due to the simplicity of their development, interpretation, and deployment, traditional machine learning algorithms have a long history of use in fraud detection and have been the backbone of fraud detection systems until recently. These algorithms include logistic regression, decision trees, and support vector machines. Of these algorithms, logistic regression is the simplest and least costly to implement, but its assumption of linearity makes it less robust in practice and less able to capture the heterogeneous distribution of actual fraudulent and legitimate transactions. Decision trees handle discrete variables well, but their risk of overfitting data makes them unreliable for fraud detection (Wu et al., 2023). Support Vector Machines (SVMs) can be made robust to overfitting, unlike decision trees, but present challenges in their application, resulting from unsuitability in working with a large number of instances or categorical variables.

(ii) **Deep Learning Algorithms:** More recently, a new generation of neural networks known as deep learning has enjoyed great success in a number of domains, including image analysis, predicting the stock market, and natural language understanding and translation. In the past years, deep learning has also shown strong performance in fraud detection, and deep neural networks are now becoming increasingly common in commercial fraud detection systems (Muhammad & Hossain, 2021). These networks have a number of distinct architectures that take advantage of their structure to work with particular fraud detection problems, as presented in Table 6.1.

Table 6.1 AI techniques for fraud detection and their ethical considerations.

Technique	*Functionality*	*Predictive Power*	*Ethical Constraint*	*Mitigation Strategy*
Rule-Based Systems	Detects known fraud patterns using hard-coded logic	High for historical cases	Inflexibility to new fraud types	Combine with adaptive ML models
Supervised Machine Learning	Learns from labeled fraud/non-fraud data	High-quality datasets	Risk of overfitting or learning bias	Diverse, balanced training data
Unsupervised Learning (e.g., Clustering)	Identifies anomalies in data	Useful for detecting novel fraud	May flag legitimate claims as suspicious	Post-processing review and human vetting
Deep Learning (CNNs – Convolutional Neural Networks, RNNs – Recurrent Neural Networks)	Analyzes complex patterns, including images and sequences	Very high for complex signals	Opaque "black-box" decisions	Incorporate explainable AI layers (e.g., Grad-CAM)
Natural Language Processing (NLP)	Extracts fraud indicators from unstructured text	Medium to high, depending on the data	Misinterpretation of context	Use multilingual, context-aware models
Network Analysis	Detects fraud rings via relationships	Strong for organized fraud networks	Data privacy concerns	Graph anonymization and access control
Anomaly Detection Algorithms	Highlights data points deviating from the norm	Good for unknown or rare fraud	High false-positive rate	Layered validation with statistical thresholds
Predictive Scoring Systems	Assigns fraud likelihood scores to claims	Enables prioritization of investigations	Unjust denial or delay of valid claims	Use transparency thresholds and an appeals mechanism
Reinforcement Learning	Adapts strategies based on fraud investigation outcomes	Promising in dynamic scenarios	Ethical risk of reinforcing biased outcomes	Regular human oversight and reward shaping
Hybrid AI Systems	Combines multiple models and logic rules	Enhanced robustness	Complexity makes auditing difficult	Modular design with clear decision logs
Blockchain Integration	Validates claim authenticity through immutable records	High for transactional integrity	Data governance and privacy concerns	Private or permissioned blockchain solutions
Federated Learning	Trains models across distributed insurers' data	High accuracy with enhanced privacy	Coordination complexity, auditability issues	Standardized protocols and audit layers
Adaptive Threshold Models	Dynamically adjusts fraud suspicion thresholds	Reduces manual tuning workload	May inadvertently favor certain demographics	Bias checks during retraining cycles
Real-Time Detection Engines	Detects fraud during claim intake or processing	Timely intervention potential	Errors may go unnoticed without review	Flag high-confidence cases only for automation

6.3 Predictive Analytics in Insurance

Actually, predictive analytics are at the root of the insurance business, which uses advanced statistical techniques to find patterns in data to predict better and evaluate risk. The traditional models have been built or at least backed by actuarial loss predictions, taking into account only the observed features of the premiums collected to insure these risks. Just because insurance prices are essentially calculated based on past losses, predictive analytics has been used for many years for pricing, as well as for understanding and reducing underwriting losses. The same applies, to a lesser extent, to modelling reserves, liability management, and risk appetite. Besides the underwriting phase, the predictive analytics models are also used for a wide variety of business issues for insurers: in marketing, to assess the likelihood of being converted from prospect to customer; in distribution, to identify the most profitable insurance brokers' network; in retention, to track and predict churn; to improve customer service; in claims management, to complement and guide expert's intuition for reserve estimation, fraud detection, risk assessment, litigation support, settlement evaluation, and time to settle; in operations, to improve balance sheet efficiency and capacity management; to optimize the supply chain; to detect investment opportunities; to support M&A decisions; and to suggest portfolio management changes (Margan, 2021).

After collecting the data, the next indispensable step is to build a predictive model. Three basic components are needed to do that. The first is data preparation, an essential and time-consuming process of data cleansing, data transformation, handling missing values, removing duplicated data, dealing with outliers, building new features from available attributes, selecting relevant features, and data balancing. The second is the algorithm that turns the relevant parts of the data into a model or a set of rules. Several learning algorithms are available, including neural networks, random forests, and gradient boosting, and the actual challenge is to find and tune the right one for a given problem. The third is model validation or performance assessment, that is, measuring how well the model performs. There are several ways to do that as well, including cross-validation, looking at out-of-sample metrics, using penalty functions, and measuring the costs of the misclassifications (Choi et al., 2024).

6.3.1 Data Collection and Analysis

Data collection is fundamental to any machine learning application, including fraud detection. Because finding and mitigating wrongdoing is often a matter of trying to identify a needle in the proverbial haystack, the power of analytical algorithms is especially reliant upon the availability of high-quality data. For insurance fraud detection, this means a sufficient quantity of well-structured internal data on historic policyholders, including applicants, claimants, beneficiaries, and agents, over a significant time frame. Such data might cover claim payments, often segmented by type of claim, associated costs, payment methods, and time taken to settle or refuse claims, as well as information associated with applicants and beneficiaries, such as names, social security numbers, quotas and personas, which can be integrated with external data to provide more complete contextual information (Margan, 2021). Additional internal data sources that can be vital for detecting fraud include information about suspicious third parties; data on non-fraudulent claimants and approved claims, some of which could include outlier examples; policy history; the likelihood of certain events based on geographic location; the customer relationship management history; or anything else that might help to formulate patterns of likely undesired behavior. Analytical algorithms can feed such data into supervised learning models to make predictions about whether claims are likely to be fraudulent or not. Other internal data sources available for unsupervised learning models to assess how claims compare to similar claims in the past include historical, industry-standard fraud scoring; the suspected motives and opportunities for fraud; and claims data enriched with external and social media data. Given that sample runs of various supervised and unsupervised models can cost very little, the money that insurers would need to invest in collecting and cleaning the data is often better spent in these areas instead (McDonnell et al., 2023).

6.3.2 Building Predictive Models

Once the data has been collected and preprocessed, including quality checks and data cleansing, it is time to build the predictive models. In general terms, predictive modeling can be defined as a process for building a mathematical description of the relationship between two sets of random variables. The set of independent variables is called predictors, while the set of dependent variables is called the prediction variables, which can either be continuous or categorical, according to the nature of the data. In the insurance fraud detection context, the predictors can be either extracted from the data that have been collected or from other data sources. Other than manual feature engineering, machine learning techniques can also be used for automatic feature engineering. The prediction variable can be defined according to the business problem or model. In case of risk score modeling in which the claim has to be assigned a score according to the claim attributes, the prediction variable is a score, either continuous or discrete (Braun & Matthes, 2018). Examples of business problems requiring risk score modeling are description-level fraud prevention, which helps in avoiding fraudulent claims from being settled; auditing guidelines in post-settlement audits; and fraud-ledger allocation in the ledger management of investigators. In case of definitive detection modeling, in which the aim is to confirm or dismiss the entity as either fraudulent or benign, the prediction variable is categorical: either fraudulent or benign. Predictive modeling has also been used for a secondary objective of business problems, wherein a definitive model also predicts a set of ignored cases, which helps achieve cost optimization from the investigator allocation process. Examples of business problems with ignore-case optimization for cost optimization are auditor allocation in the auditing guidelines and fraud-ledger allocation in the ledger management of investigators (Jouini & Sethom, 2023).

6.4 Case Studies of AI Implementation

Insurance fraud is an old problem faced by insurers, which has recently taken on new forms as technology has created unique avenues for exploitation. New methods of detection and investigation are required to meet these new schemes. We describe some recent work utilizing artificial intelligence to detect or combat fraud. One of the oldest forms of insurance fraud is the orchestrated auto accident with inflated or false claims for damages. A model was developed to detect these types of claims at companies in the insurance market using the decision tree algorithms CART and CHAID, trained on over 35,000 claims. An insurance company often must go through a long cycle of receiving a claim, investigating it, and then ultimately paying the loss. This model was shown to be very helpful in quickly screening incoming claims. The model was able to rapidly classify incoming claims from an automated claims reporting system with 92% accuracy. This reduced the number of questionable claims needing to be adjudicated by a claims adjuster by about 60% over three years (Choi et al., 2024). The address used in the claim forms was utilized along with the complainant and insured party details as features in the model. Results indicate that a 50% saving in fraudulent claims resulting from fraud ring activity is achievable, thus enhancing technology application as illustrated in Figure 6.2.

In another auto insurance fraud model similar to the previous case, decision trees, along with 11 other machine learning techniques, were developed to predict the likelihood of fraud. The sample included 11,165 policies and 46 policies were marked as fraudulent. A final model was produced which used a mixture of the decision tree and logistic regression techniques. In the insurance industry, there is always a risk of a small false-positive rate being very harmful. To mitigate this risk, a

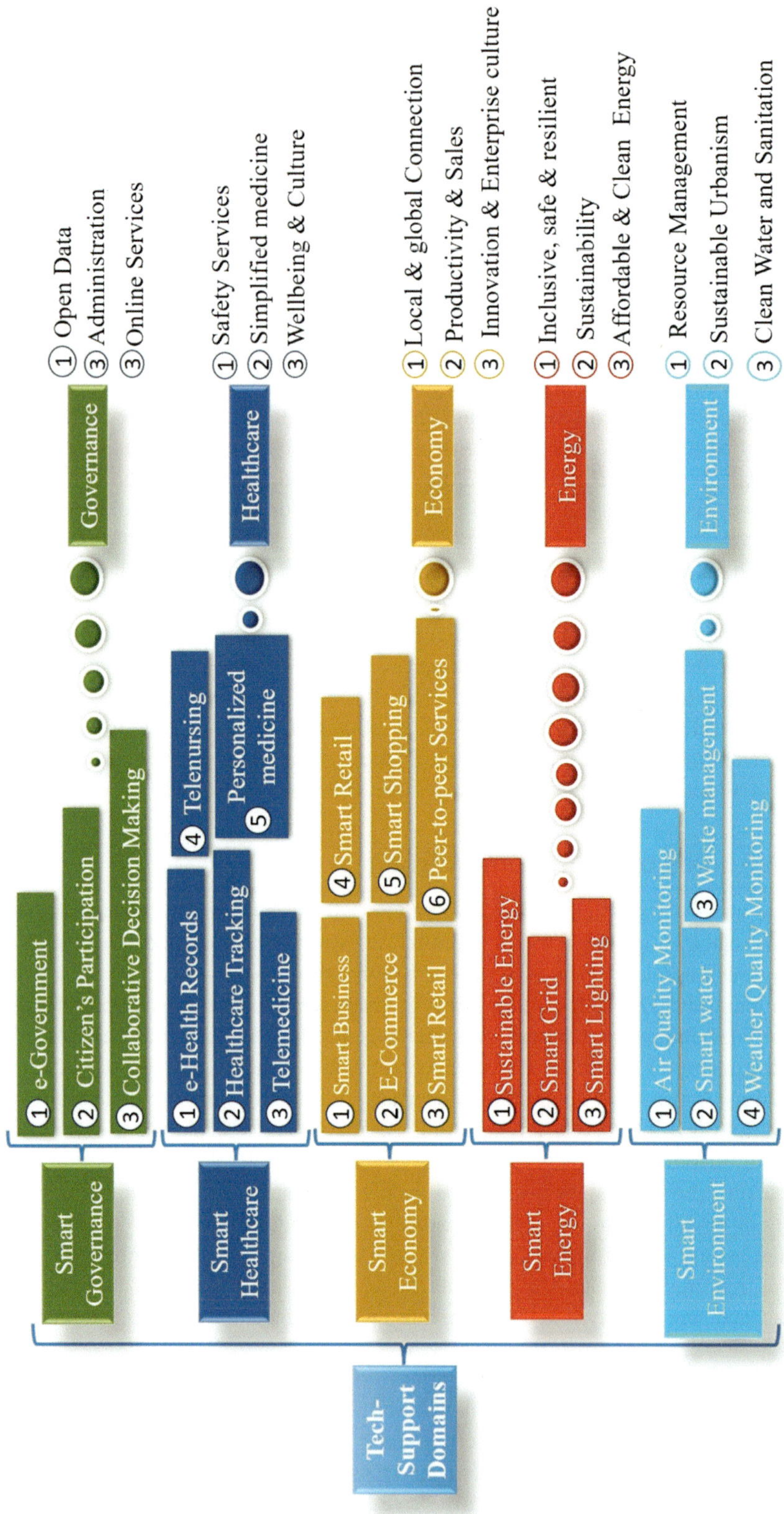

Fig. 6.2 Insurance tech-support domain.

combination of anomaly detection and rule-based approaches was used in this application. The model predicted the fraudulent cases with 70% precision and 45% recall. Although the abovementioned applications have demonstrated real-world success, there have also been failures. Companies create machine learning models and deploy them into production, only to have them fail or produce less-than-desired results. There are numerous challenges that could contribute to this: dirty data, poor features, incorrect choice of algorithm, or absence of automated tools to take care of these challenges (Murphy & Moosa, 2021). As a possible attempt to help others from heading down the same path in their insurance and other endeavors, we reviewed numerous recent case studies concerning model failures and present some lessons learned.

6.4.1 Successful AI Applications

AI has been successfully used in applications traditionally, developing in-house capacities for anti-fraud models that far outperform traditional predictive analytics. Claim approval automation using AI is increasingly seen in many industries from underwriting to fraud prediction to supervisory process management. With the COVID pandemic leading to a surge of claims, the insurance industry is using AI along the whole claim value chain: personalizing the claim experience and automating fraud prediction. The insurance industry estimates that in the next years, between 20% and 25% of claims will be subject to an AI-based fraud detection model, with such models expected to reach a 90% accuracy. Fraud recognition modules of chatbots will ask users questions based on stolen identity data to detect inconsistencies. Customers at the other end will get instant claim decisions/settlements (Philip & Suresh, 2024). An expansion of claim screening is also expected for "saving checks" by specialized vendors.

6.4.2 Lessons Learned from Failures

While some insurance companies or organizations successfully implemented an AI or ML solution to tackle insurance fraud, others faced embarrassing moments. One might wonder what lessons we can learn from these events. In this section, we summarize lessons from two case studies of failed AI attempts.

(i) In 2017, a company trained its chatbot agent to replicate the speech patterns of users interacting with it. The goal was to learn, and subsequently apply, the social interactions on a social media platform. Within 24 hours, the chatbot started using racist and sexist phrases, and blasphemous comments issued from it. The company had to cease the chatbot's actions. A more detailed investigation showed how people manipulated the chatbot by inputting improper commands. As such, an important lesson learned is that when a system is trained using ML, the sample data that is used to train or refine the model must be clean, and free of noise or incorrect examples.

(ii) In March 2018, another company faced backlash when its photo search product used an algorithm that classified individuals inappropriately. The cause of this fatal flaw was that the team used a biased dataset with heavily imbalanced gender and race representations. As such, a lesson learned from this case is that when a data-centric algorithm is used, the sample data upon which the algorithm is built determines the performance of the algorithm and must be valid and reliable.

6.5 Ethical Considerations in AI Use

AI systems are being increasingly incorporated into various facets of life, from a range of domestic practices to penal decisions, credit scoring, and welfare and healthcare provisions. However, despite their apparent benefits, these systems are not free from ethical concerns. Ethical questions can arise surrounding the intention of the intervention, the (potential) interest of the affected individuals, the method used, and the procedure followed. Namely, questions surrounding the consequences of (intended or unintended) actions, the fairness of the decisions taken, the accountability of the decisions made, and the transparency of the decision process must all be taken into account. In particular, when deploying systems to replace human actors' decisions with algorithmically defined outcomes, it should always be asked what the justification is for any disallowing of the individual right of taking responsible actions. Fair outcomes have two basic meanings; first, in some applications, ethical fairness can be strictly quantified, and a specifically designed algorithm can optimize that fairness measure (Golden et al., 2016). Second, all applications require a constant checking of the fairness of the outcomes and the underlying algorithm. Addressing the disproportions in outcome distributions directly is important, and the software makes it easy to do that. The algorithms allow deploying disproportional ratio constraints or simple threshold functions, thus speaking more generally of proximity constraints, which guarantee a fair modeling of the different categories of the applied features. For instance, one can ensure that an assigned rule disproportionately treats at most 5% of some specified group in the positive class if the overall percentage in that group does not exceed 1% of the total population. Ultimately, the most appropriate measures and checks ensure that provided explanations are understandable and intelligible to the user affected by the algorithm. It has been shown that the average time to the first question—"What does this all mean?"—was significantly reduced when intuitively understandable explanations, though at the cost of trust decisions from dummy, were presented, rather than reasonably dubious, complexly justifiable ones (Murphy & Moosa, 2021).

6.5.1 Bias and Fairness in AI Algorithms

The increasing use of AI algorithms in decision-making processes affects many aspects of modern life. Nevertheless, while AI has the ability to massively increase the efficiency and predictive power of many processes, it also creates ethical issues and may amplify existing societal biases. These issues are especially relevant in processes related to criminal justice and often impact the lives of many vulnerable people. For this reason, the algorithms need to follow specific fairness constraints. In this section, we briefly present these issues, both from a real-world standpoint of socio-economical implications and from the technical aspects controlling whether the algorithm is fit for purpose. Given the mistaken assumption that algorithms are objective and impartial, the use of machine learning in sensitive and high-stakes domains, such as the prediction of creditworthiness, job recruitment, or criminal recidivism, is becoming increasingly widespread. However, a mounting body of evidence shows that ML-based prediction can be biased against individuals because of sensitive attributes, such as gender, age, race, and disability status. Bias in AI can originate from various elements of the predictive process. The data used to serve as input to the algorithm might be unbalanced. Sensitive attributes might themselves be missing, but their effect might still be captured through proxies contained in the dataset. Algorithms might be unable to correctly generalize to some subsets of individuals or applied to a scenario that is different yet related to the training one (McDonnell et al., 2023). Making predictions on future events is notoriously difficult, and AI techniques implement what is regarded as the best predictive approach in the given instance. The serious socio-economical implications of biased prediction have created a sense of urgency in devising solutions that help alleviate human bias rather than enhance it.

6.5.2 Transparency and Accountability

In this section, we explore how the design of AI for insurance claims decisions can both promote and inhibit transparency and accountability. Research on AI proliferates capabilities, delivering ever more flexible prediction engines at ever lower costs, while concern grows that the methods are predicated on obscure processes that hinder investigation into predictive accuracy and error. Novel ways of obfuscating information and deflection are not limited to the explanatory statements that accompany some AI systems. Such methods can be intentional, producing obfuscation to deceive, or unintentional, through the massive complexity that attends many machine processes. The issue is more than one of "trust," however crucial that issue is to any public acceptance of AI. Erosion of "trust" is not limited to AI—any decision that has major implications for a person or an organization may suffer from lack of trust, especially as the stakes grow (Gramegna & Giudici, 2020). While the increasing opacity of decision-making associated with ML/AI may shift the concern for accountability at the micro level, to the policy end, it does not remove the accountability issue. Who is to be responsible for the decision's accuracy, and the consequences of erroneous predictions? Accountability is less an afterthought for AI systems used in claims decision-making, however flexible they may be. As noted earlier, insurance companies must maintain an appropriate "paper trail" of all policyholder behavior, including both predicted and actual claims costs and policy lapses, as well as coverage purchase decisions and timing, product design, pricing, and marketing decisions. This transparency means it is easy to assess the relative predictive power of the AI tools and any other predictive tool that may have been used. A good decision audit helps ensure accountability (Braun & Matthes, 2018).

6.6 Regulatory Frameworks and Compliance

When discussing fraud detection, machine learning in general and AI in particular have been hailed as revolutionary tools, combining what was once the work of hundreds of experts, team decision-making, and rule-based systems to terrible effect, while knitting together thousands of fraud indicators into identifiably clusters of catastrophically flagged results. These clusters are then fed back to investigators for improved manual filtering. And all this done during a lull in prime time viewing for attempted insurance fraud. No wonder insurance companies have raced to deploy these models! While it is hard to argue with the results achieved by these efficiency monsters, that efficiency is, as we have noted throughout, achieved at the expense of the subtly and ethically aligned design demands of AI systems. For that reason, regulators are calling for granular algorithm explainability, fairness auditing, and consumer, segment, and group protections (Owens et al., 2022). The future global battle will be to preserve the ESP, that is, efficiency, scalability, and profitability of these systems, while reserving a place for truthfulness, fairness, and ethical alignment. There will, then, be a global demand for both external and post hoc AI monitoring tools to meet these challenges. Cyber insurance, which emerged to cover the political, delinquent, and state-driven intrusion insurance requirements of companies protecting themselves against increasing Large Language Model (LLM) and cybersecurity perimeter breaches, has grown to require tailored policies and expert judgmental review by underwriters for security perimeters at increasing premiums. This demand, however, requires review of the AI-enabled models and prompt engineering used to define the LLM. What is still missing is a call from regulators for the AI and tech companies deploying these models to take responsibility for their ethico-moral implications, whether destruction of competition by monopolization of cybersecurity tools or macro-financial by blackouts crippling entire economies (Shi & Gan, 2023).

6.6.1 Current Regulations Affecting AI in Insurance

Although modern regulators have produced a variety of sector-specific rules that could be construed as AI-related, many types of businesses today are subject to regulations impacting how they manage personal data. Regulating insurance-specific AI activity is a relatively new endeavor at the state level. Many states have antidiscrimination and disclosure requirements governing the underwriting process. This is designed to ensure companies operating in the insurance industry enhance their cybersecurity infrastructure and protections of consumer data. Explicitly anti-fraud-related regulations are less common, but encourage insurance companies to avoid faulty practices or systems that lead to errors in insurance decisions. Existing laws generally prohibit carriers from engaging in fraud through false information related to rates, classifications, coverages, and applications for policies. Regulations that establish professionally acceptable business practices for how insurance is conducted and supervised create a spectrum of rules that vary among states. But although fault-based carrier regulations require insurers to avoid bad faith conduct that results in unreasonable delays in claim determination, the court found that insurers had a statutory obligation to act in good faith only after they have received a claim by an insured (Abdulkadir Isa & Fernando, 2023). Specifically, the good faith reasonableness standard applies only to the insurer–insured relationship once a claim has been presented. The good faith reasonableness standard expressed in the court's decision does not regulate bad faith conduct on the part of the insurers on the front end of the transaction.

6.6.2 *Future Directions for Regulation*

The preceding discussion naturally leads us to consider how future AI regulations should be framed. Essentially, we must strike a balance between the positive and negative aspects of using AI in insurance. On the one hand, regulations must not be overly restrictive, stifling insurance organizations from implementing the most effective detection and deterrent methods possible, as those would ultimately benefit insurance markets and policyholders. On the other hand, we must avoid a situation where the predictions made by methods based on AI systems result in disruptive and possibly exclusionary practices, perpetuating bias and discrimination either toward specific insurance applicants or groups of policyholders based on factors such as socio-economic status, age, gender, and ethnicity (Choi et al., 2024). As AI's ability to discriminate and sort individuals and groups based on increasingly flexible user-defined rules increases, so do its potential negative consequences. Technologies should be used for the common good and, if we want to preserve our future societies, regulations must acknowledge this. To this end, a future regulatory framework for AI in insurance should establish more precisely than is currently the case how the broad set of existing horizontal regulations already established could be interpreted and adapted to AI-specific cases in the context of insurance markets. Furthermore, we must advance on developing more selective regulations, for instance, on aspects related to transparency, explainability, and robustness of insurers' AI models, especially for sensitive applications such as those predicting insurance fraud (Murphy & Moosa, 2021). Specific future guidelines can also help this process to ensure a compliant, effective, and ethical use of AI systems in predicting fraud and other risky behaviors, as presented in Table 6.2.

Table 6.2 Balancing predictive power and ethics in fraud detection workflow.

Fraud Detection Step	*AI Role*	*Predictive Strength*	*Ethical Risk*	*Best Practice/Tool*
Data Collection	Aggregates structured and unstructured data	Foundation for prediction	Privacy breaches, data misuse	Consent-driven collection, GDPR–General Data Protection Regulationcompliant systems

Contd.

Table 6.2 *Contd.*

Fraud Detection Step	*AI Role*	*Predictive Strength*	*Ethical Risk*	*Best Practice/Tool*
Data Preprocessing	Cleanses, transforms, and normalizes inputs	Reduces model noise	Hidden biases during selection	Bias detection tools (Aequitas, IBM AI Fairness 360)
Feature Engineering	Extracts fraud-relevant patterns and features	Enhances model discrimination	Risk of using proxies for protected characteristics	Ethical feature selection and domain review
Model Training	Builds predictive fraud classifiers	Central to detection accuracy	Training on imbalanced or biased data	SMOTE–Synthetic Minority Over-sampling Technique, fairness-aware model validation
Scoring and Risk Classification	Assigns fraud probability to new claims	Enables prioritization	Potential stigmatization or false accusations	Provide confidence intervals and human override options
Real-Time Flagging	Flags transactions during processing	Enables early detection	Customer mistrust from false alerts	Dual-layer approval (AI + human)
Case Triage and Investigation	Ranks claims for further review	Optimizes fraud analyst workload	Bias in triage leads to unequal treatment	Incorporate human judgment for contextual evaluation
Explanation and Audit	Provides interpretability for AI decisions	Builds trust and accountability	Lack of transparency in complex models	LIME – Local Interpretable Model-agnostic Explanations, SHAP – SHapley Additive exPlanations, model traceability logs
Appeals and Dispute Resolution	Informs dispute process with AI-based reasoning	Helps clarify and resolve conflicts	Unfair rejection without rationale	Human-verified explanations and appeal channels
Post-Decision Review	Analyzes feedback and outcomes for model improvement	Improves model adaptiveness	Risk of amplifying existing biases	Implement differential performance audits
Regulatory Compliance Monitoring	Verifies alignment with legal and ethical standards	Maintains legal defensibility	Overlooked risks in fast-evolving models	Use legal-tech solutions for compliance tracking
Feedback Loop for Learning	Incorporates investigation outcomes into retraining	Adaptive performance over time	Reinforcement of flawed assumptions	Human-in-the-loop retraining with fairness scoring
Stakeholder Communication	Summarizes fraud risk decisions to stakeholders	Promotes informed decision-making	Complexity of explanation impedes understanding	Use visual tools (dashboarding, XAI explainers)
Continuous Monitoring	Detects model drift and performance degradation	Sustains long-term efficacy	Ethical drift due to unnoticed bias	Monitor with performance fairness dashboards

6.7 Balancing Predictive Power and Ethical Constraints

The last few decades have seen a sudden rush toward an ongoing interested adoption of increasingly complex predictive models. Deep neural networks significantly outperform traditional regression and tree-based models on an extremely wide range of problems across virtually all domains, and, admittedly, the increase in predictive performance has made the introduction of deep learning models to a problem hard to resist. However, many of these models suffer from listing one of the defining features of predictive models for a long time: being explainable. This has led to a new direction in developing tools. One is eXplainable AI. We argue here that an even more fundamental concern (of which the explainability problem is a subset) is that of ethics, specifically, doing no harm. We believe that addressing this concern is a prerequisite to building (and using) appropriately designed eXplainable AI in companies and that ethical restrictions should at least be considered alongside predictive performance in determining the architecture of the chosen models for any specific predictive application. We illustrate this argument, to consider balancing AI model choice and the framework in guiding AI-model development using the predictive insurance fraud literature as the application example. More specifically, we analyze how the models used to predict suspicion of fraud across areas such as the USA and Europe tend to bypass ethical questions (Ding & Zuo, 2024). To the extent that any of these assumptions are violated, there is a serious ethical justification for the AI model used, to implement unfair insurance fraud prediction decisions (in favor of some groups and against others).

6.7.1 Strategies for Ethical AI Implementation

Numerous methodologies have been proposed for implementing ethical AI within the business enterprise in practice. These typically focus upon developing frameworks that draw from existing guidelines and best practices for specific contexts and use cases. These earlier proposals include a tool for contrasting real-world AI decision-making systems with best practice principles, an ethical AI canvas developed at a university, an AI ethics framework for business and society, and an AI ethics framework, the responsible AI framework, the responsible use of artificial intelligence tool, a trust and transparency framework, and a concept of an AI Public Company Accounting Oversight Board (PCAOB)—drawing upon the precedent of accounting supervision boards to assure ethical AI deployments at scale. Most recently, a proposed digital good governance framework draws upon the aforementioned principles and guidelines to support public officials, practitioners, and decision-makers—especially at the organizational level—in ensuring that principles of responsible, trustworthy, and ethical AI are put into practice in a context-sensitive manner. It offers a series of contextualized questions about the goals, operations, impacts, and outcomes of an AI project that are designed to prompt leaders in policy and decision-making positions to consider the impacts of AI upon the public (Bermúdez et al., 2023; Pnevmatikakis et al., 2021). The questions can be used to inform and structure discussions about ethical AI for AI practitioners, businesses, and the public sector, enabling them to develop tailored responses that address the ethical implications of AI for deployment.

6.7.2 Stakeholder Perspectives on AI Ethics

Insurance and insurance fraud targeting the industry are both ubiquitous and critical components of society. However, insurance fraud is becoming a highly influential issue due to its increasing economic impact on the whole insurance system, which is now reaching quantifiable measures. In combating insurance fraud, in addition to a practical perspective, there are ethical dimensions in the decisions of the insurance actors involved that will benefit from deep examination. This is yet more necessary when advanced algorithms of AI are employed in the decision-making processes related not only to the detection of dubious claims but also the estimates of the claim values. We'll consider that the term "AI" here includes not only intelligent algorithms and systems at the stage of development and implementation, but also automated decision-making where such algorithms are adopted to assist the business operations. Indeed, decision-making about fraud detection and estimate of amount may be already referred to as "AI-driven." The term "stakeholders" refers to any parties affected and engaged by the process of AI development and service, including the potential claim filers or insured persons and general society, as well as the parties running or using the insurance business and the AI-providing companies with their profit and corporate reputation at stake. Then what to consider in insurance fraud efforts by means of AI? This question is important and general enough to apply to any service or business processes, not limited to insurance (Sachan & Muwanga, 2023). However, AI for insurance fraud detection and damage estimate may attract sensitivity both from potential claim filers and society at large since it relates to not only the financial loss and damage verification of the stakeholders but also the potential infringement upon privacy and fairness-informed concern.

6.8 Future Trends in Insurance Fraud Prevention

Insurance fraud is evolving as technology continues to advance and cybercriminals find new and innovative methods to undermine the insurance sector. It is evident that the landscape of insurance fraud will be different in a few years. Emerging technologies such as AI and predictive modeling will guide the future of the insurance industry. At the same time, changes in the industry's business models will impact how insurance fraud happens. Public expectations regarding security and privacy—and regulations concerning the latter—will also change. As various technologies converge and solutions become increasingly more complex, insurers will need to constantly adapt to these changes. In three key areas, the future work of insurers to combat insurance fraud is concerned with: emerging technologies, AI in insurance, and preparation for negative developments (Murphy & Moosa, 2021).

Various emerging technologies have enabled new forms of crime and new ways of committing crimes. The insurance industry is particularly vulnerable to the future developments of technology and applications such as digital twins, the metaverse, and synthetic identities. Insurance companies are thus often the first to face challenges from new technologies. They should take the lead in the development of applied solutions in these domains. AI will dominate a whole range of industry-wide issues in the foreseeable future. Its deployment will increase the efficiency and speed of business processes while at the same time lowering costs. It will also free up staff to work on more added-value projects, and allow insurers to better personalize their offerings and enhance customer service. Companies risk overdependence on technology and will be challenged to balance a strong human factor with the deployment of technology. Minding privacy when developing insurance products and keeping accountability when these products are used are crucially important (Choi et al., 2024). Insurers are usually quick to embrace technology, especially if this can serve their bottom line, yet cause societal negative side effects.

6.8.1 Emerging Technologies

The insurance sector is constantly striving to improve its financial performance by merging digital and corporate strategies to enhance organizational efficiency, reduce costs, improve customer satisfaction, and boost revenues. One of the problems facing the insurance industry concerns more fraudulent activities each year. The amount of insurance fraud has increased due to the increasing digitization of daily lives. Insurers have intensified their anti-fraud measures and have started using artificial intelligence and technology-based approaches to combat insurance fraud. Their use is intended to alleviate the substantial losses caused by insurance fraud, but without forgetting the ethical aspect, particularly relevant in these kinds of contexts, as well as data privacy regulations. Emerging technologies for risk and fraud analysis comprise both new types of data and improved technologies to analyze current and evolving claims and claimants' behavior. With regard to new types of data, the new forms derive from new or improved techniques that capture movements, emotions, and location, the Internet of Things that constantly creates "the data business," and the extensive use of social networks that generate a vast amount of data on individuals and their environment. The new types of technology concern, for example, machine learning and deep learning, which allow the analysis of nonstructured data in text, images, and videos, as well as the development of quantum computing, which will help speed up and improve the use of brain emulation and general reinforcement learning (Arockiam & Pushpanathan, 2023; Wall, 2022). In addition to more advanced technology, insurance fraud detection could also benefit from the exploration of different aspects of the cooperative and noncooperative behavior of fraudsters, and of the introduction of multi-agent systems and simulations.

6.8.2 Predictions for the Future of AI in Insurance

Using advanced machine learning techniques to mine data for hidden insights and structures has been one of the biggest technological breakthroughs in the last decade. With ever-increasingly large and complex datasets becoming available, such techniques seem to be poised to become the prime enabler of new AI and driving disruption across every traditional industry sector, including insurance. Insurance is a field in which data has always played a central role. Hence, the application of AI to insurance seems like the next natural step, promising outcomes ranging from increased manual productivity through improved customer experience to enhanced risk detection and vacancy prediction (Golden et al., 2016; Philip & Suresh, 2024). Just as the application of the first wave of AI to insurance drove disruption across large parts of that market and its service providers, the application of new AI has the potential to create both similar benefits and dislocation across the major segments of the insurance industry—including both automating tasks and the user interface, as well as delivering improved prediction accuracy, demand forecasting, and renewed focus on underwriting fueled by critical knowledge graphs that allow insurers to identify profitable micro-niches in the market landscape. Industry analysts expect that the majority of the world's top insurers will have adopted AI and machine learning technologies within the next five years. This is likely to result in hundreds of billions of dollars of savings in operational costs. AI has a major role to play in the optimization of damages by supporting insurers in their goals of improving their customer service and offering quality advice and support to their clients, increasing fraud detection rates, and investing the least number of resources in the investigation and other operational costs. If AI is widely adopted for this purpose, it is likely to have a considerable impact on the reduction of fraudulent claims, and finally on the reliable operation of the insurance industry, as well as on the measures for its supervision (Choi et al., 2024). By becoming more adept at spotting fraud signals in the 70% to 80% of claims that are not fraudulent, as opposed to focusing on the 20% that are, insurers will create a much smoother claims experience for legitimate customers.

6.9 Conclusion

Artificial intelligence techniques hold great promise in further identifying suspicious claimants in insurance settings, thus allowing industry experts to devise further investigation plans regarding these individuals. The potential for improving insurance fraud detection ahead of actual investigators with the administration of suitable AI techniques is maximized by their development for case-specific needs and concerns. The need for the balancing of such predictive power with specific ethical concerns is driven, in great part, by the fact that AI techniques are generally seen as black-box systems with respect to the real-world processes. As such, the predictive similarities that different AI systems might develop and that might be optimal for certain datasets are potentially pointing toward different explanations for each of the systems that are due to the different preprocessing, feature extraction, or other custom hand-engineering techniques adopted in the designs and implementations of these systems. Human society has very different tolerance levels with respect to punitive actions against wrongdoers, let alone their classification, as compared to setting policies to regulate the collection and dissemination of information regarding non-wrongdoers, since the latter affects the privacy of the citizens. As such, the problem of modulating any degree of false positives is very different in the two cases. The case of the detection of wrongdoers with respect to their classification is no different, and as such, using AI raises different ethical concerns in the two branches of the insurance business processes. It is reasonable to believe that over time, as research in these applied ethical problems progresses, a general framework will arise, proposed perhaps by some mixture of policy experts, politicians, and lawyers that will apply to most business sectors.

References

Abdulkadir Isa, U. and Fernando, A. (2023). Explainable AI and Interpretable Model for Insurance Premium Prediction. *Journal on Artificial Intelligence*, *5*(0). https://doi.org/10.32604/jai.2023.040213

Alam, A.S.A.F., Begum, H., Masud, M.M., Al-Amin, A.Q. and Filho, W.L. (2020). Agriculture Insurance for Disaster Risk Reduction: A Case Study of Malaysia. *International Journal of Disaster Risk Reduction*, *47*. https://doi.org/10.1016/j.ijdrr.2020.101626

Arockiam, J.M. and Pushpanathan, A.C.S. (2023). MapReduce-Iterative Support Vector Machine Classifier: Novel Fraud Detection Systems in Healthcare Insurance Industry. *International Journal of Electrical and Computer Engineering*, *13*(1). https://doi.org/10.11591/ijece.v13i1. pp756–769

Bermúdez, L., Anaya, D. and Belles-Sampera, J. (2023). Explainable AI for Paid-Up Risk Management in Life Insurance Products. *Finance Research Letters*, *57*. https://doi.org/10.1016/j.frl.2023.104242

Braun, D. and Matthes, F. (2018). Generating Explanations for Algorithmic Decisions of Usage-Based Insurances Using Natural Language Generation. *Lecture Notes in Informatics (LNI)*, *P-279*.

Choi, J.H., Choi, Y., Lee, K.S., Ahn, K.H. and Jang, W.Y. (2024). Explainable Model Using Shapley Additive Explanations Approach on Wound Infection after Wide Soft Tissue Sarcoma Resection: "Big Data" Analysis Based on Health Insurance Review and Assessment Service Hub. *Medicina (Lithuania)*, *60*(2). https://doi.org/10.3390/medicina60020327

Ding, H. and Zuo, X. (2024). Construction of Insurance Consumers' Purchasing Behavior Model Based on Big Data Analysis. *Applied Mathematics and Nonlinear Sciences*, *9*(1). https://doi.org/10.2478/amns-2024-0006

Golden, L.L., Brockett, P.L., Ai, J. and Kellison, B. (2016). Empirical Evidence on the Use of Credit Scoring for Predicting Insurance Losses with Psycho-Social and Biochemical Explanations. *North American Actuarial Journal*, *20*(3). https://doi.org/10.1080/10920277.2016.1209118

Gramegna, A. and Giudici, P. (2020). Why to Buy Insurance? An Explainable Artificial Intelligence Approach. *Risks*, *8*(4). https://doi.org/10.3390/risks8040137

Jouini, O. and Sethom, K. (2023). AgriBIoT: A Blockchain-Based IoT Architecture for Crop Insurance. *Lecture Notes in Networks and Systems*, *655 LNNS*. https://doi.org/10.1007/978-3-031-28694-0_32

Margan, S.K. (2021). Drifting into Algocratic Insurance? In *The AI Book: The Artificial Intelligence Handbook for Investors, Entrepreneurs and FinTech Visionaries*. https://doi.org/10.1002/9781119551966.ch20

McDonnell, K., Murphy, F., Sheehan, B., Masello, L. and Castignani, G. (2023). Deep Learning in Insurance: Accuracy and Model Interpretability Using TabNet. *Expert Systems with Applications*, *217*. https://doi.org/10.1016/j.eswa.2023.119543

Muhammad, G. and Hossain, M.S. (2021). Deep-Reinforcement-Learning-Based Sustainable Energy Distribution for Wireless Communication. *IEEE Wireless Communications*, *28*(6). https://doi.org/10.1109/MWC.015.2100177

Murphy, S.D. and Moosa, S. (2021). The Views of Public Service Managers on the Implementation of National Health Insurance in Primary Care: A Case of Johannesburg Health District, Gauteng Province, Republic of South Africa. *BMC Health Services Research*, *21*(1). https://doi.org/10.1186/s12913-021-06990-4

Owens, E., Sheehan, B., Mullins, M., Cunneen, M., Ressel, J. and Castignani, G. (2022). Explainable Artificial Intelligence (XAI) in Insurance. In *Risks* (Vol. 10, Issue 12). https://doi.org/10.3390/risks10120230

Philip, B. and Suresh, G. (2024). Cultivating Resilience: An In-depth Exploration of Agricultural Insurance Initiatives and Their Transformative Role in India's Farming Landscape. *Universal Journal of Agricultural Research*, *12*(1). https://doi.org/10.13189/ujar.2024.120109

Pnevmatikakis, A., Kanavos, S., Matikas, G., Kostopoulou, K., Cesario, A. and Kyriazakos, S. (2021). Risk Assessment for Personalized Health Insurance Based on Real-World Data. *Risks*, *9*(3). https://doi.org/10.3390/risks9030046

Sachan, S. and Muwanga, J. (2023). Integration of Explainable Deep Neural Network with Blockchain Technology: Medical Indemnity Insurance. *CEUR Workshop Proceedings*, *3554*.

Shafik, W. (2024). Deep Learning Impacts in the Field of Artificial Intelligence. In *Deep Learning Concepts in Operations Research* (pp. 9–26). Auerbach Publications. https://doi.org/10.1201/9781003433309-2

Shafik, W., Kalinaki, K., Fahim, K.E. and Adam, M. (2024). Safeguarding Data Privacy and Security in Federated Learning Systems. In *Federated Deep Learning for Healthcare* (pp. 170–190). CRC Press. https://doi.org/10.1201/9781032694870-13

Shi, X. and Gan, L. (2023). Equilibrium in Competitive Insurance Markets with Medical Tourism. *Studies in Microeconomics*, *11*(2). https://doi.org/10.1177/23210222211051439

Wall, J. (2022). *Keynote Speech 4: A Conversational AI Approach to Detecting Deception and Tackling Insurance Fraud.* https://doi.org/10.1109/icicis52592.2021.9694118

Wu, Q., Ma, H., Sun, J., Liu, C., Fang, J., Xie, H. and Zhang, S. (2023). Application of Deep-Learning-Based Artificial Intelligence in Acetabular Index Measurement. *Frontiers in Pediatrics*, *10*. https://doi.org/10.3389/fped.2022.1049575

7

Dynamic Pricing and Personalization: Ethical Implications of Behavioral and Big Data in Premium Models

Wasswa Shafik

7.1 Introduction

Dynamic pricing (DP) describes a practice within marketing where prices for products and services are charged that reflect deficiencies and are above the actual value of the product or service offered to customers, for example, in times of emergency or impossibility. The rationale behind this practice is that a product or service is the most valuable to customers in certain emergencies or shortage situations. These situations are rare but are connected with high customer willingness to pay, for example, for companies that fly stranded customers back to their homes with special flights. An example of companies that apply a dynamic pricing strategy during a crisis is American Airlines, which applied surge pricing during the holiday season out of New York, which is a popular destination in times of crisis. Crisis pricing includes different possible price manipulation strategies, especially if the company possesses monopoly power during the crisis. They differentiate between monopoly prices, crisis profit prohibition, price gouging, charging excessive prices, price discrimination, and surge pricing (Papachristou et al., 2023). This context highlights significant ethical issues discussed within this chapter.

Shared economy platforms like Airbnb or Uber mostly apply demand-based dynamic pricing, which is derived from commodity and paper money pricing in the 19th century. However, academic research has deals with dynamic pricing since the late 1970s. The first market examples for the model of perfect information have occurred since the 1950s. The theoretical foundations are dynamic programming, real options pricing, and price discrimination. The first systematic empirical studies on dynamic pricing were conducted in the fields of rail transport and hotels, although transport companies like Southwest Airlines had already applied dynamic pricing in the 1980s. Due to modern technologies, many industries apply dynamic pricing today. For online book retailers, dynamic pricing is part of their core value proposition. However, in summer 1999, Amazon externalized its recommender system to promote co-purchases since it produced problems due to the high fluctuation of prices (Gumz et al., 2022). At the same time, the recommender system also drives co-purchase suggestions of online book retailers.

7.1.1 Definition and Concepts

Introduced in 2004, dynamic pricing describes a practice by which "the prices of goods and services vary with the level of demand." This means that a single consumer does not have to pay the same

DOI: 10.1201/9781003747659-7

price for the same product at the same time. Its introduction is made possible through recently developed technologies that allow service providers to collect and analyze large amounts of user data. In practice, e-commerce companies, airline booking platforms, hospitality companies, or ride-sharing platforms apply the concept of dynamic pricing. Dynamic pricing is also known as personalized pricing, second-degree price discrimination, first-degree price discrimination, or personalized pricing (Franzén, 2023).

Dynamic pricing as a new business model is, unlike traditional business models such as the premium or freemium models, characterized by mass or uncoordinated giving. It provides no palpable relationship between the providers and their consumers. However, what sets apart the dynamic pricing from some other business models that apply the concept of maximizing long-term profits through mass or uncoordinated giving is that they exist without any ulterior motive. In principle, the dynamic pricing model may be described as a "money-maximizing policy...which sells so far at a discount price that its total revenues are maximized, but no farther." Put differently, the purpose of dynamic pricing is not necessarily to build long-term relationships with consumers but to achieve a goal (the maximization of revenue) in the short term. Yet, service providers pursuing a long-term perspective while engaging in practices of dynamic pricing likely succeed. With these characteristics in mind, we wish to add that we do not consider the practice of price discrimination as unethical per second (Dida et al., 2023). Price discrimination can be understood as the practice of charging different prices for the same product without a difference in the cost associated with its production.

7.1.2 Historical Context

Catching up with the evolutionary path of dynamic pricing provides significant informational value on the origins of its technological, commercial, and ethical dimensions. The historical snapshots outlined in the following text present numerous examples of the various traditional forms of dynamic pricing in operation long before the era of the Internet and big data. This may come as a surprise to observers in search of relatively recent predecessors with few experiencing these earlier practices. Whereas it has become commonplace to associate the emergence of dynamic pricing with modern technological possibilities, such as the real-time use of big data, artificial intelligence (AI), and algorithmic decision systems, it is significant to recognize that dynamic pricing has a much longer history, and one which had become deeply rooted in the commercial practices of selected industries long before the creation of the Internet. In fact, the origins of dynamic pricing appear to date back to the ancient Greeks. Among the many examples presented are merchants who charged different prices for textiles depending on the distance the customers had come from: the same store would employ price distinctions for buyers who lived different distances from the store, while it would add a different price depending on how wealthy the customer was believed to be. Today, we refer to professional services as typically suggesting a personalized pricing model to the extent that lawyers or doctors are charged according to the service provided and the time and resources expended, along with other variables in the pricing model, such as the wealth of the client (Walker, 2020). Newspapers began utilizing segmented pricing models long before the arrival of the Internet, with out-of-town papers charging higher prices than those serving local readers on the basis that the subsidized local editions were as good, and with possible development costs of the paper broken down between the advertisers and the readers. Another of the earliest forms of dynamic pricing was the advanced purchase discount based on the tiers as presented in Figure 7.1.

7.1.3 Technological Advancements

The changed state of affairs is best articulated: "The future is already here—it is just not evenly distributed." Demand and supply management systems, revenue management systems, yield

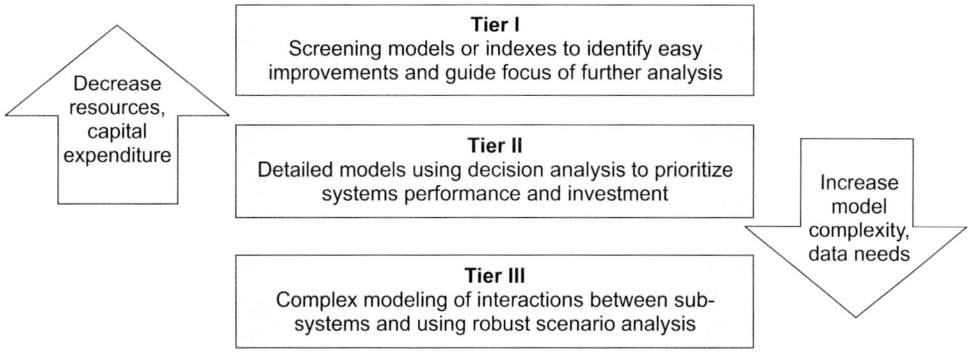

Fig. 7.1 The "three" tiers of insurance operations.

management, geo-fencing, and business intelligence have made it possible in practice to collect actuarial probabilities of all demand states for all supply states over long future time horizons. These systems capitalize on the interoperability of capabilities in credit card processing, geographic information systems, telecommunication, satellite, wireless technologies, and air travel systems. They rely on databases stocked with billions of transaction records. Credit card processors amass transaction details on individual customers, which flow into treasury databases of banks; major cardholders are retailers. Data on end consumers, including other service industries, go to their competing banks. Specialized companies build extensive aggregation databases and create customer profiles, providing privacy protection options. The sophistication of assessment of individual and group customer willingness to pay made available by modern analytics and business models—based on data sciences and the availability and reduction of costs of algorithm-guided computing—opens up a design space that was heretofore unthinkable for industries in consumer and business products and services, alongside non-for-profit organizations involved in public goods provisioning. Of particular importance are the technology advancements in communications and IT. Alongside the rapid advances in data collection, there have been huge strides in the collection and application of artificial-intelligence-based big data analytics (Hyun, 2022). The data are also used in combination with advanced algorithms that are increasingly quicker in processing customer clicks and adjusting prices using paywalls similar to testing, which allows personalized pricing in real time.

7.2 The Role of Big Data

The emergence and growing prevalence of big data—a cultural, technological, and scholarly phenomenon that rests on the interplay of technology, analysis, and the surreptitious nature of the data—have attracted both interest and criticism. As the technology and methods associated with big data have dramatically improved both in capability and accessibility, so too has its use in developing and implementing organizations' pricing strategies. However, a disconnect remains between big data methodologies available to market decision-makers and their corresponding consideration of ethical implications associated with the analysis of the data, particularly within the domain of pricing. The ability to develop and leverage big data strategies both at the organizational and individual levels creates ethical questions regarding transparency and information asymmetries. Data collection methods most commonly associated with big data are made possible through the digitalization of most aspects of our everyday lives, including web-based and mobile phone interactions, interactions via ubiquitous networks, and data generated by physical devices such as vehicles, medical equipment, and appliances (Moser et al., 2022). Individual actions online in the form of clicks, likes, comments, pins, shares, checks in, purchases, follows, and hashtags direct attention for sale to corporations that analyze and aggregate the information as a product.

Similarly, in build-your-own data models that allow users to self-serve, consumers become increasingly self-motivated to deliver information directly to organizations through promotion or discount incentives in the form of surveys, loyalty programs, and applications that provide organizations with immediate access to consumers' data. Collectively, data from these sources is stored in large, often complex, and unstructured databases. Analytical techniques associated with big data—particularly predictive modeling—also have a major influence on pricing decisions. The purpose of predictive modeling is to anticipate a specific outcome, usually to increase revenues, improve conversion rates, or reduce losses. Predictive models analyze patterns from historical data in order to inform future behavior, consumer perceptions, or decisions. Techniques such as offer recommendations and pricing optimization ensure the right message is reaching the right individual by allowing organizations to better tailor their interactions with each customer in real time, based on what they predict is the most relevant experience. The techniques and processes inherent in predictive modeling allow organizations to exploit pricing differentials magnified by the extensive use of digital channels and the personalized response model characteristic of premium pricing strategies (Papachristou et al., 2023).

7.2.1 Data Collection Methods

The segmentation of consumers based on preferences is an important issue for marketers. Traditionally, companies would rely on explicit consumer preference information; today, however, advanced analytics enables managers to infer consumer price sensitivity or product or service preference information by analyzing other consumer touchpoints. Over the years, data collection and analysis capabilities have vastly improved. While market researchers had previously had to publicly ask consumers many questions to gather data, wearable sensors, smartphones, and data-sharing have become commonplace. Through the ubiquitous technologies, governments and other organizations can observe and monitor consumer behavior remotely and imperceptibly, providing researchers with invaluable amounts of real-time data. In short, big data offers exciting new opportunities for consumer behavior research. Today, growth in both the quality and quantity of data available enables behavioral research questions to be addressed in ways that were previously impossible. It is now far easier to gather information on a larger scale, more quickly, and inexpensively. Simultaneously, the types of data available are growing exponentially, with more and better data on maintained information streams, active social networks, sensor technology, electronic transactions, mobile communications, digital credit systems, metadata, and research-sharing databases. In addition to the aforementioned developments in data, analysis capability is also advancing rapidly, using techniques not previously available, such as natural language processing techniques, text mining, network visualization, machine learning (ML), and model-based computational inference methods (Reuter et al., 2016). By dramatically expanding the horizons for the marketing science field, big data creates challenges, as well.

7.2.2 Data Analysis Techniques

In this chapter, we will present the available data analysis techniques for deriving insights supporting companies' pricing policies and enhancing the customer experience. We categorize these techniques, according to the data type, into two groups: statistical methods and machine learning approaches. We focus more on machine learning algorithms than on statistical ones, which have been extensively presented in other chapters. Statistical methods are widely used to explore big data and commonly include bivariate techniques such as t-tests, chi-square tests, and correlation measures. When examining multiple predictors, Analysis of Variance (ANOVA) or regression analysis are two methods most frequently applied, and special types of regression, such as time-series forecasting, logistic regression, and generalized additive models, are also used. Hierarchical linear modeling has the advantage of catching the multiple levels of customer data. When using big data, the number of predictors is usually large relative to the number of observations. Therefore, researchers apply penalties or compute principal component analysis in order to reduce dimensionality. Hierarchical modeling, approaches, and cross-validation methods have been introduced to the machine learning literature. The exponential growth of innovative machine learning techniques over the last few years has changed data science, enabling the analysis of massive amounts of customer data with software packages that require little prior knowledge of machine learning (Franzén, 2023; Gumz et al., 2022). The motivation and benefits of machine learning are well understood within the community, but have yet to leave the confines of the technical research community and make their way into practical guidance for applied researchers in economics and management.

7.2.3 Applications in Pricing Strategies

As emphasized in the market for experience goods, the selling firm has privileged access to qualitative information about the preferences and tastes of the interacting customer that, by its fading self-selection and switching costs, cannot easily recover or imitate. When combined with big data technology, this empirical qualitative position yields the implementability of specific pricing strategies that reward loyal customers by charging them individually lower prices, or, more generally, less than market-average prices, than casual customers. Conversely, third parties can easily use the same technology to detect more accurately the best offer in order to avoid incurring the potential reputation costs implied by negative feedback from disappointed experience-good consumers. Purchasing data, together with web-tracking tools, also allows the selling firm to estimate the price sensitivity of its customer base accurately (Dida et al., 2023). First, its web analytics tools enable it to evaluate the long-term elasticity of demand for a product with respect to its online price. Specifically, from the observed demand fluctuations associated with the time-specific realizations of the online price, it is possible to compute the time-invariant price elasticity of demand. By purchasing additional data on the customer characteristics that the firm does not collect on its own, it is then able to assess the cross-sectional heterogeneity of time-invariant price elasticities based on the customer characteristics at its disposal. Second, through the same web-tracking and purchasing data, a firm can also monitor the customer search behavior, that is, the comparison shopping that occurs before the final decision to buy, and the associated time-varying cost of search. In particular, a negative elapsed time between visits may be indicative of a shopping-around behavior (Hyun, 2022). Online search is indeed thought to be an important driver of price competition in markets with differentiated goods.

7.3 Behavioral Insights in Pricing

Today's flexible, service-driven, and advanced economies are replete with idiosyncratic opportunities and risks that brands face throughout the life cycle of a product. Various social media platforms and local e-commerce websites help consumers very easily communicate their wants and needs to marketers. They also contribute to nurturing hype and affinity behind brands that use these platforms smartly, and thus, actually build incentives behind pricing. Using the behavioral insights perspective of type M and type H promotion models, this section offers a review of the various behavioral price promotion strategies implemented successfully by research and by practitioners alike to widen the effectiveness of pricing and non-pricing promotion marketing, and to drive brand equity and build brand loyalty.

(i) Consumer Behavior Analysis: Although marketers have long practiced such behavioral price promotion strategies, a real "science" behind them has just gained attention in the last decade. A voluminous number of research pieces published have attempted to detect and identify "the idiosyncratic way hype" about consumer responses to various promotions across consumer subsegments. The major findings of this empirical body of research have indeed uncovered some consumer behavior axioms. For example, marketers should favor "general images," "flow state," "new event orchestrator," and/or "price promotion incentives" as instruments of "economic/affective signals" rather than directly felt "fun-feeling discounts." Percent-off promotions induce more short-term utility via the "shock effect" than upscale enhancing "hype-warranty" premiums do (Moser et al., 2022). But the ability of the latter to evoke policy-hinting optimally synchronized consumer actions, "inducements," surely outperforms the former.

(ii) Psychological Pricing Strategies: However, certain "hints" seem to spoil the latent strength of the "hype-warranty" premium strategy. For example, consumers seem to feel more hypersensitive about "price and promotion labelling schemes" when they are fleecing the retailer for their impulse purchasing wrath.

7.3.1 Consumer Behavior Analysis

A plethora of variables stimulate B2C buyers to choose one offer or another. Usually, marketing departments have to deal with years of gathered experience and put this knowledge into rules of thumb. They then deal with customer demand to implement a successful pricing strategy. With the rise of digitalization, major tech companies now export billions of dollars thanks to the intelligent use of algorithms and relevant data. These companies, however, are the exception to the rule. Most other firms still consider the application of algorithms and the use of data an exciting idea, but mostly do not manage to put them into practice due to a lack of resources, knowledge, or budget. However, these companies still have to deal with behavioral differences between inequality and equality aversion, identity and reference points, loss aversion, perceived value, and fairness that characterize their customers. The demand for more individualization of B2C goods and services remains the key driver for digitalization, as customers want to be addressed in a more resonant manner. Nevertheless, most companies operate under margin pressure and so far refrain from giving customers the requested attention. Behavioral insights into these specific circumstances of B2C sellers and buyers are helpful. The behavioral decision-making research branch goes back to the early work of a psychologist when he outlined his cognitive dissonance theory in the 1950s. Other seminal contributions came from various researchers, to name but a few. For a long time, consumer modeling of B2C demand was described more by conjectural rather than behavioral economics. The asymptotic growth of empirical research boosted insights into consumer habits and ideas (Jin et al., 2024). Large datasets allowed new modeling approaches to consumer choice, such as, among others, random utility modeling, factor analysis, and discrete choice analysis.

7.3.2 Psychological Pricing Strategies

The behavioral research on judgment and decision-making has revealed many fascinating insights on how individuals evaluate the world around them and how they form preferences. Pricing is also a part of this world, as consumers tend to rely on heuristics for price presentation, reduction, and comparison. While obviously not all consumers might react to pricing strategies in a way that can be predicted in advance, there are at least some general principles or insights regarding pricing strategies derived from psychological research that are worth highlighting. The first insight is price endings. First, the traditional prices ending with nine or, often, also five convey the message of being discount prices. This makes sense for stores that try to be the low-price sellers and that position themselves as being additionally cheaper than their competitors. The second idea is that it conveys the message of inexperience or the low quality of the item being sold. For instance, applying it to an expensive hotel or restaurant would look out of place. However, for luxury products, such as luxury automobiles or luxury watches, or high-end luxury hotels, using a nine-ending or five-ending price does not create the same "low quality" message as the idea of the hotel or restaurant conveys. The second area deals with price reductions during a shopping excursion. In fact, it might be quite shocking to discover how easily a retailer can change consumer evaluations of items during a shopping excursion by simply changing the type of pricing strategy that is applied or presented. And how expensive discounts might look if they are compared to the normal price. In fact, giving the retail customer the idea that he is receiving a particularly effective discount might go a long way toward positioning a store chain (Leitner-Hanetseder & Lehner, 2023; Nassar & Kamal, 2021a). For that reason, one can find many other price-based differences that might lead the consumer to compare different retail chains or retail outlets belonging to the same chain.

7.3.3 Case Studies of Successful Implementation

Numerous companies across various sectors have successfully implemented psychological pricing models. In retail, both Walmart and eBay have adopted odd–even pricing. Amazon is known to use charm pricing to appeal to consumers, and Gap applies price anchoring. In beauty, Estée Lauder has been found to use charm pricing and Lucky Brand to engage in price anchoring. Another example can be found in automotive, where Mercedes-Benz has recently developed a new way of engaging consumers with price anchoring, psychological pricing, and the use of social media influencers' weird offerings. Travel and entertainment have also witnessed personalized psychological pricing. Recently, some airlines have specially identified unserved flights and optimized their prices accordingly. Companies are now rethinking how to price their products and take a dual pathway approach to psychological pricing, using simpler pricing rules while addressing the complexity of user demand (Gligor et al., 2021). Lastly, B2B companies are rationalizing and optimizing customer-specific pricing by applying algorithms, behavior monitoring, and pricing best practices. Powered inclusive tech is developing new levels of dynamic pricing in three areas. First, for the budget constraints for low-capital customers whose trust in a new product reduces their perceived risk, there are new levels of odd offshore pricing being offered. Second, for the socioeconomic segmentation of big data and intelligent prospects, there are new levels of odd-neighbour pricing being offered based on social technological connectivity brand share. Third, for customers with a high willingness to pay but with a variable purchasing frequency, there are new levels of odd-opportunity pricing being offered that incentivize spontaneous product exploration. Finally, smart dynamic pricing using big data will offer consumers new levels of heuristic-driven sabbatical pricing that simplifies the complexity of pricing and focuses on the consumers' complementary or substitute purchases at specific times (Nassar & Kamal, 2021b). The marketing of products is more than just establishing a customer price; it is also important to consider how every other aspect of the marketing mix will impact consumer choice and purchase behavior mix as optimal capital pricing, as some sources of dynamics are presented in Table 7.1.

7.4 Personalization in Premium Models

In contrast to common products that come at lower or generalized price levels, premium offerings are intended for specific customer groups or even single customers. They provide matching experiences, adding-value benefits, or tailored solutions. These premium values need to include product quality, brand image, and extraordinary services that qualify the product to a unique final price in contrast to

Table 7.1 Sources of behavioral and big data in dynamic insurance pricing.

Data Source	*Collected Data Types*	*Use in Pricing Models*	*Ethical Concern*	*Mitigation Strategy*
Telematics (Auto Insurance)	Speed, braking, mileage, location	Risk scoring and dynamic premium adjustment	Location tracking, surveillance	Data minimization, informed opt-in
Wearables (Health Insurance)	Steps, sleep patterns, and heart rate	Incentivize healthy behavior, tailor premiums	Health data sensitivity, exclusion risk	Encrypted storage, opt-out choices
Smart Home Devices	Sensor data (smoke, intrusion, temperature)	Risk mitigation discounting	Data misuse, consent complexity	Explicit device-level consent
Social Media Activity	Posts, connections, lifestyle indicators	Risk inference through sentiment/ lifestyle analysis	Profiling, inferred traits without consent	Prohibit use without user-initiated sharing
Purchase and Financial Records	Spending patterns, transaction history	Credit-based risk analysis	Socioeconomic discrimination	Limit the use of financial proxies
Web Browsing History	Clickstream data, content interaction	Personalized offerings and pricing	Invasive data harvesting	Cookie transparency, user agency
Claim History and Interactions	Past claims, complaints, inquiries	Behavioral risk prediction	Penalization for honest claimers	Adjust scoring fairness over time
IoT Devices (General)	Device usage logs, environmental context	Preventive behavior modeling	Consent and scope of data use	Device-specific opt-in policies
Email/ Communication Metadata	Timing, frequency, tone (via NLP)	Behavioral profiling	Intrusion into private life	Restrict to user-facing communications
Mobile App Usage Patterns	App types, usage frequency, geo-tracking	Demographic and behavior profiling	Potential for implicit discrimination	Transparency in T&C and data dashboards
Credit Scores and Banking Data	Creditworthiness, loan history	Premium tier placement	Penalizes low-income users disproportionately	Multivariate fairness checks
Location and Mobility Tracking	Commute habits, visited zones	Risk exposure modeling (e.g., crime-prone areas)	Reinforces geographic bias	Regional normalization strategies
Public Records and Licenses	Driving record, licenses, convictions	Verified data for underwriting	Disparate treatment of marginalized populations	Contextualized adjustments
Online Reviews and Feedback	Tone of reviews, patterns in feedback	Trustworthiness proxy in shared economy insurance	Sentiment bias, misinterpretation	Exclude from the pricing model unless verified

competitive products, justifying the premium pricing. In many cases, premium service solutions such as extensive and personalized pre- and post-sales services are required. Apart from very exclusive offerings having a unique added-value proposition, the personalization of customer experience and solution management is the identifying factor of premium models (Urmila & Mamatha, 2024). The designer of product- and customer-side premium experiences has to find the ideal combination of how and to what extent the personalization should differentiate the customer experience from competitors' common solutions. Usually, the personalization process follows a four-stage structure using various technologies or psychological nudging techniques. First, customer segmentation is commonly based on simple criteria such as demographics, socioeconomics, location, company size, and industry, but they usually do not show adequate correlations to behavior, preferences, and consequences. Behavioral characteristics such as technology affinity, availability of assets, previous experiences, expectable future behaviors, as well as psychological profiles from big and behavioral data are applied to identify the behavioral clusters and segments with similar expectable reactions. Customer profiling based on primary, secondary, and behavioral data is the second stage. Customer propositions are developed and tested in the third stage, and the price hedonic demand development is confirmed in parallel. Based on the convincing results of these stages, personalized nudging or intervention and dynamic pricing become the final and ongoing controlling activity of the personalized revenue management process (Duchesneau et al., 2024).

7.4.1 Definition and Importance

The focus on consumer demands and a continual search for differentiation have led brands to seek ways to offer increasingly customized products and services. However, with a few exceptions, the initial novelty of personalization has somewhat lost its luster, resulting in significantly diminished returns. Consumers are becoming resistant to mass personalization, particularly in the digital realm. Given this context, it is interesting to consider what distinguishes premium brand personalization practices operating in markets characterized by an emphasis on quality, excellence, and prestige. Nearly all collaborating brand managers mentioned the importance of developing a deep understanding of the consumer and referred to the growing sophistication and variety of data sources at their disposition in collecting consumer insights for this purpose. However, with the notable exception of the increasingly prominent brand models, premium brands are often creating personalized experiences for what they perceive to be homogeneous target segments (Papachristou et al., 2023). Consequently, it is important to determine what effective personalization looks like in the context of premium brands and one-off luxury brands, and what data-driven techniques these brands are deploying. The apparent ubiquity of segmentation leads many to ignore its importance both as a discipline in itself and as a critical component in the new era of big data. Underlying all commercialism is the expectation that organizations will tailor solutions and experiences to the true wants and needs of specific consumer groups as opposed to delivering standardized products that seek mass adoption. Indeed, recently published accounts of the enormous data analysis efforts undertaken by popular brands demonstrate the centrality of data and advanced algorithms in fulfilling this promise. For premium brands that are generally not oriented toward a model, there is often the added complexity of trying to gather consumer data over multiple touchpoints in order to arrive at a clear identification of consumer program needs and desires (Reuter et al., 2016). Even if a premium or luxury brand is executing multiple touchpoints online, it typically does not control the entire consumer journey.

7.4.2 Techniques for Effective Personalization

Personalization in premium business models requires a careful definition of the criteria by which customers are differentiated. Choices also often depend on a specific firm's competitive strategy. Some characteristics can be employed swiftly to personalize a product or service at limited costs, while differences in taste that are difficult and costly to identify, be it documentable attributes or even choices seen along customers' lifetime, provide the basis for a most rewarding long-term customer relationship. No personalized offer can become a long-term market success unless it at least keeps pace with customers' evolving needs and preferences over time, regardless of whether these are determined by age or life-cycle effects, changes in living or purchasing conditions, or simply by temporary trends and fads. Keenly devised personalization techniques or mechanisms have become a matter of life and death for many firms (Gumz et al., 2022). A common mechanism to define, elaborate, and implement customer differentiation can be found in customer relationship management approaches. Various models and techniques exist that capture customer lifetime or value for a specific firm, project the evolution of a specific customer relationship over time based on prior transaction history, and eventually allow for precisely forecasting response probabilities to personalized offers. These models can rely on transactional data relating to prior purchases as well as detailed attributes on a customer or segments of customers' characteristics and buying processes. The predictive power of various models has recently been explored to optimize decision-making, such as determining optimal prices and price changes, for personalized airfare pricing. In doing so, better-fitting models involving insightful data also help achieve a better understanding of a firm's customers, using Managed Detection and Response (MDR) as presented in Figure 7.2. Such personalized decision-making approaches are already widely employed by airline companies as a key factor for their limited-price-variability strategy using the MDR approach (Walker, 2020).

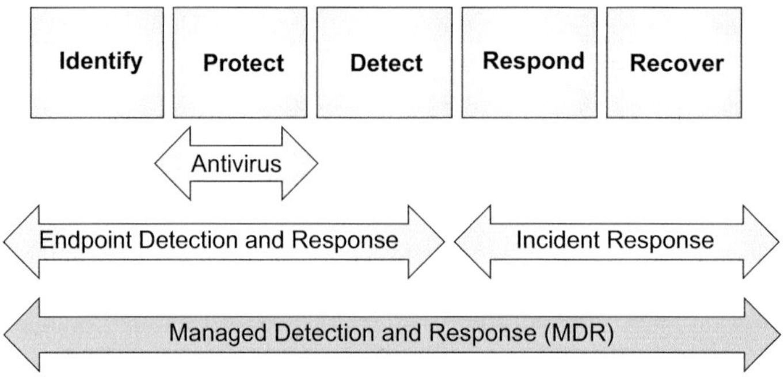

Fig. 7.2 The MDR.

7.5 Challenges and Limitations

Despite the fascinating potential brought by behavioral and big data to improve a premium model's personalization strategy and increase its associated revenue, careful considerations have to be made to install any personalization at risk of infringing privacy and ethical implications. To navigate these challenges and limitations, first, corporate accountability should not only be restricted to applying the cybersecurity category of safeguards that prevent unauthorized access, but also take proactively preventive measures to ensure that the collected data is irretrievable. These restrictions should not only be based on technical solutions, such as hardware and software in order to keep the information safe from others, especially hackers and improper use by the data controller, but on strict transparency requirements that allow consumers to limit their participative discretion in an imbalance of control over data collection and its further use, otherwise dubbed the Faustian bargain. Second, ethical characteristics of hoarding and distributive justice should be addressed. Not all consumers are safe to be very sensitive contributors of their engagement. If their secret is exploited, furthermore redistributing value through personalized offers—solely based on individual profiling and favor from subsets of high-consuming customers—affects their reputation. Or, do they feel exploited, commodified, and disrespected when loyalty is offered against one-time nudging, to die among other products brought to their attention (Moser et al., 2022; Nassar & Kamal, 2021a)? Finally, if consumer welfare depends on selective practices, the engagement booth hosts knowledge acquisition in either direction, eventually without duties either neural or extra-monetary. A balance of trade deficits, where transfer payments circulate over unequal bases of reciprocity among socioeconomic categories, benefits some and harms others; given selective equality, distributors should abide by collective conditions of commercial equality, complying with behaviors similarly in all sales, be it seen to consumers or by monetary surging to decision agents.

7.6 Ethical Considerations

Models are commonly used to justify the existence and allow operating premium models that employ differential privacy prices and explicative variables that allow estimating demand and thus the maximum willingness to pay. This is done assuming enough homogeneity among customers in order to avoid selling at a loss to consumers on the premium tier or overexploitation of consumers on the discount tier. Several ethical aspects arise from the use of DP in price personalization, data privacy, the trust of users toward a company that tracks their data, unequal treatment, and discrimination (Leitner-Hanetseder & Lehner, 2023).

(i) Big data in premium models enables highly personalized prices so that customers can be treated unequally based on their type and hopes. The price would presumably be highly inelastic. Being a once-in-a-lifetime event, the supplier may be charging a price based on the average event price elasticity. But given acting utilitarianism, if unequal treatment provides the firm the highest surplus, it feels pragmatic to support it with possible resulting short- or even longer-term upsets. Utilitarianism supports any act of fact as long as the benefits outweigh the costs; DP can be considered unethical. This is particularly the case if too much surplus is expected from tracking the data to personalize prices, and nothing is passed on to the consumer who generated the amount passing on.

(ii) Data privacy has gained momentum in mass communication and significant steps are being taken with regulations. This means that if the customer is not willing to share his or her data for free, the consumer should receive some discount. If such data are thus high, why would a firm not just provide the customer with linear prices. Ultimately exists the hierarchical approach to utilitarianism, as the firm benefits by just obtaining what was invested by analysis, using its understanding of the consumer to increase the likelihood to connect with the customer. Too much possession of a company can lead to ethical issues.

7.6.1 Privacy Concerns

Dynamic pricing holds the potential to violate consumers' privacy by collecting granular information about their preferences, price sensitivity, and willingness-to-pay. By doing so, businesses may create highly detailed consumer profiles, which may include sensitive information. While such information is used to ensure higher conversion rates for online purchases, at the same time it is on the border of ethical and legal grounds on how much information needs to be disclosed when collecting and using information about consumers. Targeted display ads are known to track consumers throughout all interests and previously visited websites, triggering ads for similar items or categories, which are stored in data warehouses and data lakes accessible to both companies and third-party vendors. Most disclosure statements, which consumers cannot bypass, only disclose that their data will in some form be shared, sold, or leased for analytical and marketing purposes. They never disclose who would gain access to that information and thus are primarily designed to navigate the fine line between ethical and legal use of information (Gligor et al., 2021). The use of information to influence future behaviors, including the nudging behavior, is prone to therefore bordering manipulation since companies use the same data-driven analytical methods to elevate profitability than with the social-science-glass paradigm that those companies aim to violate.

7.6.2 Transparency and Consumer Trust

Dynamic pricing relies on technology-mediated algorithms, which operate in a black-box manner. As the rationale of price differentiation is concealed for consumers, their information might appear exploitative. The difficulty to inspect algorithmic decisions and the appropriation of pricing without enhancing added value is likely to remove consumers' confidence in the pricing strategy. However, transparency concerning the adjustment of pricing mechanisms by suppliers, especially for personalized settings, can foster confidence. With the increased adoption and reliance on big data strategies, questions of ethical business decisions arise. Various recommendations on how to employ big data exist, and methods are proposed that can handle the ethical implications for decision-making. Pricing and personalization strategies could indicate power distance and lack of trust between supplier and consumer. Accordingly, a differentiation exists whether big data use is bilateral or unilateral. In the latter case, a more careful examination suggests the promotion of the idea of potential trust gain through personalization techniques (Mukhopadhyay et al., 2024). Similarly, it is stated that transparency is one of the major triggers of consumer trust and engagement.

Trust and goodwill between supplier and consumer may play a role even stronger than criticisms on privacy violations. For example, if the supplier asks consumers to reveal personal information when they feel their privacy is being threatened and consumers comply with it, this may indicate a higher trust level. This is backed by the indication that higher customer-related data collection and higher commitment can lead to more trust. It is stated that consumers are more favorable toward ads tailored with their external information than general ads if trust in the company is higher and the company has used their information for a longer period. This indicates that the effects of personalized marketing on consumer attitudes can differ not only along consumer characteristics but also depend on the type of products involved, how the ads are identified, and how they are aimed at consumers (Giannakopoulos et al., 2024). Given this context, we discuss the role of trust and transparency concerning the behavioral bias toward pricing methods.

7.6.3 Fairness and Discrimination

Recent research has indicated that machine learning algorithms can discriminate against certain groups in society, with serious ethical implications. Discrimination can exist even if the algorithm is not expressly choosing to discriminate. For example, implementing a pricing algorithm based on customer behavioral data can lead to customers in different regions of a city paying different prices for the same product. Customers from lower-income neighborhoods are likely to be targeted and to pay more if their behavior is characterized by more visits to the store, more extensive review reading about a specific product category, spending more time browsing over long periods, and more interactions with customer service. Dynamic pricing applied in certain industries has the potential to hurt disadvantaged and sensitive individuals and groups (Aldboush & Ferdous, 2023). For example, implementations of price discrimination in the airline and hotel industry can lead to customers who have less mobile work schedules—such as lower-income customers (receiving the least financial benefit from price discounts and reductions)—dealing with the biggest price differences while those who are capable of paying higher prices enact price discrimination as they are allowed to book flights or hotel rooms at higher prices. The same implications exist with respect to discriminatory marketing measures based on user behavior on the web. For example, an online discount retailer might charge higher prices for the same items to loyal customers, viewing them as being willing to pay a premium price. This kind of price discrimination seems rather cruel and unacceptable. Nevertheless, although questionably ethical, this strategy would not be illegal. However, whose interests are being served? A member of a group possesses more consumer surplus than a member of another group, but the reverse is true when considering the entire group. The plane's belly cargo space, with its corresponding excess capacity, can certainly be thought of as a repository of storage vertically dedicated to less affluent travelers who can fill that space only with much lower prices than more affluent travelers flying in the cabin (Hulsen et al., 2023).

7.7 Regulatory Framework

Since the nutshell report of the committee published in 1977, which emphasized the concept of ethical marketing and recommended to put a special badge on advertising messages liable to manipulate people at risk of persuasion, ranging from the disregarded to the cognitively limited, marketing manipulations have been extensively regulated at a specific community level in a wide variety of branches. These regulations mainly originate from the elaboration of various codes of ethics by chambers of commerce and by trade unions and other stakeholders in other countries. These codes are entry points for the clauses of business contracts or collective contracts. By screening, analyzing, and clustering these codes, categories related respectively to marketing manipulations or ethical topics of research are elaborated, and a database is built. Here emerge two potential considerations about these marketing regulations. The first is related to hygiene factors for ethical marketing (Papachristou et al., 2023). A charter for a "New Helsinki" was issued, whose primary objective is to propose clear and transparent rules in the digital world, aiming for a collective harmony prosperous for all and beneficial for all the actors of the digital economy. This neutrality and transparency are also present in the communication strategy of major tech companies, which concentrates on the operation of a program to finance the activities of publishers, respecting the aforementioned ethical commitment. The second consideration concerns behavioral targeting, since it presents many solutions for the ethical issue faced by digitized firms in today's economy. On the one hand, it considers the firm as a guardian against risks of manipulation—this is the principle known as "relative responsibility of the consumer"—by configuring the online experience according to the values to be respected by the advertising industry, values which are objectified by the audience of the interested publishers (Walker, 2020).

7.7.1 Current Regulations

One of the most important laws governing privacy and security in the United States is the Privacy Act of 1974. The act limits the use of data by federal agencies. It requires that all federal agencies "give the public notice of the existence and character ... of the systems of records ... maintained," and that they make no "use ... of the information in the system of records for ... a purpose or purposes other than the ... purposes ... for which it was collected." Given the limited breadth of the act, many federal agencies have ignored these requirements and have increased the amount of data that they leak to private entities. The act is also quite out of date and is missing protections for digital data storage leaks from the private sector. Sparing any severe changes, the act would appear not to help protect any present personal information use systems. In the private sector, the primary law governing the operation of websites is a law that governs the collection of data from children online, prohibits disclosure of identifiable census data, prohibits certain entities from disclosing health-related information, and governs the collection and sale of personal financial data. In addition to these regulations, statutes allowing a private right of action for data misuse allow certain entities to sue companies for misuse, including lawsuits against data brokers, and violations of securities law can trigger the use of debugging security checks to mitigate algorithmic market abuse (Jin et al., 2024). These laws regulate only limited facets of the data maintenance systems that have formed around dynamic pricing and personalization, and their auxiliary systems.

7.7.2 Proposed Changes

We would rename the terms "adverse selection" and "moral hazard" as "behavior management" and "data manipulation", respectively. The intent is, respectively, to advocate, on the one hand, limiting and/or preventing the adverse manipulation of consumer behavior by companies via AI and big data applications, and to set ethical and transparency limits to the negative bias of consumers, whereby they seek to manipulate the system to their advantage. Disclosure and transparency should be respected in both directions. Marketers have the responsibility of avoiding negative bias. On the other hand, consumers must not abuse it. The two-way mandatory information collaboration should apply equally to dynamic pricing, personalization, and product/service quality (Gligor et al., 2021; Leitner-Hanetseder & Lehner, 2023). The capability to avoid data manipulation and abuse should be implied in consumer protection regulations.

(i) The regulation of dynamic pricing and personalization (DP&P) de jure recommended that strategies against DP&P negative biases should be discussed as an extension to the principles for ethical, moral, and consumer protection in data-driven marketing models provided by the several codes and charters of marketing conduct currently used de facto. Current documents on marketing ethics do not normally mention the possible manipulation of consumers´ behavior in one direction, but should adapt to the dynamic pricing and big data context.

(ii) Regulation on transparency and ethical calibration of DP&P requests would suggest the adoption of clear procedures for data collection and methods to avoid their possible biasing. They would also have to set up practical ethical guidelines to avoid discrimination by avoiding self-fulfilling prophecies triggered by price positioning and DP&P decisions. The proposed regulations would clarify the limits of sharing and monitoring consumer information as far as employed decisions are biased; and prior warn that consumer consent would be required for sensitive segmented vigilant pricing and segmentation strategies.

7.7.3 Global Perspectives on Regulation

Cultural and traditional anchors are the steel cables that guide and regulate modern transactions at a personal level. For different countries and peoples, for different majorities and voting blocs, and at different stages in the economic cycle, these regulate the transaction. In the initial days of the internet, for example, targets went free. However, as predicted by some modern schools of economics, there was continued panic regarding privacy considerations during transactional activities. Primary inducements for the development of these artificial regulations are the exacerbated inequalities in wealth and income distribution within nations, or the unequal exploitation of artificial inequalities internationally between nations, although many of the developing nations are creating, controlling, and profiting from completely new models of business and guides for action. Attempts by various governments have recently been made to regulate personalization and targeted advertisement fraudulently creating enhanced revenues for websites through noncontingent theft, or thievery of tradable cultural or traditional properties of nations and collectives of peasant producers (Nassar & Kamal, 2021b). Legislation in progress flows out of the increasing user and media pressure by governments—for example, the Digital Markets Act and Digital Services Act, respectively, the statement that AI-guided action shall not be inappropriate, or the rules proposed on targeted ads on gambling and food delivery.

7.8 Future Trends in Dynamic Pricing

Dynamic pricing has become a widespread and popular practice pioneered by airlines and adapted for sport and entertainment event ticketing, hotel room, rental car, and e-commerce sales, to name a few. The state-of-the-art of dynamic pricing system architecture commonly includes analytic functionalities, yield management algorithms, change management, price realization, and price-sensitive customer profiler. System architecture development investments have been largely compensated and at the same time propelled by the sales and revenue growth of the related sectors. Predicted social and technological developments will likely continue to refine the DP system architecture and the key properties of the prevailing industry models and selected applications. Emerging technologies, such as mobile computing and real-time analytics, fundamentally alter the economics of the dynamic pricing model implementation (Urmila & Mamatha, 2024). Evolving consumer expectations nurture the development of new DP models for new classes of products and services, such as experience goods, in a growing number of industries, such as banking and insurance, where dynamic pricing is still in its infancy. The captivating consequences of possible penetration of dynamic pricing on the experience-goods-related market structure, performance, and evolution make it a particularly interesting application. At the same time, publicity subsidies may alter consumer expectations about the management of price customization, making that a two-way road, with customers as well as businesses adjusting price-perception-related behavior. Market concentration and dynamic pricing are related in an intriguing way. Price discrimination is about charging different prices to different customers. Dynamic pricing is a specific variable pricing implementation model when consumers are inquiring or trying the product or service before committing themselves to an ex-post decision to purchase. The increased economies of scale linked to the applications of high-fixed-cost, high-volume, low-profit-margin premium business models rely on a high frequency of dynamic pricing and third-party purchase monitoring (Mukhopadhyay et al., 2024). These considerations suggest that Date of Services (DOSs) pray for low levels of DP third-party intervention, wanting to be perceived as implementing a well-orchestrated strategy of accepted DP for direct purchase only, in the highly established market concentration of monopolistic competition cases.

7.8.1 Emerging Technologies

Understanding the impact of emerging technologies on future trends in dynamic pricing can help businesses prepare for the possible challenges that could arise. The development of sophisticated technologies has enabled the automation and optimization of pricing operations. Such technologies include artificial intelligence and machine learning, customer-centric recommendation systems, and blockchain technology. The use of AI algorithms has made the prediction of consumer behavior more efficient and accurate, and allows for product pricing in real time, which was impossible before. With rapid advances made in big data analytics and sensor technology, optimal pricing decisions can be made based on changing external environmental conditions in real time (Aldboush & Ferdous, 2023).

Recently developed complex and heuristic algorithms mimic expert pricing decisions, which would previously have required significant time and effort to emulate. Moreover, AI and machine learning have transformed businesses and consumers' daily lives, creating opportunities and challenges across sectors from manufacturing to transportation. In fact, pricing influence through recommendation systems such as triggered email, personalization, browsing behavior, collaborative filtering, and user characteristics offers an insight into the likely future use of AI in dynamic pricing. Lately, recommendation engine algorithms have become the stimulus for impulse buying, not only for books but also for groceries, apparel, jewelry, and electronics. Blockchain technology can facilitate trust and transparency in consumer–business transactions. In addition, it can overcome the threats by possessing one entity, such as a company, that controls all the data related to blockchain technology. For example, centralized networks can lose data, which could be sold for prices much lower than their true value, creating their crisis (Reuter et al., 2016).

7.8.2 Evolving Consumer Expectations

An important factor determining the optimal business model of a company is consumer behavior, which is continuously changing, especially in recent times. While traditional behavioral economics presumed that consumers strive toward maximum economic utility, contrary results have been documented by various empirical studies. Consumer expectations can diverge from economic maximization motives, leading to brand loyalty and equity, with consumers accepting lower price/performance ratios than competing offerings. These discrepancies between pricing models and consumer preferences can have a strong impact on the pricing power of organizations that are acting rationally. With an increase in online access to useful news and data, it is likely to assume that consumer behavior evolves toward rationalist maximizing strategies (Franzén, 2023). However, the success of premium and luxury models in the digital world is based on innovative services and a brilliant communication strategy. Digital services generate strong interest among consumers, and their rapidly evolving expectations are not solely based on pricing but also encompass strong wishes regarding product and service quality, exclusivity, and convenience. Companies are confronted with the challenge of meeting these demands driven by their digital concept while still justifying high price levels and margins to their customers. An open question is to what degree the new forms of demand, enhanced by advanced digital and social technology-enabled services and products, including artificial intelligence, will affect the balance between brand equity and consumer behavior toward digital exchanges in the luxury and premium markets, separating them from traditional goods and services. Potentially, companies in these segments become redundant or cannot manage the new service requirements imposed by consumers anymore, losing their right to charge high price levels (Moser et al., 2022).

7.8.3 Potential Impact on Market Dynamics

Dynamic pricing is a powerful demand management tool for allocative efficiency, which has long been argued to increase total market welfare. Yet, the introduction of dynamic pricing has in parts led to a decline in the level of discounted prices in the market. The overall effect of variable pricing on consumer benefits remains ambiguous. Promotions are on the decrease; however, the periods around which promotional discounting is less intensive may come to represent alpha and omega for brand owners with financially driven investment criteria. Overall balance sheets indicate a mixed picture with parts of traditional industries economizing on promotional spending and newer electronic industries stepping up their targeting. The long-term effects of big data and micro targeting on pricing dynamics, promotional levels, and consumer price expectations are among the many open questions. These uncertain market dynamics are caused by the rapidly changing operating environment due to digitalization and disruptive technologies. Profitability of traditional industries is increasingly dependent on promotional activities, which aim to protect revenue and customer base. The increased involvement of big data, micro targeting, and machine learning in personalization pricing strategies has not so far been able to find a lasting inverse relationship to promotional intensity despite the preposition of a potential double optimization effect stemming from more granular consumer profiles (Nassar & Kamal, 2021a). What is true, however, is that personalized DP systems have explicit potential to tackle the retailer dilemma regarding profit reversal under DP. Generating rich first-party data from loyalty programs can reduce the chances of the competition finding and serving price-sensitive consumers when introducing DP, as presented in Table 7.2.

7.9 Case Studies

In this chapter, we develop cases and examples from different markets, industries, and types of pricing strategies. To the best of our knowledge, no study has yet developed an overview of diverse

Table 7.2 Ethical challenges and design strategies in dynamic premium modeling.

Ethical Challenge	*Description*	*Risk in Practice*	*Design Principle/ Strategy*	*Example Tool/ Approach*
Price Discrimination	Charging different prices based on personal data	Penalizes high-risk groups unfairly	Fairness-aware pricing frameworks	IBM AI Fairness 360, Fairlearn
Lack of Transparency	Users are unaware of the pricing logic or data use	Distrust, poor informed consent	Explainable pricing algorithms	SHAP (SHapley values), model cards
Consent Ambiguity	Vague or bundled consent for behavioral data	Undermines autonomy	Granular, modular consent options	Privacy dashboards, consent management platforms
Exclusion of Vulnerable Groups	Algorithms may exclude high-risk or non-digital users	Insurance inaccessibility	Inclusive design, minimal viable coverage	Social impact audits
Proxy Discrimination	Using variables that indirectly encode sensitive traits	Hidden bias, algorithmic redlining	Adversarial debiasing, proxy detection	AI auditing pipelines (e.g., What-If Tool)
Over-Personalization	Treating customers as data profiles rather than individuals	Narrow service access or manipulation	Human-centric personalization	Context-aware personalization frameworks
Regulatory Noncompliance	Breach of data laws (e.g., GDPR – General Data Protection Regulation, CCPA – California Consumer Privacy Act, DPIA – Data Protection Impact Assessment)	Legal and reputational consequences	Compliance-by-design architectures	Automated audit logs and DPIA tools
Inequitable Data Access	Large firms access richer data ecosystems	Market concentration, reduced competition	Data-sharing with ethical governance	Federated learning consortia
Overreliance on Prediction	Penalizing predicted, not actual, behavior	Preemptive denials or pricing	Include corrective pathways and appeals	Transparent appeals process with human oversight
Model Drift and Unfair Outcomes	Model behavior changes over time due to new data	Unexpected discrimination	Regular fairness and performance reviews	Model monitoring platforms (e.g., Evidently AI)
Feedback Loop Amplification	Reinforces patterns from past data	Bias perpetuation (e.g., same groups flagged again)	Counterfactual simulation and bias flipping tests	Data shift diagnostics and rebalancing
Ethical Oversight Deficiency	Limited multidisciplinary review	Narrow, tech-centric decision-making	Cross-functional ethics boards	Algorithmic impact assessments (AIA)
Manipulative Pricing Practices	Adjusting pricing to nudge behavior or spending	Exploits behavioral vulnerabilities	Ethical nudging, transparency of intent	Behavioral-science-informed ethical review
Lack of an Appeals Mechanism	No recourse to challenge personalized premiums	Perceived injustice	Human-in-the-loop appeals with full rationale	Explainability dashboards for customer support

experiences with dynamic pricing of consumer goods using behavioral data, nor the personalization approach to dynamic pricing. The examples listed in this chapter are selected not just because of the industries/pricing strategies they represent, but also because each of them carries unique lessons. Some of these lessons are things that the implementation teams "did right." Others are lessons learnt from mistakes or oversights committed in the trials recounted. Unlike most papers in the field of pricing, we use empirical case studies to examine the market response to consumer pricing research. The rationale for our approach is simple. Only a small number of companies have used dynamic pricing models of consumer behavior (Gligor et al., 2021). Testing the predictions of market response models against choice data in these test markets (especially at the model-building stage) is difficult, since price responsiveness is influenced by many factors that are rarely modeled, and many of which are not constant across demand estimations. However, real-world implementations offer more realistic testing grounds for larger and more complex restrictions on consumer purchasing behavior pricing models.

7.9.1 Successful Implementations

Dynamic pricing and personalization have penetrated virtually every industry today, but their implementations in certain markets stand out for their success and exposure. Ride-sharing service operates on the basis of dynamic geo-temporal demand forecasting models. In this particular case, its success does not stem from devising novel algorithms for predicting demand, but from being the first mover in a market that grew rapidly and considerably already. With real-time, whenever-you-need-it access to transportation services, citizens largely accepted ever-changing pricing, with dynamic pricing reputed to guarantee faster pickups. In comments that echo during the other case studies outlined in this section, the implementation has met mixed opinions among economists and wider audiences. While many praise its introduction of surge pricing, which allows price increases during peak-demand periods, fundamentally re-allocating resources to the most productive uses, others lament how surge prices can burn significant amounts of cash within minutes, nay, seconds (Urmila & Mamatha, 2024). Entertainment streaming platforms that retail access to large libraries of music and audiovisual content have taken discounting or dynamic pricing and personalization methods for customer segmentation to extremes. These case studies typically revolve around either discounting or personalization for customer segmentation in subscription-based income models—the two methodologies are similar if users churn during the lifetime of a subscription—and have met largely positive reception among both economists and consumers alike. The implementations entail mass adoption of data-driven techniques for pricing at many different levels—product-specific prices, customer-segment-specific pricing, and geo-location-specific pricing (Giannakopoulos et al., 2024).

7.9.2 Failures and Lessons Learned

Cases where dynamic pricing has backfired, particularly when coupled with inadequate consideration for behavioral issues of customers, teach valuable lessons about the ethical considerations of pricing work. One of the most high-profile failures came in 2011, when a dynamic pricing algorithm substantially elevated its prices on the night of a terrorist attack in France, especially just as people in the area were trying to book rides for their safety. Similarly, in 2018, thousands of passengers faced massive price spikes on tickets from airlines trying to head to Florida, when a strong hurricane was heading toward the state. Paying prices in excess of four to five times the average price was a common occurrence, especially when trying to flee from the hurricane within 24 hours of flight. The public backlash in these cases was overwhelming. Besides the reputational damage, the companies were also subject to heavy fines by the regulatory authorities for using algorithms without the necessary ethical and appropriateness considerations. Another case that elucidates the ethical implications of algorithmic pricing comes from e-commerce. A retailer was revealed to be dynamically adjusting its prices for consumers based on intraday or interday effects. This retailer used a smartphone or tablet that displayed signs of a customer who returned to the retailer's site after three years to buy something on their wish list. The price indicated on the product for that customer was substantially higher than the price for other customers. Public reaction was vociferous; the practice violated the principle of fairness, undermining the public's confidence in the retailer in the long run (Jin et al., 2024; Nassar & Kamal, 2021b). Apparently recognizing this, the retailer stopped the practice soon thereafter.

7.9.3 Comparative Analysis of Industries

In the previous sections, we analyzed a number of examples of industries where personalized pricing (especially dynamic and algorithmic) has been implemented. This gives us some first ideas about the main traits of dynamic pricing in the real world. In particular, we can compare, in a simple way, four different areas of industry where algorithmic, automated dynamic pricing has been implemented and theorized: e-commerce (typically, travel accommodation and travel tickets, but more recently also fashion clothing and groceries), ride-hailing, on-demand services, and last, a whole set of markets that matter to consumers, but mainly housing and internships. These industries are seeing the emergence of a problem of bias-less allocation that recently led to candidate algorithms which seek to bring fairness in these markets. First, concerning e-commerce, we think that its main trait is the fact that the consumer faces relatively high costs for changing the provider, but on the seller's side, there are zero costs associated with changing price strategy and betraying consumer trust. That means—at least until consumer trust is broken down, and it desperately moves to more traditional or collaborative platforms, or to negotiating price reactions as a form of catalyzing transparency or volatility more frequently than on other services—successful systems develop collaborative relationships and explore consumer behavior, which exploit asymmetric information sometimes to the limit of collusion (Papachristou et al., 2023; Reuter et al., 2016).. Second, demand predictability versus uncertainty on other sides leads ride-hailing price discrimination trends to be more limited in scope and, to intraday or interday effects, be far less effective to explore consumer surplus than other daily services with far less predictable demand.

7.10 Conclusion

The presented contents summarize the empirical entanglements, theoretical results, and normative assumptions that were exposed in previous sections. The following chapters go through the main reflections and contributions that were organized within the first seven chapters of the monograph. The text also deals with some possible future research paths. Overall, the objective is to provide a broader view of the presented work, while triggering critical thoughts on technological developments that exploit the economic potentiality of behavioral and big data. This chapter recaps previous work and puts forward some ideas for future research. Research has presented results and cautions about the implications of behavioral targeting and dynamic pricing. Despite the potential advantages to both consumers and retailers that these models promise, they can easily lead retailers to adopt unethical behavior, obtaining short-run competitive advantages by monetary exploitation of consumers. Researchers and regulators must protect consumers from monetization and exploitation flows that stem from models based on personal data collection and exploitation, combined with data processing techniques of consumers' internet behavior. For this reason, particular attention should be paid during the modeling and commercial exploitation stages of these models. Artificial intelligence and machine learning implications on marketing ethical issues are specifically described. A final consideration that we want to emphasize is that digital advertising and AI technology are becoming more and more democratized. With this democratization comes temptation to exploit. It is very easy to lose sight of the ethical aspects and responsibilities of this technology-driven model. We hope that our work can contribute to increased sensitivity and help inside the AI/ML for digital advertising modeling, research, and execution communities.

References

Aldboush, H.H.H. and Ferdous, M. (2023). Building Trust in Fintech: An Analysis of Ethical and Privacy Considerations in the Intersection of Big Data, AI, and Customer Trust. *International Journal of Financial Studies*, *11*(3). https://doi.org/10.3390/ijfs11030090

Dida, H.A., Chakravarthy, D. and Rabbi, F. (2023). ChatGPT and Big Data: Enhancing Text-to-Speech Conversion. *Mesopotamian Journal of Big Data*. Vol. 2023, Issue 2023, pp. 31–35. https://doi.org/10.58496/mjbd/2023/005

Duchesneau, E.D., Klepin, H.D., Hanchate, A.D., Lin, M.Y. and Bluethmann, S. M. (2024). Big Data for Geriatric Oncology Research. *North Carolina Medical Journal*. *85*(1). https://doi.org/10.18043/001c.91420

Franzén, A. (2023). Big Data, Big Problems: Why Scientists Should Refrain from Using Google Trends. *Acta Sociologica (United Kingdom)* Volume 66, Issue 3, Pages 343–347. https://doi.org/10.1177/00016993221151118

Giannakopoulos, N.T., Terzi, M.C., Sakas, D.P., Kanellos, N., Toudas, K.S. and Migkos, S.P. (2024). Agroeconomic Indexes and Big Data: Digital Marketing Analytics Implications for Enhanced Decision Making with Artificial Intelligence-Based Modeling. *Information (Switzerland)*, *15*(2). https://doi.org/10.3390/info15020067

Gligor, D.M., Pillai, K.G. and Golgeci, I. (2021). Theorizing the Dark Side of Business-to-Business Relationships in the Era of AI, Big Data, and Blockchain. *Journal of Business Research*, *133*. https://doi.org/10.1016/j.jbusres.2021.04.043

Gumz, J., Fettermann, D.C., Frazzon, E.M. and Kück, M. (2022). Using Industry 4.0's Big Data and IoT to Perform Feature-Based and Past Data-Based Energy Consumption Predictions. *Sustainability (Switzerland)*, *14*(20). https://doi.org/10.3390/su142013642

Hulsen, T., Friedecký, D., Renz, H., Melis, E., Vermeersch, P. and Fernandez-Calle, P. (2023). From Big Data to Better Patient Outcomes. *Clinical Chemistry and Laboratory Medicine*. *61*(4). https://doi.org/10.1515/cclm-2022-1096

Hyun, W. (2022). Big Data: An Overview and Its Applications in Medicine and Aviation. *The Korean Journal of Aerospace and Environmental Medicine*, *32*(2). https://doi.org/10.46246/kjasem.220016

Jin, K., Zhong, Z.Z. and Zhao, E.Y. (2024). Sustainable Digital Marketing Under Big Data: An AI Random Forest Model Approach. *IEEE Transactions on Engineering Management*, *71*. https://doi.org/10.1109/TEM.2023.3348991

Leitner-Hanetseder, S. and Lehner, O.M. (2023). AI-Powered Information and Big Data: Current Regulations and Ways Forward in IFRS Reporting. *Journal of Applied Accounting Research*, *24*(2). https://doi.org/10.1108/JAAR-01-2022-0022

Urmila, M. and Mamatha, K.R. (2024). Consumer Behaviour Using Big Data Analytics. *International Journal of Research Publication and Reviews*, *5*(1). https://doi.org/10.55248/gengpi.5.0124.0218

Moser, K., Choo, K.K.R. and Le-Khac, N.A. (2022). Database Forensics for Analyzing Data Loss in Delayed Extraction Cases. *Studies in Big Data*. *116*. https://doi.org/10.1007/978-3-031-16127-8_6

Mukhopadhyay, S., Singh, R.K. and Jain, T. (2024). Developing Big Data Enabled Marketing 4.0 Framework. *International Journal of Information Management Data Insights*, *4*(1). https://doi.org/10.1016/j.jjimei.2024.100214

Nassar, A. and Kamal, M. (2021a). Ethical Dilemmas in AI-Powered Decision-Making: A Deep Dive into Big Data-Driven Ethical Considerations. *International Journal of Responsible Artificial Intelligence*, pp. 1–11, *11*(8) .

Nassar, A. and Kamal, M. (2021b). International Journal of Responsible Artificial Intelligence Ethical Dilemmas in AI-Powered Decision-Making: A Deep Dive into Big Data-Driven Ethical Considerations. *International Journal of Responsible Artificial Intelligence*.

Papachristou, N., Kotronoulas, G., Dikaios, N., Allison, S.J., Eleftherochorinou, H., Rai, T., Kunz, H., Barnaghi, P., Miaskowski, C. and Bamidis, P.D. (2023). Digital Transformation of Cancer Care in the Era of Big Data, Artificial Intelligence and Data-Driven Interventions: Navigating the Field. *Seminars in Oncology Nursing*, *39*(3). https://doi.org/10.1016/j.soncn.2023.151433

Reuter, C., Ludwig, T., Kotthaus, C., Kaufhold, M.-A., von Radziewski, E. and Pipek, V. (2016). Big Data in a Crisis? Creating Social Media Datasets for Crisis Management Research. *I-Com*, *15*(3). https://doi.org/10.1515/icom-2016-0036

Walker, A. (2020). Internet of Things-Enabled Smart Sustainable Cities: Big Data-Based Urban Governance, Wireless Sensor Networks, and Automated Algorithmic Decision-Making Processes. *Geopolitics, History, and International Relations*, *12*(2). https://doi.org/10.22381/GHIR12220208

8

Detecting and Mitigating Algorithmic Bias: Technical and Ethical Interventions in Insurance AI

Wasswa Shafik

8.1 Introduction

Artificial intelligence (AI) refers to any computation that displays intelligent behavior through the emulation of cognitive functions associated with the human mind, such as learning and problem-solving. AI encompasses a plethora of technologies and frameworks, stimulating innovation across industries. In particular, algorithms involving machine learning (ML) are becoming prevalent in the insurance sector due to their predictive performance across numerous applications, such as assessing risk through predictive underwriting, improving customer experience via AI chatbots, automating claims with computer vision, developing hyper-personalized services via customer segmentation for fraud detection, pricing, and financial forecasting. The vast amount of data generated by insurance activities has made the use of AI a compelling proposition. The term insurance AI can be defined as any AI application that affects the insurance industry, enabling insurers to operate efficiently, thereby accelerating the deployment of AI innovations in data generation, preprocessing, modeling, and deployment/mining. Despite the benefits that InsurTech has gained through the use of AI, scholars have voiced concerns regarding the absence and lack of explainability behind the AI decision-making process. This "lack of understanding" of such algorithms is due to the intricate nature of these algorithms, containing millions of millions of parameters (Akter et al., 2021). As such, InsurTech companies using such predictive models have faced activist opposition, leading to explanations being necessary to ensure that the unique requirements of the insurance industry are not only considered but also met.

The research on algorithmic bias is still in its early days, but a typology of possible bias types is emerging. The first bifurcation is between data bias and model bias, where the term data bias is shorthand for bias stemming from how the training data was selected and prepared, while model bias covers bias arising from how a model is specified and trained, independent of the training data. A second potential bifurcation is into human bias and machine bias, where the term human bias is shorthand for how humans influence the selection, preparation, or transformation of the training data. Many researchers narrow their focus to data bias and criticize the field for neglecting ways in which algorithmic models could and should be less insensitive to the potential for bias stemming from the use of data alone, ignoring for the moment that the borderline between data and model bias can be a matter of research priorities. Among many potential forms of data bias, the easiest to locate fall under the heading of bias arising from the processes of labeling or transforming the training data and seem

DOI: 10.1201/9781003747659-8

especially relevant for algorithmic decision-making. For example, images portraying black skin may be labeled as "not suitable," while those labels are also applied to people with lighter skin. Without corrective controls to account for this selection bias, the model will automatically be biased against people of color, as it will recognize lighter skin as preferable, ignoring variations such as skin color and hair texture that often distinguish ethnic groups. The second main type of stated algorithmic bias, model bias, refers to bias inherent in the choices made in the design of the model, regardless of the contents of the training data (Dwork & Roth, 2013). For example, an algorithmic model designed to assess social creditworthiness but centered entirely on credit history without considering outside factors could be biased against lower-income individuals needing loans and financial access.

8.1.1 Data Bias

The phrases "garbage in" and "garbage out" remain true when it comes to algorithms and the data that trains them. Insurance organizations are liable for protecting their clients, and many are working toward delivering balance and fairness within their AI models; however, selecting data that is polluted with biases can have a severe consequence on the outcomes of the algorithm used for modeling and predicting risk. At the highest level, data used in AI is categorized into two different groups: features and labels. Features are information or metrics that are used for training a model, while labels are the class output that allows AI algorithms to make predictions, and that is used to assess how accurate the algorithm is. For instance, in a model built to predict the probability of a house fire, data used in training the model may contain features indicating the materials that were used to build the home, size of home, the location of the home, the owner's burning habits, and the model would be labeled as a "house fire" or "no house fire." Data bias is a major cause of algorithmic bias in the datasets used to build, train, and test AI models. For risk selection, predictive models are often trained using historic data on clients and claims. If this historic data is biased, so will the build model. The model will favor the same groups or types of people the biased historic data favored, leading to the approval or denial of policies involving certain groups or individuals that may not truly deserve to be treated this way. For example, the data used may result in AI models directing insurers to charge protected classes higher rates than unprotected classes while also denying claims from the protected classes more often than claims from unprotected classes (Bode et al., 2024). This use of biased data could have serious consequences for both insurers and clients and is an area that regulators often focus on in insurance.

8.1.2 Model Bias

While data bias is the most visible aspect of algorithmic bias, and the best-known form of bias, it is not the only type of bias that is relevant for machine learning. Model bias, which is more subtle but equally important, is likely to be most relevant in understanding bias in modern insurance models. Model bias refers to constraints that are inherent to the models and architectures being used, but do not stem from the data that is provided to them. In general, a machine learning model learns to approximate a phenomenon, such as predicting the likelihood of a claim based on features of the risk. To be deployable, the model must be able to approximate the phenomenon accurately. In addition, the model must also be able to generalize from the training data, meaning that it is able to produce accurate predictions for unseen data points. The quality of estimates and predictions from a model hinges on the model's ability to approximate the underlying phenomenon accurately. If the model is not able to approximate the phenomenon closely enough, it will produce biased predictions. Model bias can be seen in cases where wider sample spacing results in areas with poor prediction accuracy, and becomes particularly salient for phenomena that have sudden and localized transitions. Many assumptions that are made for model fitting are made to ensure generalizability.

Common practice, in many fields that leverage machine learning methods, is to limit model and algorithm choice to those whose generalized model output will either have desirable properties or whose structure and flexibility will make generalization to predictive accuracy across the entire feature domain reasonable (Bond et al., 2019). This exclusion principle can lead to adverse outcomes if the generalized form of an accepted algorithm at any level is unduly biased. This is especially relevant in the insurance domain.

8.1.3 Human Bias

Humans design machine learning algorithms, resulting in initial design bias. They also clean training datasets, select features, and devise the utility functions that map the algorithm's output to its observed performance. As a result, human biases frequently permeate the ML pipeline. Model bias then arises indirectly as a consequence of intuitive choices made by a human, either while designing, building, or deploying an algorithm. These choices can be imprecise, uninformed, or "wrong." They could also reflect the designer's values. It is also quite likely that designers may not share the same background or culture as the affected group. This problem is particularly prevalent in insurance ML systems for multiple reasons. These reasons range from the crucial importance of the utility functions to several practical shortcomings in the ML design pipeline (Engelmann, 2023). For instance, the choice of utility function can considerably influence the operation of an algorithm, especially for high-stakes tasks. Utility functions that aspire for different quantities can easily conflict with each other during deployment, while some algorithms are also more flexible. Heterogeneous requirements are of primary importance for ML insurance systems, and one function may not suffice. For example, "optimal" is subjective when it comes to quantifying risk assessment. Optimal economic utility does not necessarily imply systemic accident benefits. These differences in opinion can reflect the prevailing social consensus or the underlying inference employed to interpret the output. "Best" performative criterion is generally in conflict with how best risk exposure is actually controlled (Obreja, 2024). Determining which group is most favored by the system is indeed a real dilemma, given the intense public pressure in recent years concerning equity and fairness concerns in many crucial social domains, including justice, hiring, and lending, depending on cyber resilience privilege as demonstrated in Figure 8.1.

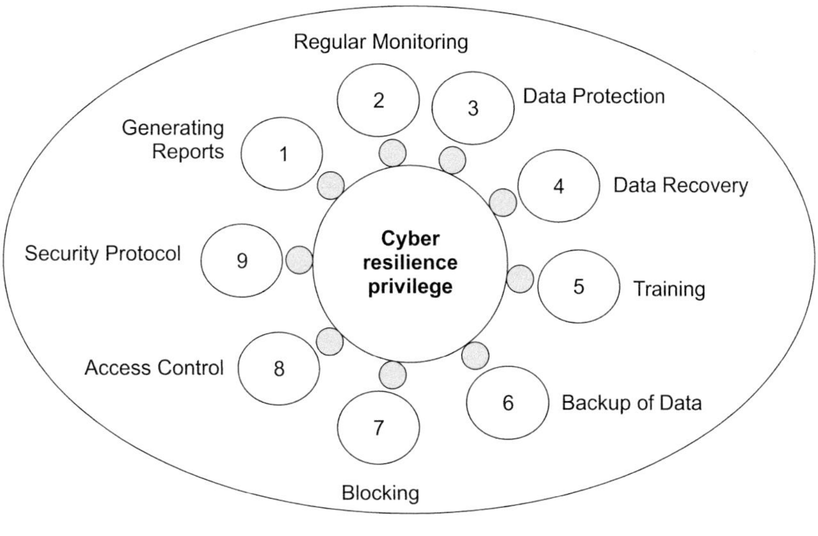

Fig. 8.1 Insurance cyber resilience privilege.

8.2 Impacts of Algorithmic Bias in Insurance

Algorithmic bias in insurance can lead to harms even without malicious intent from insurance companies. For example, consider an InsurTech company that develops a model that serves as input for underwriting but fails to account for the different treatment of protected classes. While it seems that the model is doing this automatically, the company is passing along background risk factors that correlate with "bad" risk and are in fact correlated with race or protected class status. The original, simple model using observable risk as inputs would also serve as a proxy and cause the company to be denied insurance coverage in order to open itself up to underwriting. These harmful effects may arise from predictions being derived from proxies with little illumination. People in protected classes, for example, may not look safe to a policymaker. In many cases, the probability that a protected person would have an adverse risk event is higher than that of a corresponding non-protected person; it is not because the model is biased, but rather because they are correlated in the general population. An insurance company could charge the entire class huge prices, but very few would buy. Each protected-class risk, however, pays much lower prices, and the adverse selection pushes premiums for protected classes even lower. The insurers stand to lose a lot over time. In these cases, protected classes must demand premiums from insurance companies for targeting and charging prices on the basis of race or other sensitive characteristics, or face adverse selection and pick up the bill (J. Zhou et al., 2023). Alternatively, the company can self-insure to cover, in the long run, the adverse selection losses.

8.2.1 Case Studies

A foundational case study of risk classification is that of the life insurance industry. Until the mid-1800s, insurance policies covered property and were not classed by risk. Then, actuaries modeled the mortality for various classes of people using differential tables—for example, a person's risk of death at each age was modeled by age, gender, and occupation. In particular, the first such complex models showed that unskilled laborers had far lower life expectancies than middle-class people. This led to class-segmented policies in which the very poor would pay more than their probability of death would warrant; however, single premium investments would continue to serve as a form of forced savings, paying out a benefit upon death. However, insurance is highlighting risk segmentation and therefore discouraging representatives of higher-risk segments from proceeding in the purchase of insurance policies. In this case, highlighting risk segmentation harms those who will be treated discriminatively by the insurance institution. The US. natural disaster is that of fire, by which there was a lasting moral hazard problem, leading insurance companies to withdraw from the marketplace altogether. In the late-nineteenth century, the loss of life from fires in America started notably rising because increasing urbanization and increased immigration of the poor-led services for fire retardation could not keep up with the increase in fire risks. The suggestion was made that the risks of the poor be borne collectively, but continued risk segmentation would ensure that within the group of the insured, the poor would bear a higher risk than the rich and so suffer significantly from near bankruptcy about potentially such losses when they occurred (Braun & Matthes, 2018; Gerlick & Liozu, 2020). The insurance clearly told poor people without insurance against fire that they could lose all their worldly possessions at any moment. In the late-nineteenth century, privately organized insurance against monumental losses was impractical, leading to calls for state involvement in mutual insurance.

8.2.2 Financial Consequences

Insurance biases in AI, ML, and big data can have enormous financial costs. The Prudential Regulation Authority and Financial Conduct Authority have stated that financial misconduct is often driven by a “culture of making money” without adequate emphasis on fair outcomes. It has been pointed out that algorithmic bias is a type of model mis-specification and predicted that insurers would underestimate the impact of model risk on profits, noting that the consequences are considerable, ranging from severe loss, regulatory censure, and even charges of misconduct against individuals for model failure, inadequate model validation, or inadequate model oversight from a Chief risk officer (CRO) or board. The potential impact of this bias-related model risk is increasing due to the growing use of extreme ML methods—decision trees, random forests, and boosted trees, which are highly sensitive to inputs. For example, it has been examined how different input variables changed the decisions of a random forest, showing that extremely small perturbations to a single input variable could flip the classification for a significant percentage of the observations in a random forest model for a specific condition in dog breeding. Other writers have also predicted that ML in insurance will suffer from mis-specification, meaning the nonexistence of a sufficiently accurate model in the model space. Big data has made it possible for insurers, especially motor and health insurers, to create extremely sophisticated pricing models. By definition, no model can perfectly predict insurance claims, but with detailed scoring, the optimal model may be more capable than previous models were. However, as insurance pricing becomes more precise, the financial consequences of model mis-specification will also increase, with thousands of policyholders being heavily overcharged and large numbers of rule-violating-allowed claims still being paid annually (Y. Zhou et al., 2023). Concerns have already been expressed about the swelling market for insurance created by predictive modeling algorithms.

8.2.3 *Reputation Damage*

Algorithmic bias in insurance exposes practitioners to the reputational consequences of broken public trust. A primary objective of insurance, balancing the risk pool while safeguarding good-faith policyholders, is incompatible with creating a toolset upon which to subject the most vulnerable. Society’s increasing reliance on automated decision-making systems belies a responsibility of preserving and increasing public faith in the professions that develop and utilize them. Societal error in judgment regarding privacy, security, accountability, and social responsibility implicates the insurance profession in its overt regulatory role. As a result, insurance, perhaps more than any other sector, is uniquely subject to sharing blame for errors of third-party AI firms. Social trust in the insurance industry is at risk of banking-like scrutiny: overreliance on statistical models could prompt an unjust intent. It is, moreover, arguably more difficult for actuaries, who typically model risk for commercial purposes, to garner public support. The leverage of the insurance industry is far-reaching, influencing third-party institutions such as financial market exchanges, the lending and credit card services vertical, and healthcare. The realization of commercial interests by risk-bearing entities is a necessary cost of doing business—the effort toward “profit” is reduced to technicality and semantics—and, in the case of insurance, provides a provisional boundary between commercial interest and public good. Trust in insurance is thus predicated on acting in the best interest of the population. Algorithmic bias compels scrutiny impossible to deflect completely: culpable parties are difficult to identify and assign blame (Bode et al., 2024). Indeed, the reputational risks associated with algorithmic decision-making in insurance reflect the stakes of capriciously deciding recent data yield incorrect statistical conclusions: racism, sexism, ageism, and an ever-expanding list of “-isms” disallow the regulatory-friendly “nothing to see here” rejoinders to increased liability, as detailed in Table 8.1. Society asks: if we could reasonably expect that AI tools will produce pronouncements ill-befitting the adversity modeling addressed, should tools-ranking tools be trusted?

8.3 Detecting Algorithmic Bias

Detecting algorithmic bias, or more generally, evaluating algorithms’ effects or performance, is a crucial first step in mitigating and understanding mitigation. This task can be complex owing to the

Table 8.1 Common bias types in insurance AI and their detection techniques.

Bias Type	*Definition*	*Example in Insurance*	*Detection Technique*	*Challenges in Detection*
Historical Bias	Bias is encoded in historical data, even if the model is fair	Lower claims approval for certain zip codes due to past prejudice	Dataset analysis, bias audits	Data sparsity, lack of context
Sample Bias	When training data doesn't represent the target population	Overrepresentation of urban drivers in telematics data	Distribution comparison (e.g., Kolmogorov–Smirnov test)	Hard to detect if demographics are missing
Measurement Bias	Inaccuracies in how features are recorded	Inconsistent reporting of health symptoms in self-reported datasets	Feature quality audits	Subjective or noisy data
Label Bias	Ground truth labels contain human bias	Manual claim denials reflecting systemic discrimination	Cross-validation with debiased labels	Labels are rarely audited manually
Proxy Bias	Use of variables that correlate with protected features	Credit score as a proxy for race or socioeconomic status	Correlation and SHAP (SHapley Additive exPlanations) value analysis	High correlation does not imply intent
Aggregation Bias	Applying a uniform model to diverse subgroups	Same underwriting model for both rural and urban clients	Disaggregated performance analysis	Group boundaries may be unclear
Representation Bias	Lack of minority group data in the training set	Minority ethnic groups are underrepresented in actuarial tables	Sampling audits, fairness metrics per group	Limited access to protected attribute data
Automation Bias	Overreliance on AI predictions without human checks	Denial of claims due to model flag without manual review	Workflow analysis, human-in-the-loop inspection	Lack of transparency in the decision path
Feedback Loop Bias	Models reinforcing existing decisions based on their predictions	Fraud detection systems learning only from past flags	Temporal analysis, data pipeline audits	Self-fulfilling predictions are hard to track
Intersectional Bias	Compound bias affecting overlapping identities	Worse outcomes for older women from specific regions	Intersectional subgroup analysis	Requires rich, granular demographic data
Evaluation Bias	Metrics that favor the majority groups or overlook key disparities	High global accuracy masking poor performance on minorities	Use of group-specific metrics (TPR - True Positive Rate Parity, etc.)	Requires fairness-aware Key Performance Indicator (KPI)
Deployment Bias	Bias introduced when the system is used differently than intended	Claims app used differently by younger versus older clients	Monitoring real-world behavior	Misuse often goes unnoticed
Emergent Bias	Bias that arises over time through societal shifts or model updates	New forms of exclusion from updated telematics inputs	Continual model evaluation	Need for long-term monitoring
Confirmation Bias (Human)	Users accept AI outputs that confirm expectations	Underwriters blindly accept model's denial for certain profiles	Human–AI interaction audits	Cultural/ organizational inertia

number of ways in which an algorithm can fail different groups of people across different parts of the input action or output space. Such a naked-eye understanding of the outcomes can be guided in multiple ways based on existing admonitions for model evaluation. Detection may be done for predictive performance or model evaluation for the particular task of interest, whether it be link prediction in the case of a recommender system or accuracy in the case of a classifier. Additionally, detecting algorithmic bias and more generally evaluating model effects can be aided by systematic external audits, bias detection tools, and visualization techniques. We outline some of the existing techniques next, with a particular focus on social media algorithms. In the statistical discrimination literature, there is a long tradition of employing statistical tests, or statistical proxies, based on correlations, discrepancies, and divergences of outcome probabilities given sensitive features and other features. Such a traditional statistical bias detection approach is a commonly used first step in algorithm auditing but is also applicable in the context of algorithm fairness. Much of the current scientific literature on algorithm auditing has taken inspiration from these statistical methods and procedures. In machine learning, these have been further expanded to include metric-based frameworks that consider multiple group types and different types of errors, optimizing them on the training set, and then reporting them on the validation dataset with group membership derived from sensitive features or group membership predicted via the sensitive features classifiers (Bond et al., 2019). Nevertheless, because testing demographic disparity is a common concern and initial step, we use the term statistical methods interchangeably with the above-discussed elements of statistical discrimination.

8.3.1 Statistical Methods

Statistical models, especially logistic regression and its extensions, have been widely embraced for detecting and measuring algorithmic bias in security and related AI systems. The key ingredients of these methods are the model predictors, the more precise term for independent variables; among them, a group identity attribute (often a protected attribute such as race or gender), the output or decision predicted by the use of security AI, and the model target of the statistical model, which is usually a measure for the "success" of the AI's prediction, such as prediction accuracy. The structure and coefficient estimates derived from the statistical detectability model are used to assess whether group attributes alone play a significant role in predicting the AI decision or system performance; in effect, such assessment is an empirical test for potential use and efficacy, validation, and performance guarantee of the AI system. Why use this test for detectability rather than good old testing for equality? Simply, testing for the statistical significance of the group attributes cannot be explained or justified with known patterns of sensitive mobilization either because such factors are simply ignored or not readily amenable to the controlling work of theory or practice. Methods for testing the joint effects of all variables associated with a certain group attribute are notoriously weak; for that matter, whenever joint equality holds, equality testing cannot explain joint departures due to other data than standard estimators, all it says about the variation of the group mean values of the sensitive mobilization variables. However, the coefficient estimates of statistical bias detectability models answer some of the most important questions and feature a rich toolbox of model choices and methods for answering them (J. Zhou et al., 2023). Recent advances in statistical learning provide formal links to popular elements of some of these statistical detectability tools by linking them to predictive machine learning models.

8.3.2 Algorithmic Audits

Existing statistical approaches to bias detection, such as measuring disparate impact and assessing model performance on subgroups, have notable limitations. In particular, statistical methods require clearly defined demographic groups, can only support specific definitions of fairness, and may lead to biased decisions regarding model fairness based on simplistic metrics. For example, failing a statistical fairness test is typically sufficient to reject a model, while passing a fairness test does not guarantee that a model is unbiased. Furthermore, these methods typically do not utilize additional data pertaining to the context and potential impact of algorithmic decisions, which can greatly influence the real-world risks associated with biased outcomes. Due to these limitations, algorithmic audits have been proposed as a more holistic way of assessing algorithmic bias. Algorithmic audits use domain-specific data and expert knowledge to build a contextualized understanding of a model and its impact on real-world populations. This may include understanding how input data is gathered, modeled, and preprocessed, the underlying data that the learned model represents, the population that experiences the model's predictions, the ultimate effects that these predictions have on individuals and broader groups, and how the model makes predictions. Since these factors operate within a broader socio-technical system, algorithmic audits are inherently interdisciplinary in nature, often requiring input not only from information scientists but also from legal, technical ethics, and domain experts. Such audits are often expensive and time-consuming, meant to be performed on model instances that are already being actively used to make predictive decisions or are running in production (Gerlick & Liozu, 2020). However, they often provide the most accurate and actionable results since they can leverage domain-relevant data that allows for the contextualization of quantifiable outcomes.

8.3.3 Bias Detection Tools

It is also important to mention that the previous tools still require proficiency in some programming language, usually Python, in order to detect bias with them. In contrast, there are commercial tools to audit insurance AI from a commercial provider which allow via a graphical user interface to do testing without programming. Of these tools, Fiddler.ai, Apurva.ai, and H2O.ai are available to the insurance sector. This is a direct consequence of the effort done by the New York Department of Financial Services, which has pointed on different occasions in the recent past that the insurance companies under its jurisdiction should have a record tracking of their AI algorithm. A tracking record of the AI algorithm can also serve for auditing purposes. Aligning with the recommendations of the Department of Financial Services, we encourage not only keeping a permanent record of how any possible bias is detected, but also sending anything suspicious to specialized vendors that have knowledge in dealing with bias. Strikingly, a recent study notes that very few insurance companies have incorporated bias frameworks. It is then more than advisable to request these vendors' tools as a checklist to accompany the insurance company's AI-based service implementation, so that, in case an infraction goes to court, the tool validates that the insurance company detected bias. Putting together the SHAP values on the different outputs, say in the case of credit scoring models, prompts a suspicious behavior visualization (Dwork & Roth, 2013).

8.4 Mitigating Algorithmic Bias

Detecting and measuring algorithmic bias is the first step toward using responsible AI. Developers must take further steps toward providing assurance that biased models will not be deployed, nor that they will be retrained in the future. This section lists the techniques that may be used to mitigate algorithmic bias, focusing on three main directions:

(i) Pre-procedural and post-procedural bias detection, where mitigation refers to the data curating steps normally employed to create a model-mining dataset.

(ii) Model evaluation, where model mitigation refers to the excessive evaluation of model performance through models specially selected because performance seems good.

(iii) Preprocessing, in-processing, and postprocessing bias mitigation, where mitigation refers to the use of sampling, modified problematic functions, and a posteriori adjustment.

The state of the art of mostly discussed bias mitigation techniques is included, but neither is it exhaustive nor does it mean we are encouraging all processes to be followed on data when training AI. Data is at the heart of any ML initiative, and the process of collecting, refining, and curating data for mining is as important as it is for any human-created model. In this sense, any bias mitigation in AI models usually starts with a complete, diverse, and representative dataset. This is often a difficult endeavor, especially in niche markets like insurance. Unfortunately, the inherent need of the insurance business to be able to build and rely on datasets that allow for statistical representation of low probability events presents an increased risk of working with incomplete datasets gathered using unclear reasons. Bias might be inherently encoded in the data. It might also be a consequence of the data processing activities, so care needs to be taken to critically evaluate these stages. A design centered on ethical principles has to be defined prior to the data collection design. Criteria on selection, use, representation, measurement, privacy, and support need to be released and followed to gather high-quality data for model mining (Bond et al., 2019). Effort should take place on considering data that can allow for knowledge discovery.

8.4.1 Data Collection Strategies

A fundamental approach to mitigating algorithmic bias is to perform careful data collection. The algorithmic challenges which we examined mostly stemmed from the low quality of existing datasets. We argue that the field will benefit tremendously from dedicated efforts in creating representative datasets. To support and incentivize these collective efforts, we hope the following questions will provide some guidance to practitioners and users who decide to engage in the relatively more laborious path of collecting new data. What data is missing from existing datasets? The pivotal point in deciding when to collect new data is when one discovers that existing datasets will deliver poor performance estimates for the task at hand, or worse, that the performance of the system will be poor when deployed. System performance estimates are often triggered by relevance gaps for input feature values that are not represented in the current dataset. For example, a sentiment classifier with a large relevance gap can perform badly on test instances containing sensitive identity terms or terms relating to a stereotype, such as "I am very sad because my mother insists that I must be a doctor." All of the quantification algorithms may also signal a performance gap for a certain group. In this case, sensitivity to relevance gaps might hinge on the presence of the minority group in labeled test data (J. Zhou et al., 2023). Another signal of minority non-representativeness is minority group size: very low minority density may be dangerous indeed, as well as highly unbalanced datasets.

8.4.2 Model Evaluation Techniques

Evaluating machine learning models is often done using accuracy-based evaluation metrics, such as precision, recall, and F1-score. However, the majority of machine learning models are designed for a single objective: maximizing the model's accuracy on unseen data. There is, thus, little regard for the model's performance on different segments of the data. Orthogonal to this accuracy-based objective, it is essential to ensure that the model satisfies the relevant fairness criteria for predictions. Otherwise, a biased model can make unfair predictions for certain segments of the population, which can result in social harm or legal complications. While the topic of privacy in model evaluation is not new, the subject of fairness in model evaluation has grown rapidly in recent years. Further, for the insurance context, multiple fairness criteria may need to be satisfied simultaneously, such as the disparate impact, disparate acceptance rates, and disparate error rates. A challenge here is that these fairness criteria often contradict each other, thereby creating an imbalance between the competing objectives. These competing objectives and trade-offs can exacerbate algorithmic bias even further if one maximizes accuracy under this evaluation paradigm. This has led to growing interest in evaluating fairness in machine learning systems, including metrics for problems in which model evaluation has been studied traditionally, such as supervised classification, ranking, regression, etc. These issues can become even more complex with the introduction of novel machine learning paradigms, such as deep learning, transfer learning, and semi-supervised learning (Obreja, 2024). Due to this complexity and the heavy reliance of a particular application domain on such evaluative procedures, it is essential to use these strategies in conjunction with domain expertise to promote responsible design and deployment for models used in sensitive applications.

8.4.3 Bias Mitigation Algorithms

While data and modeling approaches hold promise, they cannot be relied upon alone to mitigate the impact of bias within insurance machine-learning systems. This is because enhancements and tweaks to data and modeling are often mere band-aids, occluding stickier issues at root with the potential to have more meaningful, experiential, and far-reaching implications within the insurance industry. Further, rather than meaningfully erasing model or data bias, mitigation algorithms may result in new, untested forms of bias introduced exogenously into a model, reframing, refracting, and transforming bias rather than erasing it. While commonly discussed in other domains, the application of debiasing algorithms in the insurance space is nearly unprecedented. In particular, non-insurance specific codecs have been applied in insurance-like contexts. A bias mitigation algorithm typically employed in racial bias mitigation settings utilizes explicit representation learning for ideas such as disparate treatment and impact, training biased generative models to construct latent features so that the generated instances satisfy certain fairness properties. A multichannel bias codec can be applied to multidimensional mediation and moderation effects, and another employs joint distributional predicted probabilities as pseudo-targets for calibration within settings with at-risk or sensitive subgroups. All three codecs are integrated via the deep neural networks within an insurance model (Bode et al., 2024; Bond et al., 2019). While no harm is explicitly caused by the application of such codecs in the insurance context (and, thus, such codecs may actually reduce, rather than influence, disparities), negative effects may emerge from the unintended creation of group-selection effects or from model overfitting or underfitting.

8.5 Ethical Considerations in Insurance AI

As AI increasingly influences every aspect of our lives, it is imperative to consider its ethical implications. In the insurance sector particularly, use of AI not only raises ethical concerns, but also has a potentially disproportionate and devastating effect on policyholder welfare. With the power of profit maximization as a driving force, some companies may use AI in ways that magnify inconsistency across classifications, exacerbate existing biases, and lead to an opaque claims process where liability is assigned to policyholders without transparency or even explanation. The peril is that AI is used as a tool for exploitation rather than a technology that enables fairness and equity. Some of the most obvious reasons for regulatory intervention stem from ethical considerations. Addressing issues such as fairness, transparency, and accountability are thus some of the most intuitive arguments in favor of regulating the use of AI in the insurance industry. Fortunately, these ethical considerations are not only about "prohibition of abuse," but can also be seen as guiding principles that drive the responsible and beneficial use of AI inside certain guardrails. As is true with the development of any complex technology applied to publicly impacting activities, the trust factor is vital in the determination of its success, and the AI-enhanced insurance sector requires some foundation of fairness and reasonable explanations in predictions and decisions. Insurance companies are more concerned with the potential criticism stemming from the opaque nature of decisions made solely based on risk predictions. Existing risk-based pricing may be viewed as unfair due to the resulting unmet demand for high-risk clients. The problem stems from the fact that policy prices are solely based upon predicted risk and do not reflect an individual's preference for risk cover (Braun & Matthes, 2018; J. Zhou et al., 2023). Risk-based pricing is mostly antithetical to the principle of providing a safety net and maintaining social stability, especially in property insurances.

8.5.1 Fairness and Equity

Modern discussions about fairness draw from multiple theoretical perspectives, including distributive justice, corrective justice, and deliberative democracy. With respect to insurance, two central issues are often collapsed into one—pricing fairness and broader societal implications—and relatedly many disparate forms of harm are attributed to "unfair" pricing models. On the one hand, there is the question of whether specific individuals (or even groups) are treated fairly in the considered action. On the other hand, there is the question of whether AI processes and the pricing models they produce shift burdens on to particular subpopulations or create aggregate societal effects which are considered unfair. As with all pricing mechanisms, those employed in insurance are necessarily selected to meet certain objectives from a broad set. In commercial insurance markets, pricing is primarily intended to balance risk across customers—with the distribution of that risk being largely determined by the broad constellation of other factors—and therefore to contribute to the stability and sustainability of insurance markets. In this narrow sense, the empirical patterns of risk within data would suggest that some low-income individuals—typically younger individuals with poorer driving records or those living in urban areas with higher crime rates—are essentially charged more "fairly" than higher income customers (and thus suffer lower risk of under-insurance) (Archambault et al., 2024). The idea of fair pricing in this context is based on two aspects—specified requirements of social justice such as upholding the rights to equal and dignified treatment of individuals and groups in society that contribute to underwriting political action are often crucial.

8.5.2 Transparency and Accountability

Civil society proposes to implement transparency and accountability in AI across financial sectors, alongside a selection of regulatory proposals dedicated to the insurance sector. Transparency in algorithmic auditing makes asset managers and banks responsible for the efficiency and fairness of their models. However, these sectors are necessary intermediaries, with huge impacts and externalities for clients and related actors, against which they have no power whatsoever. It is therefore crucial that these sectors, and now increasingly insurance companies too, are interrogated, compelled, and regulated. Furthermore, no industry other than the tobacco industry has been specifically targeted for such a long time. The concentration on transparency and accountability in AI across investment, banking, and insurance is therefore a major victory for the Financial Transparency Coalition. Their request is simple: "Publish your data. Present it in a format that others can analyze easily. Share your insights on the social and environmental effects of the projects you are funding. Introduce a system for auditing the effects of your policies. Support independent researchers, who will often have more expertise than anyone in your organization." However, beyond requesting a few arbitrary standards and obtaining a few reports based on them, the difficulties associated with transparency and accountabilities are the same as their common sense. The Dutch Merchant Bank, responsible for the delayed tax system of the Dutch public sector, asked for a shareholder report on an algorithm to process all lender applications, about the company developing this algorithm to render the report trustworthy (Shafik et al., 2025; Singh et al., 2024). No such report exists. What should be in that report? What would just transparency—and not just accounting tricks—entail? What makes a reliable shareholder report for an AI, a model, on a remotely exploitable architecture, accessing internally and externally sensitive data? This XAI is largely challenged by the data quality on which these AI models are trained on as illustrated in Figure 8.2.

Fig. 8.2 Data quality.

8.5.3 Regulatory Compliance

The utilitarian and consequentialist view of AI ethics invokes a concept of prosperity that involves increased wealth, increased safety, increased comfort, increased leisure time, the preservation of the environment, and improved human experience in general. Under this broad positive-utility definition, it is the duty of AI engineers not just to comply with the law and protection but also to use every resource available to align with the above-stated prosperity principles. According to this argument, the AI engineer's role is not just to mitigate risks and to develop ethical AI within legal boundaries, but to proactively maximize benefits for everyone in the relevant collective in the future. This approach to the role of an AI engineer may be experienced as somewhat overwhelming. Requiring that insurance AI, in the development and operational phase, complies with the relevant laws and works within legal boundaries is of central importance. Throughout this chapter we show how the use of AI for the provision of insurance products, in every relevant step of the process, must comply with legal rules and guidelines from data privacy to lending discrimination to unfair commercial practices. Areas of insurance and other sectors that can easily be affected by bias or other ethically wrong behaviors of the AI are protected by specific behavioral laws and are under the watchful eye of regulators responsible for ensuring compliance. The goal of these laws is to ensure a neutral effect of the decision taken using the AI, whether affected by bias or not. In several jurisdictions, companies can be sanctioned not only for discriminatory results of using AI or for a potential bias in the data but also be sanctioned for failing to put in place transparency controls or algorithms able to flag when a potential bias in the AI could become a risk (Shafik, 2024b, 2025). Furthermore, penalization may result from failing to take action to mitigate such risk.

8.6 Technical Interventions for Bias Mitigation

In the previous sections of this chapter, we have covered a number of challenges in detecting and understanding bias in AI-based systems in insurance; however, it is also crucial to offer ways to mitigate this bias to aid actuaries and other practitioners in insurance in implementing their systems in a fair manner. Therefore, we now discuss various technical interventions that could help model developers and deployers in the mitigation of algorithmic bias. One type of intervention we cover is that of algorithmic fairness frameworks and toolkits, but these in essence offer to mitigate model bias and are model-agnostic. We then discuss the potential need for bias-aware real-time monitoring systems as well as feedback loops for bias mitigation that are specifically tailored to mitigating bias in the domain of insurance. A large body of research has been published in the area of algorithmic fairness, including numerous fairness toolkits that implement various algorithms for removing or mitigating sources of algorithmic bias. Fairness toolkits allow users to better quantify bias within their model pipelines, for example, via pre- and post-hoc evaluation techniques, and then make changes to their pipelines designed to reduce unwanted bias by changing how data is either extra or post-processed before or after modeling, changing the model during training to minimize some fairness metric while minimizing loss, or chaining different pre-, in-, and post-processing techniques together. Depending on the type of monitoring required, frequently checking models for undesirable performance could be simple, such as with a large suite of automated tests, or difficult, such as examining a complex model. Testing for level setting could be automated, while those tests that sought to check for catastrophism may not be apparent until a rare high-severity low-frequency event occurs with undesirable model behavior (Shafik, 2024a). Using such an error of the first kind while having little ability to quantify error of the second kind could be troublesome, and in a worst-case scenario could put burden on the infrastructure. These factors plus the insurance should aim to offer seamless transaction experience for users, and present challenges in operating real-time monitoring systems also in conjunction with mitigation strategies like feedback loops that rely on periodic model retraining.

8.6.1 Algorithmic Fairness Frameworks

Various frameworks measuring algorithmic fairness have been proposed in the literature. A principled review of over 75 fairness definitions with an emphasis on the statistical underpinnings of each definition is provided, which helps fully organizing the definitions into the following categories: group fairness, individual fairness, causal fairness, counterfactual fairness, disparate impact, and error rate balance. There is often considerable tension between many of these fairness definitions, and it is known that certain definitions are reinforced while others are contradicted. This leads to a difficult balancing act when applying and evaluating algorithms with respect to fairness monitoring frameworks. The group fairness framework is the most common and straightforward lens through which to evaluate fairness, treating all individuals within a specified demographic group as equally deserving of equitable algorithmic treatment; a characteristic that makes evaluating a large family of language-based algorithms aligned with this principle very simple. Formalized fairness definitions and procedures must be employed when evaluating models, as without careful attention, algorithms may be built with no concern for appropriate monitoring or evaluation (Dwork & Roth, 2013). For example, disparities in recidivism risk prediction for African American and Caucasian defendants in an algorithm that evaluated mistakes and correct predictions made jointly using two binary-state crowd indicators and that did not evaluate theater or classification disparities.

8.6.2 Real-Time Monitoring Systems

Bias in AI models can only be monitored effectively if there are dedicated monitoring systems that check model decisions and identify bias issues in real time or after certain time periods. Multiple methods can be designed to check critical metrics on a continual basis to identify bias issues. In this paper, we outline dedicated monitoring systems in the context of insurance and describe their possible architecture and data requirements to ensure the systems perform faithfully. Thresholding predictions in order to summarize what the model does is a sensible strategy to exploring AI outcomes and decisions. Summarizing is usually done with the help of ad hoc summary statistics such as distributions of predicted outcomes stratified by categories such as gender or race. In order to better understand model predictions and enable interpretable AI in production, a bias monitoring infrastructure in real time seems only appropriate. Different ideas can be pursued here; one, for example, measures with a real-time bias optimizer the thresholds of how often the algorithm is unfair. This threshold can be aligned with the insurance company's bias with minimum expectations, and can compare expected metric decisions of the model to estimates published in the company politics against human actuarial estimates. For executive non-tech people, the translation of model output or lack thereof is usually a difficult thing because they lack the math and technical expertise to understand the outputs (Akter et al., 2021). It seems only wise to push the research agenda toward more abstract measures that go far beyond traditional AI performance functions.

8.6.3 Feedback Loops

There are recognized limits to post-hoc adjustments; a crucial utility of bias mitigation methods is that they can be incorporated into the training process, rather than being flipped on at the end of training. In so doing, we can maintain fairness in a more principled way, instead of via a reactive adjustment later on. Bias-averse training schemes leverage direct penalty methods by which we integrate specialized loss functions into the training process, applying penalties when possible model outputs are deemed unfair. Humans use predictions as inputs for additional models, looped over time. If predictions from the initial model exhibit a predictive bias, the feedback from the second-stage model will push the outputs of the initial model in the same biased direction. This setup parallels many important applications in finance, marketing, and other domains, where human behavior is sensitive to the output of an ML model; thus, activity will be affected by the policy/prediction of that model. We use the term human-in-the-loop in a broad sense, incorporating both economic utility and societal impact. Reasons for monitoring and addressing feedback loops may include concern regarding sensitivity to inaccurate predictions—for instance, a credit risk model that exerts real-life effects by driving market participants away via inaccuracies will increasingly amplify its effect as it becomes entrenched. A monopoly feedback pathway may thereby funnel the cumulative influence of a biased model onto the population, on the basis of predicted measures that bear a bias or error, such as risk of noncompliance; individuals focused on avoiding noncompliance will be less likely to act in a way to promote model recalibration (Obreja, 2024; J. Zhou et al., 2023). Efficiency and growth will suffer; and those citizens at risk of actioning an impulsive response to the initial social change will react according to a policy that amplifies the original model effect, as presented in Table 8.2.

8.7 Policy Recommendations

Increasing use of AI within insurance introduces new monitoring and compliance considerations for regulators and could exacerbate regulatory concerns in markets that are already of intense interest. Legislative and regulatory scrutiny is at an all-time high and some legislative efforts are focused on AI specifically. Data bias, algorithm bias, and new uses of AI, such as autonomous systems, are

Table 8.2 Bias mitigation strategies in insurance AI models.

Intervention Type	*Technique/Approach*	*Stage of Application*	*Insurance Application Example*	*Limitations/Trade-Offs*
Preprocessing	Reweighting, resampling, data augmentation	Before model training	Adjusting training data to balance urban/rural profiles	May distort real-world distributions
Fair Feature Selection	Excluding or transforming proxy variables	Feature engineering	Removing ZIP code as a proxy for race	Risk of performance drop if over-pruned
Adversarial Debiasing	Training model to be accurate while fooling bias detector	During model training	Fraud detection not correlated with age or race	Computationally expensive
Fair Representation Learning	Embedding data into a latent space that removes bias	During training	Embedding behavioral data without gender/ race info	May reduce interpretability
Postprocessing Corrections	Equalized odds postprocessing, reject option classification	After training	Adjusting outputs to equalize approval rates	Reduced model confidence
Explainability Techniques	SHAP, LIME, counterfactual explanations	Across model life cycle	Explaining why a claim was denied	Complex for end users to interpret
Bias Auditing Tools	AI Fairness 360, Fairlearn, What-If Tool	Model validation	Periodic audits for underwriting systems	Need domain-specific tuning
Intersectional Fairness Checks	Analyze outcomes across overlapping group identities	Model evaluation	Assess impact on older minority women	Data granularity may be insufficient
Governance Frameworks	Ethics boards, model risk committees	Oversight and policy level	Third-party review of pricing algorithms	Requires strong organizational buy-in
Regulatory Alignment	Compliance with GDPR, EO 13985, AI Act	Legal/compliance	Ensuring "right to explanation" in premium adjustments	Regulations evolve slowly
User Appeals and Recourse	Human-in-the-loop escalation systems	Deployment	Allowing clients to contest denied claims	Needs strong process design
Fairness Constraints in ML	Constrain loss functions to enforce group fairness	Model training	Force fraud detection to have equal TPR across groups	Accuracy trade-off
Causal Inference Techniques	Identify and remove causally linked biases	Data and model design	Understanding the impact of sociodemographic features	Requires expert causal modeling
Continuous Monitoring	Live system drift and fairness tracking	Post-deployment	Detecting emerging bias after market entry	Resource-intensive to maintain

predominant areas of focus for regulators. There is a need for a more coordinated and coherent approach for federal oversight of AI. Since then, some US states have begun to legislate their own standards for algorithmic risk assessments, while other states have issued executive orders creating task forces and commissions to study the issue. Those actions at the legislative, executive, and regulatory levels highlight a growing consideration for algorithm use in insurance in both the private and public sectors. However, creation of constraints and rules around the use of AI in insurance and establishment of the minimum required standards in such areas as audit, testing, transparency, and explainability will require the advance of research, practice, and dialog in this emergent area. In addition to studying biases in existing algorithms, monitoring the introduction of new algorithms into the market is necessary, especially in the event that the new algorithm is not subject to a sufficient prior review (Braun & Matthes, 2018). This provides an exploration of best practices for the insurance industry, outlines some areas where standardized technical requirements could better ensure consistent risk management, and discusses a collaborative approach that insurers can adopt with regulators as part of a larger effort to implement guidance.

8.7.1 Best Practices for Insurers

As AI decision-making systems used in insurance become ubiquitous, it is becoming increasingly important for insurers to take actionable steps to ensure that their systems are not committing algorithmic harm through biased predictions. The most effective and efficient way to preempt the need for costly remediation down the line is to make systematic and rigorous ethical and regulatory considerations part of the AI development and deployment process, from inception through implementation. The following list, although not comprehensive, identifies steps within this iterative process that can serve as a guide for how to do so: Identify potential harms from the use of AI in insurance. Insurers should commence with careful consideration of how proposed algorithmically assisted business use cases could be utilized or misused in ways that could harm vulnerable populations. Organizations should consider these harms by engaging stakeholders both within the company as well as outside of it, including employees from different divisions who may raise different issues, executives who may be aware of factors concerning the company's overall objectives, and leaders from the communities being served. Working groups that include members from within the company as well as stakeholders, including experts in the community who may be affected, can also provide value. Concerns that these groups identify could include questions like: how will the algorithmic system's decisions affect customers (Gerlick & Liozu, 2020)? Are there any groups that the system may discriminatorily or negatively impact? What are some potential ways the predictions could be misused?

8.7.2 Industry Standards

A discussion on standards for responsible AI in insurance has been going on for several years. Recommended principles for the responsible use of AI include considerations for availability of data, regulatory and legal compliance, stakeholder needs and societal impact, reliability, explainability, and validation. This has been discussed at length, including data bias mitigation and algorithmic discrimination assessment and mitigation, fairness by design, explainability and transparency, and predictability, reproducibility, and stability. In the auto insurance space, there is a focus on algorithmic discrimination and fairness testing, transparency and explainability, data security and privacy, and accountability. Similar sentiments have been expressed regarding principles for the responsible use of AI. Various organizations have also outlined principles for a trustworthy AI (Bode et al., 2024). There are ongoing developments in various AI system standards.

8.7.3 Collaboration with Regulators

Detecting and mitigating issues of algorithmic bias is a relatively new area of risk in insurance underwriting. Data and technology risks rarely occur in isolation; there is presently no robust and widely implemented system of external assurance to mandate and verify compliance of good practices by the insurance sector. The move toward increased scrutiny of algorithmic bias and risk needs to happen quickly in order to build a foundation of stakeholder trust, for the sector and for the future. We reiterate that there must be close collaboration between insurers, the Data Protection Commissioner, the Central Bank of Ireland, and the Data Protection Commission. The development of appropriate guidelines, regulations, and assurance mechanisms should be undertaken transparently, forging input from the industry, regulators, oversight bodies, academia, consumer protection groups, and the data protection community. Guidelines should be based on the principle of minimum viable regulation, providing the appropriate level of oversight for those companies more directly at risk of data or technology-related issues (Raza et al., 2023). Such an effort should be designed to be iterative, allowing the guidelines to develop in scale and scope as our understanding of the risks and consequences becomes clearer. While the current landscape may seem overwhelming, we urge all involved to take guidance from the ethical considerations outlined in the Foundations of Algorithmic Fairness section as insight for the UK's Treasury InsurTech Sandbox.

8.8 Future Directions in AI Ethics

Machine learning has attracted much debate in recent years: heated agreement on its potential for social good is countered by equally heated disagreement regarding its ethical implications, be it for news dissemination, political discourse, economic disruption, privacy enrichment, or nascent cognitive enhancements. And yet—and perhaps precisely because—we forecast further growth in the investigation of ethical principles for AI and machine learning research, development, and deployment. Here are three aspects standing for future directions in AI ethics that we find particularly relevant.

(i) Developments in AI technology continue at a rapid pace. While this is true for both foundational advances such as large language models, it is also true for further applied developments such as algorithmic claim recommendation, and new developments in economic activity tracking and prompt engineering. These advances pose novel ethical challenges. Will new predictive capabilities increase the risk of algorithmic discrimination? Will new infrastructure for digital media dissemination raise issues of transparency and reliability? Will emerging tools for criminal justice such as agency estimation and recidivism risk estimation increase the risk of wrongful conviction or violation of due process?

(ii) Global perspectives is the one factor determining the extent to which technology influences action is its perspective, governance, and totality of the group it is assisting. It becomes especially interesting when we speak of other than Western societies, cultural groups, or ethical models. Do the principles we live by in regulating technologies of, for example, autonomous driving, healthcare, or crime prediction also hold true for Western governments engaging with other software as an economic and social tool? Or is the obligation toward citizenry not necessarily one of simple governance: are other forms of IA deployment legitimate or crucial in their own right, such as those by nongovernmental organizations seeking to change the political landscape on the ground?

8.8.1 Emerging Technologies

The transformational potential of modern AI stems not only from its remarkable capabilities today, but from the rapid pace of research and investment that seeks to improve these capabilities, explore new applications, and commercialize new products. Several approaches in particular may lead to large-scale changes in the development and deployment of AI systems in the near future: trends toward more general AI systems, as well as more multimodal systems that respond to different forms of input and produce different types of output, with associated improvement in capabilities;

better AI systems enabled by expanding computational availability, with powerful new chips from leading semiconductor manufacturers, as well as utilized developments in AI algorithms that reduce the amount of training data and hardware resources required to achieve higher-quality performance; sectors of the economy which are underserved by AI today that will see an influx of new commercial systems due to increased demand for AI-powered products. These changes will enable new applications in AI and accelerate more thorough integration of AI into numerous domains already utilizing AI in critical decisions for insurance modeling and operations, such as healthcare, and related disciplines such as finance, which grapple with mitigating algorithmic bias and its many complex ethical, social, and legal implications (Bond et al., 2019). While the ethical considerations surrounding AI-powered solutions in some domains are already being scrutinized and debated, those in additional areas may see new systems emerge without appropriate consideration of their possible negative effects and publicly discuss their constructive incorporation into domestic and international legal frameworks.

8.8.2 Global Perspectives

There is growing concern and commitment to managing fairness and equity issues in AI across the world. Private firms and national governments across the world are piloting fairness checklists and guidelines. The release of a high-level expert group made a number of recommendations for the creation of comprehensive policies for responsible AI innovation and deployed a checklist for ethical AI. Other organizations are also moving toward creating responsible AI ecosystems. In 2017, a global initiative was launched for ethical considerations in artificial intelligence and autonomous systems with the aim of aligning the innovative capabilities of technology with human values; in 2019, the initiative released its ethically aligned design to provide ethically sound design guidelines. Following Canada, the USA published its own guidance on the use of trustworthy AI by federal agencies. There are also multiple technology-driven initiatives proposed to identify, measure, and mitigate algorithmic bias across various domains, including unemployment, healthcare, and online advertising, to name a few. However, while there exists a growing awareness of the need to protect individuals from the harmful impact of algorithmic bias, the solutions are still very much in development. Organizations are in various stages of aiding local and national governments in combating algorithmic bias. Moreover, while the institutions have put in effort and committed time and resources to outline high-level principles, there are international differences, challenges, and trade-offs with respect to the principles (J. Zhou et al., 2023). The implementation of AI technologies has resulted in various issues worldwide, including algorithmic bias, infringing on religious freedoms, and in some cases a manifested loss of life.

8.8.3 Public Awareness and Education

To create an ethical artificial intelligence framework that is more equitable, it is essential to engage with the public and educate people inside and outside organizations that are developing, implementing, and deploying the technology. It is important to ensure that people who are affected by the technology are included in algorithmic decision-making, as data scientists, computer scientists, software engineers, and others working on these teams are not always representative. The AI community in particular needs to take seriously the responsibility of talking about bias and inequity in technology so that all people can have a greater understanding of how systems have been biased and what impact they have, and how systems can be created to be more equitable. The difference in the prevalent conversation around automation and especially algorithmic bias in the media, in policy, and among civic groups is also something to consider: it is not enough to raise awareness of the bias, but one must also create a cohesive understanding of when people are being harmed, in what ways, and what practical changes can be made to create more equitable systems. Tangible solutions are needed to some of the technical challenges people face as they discover error-filled models (Braun & Matthes, 2018). A unified understanding must also be cultivated among researchers from all disciplines that associates the act of democratizing and opening up tools with the well-intentioned goal of closing the gap of equity. Programs and initiatives promoting algorithm transparency may even benefit from advocacy from the computing community.

8.9 Conclusion

Insurance is a key site of algorithmic decision-making. AI tools are determining who is, and who is not, able to afford and access essential products, and these decision-making systems must be fair and accountable. However, there are few up-and-running processes for ensuring the accuracy of insurance-related algorithmically driven decisions or appropriately reviewing the fairness of AI and ML tools designed to assist with such decisions. To that end, this paper helps insurance experts and additional stakeholders recognize how bias can arise in AI-assisted tools applied across the insurance life cycle. In addition, we provide concrete steps for rooting algorithmic bias out of such tools and for ensuring the accuracy of insurance-related algorithmically driven decisions. In particular, we emphasize that it is essential to recognize that insurance claims and underwriting are inherently high-stakes scenarios, as biased decisions based on protected attributes can have deep impacts on the lives of those affected, potentially steering consumers toward unhealthy and financially ruinous economic states. Overall, the insurance field would greatly benefit from the implementation of external algorithmic audits of AI- and ML-assisted decision-making tools across the insurance life cycle. Furthermore, such audits would significantly benefit from regulation and incentivization, leading to a de facto demand from insurance providers for transparency in the tools they use. For this, the proposed tools would serve as an outline for external auditors to gain insight into the workings of the AI systems in the context of insurance and would serve as a guideline for insurance institutions looking to optimize their AI tools. In all, our proposed tools would help mitigate common algorithmic biases and help standardize the auditing process of AI tools in the insurance domain—a process that is currently far from being risk-free and still in its infancy.

References

Akter, S., Dwivedi, Y.K., Biswas, K., Michael, K., Bandara, R.J. and Sajib, S. (2021). Addressing Algorithmic Bias in AI-Driven Customer Management. *Journal of Global Information Management*, *29*(6). https://doi.org/10.4018/JGIM.20211101.oa3

Archambault, S.G., Ramachandran, S., Acosta, E. and Fu, S. (2024). Ethical Dimensions of Algorithmic Literacy for College Students: Case Studies and Cross-Disciplinary Connections. *Journal of Academic Librarianship*, *50*(3). https://doi.org/10.1016/j.acalib.2024.102865

Bode, I., Huelss, H., Nadibaidze, A., Qiao-Franco, G. and Watts, T.F.A. (2024). Algorithmic Warfare: Taking Stock of a Research Programme. *Global Society*, *38*(1). https://doi.org/10.1080/13600826.2023.2263473

Bond, R.R., Mulvenna, M. and Wang, H. (2019). Human-Centered Artificial Intelligence: Weaving UX into Algorithmic Decision-Making. *RoCHI 2019: International Conference on Human–Computer Interaction.*

Braun, D. and Matthes, F. (2018). Generating Explanations for Algorithmic Decisions of Usage-Based Insurances Using Natural Language Generation. *Lecture Notes in Informatics (LNI)*, *P-279*.

Dwork, C. and Roth, A. (2013). The Algorithmic Foundations of Differential Privacy. *Foundations and Trends in Theoretical Computer Science*, *9*(3–4). https://doi.org/10.1561/0400000042

Engelmann, A. (2023). Algorithmic Transparency as a Fundamental Right in the Democratic Rule of Law. *Brazilian Journal of Law, Technology and Innovation*, *1*(2). https://doi.org/10.59224/bjlti.v1i2.169-188

Gerlick, J.A. and Liozu, S.M. (2020). Ethical and Legal Considerations of Artificial Intelligence and Algorithmic Decision-Making in Personalized Pricing. *Journal of Revenue and Pricing Management*, *19*(2). https://doi.org/10.1057/s41272-019-00225-2

Obreja, D.M. (2024). When Stories Turn Institutional: How TikTok Users Legitimate the Algorithmic Sensemaking. *Social Media and Society*, *10*(1). https://doi.org/10.1177/20563051231224114

Raza, S., Dolatabadi, E., Ondrusek, N., Rosella, L. and Schwartz, B. (2023). Discovering Social Determinants of Health from Case Reports Using Natural Language Processing: Algorithmic Development and Validation. *BMC Digital Health*, *1*(1). https://doi.org/10.1186/s44247-023-00035-y

Shafik, W. (2024a). Factors Affecting Green Purchase Behaviors for Small and Medium Enterprises (SMEs) in Uganda. In *Entrepreneurial Strategies for the Internationalization and Digitalization of SMEs* (pp. 198–224). IGI Global. https://doi.org/10.4018/979-8-3693-3518-5.ch009

Shafik, W. (2024b). Generative AI for Social Good and Sustainable Development. In *Generative AI: Current Trends and Applications* (pp. 185–217). Springer.

Shafik, W. (2025). Generative Artificial Intelligence for Social Good and Sustainable Development. *Generative AI: Disruptive Technologies for Innovative Applications* (pp. 153–185). Wiley https://doi.org/10.1002/9781394302932.ch8

Shafik, W., Singh, R. and Kumar, V. (2025). Artificial Intelligence Transparency and Explainability in Sustainable Healthcare. In *Transforming Healthcare Sector Through Artificial Intelligence and Environmental Sustainability* (pp. 165–191). Springer.

Singh, R., Shafik, W., Crowther, D. and Kumar, V. (Eds.). (2024). *Transforming Healthcare Sector Through Artificial Intelligence and Environmental Sustainability* (1st ed., Vol. 1). Springer Nature Singapore. https://doi.org/10.1007/978-981-97-9555-0

Zhou, J., Zhang, Y., Luo, Q., Parker, A.G. and De Choudhury, M. (2023). Synthetic Lies: Understanding AI-Generated Misinformation and Evaluating Algorithmic and Human Solutions. *Conference on Human Factors in Computing Systems – Proceedings*. https://doi.org/10.1145/3544548.3581318

Zhou, Y., Wang, L. and Chen, W. (2023). The Dark Side of AI-Enabled HRM on Employees Based on AI Algorithmic Features. *Journal of Organizational Change Management*, *36*(7). https://doi.org/10.1108/JOCM-10-2022-0308

9

Explainable AI for Insurance: Enhancing Transparency, Accountability, and Client Trust

Wasswa Shafik

9.1 Introduction

Explainable artificial intelligence (XAI) provides a visualization or explanation of the model's decision at a certain instance. This is a nascent area of AI that is of paramount importance as ethical, responsible, and trustworthy AI systems need to be explainable in order to understand the actual model behavior. Moreover, for the adoption of AI in safety-critical domains such as healthcare, finance, insurance, and defense, it is crucial to explain the models' predictions to the stakeholders. XAI is extremely useful in the following situations. First, there could be a flaw with the model's design. XAI helps in debugging the algorithms. For example, assuming a model predicts a certain patient to have 0% of genetic roots to a specific tumor, but that patient has relatives having similar tumors and the patient has been identified to carry a certain gene alteration, then the model's prediction will be deemed as faulty (Minh et al., 2022).

The domain expert can use XAI methods to debug the model to understand how the model reached that conclusion. If the model had failed, then the model would need to be retrained with various candidate configurations. Second, if the model has not generalized well on the validation/test set and has resulted in misclassification for specific instances, then XAI will help the model developers figure out how the model reached that conclusion. The domain experts will be able to understand the model's behavior for specific subsets of instances. If the reasoning is different from what is expected, then the appropriate actions can be taken, and the model has not generalized well, and will need to be retrained. Third, it could be a case that the model is correct, but the domain experts do not trust the model's prediction or reasoning. If the model is a black-box model, then that will lead to rejection of the model and distrust of the model's prediction (Taj & Jhanjhi, 2022).

9.1.1 Definition of Explainable AI

AI methods, and in particular machine learning (ML) methods, have been developing rapidly in the last couple of decades. Their successes in a variety of tasks such as image and speech recognition, natural language processing (NLP), robotics, etc., have led to the increasing diffusion of AI technologies in society. Given the large number of tasks where AI systems are being used, these systems must be at the same time accurate, efficient, and useful. Moreover, AI systems are often part of big socio-technical infrastructures with, in general, a problem-detecting and a problem-solving

DOI: 10.1201/9781003747659-9

function. The goal of such socio-technical infrastructures is to address complex individual and societal problems such as, but not limited to, health issues, safety and security, economic services, etc. In light of their fundamental role in contemporary society, AI systems must be also able to explain their reasoning process and provide an account for their actions. A simple definition of XAI considers it as a set of procedures and methods that permit a human to comprehend the decisions taken by an AI system, given the submission of an input to the AI system. More formally, an AI decision function is considered explainable if it can be understood by a human at some adequate level of detail at a certain critical region around a given input in the input space. While human understanding is usually facilitated by methods that permit the reduction of the complexity of the decision function, we adopt the term XAI to capture a broader spectrum of possible methods (Lahby et al., 2021). In particular, we consider any possible method permitting human understanding as belonging to the research domain that we denote as XAI through seven practical approaches, as demonstrated in Figure 9.1.

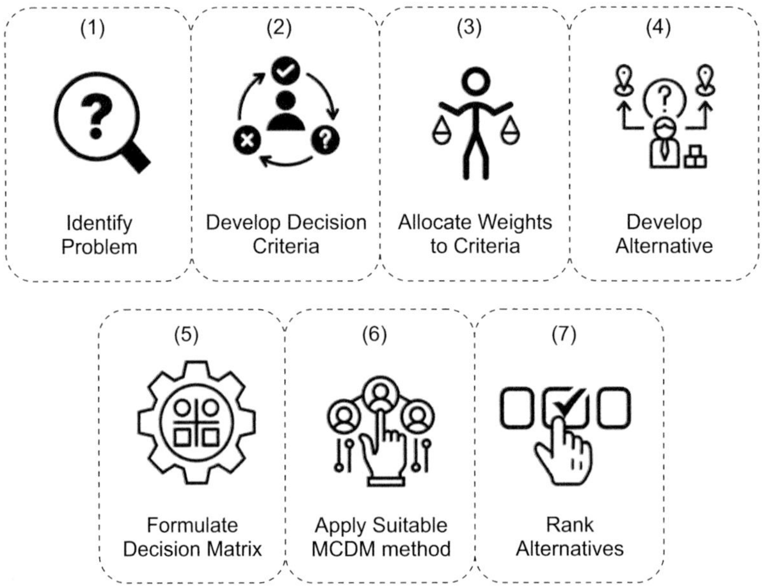

Fig. 9.1 Appropriate insurance problem identification.

9.1.2 Importance in AI Systems

Artificial intelligence systems are becoming an integral part of our lives. These systems assist us in areas such as recruiting, credit scoring, investing, and security. A financial investor may utilize AI-supported services to evaluate current market conditions and receive timely investing recommendations. These systems read news articles and evaluate the sentiments around the released information, and call for a buy or sell action. Most of these recommenders are driven by machine learning models that are hidden behind a curtain. Machine learning models learn patterns from a gigantic amount of training data. Their results after deployment are driven not by rules explicitly described by humans but by an internal mapping learned from the data. However, not all the users of these intelligent systems have a technical background. Non-expert users may not understand the inner workings of these systems. As a result, the recommendation made by the model may be rejected due to the black-box nature of the model, despite an insignificant improvement in model accuracy when compared with a baseline probabilistic model. This jeopardizes the user's trust in the model. Research in explainable AI helps end-users understand the model better through explanations (Górriz et al., 2023). To be more precise, explanations aim to increase users' faith in the model.

9.2 The Role of AI in the Insurance Industry

The introduction of AI is quickly changing all aspects of life, and insurance is no exception. The worldwide AI in the insurance industry is poised to catapult from 1.06 billion in 2022 to 39.53 billion in 2030. The use cases for intelligence in insurance are vast, including helpful automated customer service, improved underwriting and pricing, fraud detection, benefit prediction, claims handling, risk assessment, and risk modeling. AI can help make customer claims more efficient and accurate. At the underwriting phase, it can alleviate some of the decision-making burden from humans, paving the way for faster outcomes. If developed with safety features, AI may mitigate many types of human errors that lead to poor claims processing. AI is being used in a variety of different ways, including fraud investigation. Increasing volumes of fraud have burdened the insurance sector. To determine the legitimacy of claims, AI can help identify discrepancies, returning precise outcomes quickly without being hampered by volume constraints. Additionally, it can help automate repetitive tasks such as mini investigations, and incorporate geolocation, social media, and financial data into the fraud prediction process. The claim investigation and settlement speed and efficiency can be improved as it detects hidden or suspected fraud patterns. Additionally, machine learning forecasting models can predict expected claims costs at the point of sale and throughout coverage. AI can assist in identifying mitigating factors that lead to fewer claims across customer segments, either by systematically recommending that underwriters incorporate these factors into their underwriting or actuarial models or by creating predictive scoring models (Ahmed et al., 2023). Besides, unlike human agents, intelligent virtual agents can cater to customers every hour of every day, solving simple questions such as "when is my premium due," "how do I file a claim," "renew my policy," or "find an agent."

9.2.1 Current Applications of AI in Insurance

AI is increasingly relied upon across the life cycle of the insurance industry to monitor, manage, distribute, and settle risk. Insurers primarily use AI for four functions: claims processing, customer service, fraud detection, and risk assessment. When it comes to claims, it helps automate both intake and adjudication, specifically within the areas of P&C, health, and life insurance. Through case management, AI helps provide better estimations on the time and resources that are required to fully process each claim, enabling better planning and allocation of resources. Insurers have implemented virtual assistants, intelligent chatbots, fraud detection, indexing, and training and onboarding in order to supercharge customer service. Several aspects of the claims process are managed by chatbots that handle customers who require assistance 24/7, especially during peak hours. Such chatbots help usher customers through the experience of filing an insurance claim. Insurers have implemented fraud detection solutions to protect against increasingly inventive fraudsters, as fraud represents a significant portion of losses, a cost estimated at a substantial amount annually in the United States alone. AI relies on a variety of algorithms to detect suspicious claims through deep learning, neural networks, supervised machine learning, and predictive analytics to detect patterns. AI, through data management and risk modeling, has also been embedded in risk assessment processes. Such models help insurers price risk more accurately when issuing policies and completing underwriting because they can help providers more efficiently ingest and assess vast amounts of data that determine an applicant's suitability for coverage (Ponzoni et al., 2023). Predictive analytics can also be deployed to assess risk through modeling, predicting the percentage of claims to be expected, given the company's specific portfolio allocation, composition, and probable underwriting losses for each risk type through digital asset management (DAM), as illustrated in Figure 9.2.

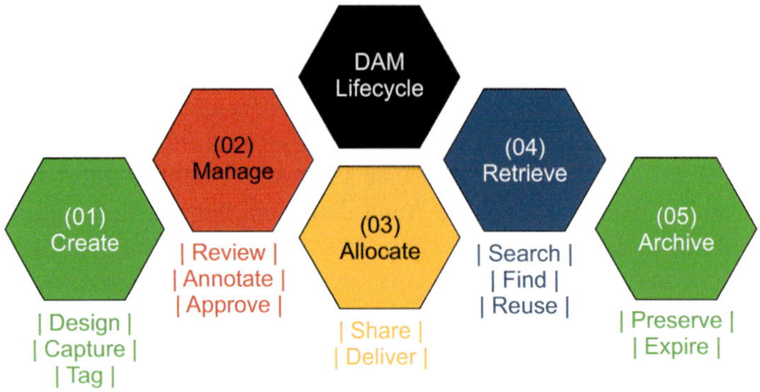

Fig. 9.2 The digital asset management (DAM) life cycle.

9.2.2 Benefits of AI for Insurers

Advanced AI technologies and increased availability of data are driving an unprecedented wave of innovation in the insurance industry. Insurance firms are often large data collectors, and financial services firms are sitting on enormous troves of sensitive, personal data about clients, such as data about finances, behavior, and health, that would make them ideal candidates for harnessing highly accurate, algorithmic predictions. Insurers have begun using AI tools to improve both the quality and efficiency of core insurance services such as underwriting, claims, fraud detection, and customer service. Insurers have begun to use AI tools in ways that would create a more efficient, customer-friendly marketplace. In particular, until only recently, insurers have used rudimentary models to assess risk—that is, might we be compelled to make a payout?—for various types of coverage, and set their premiums accordingly. Doing so serves to protect the company's solvency, but can lead to anti-competitive behavior and reduced transparency. Recent developments in machine learning technology—made possible by the synergy of enormous amounts of demographic and behavioral consumer data, advanced algorithms, and massive storage capacity in the cloud—would enable insurers to estimate the likelihood of certain behaviors occurring over different time horizons, and adjust premium prices to reflect real-time risk probability. This kind of dynamic pricing model would react to likely deep discounting by market entrants for some specific services, as well as ups and downs in insurance demand by particular localities and customers. Such generated pricing would likely create greater price fairness across demographic groups (Owens et al., 2022). Having the entire industry on the same, data-driven page, allowing for continuous fine-tuning based on millions of data points, rather than only actuarial-grade results trademarked by the major insurers, would create better market transparency and a more efficient enforcement of insurance regulations.

9.3 Challenges of AI in Insurance

AI is increasingly popular in many fields, namely, natural language processing, computer vision (CV), and speech and audio processing; and it produces many results or predictions that experts can hardly totally disagree with. However, there are a growing number of blogs and reports published that list the challenges of AI, such as problems of explainability, interpretability, etc. There are many hidden layers in the typical deep learning models; hence, even researchers are not certain how the models make a certain decision. The AI models are sometimes treated as black-box models.

However, the insurance domain has two major properties that make AI models very challenging. The first property is about sensitive data, and the other property is about social issues. Insurance is one of the markets that needs to deal with sensitive user data. The use of sensitive data is tightly related to the data protection regulation. The regulation states that one can use sensitive data for the AI model prediction only in limited and rare cases, especially focusing on important social issues such as national emergencies, severe public health crises, etc. It even states that, on the basis of sensitive data, one is not allowed to make automatic decisions that could be harmful to oneself. Hence, most insurance companies do not allow brokers or agents to sell their insurance products based on personal health data. Rather, they seem to think long and hard before building the AI model using such data. This creates an additional high barrier for insurance companies to develop models using sensitive data in compliance with the regulation. Apart from not being able to use sensitive data, there are three popular social issues currently cited as related to fairness when building AI models (Hall et al., 2022). The first issue is about bias and fairness. The second issue is about discrimination. The third issue is about stereotypes.

9.3.1 Data Privacy Concerns

Over the past couple of years, there has been an increasing skepticism about obtaining permission to use sensitive personal data for model training. Various aspects of AI algorithms can be seen as a potential violation of data privacy. First, model training and generating output predictions can involve using client-sensitive data. Second, for data vectors that are stored for model inference, it may be possible to reverse-engineer personal information from these individuals. Third, these concerns are amplified in federated systems, where private institutions, which are inherently untrustworthy, can collaborate with private institutions in order to reduce the model generalization error. AI researchers have proposed a number of methods to address these issues. Federated learning combines a number of different models stored at different institutions so that no sensitive information has to be shared. Differential privacy adds noise to the model input so that it is difficult for adversaries to reconstruct it. The input is fed into AI models only a limited number of times, and, in the case of the output being located in a small input space, especially for classification problems, it is used a limited number of times. Vanilla federated learning does not guarantee the preservation of privacy, as the only reliable guarantee is k-anonymity. The requirement of obtaining permission from individuals is not new, as regulations oblige all businesses to obtain consent before collecting any personal data. While data privacy is an issue for all businesses worldwide, it is particularly of importance to insurance companies that are entrusted with sensitive medical and financial data of clients. In particular, AI-driven risk pooling systems can potentially violate the privacy of individuals in many different conditions throughout their lives, and companies are required to preserve client data secrecy. Use cases in which federated systems can be implemented in insurance data, while ensuring data protection, are proposed (Ahmed & Zubair, 2022). As insurers create AI systems that are able to learn from federated data stored with their different business partners, it is important for them to engage in these collaborative activities to ensure that the underlying federated system used to create fine-tuned AI health monitoring models is sufficiently transparent.

9.3.2 Bias and Fairness Issues

Bias is a common issue in business intelligence applications. AI models are fed with historical data; if that data reflects a biased view of the world, the models will "learn" those biases, which can lead to bad predictions. In the case of insurance, this can concern areas such as risk assessment for credit, health, or property insurance, and the prediction of price or loss. The impact of bias on the insurance sector is increased in detriment to the insured party. When the prediction is made about the insured party and serves as the input for the insurer offering a quote that is above their risk level based on unfairly biased data, the impact of such bias is clearly misalignment and damage to the entire industry. In the insurance sector, many aspects potentially affect the attraction and retention of clients. One such aspect is the level of bias in AI-driven decisions; another is the degree of "fairness"; and both have an important connection to transparency. We can understand fairness as vice versa to bias; when a system is fair, it doesn't discriminate against a section of the population in its decisions. In insurance with respect to the insured parties, we can think of fairness violations based on protected attributes; in our study, focused on insurance services for clients, these attributes refer to protected types such as gender, ideology, language, nationality, race, sexual orientation, or other protected characteristics (Chauhan & Sonawane, 2022). The questions around fairness are of high relevance and importance.

9.4 The Need for Transparency

A growing body of regulation and legislation is covering the financial services industry ever more stringently, for safeguarding aspects such as privacy, security, risk assessment, and also transparency and explainability. Examples include non-banking FinTech regulations and general acts. At the very least, these regulatory mechanisms require companies to have clear accountabilities when working with client data for whatever reason. This is particularly important in the context of using advanced data science methods for assigning risks or fraudulent behavior assessments. These methods carry a risk of being considered "black boxes," thus contravening requirements for transparency, explainability, and accountability, based on the nature of the methods and of the data being processed, employed for operational purposes with little human intervention and little peer scrutiny. Whichever organization is entrusted with client data needs to prove its reliability to its clients. Clients will be reassured when they not only understand but also agree with an assignment of risk in order to give away pieces of private information. Digital natives expect easy and interactive ways to understand how decisions about data processing were made. Banks need to be able to explain how they determine risk assessments, and how sensitive data affects that process, when actions will be taken. An AI model will be treated as a real advisor, and is able to provide clear data explanations that are personalized for human consumption (Imoize et al., 2022). Payment systems will need to leverage AI engines that provide explanations for decisions while being asked about risks, in seconds.

9.4.1 Regulatory Requirements

AI tools have been developed for different industries to perform a variety of functions. In particular, the application of AI in critical domains—such as aviation, healthcare, and insurance—that directly affect people's lives has raised concerns about the transparency and accountability of such tools. These industries are facing increasing demands from stakeholders, including not only regulatory agencies but also clients, for increased transparency in the activities of AI tools. Governments and regulatory organizations have been developing specific guidelines, proposed regulations, and regulations on the development and deployment of AI technology, driven by their interest in minimizing the negative effects of AI. The General Data Protection Regulation emphasizes the principle of the right to explanation, which allows individuals to know the rationale behind any automated decision-making process carried out by organizations respected under the regulation. The purpose of this regulation is to allow individuals to "understand and challenge decisions that are affecting them" and to ensure responsibility regarding individuals' rights, freedoms, and legitimate expectations. The regulation lists several domain applications that do not allow for risk-free handling of personal data: credit and insurance assessments, employee monitoring, natural person profiling, training, and recruitment (Carta et al., 2022). Even in organizations that fall under the protective jurisdiction of the regulation and are unlikely to affect the security and well-being of individuals, the regulation permits a legal basis for prohibiting an organization from making solely automated decisions with respect to sensitive data if the organization fails to explain the rationale behind the decision.

9.4.2 Client Expectations

A pivotal aspect of risk consideration is accountability. More than ever people require answers to questions—such as "What do you know about me?", "How do you know it?", and "How likely am I to get hit in the street by a meteorite?"—when they are confronted with an insurance decision. The digitalization process has established a foundation for data collection and data sharing by allowing companies to have access to diverse datasets providing considerable amounts of information. The same trend enables and empowers a consumer to increase their bargaining power through comparative price and service offerings, as well as to express their opinions online and voice their satisfaction or, more importantly, their aggravation with a particular provider on social media. Whether or not they intend to inflict reputational damage, many policyholders are not completely aware of the effect of such comments, especially in a world of ubiquitousness. This may potentially cause a snowball effect aggravating the company's market position and performance. The combination of these two aspects puts a considerable amount of pressure on the insurance company. What can, or rather what should, the insurance industry do to satisfy its clients' needs for transparency? One possible avenue, which also applies to external stakeholders like regulators may be through XAI. However, releasing state-of-the-art XAI tools does not necessarily ensure the consumer's trust in the entire market. It is rather a first step into the right direction. Devising interpretable models, conducting evaluation studies to examine what constitutes a trust-enhancing form of interpretability, how the necessity for transparency relates to the insured event, and what other means there are to educate people about risk exposure in order to enhance their understanding, augmented by persuasive digital experiences for personalized interpretation, can help the entire financial industry to increase the trust threshold of clients again, as presented in Table 9.1.

Table 9.1 Explainability techniques and their application in insurance.

Technique	*Type*	*Application in Insurance*	*Strengths*	*Limitations*
LIME – Local Interpretable Model-agnostic Explanations	Local (model-agnostic)	Explaining why a claim was denied	Easy to implement, visual-friendly	Sensitive to data perturbations
SHAP – SHapley Additive exPlanations	Local and global	Explaining premium calculations based on individual features	Consistent, mathematically grounded	Computationally expensive
Counterfactual Explanations	Local	Showing alternative scenarios for underwriting approval	Intuitive for clients, promotes actionability	May produce unrealistic examples
Feature Importance	Global	Highlighting top risk predictors in underwriting	High-level transparency	Lacks individual decision detail
Partial Dependence Plots	Global	Visualizing the effect of income or age on claim outcomes	Visual interpretability	Assumes independence of features
Anchors	Local (model-agnostic)	Defining rules that "anchor" predictions for fraud detection	Offers human-understandable rules	May miss edge cases

Contd.

Table 9.1 *Contd.*

Technique	*Type*	*Application in Insurance*	*Strengths*	*Limitations*
Explainable Boosting Machines (EBM)	Intrinsic	Interpretable models for pricing	Built-in transparency	May underperform versus black-box models
Rule-Based Surrogates	Local/global	Generating simple rules to mimic deep model behavior	Simplified surrogate models	Trade-off between accuracy and interpretability
Decision Trees	Intrinsic	Transparent claims scoring system	Easy to audit and visualize	Susceptible to overfitting
What-If Tool	Interactive	Simulating premium scenarios based on client inputs	Client-friendly interface	Limited to supported model formats
Concept Activation Vectors (CAVs)	Deep learning	Understanding abstract insurance features in neural networks	Enables concept-level insight	Requires labeled concept examples
Natural Language Explanations	Post-hoc	Providing claim rejection reasons in client-friendly language	Improves communication and trust	Must ensure accuracy and avoid oversimplification
Attention Mechanisms	Intrinsic (NLP, CV)	Understanding which text or image regions drive decisions	Good for document-based underwriting	Can be misleading if misinterpreted
Saliency Maps (Visual AI)	Local (CV)	Detecting image-based damage for vehicle claims	Highlights relevant regions	Only applicable to visual input

9.5 Building Trust through Explainability

The efficient sharing of data between policyholders and insurance companies through answers to underwriting questions and during claim processing is crucial for mutual benefits. The policyholder shares personal data, and the insurer uses the data to assess the risk, estimate the basis of premium pricing, and decide on the insurance policy's validity. The firm builds a risk profile of the policyholder with a goal of protecting themselves from loss, and the consumer has an expectation that, based on the insurer's evaluation, they will receive the support promised in the event of a covered loss. To cement the relationship, transparency regarding how the firm handles the customer's experience, the pricing model, and how the claim is processed and validated are paramount. Any aspect of this process without the benefit of transparency will destroy consumer trust. To that end, companies work to build trust with clients and partners by developing models of loss prediction and incident evaluation that are straightforward, clear, and transparent. They provide clear explanations on why a particular decision or recommendation, aided by processes based on natural language processing, machine learning, visualization tools, and clear interactive dashboards, can make the final decision intuitive for both the consumer and the insurer (Fritz-Morgenthal et al., 2022; Schwalbe & Finzel, 2023; Yang, 2022). This helps not only in building trust but also facilitates the chain of accountability for both parties in the partnership.

9.5.1 How Explainable AI Enhances Trust

Doing business means making decisions that affect not only your wallet but also your social well-being, as other people's lives can be influenced by your decisions in the long run. Clearer business decisions lead to greater trust by clients and investors, thus assuring loyalty and improving performance. Trust is a powerful and delicate tool that must be carefully nurtured, as it is the basis of long and positive relationships between the service provider and the service user. As even the quality of products and the price of services cannot create a strong barrier to competition, the unique value of the company can only be found in its ability to create trust. If a company loses its customers' trust, it will pay for it in the long run. The relationship between explainability and trust then deserves a careful analysis, especially in sensitive sectors like insurance. Models in general, and AI in particular, are used to make sensitive decisions that affect the lives of millions of people. As a consequence, small changes in input data may lead to significant changes in the model's output, with severe effects on customers' lives. Employing machine learning algorithms that can be classified as black-box models raises the problem of the opacity of the decision processes that lie behind the predictions and insurance decision-making. The application of these techniques to risk management creates various concerns related not only to security but also to secrecy, communication, equality, and justice, which must be carefully considered by the company. Today, legislation not only makes fairness obligations but also requests for an explanation (Sahakyan et al., 2021). Designed to prevent and mitigate any discrimination, these rules can thus have ramifications on the technical choices of AI development.

9.5.2 Case Studies of Successful Implementation

Holistic explainability has yet to be widely implemented, but there are indeed a few successful case studies of unique applications of Enterprise Application Integration (EAI) principles that directly address these dimensions of trust in AI insurance technology. One commonplace example in insurance is within underwriting, where automated decision systems are typically seen as particularly dangerous in terms of accountability and regulatory compliance. A company works with insurers to explain tickets for complex products to clients who may be significantly underserved or are going through financial hardship. From a broad picture perspective, a more pragmatic step toward using explainable AI principles could be templated explainability at a more reduced scale. For example, a company could localize global heuristics around risk groups chosen by a model and use this to provide tailored, itemized risk group explanation when working with claims or pricing products for new clients in such risk categories. A company helps insurers explain complex products with little needed explanation effort. The result is an overview that ensures active transparency while letting models optimize the core in the large data. Another prominent and prevalent example in the insurance world of advanced AI-oriented automations is around pricing insurance products dynamically, which are the most effective tools to lower underwriting risk. These AI systems can be incredibly powerful at understanding risk in real time, but they come with increased scrutiny. Regulators hold prominent positions around making sure they report the influence of protected categories and also guarantee that the influence is just and reasonable; for example, they're not just fixing prices but are really helping ensure they reflect evolving insurance risk profiles (Goodell et al., 2023). Transparent incentivization is essential here, then allowing these dynamic pricing algorithms to relieve the challenges of insurance products but without suppressing these challenges.

9.6 Techniques for Achieving Explainability

Many different techniques have been developed for providing explanations of found AI models or their predictions. They can be split into two groups: model-agnostic methods, that can be used in connection to any models, and the use of interpretable models. The second group contains widely used techniques such as decision trees, generalized additive models, and rule-based models. Due to their intrinsic transparency and ability to provide interpretable results directly, these models are more naturally explainable, because the explanation can be derived directly from their internal structure. However, their accuracy is usually lower than the accuracy of Artificial Neural Network Model (ANN) models, and is restricted to simpler problems. Model-agnostic methods can be applied to the prediction of any black-box model; some of them are applied to the local area around the prediction point, while others provide global explanations of the behavior of the model. In the context of insurance, two important methods try to explain the input–output maps of black-box models. Despite being model-agnostic, the computation of values is not necessarily efficient for any possible model. Here, we will focus on perturbation-based or surrogate methods. Perturbation-based explanations provide insight into the functioning of the model by looking at features' contributions to the predictions. Briefly explained, one method samples random points around the prediction of interest, assumes the local area surrounding it can be approximated through a linear model, and fits that linear model to the generated dataset (Minh et al., 2022). Given how this method works, it is capable of being used with any classifier, whether it is a black-box or an interpretable one, because interpretability only comes with the linear model of the local area surrounding the point of interest.

9.6.1 Model-Agnostic Methods

Many model-agnostic techniques focus on analyzing a single model's predictions. These approaches usually provide post-hoc explanations for a model's prediction. The latter assumption refers to the fact that, given a trained black-box model, one can use the proposed method to extract an explanation for a particular data point. One type of model-agnostic technique assumes that interpretability is not a property intrinsic to the model. Model-agnostic approaches assume that the required information to perform an interpretation or explanation task is usually in the data. This category includes model-agnostic techniques that define surrogates of the trained model. The first type of approach focuses on analyzing the whole black-box model and its predictions. For instance, these methods can compute instances that were deemed confusing and would benefit from additional scrutiny, or use model-enhanced visualizations to aid the analysis of how the model interprets the input space. In the context of specific application domains, these methods can produce relatively generic results. However, when the model is used in other application domains, the added value is reduced. These methods can compute instances that were deemed confusing and would benefit from additional scrutiny. A relaxation of this type of model-agnostic method allows the model to be invariant to small perturbations on the input space (Taj & Jhanjhi, 2022). Hence, the model's behavior, and more importantly, a few confusing instances, will depend on a higher hierarchy of features that are supposed to be modeled by the interpretable method.

9.6.2 Interpretable Models

The second category of methods concerns specifically methods that produce interpretable models and thus perform inference with an inherently interpretable model. Although other methods can compensate for the lack of interpretability of the models by providing ex-post explanations, these methods have a great disadvantage in that the resulting explanation is usually only valid in a local sense; at least in principle, model-agnostic methods can always provide a local explanation, while model-specific methods can also provide global explanations. These methods produce explanations that the model is inherently interpretable. These models are intrinsically interpretable because their complexity is restricted, and they cannot capture very complex mappings between input and output vectors. The advantage of these methods is that the models provide global and local explanations for all observations, both in the training and testing datasets, uniformly, since the models use them to perform inference and these are not approximated solutions to the very complex and characteristic models, as illustrated in Figure 9.3. These methods are usually linear regression with few parameters, small trees with few nodes or splits, rule lists, and now the interpretable neural networks built with neural modules (Ridley, 2022). These models are too restricted or simply unsuitable to capture many relationships present in the data, and this will lead to poor prediction performance not only on the testing dataset but also on the training dataset.

Fig. 9.3 The complex mappings between input and output.

9.7 Integrating Explainable AI into Insurance Processes

The previous chapters explored the need for explainability in insurance AI, described various methods for creating interpretable models, and visualized the outputs and consequences of model decisions. But how might one actually go about adopting and integrating these tools into their pipeline? Here, we discuss various options for carrying out explainable AI in common insurance business scenarios, highlighting the relevant decisions at each stage along the way. If our goal is to make AI decision-making transparent and understandable to clients, then the explainability needs to be built up from the ground level, starting with model choice, construction, and training. In the use cases we discuss, we will focus on three main applications areas of insurance AI: underwriting risk pricing; claims processing and reserving; and fraud detection. Each of these tasks has an obvious need for explainability, resulting from client relationship needs, and consumers at large care about the fidelity of these insurance systems. By drawing upon these joint understandability and fidelity goals, we can seek to build a fidelity cycle into the AI underwriting and claims modeling processes, whereby models can be used to inform selection or pricing criteria better. Then, pricing insights alongside other considerations can be used to further improve the pipeline without overly sacrificing predictive performance or calibration (Górriz et al., 2023). In short, joint understandability and fidelity need not be mutually exclusive in the pipeline, and careful and informative AI modeling can be leveraged to enhance traditional sets of business tools further.

9.7.1 Underwriting

Insurance underwriting is used to determine the associated risk of insuring a policyholder and the appropriate premium to charge for assuming that risk. After a loss-generating event, insurers gather premium dollars from many insureds to cover the substantial costs of payouts to a small number of policyholders who experience losses. Failure to assess risk accurately can lead to substantial claims cost for insurers. However, judging risk is a complex assignment with equations too sophisticated to explicitly execute. Numerous quantitative and qualitative factors such as financial stability, property location, criminal records, home-safety devices, medical history, and other actuarial and demographic factors must be evaluated, sometimes across many alternatives. In addition, the underwriting decision should be made by an experienced underwriter well versed in industry nuances. But the underwriter is faced with voluminous amounts of data sourced across many disparate input files (Ponzoni et al., 2023). Understanding which factors carry the most influence, perceiving patterns across variables, and discovering associations can be difficult. Luckily, data science capabilities are a perfect complement to the skilled judgment of experienced underwriters. Machine learning algorithms calculate variable importance and reveal interactions and other complexities which, when combined with visualizations, can expose hidden patterns and relationships. Adding visualizations to the underwriter's toolkit expands the capabilities of that skilled expert, especially as the complexity of the decision-making and the scale and variety of data increase. With these capabilities, the underwriting process is transparent because the actuarial and demographic factors impacting the decision can be visualized. It also allows fiduciary responsibility and accountability, and facilitates trust for the policyholder. Using these capabilities for underwriting enables consistent, accurate decisions while also allowing the underwriter to make the final decision especially in unusual cases or clear outlier positions (Imoize et al., 2022).

9.7.2 Claims Processing

Most insurance companies promote themselves as delivering compensations through a fair and just process. For the most part, insurance companies aim to establish a level of trust and transparency through this essential flow within the company. But the dilemma lies among the chosen algorithms to drive decision-making processes. Devisors of the algorithms need to be careful, for algorithms assistance in compensation allocation may exacerbate the preexisting situation of racial, ethnic, and gender inequality. Machine learning systems for claims processing typically analyze textual information. Insurance claims typically have a large amount of text in the form of notes made by claims adjusters within working systems and by third-party vendors. Many of the notes are unstructured or semi-structured free-text language statements. The advantage of using NLP solutions in this area is that, especially as data volumes grow quickly, using machine learning in an unsupervised manner, without the answer keys of structured databases, can result in more effective automation of these processes. The explainability issue is crucial in this application area. First and foremost, if a claims processing decision is "wrong," it can unequally distribute claims payouts based on race, ethnicity, and gender among other characteristics. Insurers use words such as "deny," "unfair," "delay," "acceptable," "reject," and "investigate" when referring to possible outcomes from this decision area. Words like these raise red flags for examining decision-bias areas. At the claim level, biased decisions can cause potential reputational damage and costly regulatory audits. Hybrid NLP underwriting solutions require input and should also reference the larger available health data context. Other possible structured data sources include claims (Capuano et al., 2022). Most insurance prediction models are highly predictive, but this is not enough. Executives would like to understand better the characteristics of individuals and companies who drive the predicted values in order to develop further business strategies.

9.7.3 Fraud Detection

AI is rapidly being integrated into everyday processes in the insurance sector, carrying out assessments at greater volume and frequency than ever before. With this increased scale comes the danger that problems will be less noticeable—for example, the subtle worsening of an error rate for a small group of clients. One key way insurers are looking to supplement human checks with machines is in the detection of fraud; it is estimated that around 10% of underpaid claims are fraudulent, leading to payouts of up to $80 billion a year, with knock-on effects increasing premiums for clients. While specialist portfolios exist at some companies with dedicated fraud loss adjusters, it is generally the case that low- to mid-sized value claims are handled by loss adjusters with more general expertise. The sheer volume of first notice of loss events happening daily makes it impossible for humans alone to assess every claim. How then does it make sense to allocate resources most effectively to identify and tackle fraud cases? Once alerts are triggered on a small number of flagged claims, bespoke models focusing on fast, accurate decision-making can assist adjusters in validating suspicious claims that merit further investigation. With increased regulatory accountability, it is imperative that claims analysts are able to audit fraud detection models post hoc. For operational fraud detection systems, it is critical that ML is able to achieve conditional silos and suitable quantile coverage across different policyholder segments. These segments can be demographic, behavioral, or based on loss characteristics. Early loss detection methods were based on simple heuristics, often driven by domain expertise or naive rules of thumb. With greater sensitivity to risk selection, insurers are now able to create a fleet of models for different small subsets of claims issued at the same time, permitting more granular evaluation (Fritz-Morgenthal et al., 2022). The initial impetus to create InsurTechs focusing on fraud detection was triggered by incumbent insurers' desire for more efficient, faster detection processes, leading to the establishment of specialist companies that automate and build platforms, as illustrated in Table 9.2.

Table 9.2 Strategic benefits of XAI in the insurance ecosystem.

Stakeholder	*XAI Use Case*	*Impact on Decision-Making*	*Trust & Transparency Outcome*	*Compliance & Risk Management*
Clients/ Policyholders	Understanding claim rejections and pricing decisions	Empowers informed appeals and plan selection	Builds trust, reduces dissatisfaction	Supports GDPR Article 22 ("Right to Explanation")
Underwriters	Reviewing model-supported recommendations	Enhances human judgment and reduces overreliance	Ensures consistency in decisions	Improves auditability
Data Scientists	Debugging and refining model outputs	Identifies bias, data leakage, or drift	Enhances model robustness and confidence	Enables fairness audits and tuning
Executives/ Insurers	Explaining AI strategies to investors/regulators	Aligns with ethical leadership and corporate values	Enhances brand reputation and client loyalty	Avoids regulatory penalties
Compliance Officers	Auditing algorithm decisions for legal adherence	Detects systemic unfairness or opaque decision paths	Maintains regulatory transparency	Essential for complying with insurance laws
Legal/Regulatory Bodies	Evaluating model legality and fairness	Supports external audits and policy formation	Facilitates transparent oversight	Encourages accountability in AI deployments

Contd.

Table 9.2 *Contd.*

Stakeholder	*XAI Use Case*	*Impact on Decision-Making*	*Trust & Transparency Outcome*	*Compliance & Risk Management*
Brokers/Agents	Explaining policies based on AI recommendations	Clarifies offerings and customizations to clients	Improves communication and credibility	Minimizes legal disputes
Customer Service Teams	Resolving AI-related complaints	Provides actionable insights for grievance redressal	Increases customer satisfaction	Ensures accurate documentation of AI decisions
AI Governance Boards	Validating models against ethical standards	Guides ethical deployment practices	Upholds fairness and diversity standards	Reinforces organizational governance
Insurance Auditors	Verifying pricing and underwriting algorithms	Enables reproducibility and forensic analysis	Promotes transparency in financial models	Helps with internal and third-party audits
Product Developers	Designing user-centric digital insurance platforms	Ensures clear explainability for user-facing AI tools	Enhances digital experience	Aids in transparency by design
Risk Managers	Assessing AI-induced operational risk	Identifies potential trust breakdowns	Supports continuity planning	Provides foresight into model governance
Ethics Committees	Reviewing controversial model outcomes	Advocates for fairness, inclusion, and transparency	Drives responsible AI design	Aligns with ethical AI frameworks
Academic/Policy Researchers	Studying the societal impact	Benchmarks best practices across regions	Encourages openness and innovation	Informs AI policy development

9.8 Stakeholder Perspectives

Insurers, clients, and regulators all possess distinctive perspectives regarding explainable artificial intelligence that are involved in the intersection of insurance and AI. Insurers that utilize AI in their organizations often regard the technology with a fascination reminiscent of youth. They are full of hope for the transformative power of AI, the competitive advantage it may offer, and the potential gains from AI-driven automation. At the same time, insurers are well aware of the challenges that accompany the utilization of AI in general and deep learning models in particular. The black-box issue associated with many AI systems is one of these challenges and, importantly, a major roadblock to the industry-wide, permanent integration of AI functionalities in processes across segments. If not addressed competently, the black-box issue increases the risk of a disconnect with respect to trust and a perceived lack of accountability toward clients regarding such decisions as premium calculations or claims adjudications. A lack of client trust and the perception of poor accountability come with a risk of compliance violations and ensuing regulatory actions (Sahakyan et al., 2021). This is all the more pertinent for the insurance sector and its use of AI since these technologies and their outputs are not yet sufficiently understood, nor commonly accepted.

In a way similar to insurers and even more than insurers, clients regard AI with fascination, which may stem from the novelty and perceived cutting-edge nature of these technologies. The enthusiasm of clients is tempered by the commoditization of claims settlement procedures and premium calculation models—their perceived needs may clash with their limited opportunities to influence these processes. They may thus find themselves at the mercy of AI decisions and see the need to obtain information regarding factors, data, and variables utilized in AI processes. In addition to a demand for information, clients may also raise questions about the accuracy and reliability of model outputs. By definition, such important insurance decisions are not without emotion. The potential for personalized treatment is a delicate balancing act for insurance companies that involves using AI technologies, but only as an intermediate step toward client closeness and service quality. Again, a lack of trust on the part of clients comes with a risk of compliance violations and ensuing regulatory actions for the insurer (Minh et al., 2022).

9.8.1 Insurers

The industry-standard role of an insurer—"the party in the business of offering insurance"—summarizes, simple enough, what the essential function of an insurer is. Insurers provide solutions to assist themselves financially in the case of a detrimental event, harmful for their property or health. This customer compensation is fully reliant on the insurance premium calculation procedures, which are already prone to innuendos as to their precision and reliability, both on part of the clients and also the insurers themselves. Machines assisting these estimations can thus be seen as functional partners of the insurer's technical divisions. Their collaboration relies heavily on the abilities of algorithms to deliver outputs of high accuracy, belief, and trust for the rest of the company. The growing concern on the question how these AI algorithms are capable to generate knowledge regarding these prescreening procedures is turning slightly annoying, since it leaves the human domain of pure insurance calculations, which denote the quality of these computations are delivered by human expertise rather than hardware assistance. The insurance business is liable to every social uprising against systemic distrust which would prohibit insurers to solicit and collect their customers premiums on a broad scale. Therefore, the question toward the insurers is one of complexity reduction, either to act against the alternative of full digitalization of social relations or not to abandon the competence of technical personnel assigned to the machine outputs validation. Given how delicate discussions are, final decisions are completely left to the entire policyholder relationship network of customers and insured associations (Lahby et al., 2021; Ridley, 2022). Any years ahead could come the day of a true explainable AI, one of those solutions proficiently able to denounce "bad" risks and tell the responsible insurance actuarial for their bad prognosis, with imaginable consequences for models and insurers alike.

9.8.2 Clients

Claim underwriting and reserving decisions are inherently opaque. Clients are often left asking what factors contributed to their quote and to what extent, if any, they influenced their premium cost. AI systems used in these functions are particularly difficult to unpack. A common parting expression in digital advertising is tuning your search query. Clients query advertising for a specific intent based on specific words known as keyword matching. Companies pay different prices for their keywords. Insurance calculators allow clients to tune their quote based on small variables, resulting in large percent premium jumps. However, identifying what factors influenced their premium jump is not exact science. Traditional algorithms simply provide easy to understand, clear reasons. As such, AI offers little policyholder insight at best, and at worst is erratic. A health insurance client recently sued their provider for paying lower premiums based on their health score for years, but allowing a pregnancy exemption to provide higher premiums. Reserving decisions share many of the same transparency obstacles. Actuarial reserving reports to prepare for external audit and for regulatory review only have information for overall reserve development for large-claim segments. Data is generally not segmented by specific clients or insurance lines. Unlike insurance fundamentals, reinsurance property and casualty clients have more specific questions. What model output drives my ground-up premium or underlying excess? Are the causative variables market-related? Severity outlier-related? Changes in layer loss ratio compared to last renewal at what time series (Ahmed et al., 2023; Górriz et al., 2023)? By optimizing these questions, guiding parameterization on where to focus, and using predictive models to improve complexity and accuracy, clients are able to understand and design their reinsurance programs more efficiently.

9.8.3 Regulators

In addition to consumers and those who earn their living, insurance is unique in being an enabler at the expense of regulation, overseen by an extensive arcane set of rules designed to protect it. The questions for regulators concern what is in their remit, for example, a market that can periodically collapse. The answer is to arrange the conditions in which insurance can be profitable, accompanied by a degree of transparency and straightforwardness that would disguise any actuarial disparities. What is the reason for all these esoterica? In a world of asymmetric information, it helps the buyers more than the sellers. Insurance explains changes in premium, and it explains life expectancies. On short periods, it can be measured against short-term financials. Alternatively, on long periods, it maintains balance sheet strength. It varies according to the credit rating. But in longer term, the links to predicted claim volumes, underwritten ratings, and bankruptcy probabilities are tight. Insurance regulators have plenty of very specific rules, but these are generally for very specific circumstances and developed over decades if not centuries of experience. As a check, medical and pension schemes now lose money and necessitate regulation, the reason being a shortfall between estimated claim costs and what they charge. Life insurance is not too different, the risks involved are just a lot better hedged. Asymmetry across the group is also a lot more enforceable. At the general level also, there are credit agencies who assure quality to specific individual issuers. These have been richly rewarded for past mistakes (Ponzoni et al., 2023). In theory, basing their warning signals on insurance factors, insurers should be able to factor these considerations into their business models and premium calculations.

9.9 Future Trends in Explainable AI for Insurance

The importance of transparency and accountability when leveraging the potential of AI-based technologies in insurance distribution, underwriting, and claims assessment will only increase in the future. Society's growing demands of companies to transparently explain their actions and take responsibility for these actions have also been summarized as a call for due diligence. Such people-centric demands manifest themselves in the introduction of new or revised regulations, aiming to enable consumers to make aware decisions based on easy-to-understand criteria. Companies not complying with new regulations will rapidly lose market share, or even face bans. Explainable AI will be a useful tool in this context to gain and maintain the trust of clients and regulators alike. However, complying with regulations is a necessary but insufficient condition to implement explainable systems. New AI technologies that focus on interpretable models will additionally be needed. In this domain, there are exciting efforts in the academic community both with respect to theoretical methodologies and applied systems. Next to template-based systems that generate explainable language, also models tailored to the creation of interpretable decision logic will be developed in the future. For example, so-called differentiable decision trees provide a framework to build on traditional decision trees while simultaneously allowing for the optimization mechanisms leveraged by deep neural networks. According to this approach, models will be invented that combine the highly interpretable predictions of decision trees with the accuracy of more complex models or ensembles of interpretive models, while the interpretability will not be glossed over in the ensemble models. Similar research will emerge in other specialized domains next to insurance, such as healthcare (Owens et al., 2022). Here, models will be invented that advance the interpretable nature of decision trees but that also address other goals, such as model polarization.

9.9.1 Advancements in AI Technologies

The immense recent advancements in artificial intelligence, in a nutshell the great increase in available compute power, number, and quantity of the available data, and the advancement in AI algorithms have given rise to dramatic advances in capabilities: everything from image and video recognition to natural language understanding to autonomous vehicles. Present-day AI systems are capable of performing very effectively on various tasks such as image classification and object detection, playing certain board games, or video content interpretation. In many cases, these task capabilities operate at human likeness or better level—and with very low or no prior hand-crafted rules—raising the question in the public mind whether such task capabilities are or should be somehow synonymous with machines having a certain level of intelligence. That being said, we should note that present-day AI systems are very limited in terms of the types of tasks they can perform effectively. They are not very good on tasks requiring reasoning and common sense knowledge, nor on tasks needing skills such as planning or comprehending, nor tasks requiring the comprehension of emotions. Instead, if we do expect AI systems to handle an increasing number of existing human tasks, including in domains such as healthcare and finances where cause-based explainability are very critical, then some form of explainability is going to be essential—for a number of varied reasons that we will now discuss (Chauhan & Sonawane, 2022). In fact, current AI systems that perform with a very narrow range of capabilities raise the critical question of where we should draw the line between "intelligent" and "non-intelligent" behavior.

9.9.2 Evolving Regulatory Landscape

Insurance companies are also bound by provisions intended to shield consumers from predatory business practices. The Financial Stability Oversight Council is charged with protecting against unfair, abusive, or deceptive acts or practices. This body prohibits issuing false or misleading statements or misrepresentations, fiduciary obligations that extend to existing and future obligations of seniors with respect to their status as clients of insurance agents, and state regulations prohibiting "unfair trade practices." The Uniform Commercial Code as adopted by states reflects the obligations of insurers who do not pay claims promptly. In addition, the insurance regulators of every state restrict how rating systems work and how companies communicate about ratings to consumers. Research is underway, at the state and federal levels, to establish specific insurance-related guidelines. But there is much more to come as explainable AIs and insurers trumpeting their R&D capabilities to produce enhanced products that encounter well-funded watchdogs with heavy capabilities and rules that become particularly burdensome when misdeeds are uncovered. The demands for AI advancements to follow the mental model hungry consumers and the architects want, without the rationale pathway from the forwards to the model and back again, focused on the shortcoming that caused the problems, are daunting. The techniques described here can supply that pathway, and the confirmatory as well as the exploratory rationales that lead either to a new input or inputs that relate to the past transition from no issues to an emergence of issues or, if unavoidable, a substantive explanation as to why no adjustments were implementable (Carta et al., 2022). In particular, since this chapter references these issues in several instances, the transparency and specificity issues at the board and management levels, which are highly interconnected and depend on how well these flows function, are necessarily also top of mind.

9.10 Ethical Considerations

Recent advances in science and technology require us to espouse new ethical ways of thinking, founded on a deeper understanding of the dynamics and implications of innovation. Emerging methods and associated automation are radically changing workforce patterns and traditional notions of employment. This disruption requires careful consideration of regulatory mechanisms to manage their deployment and not only speed up or fuel a relentless pursuit of profit. We need a collective reflection on the notion of "public good," as well as on the sometimes-punishing nature of AI implementation in public and private decision-making processes. The ethical considerations of AI systems have been fervently debated for decades, prior to their massive use by private and public decision-makers. Research has focused on ethical principles, but also on the social, economic, and political consequences related to the implementation of these systems. These studies apply the ethics of technology lens, as well as the expanding field of AI ethics. These two areas have their roots in a deontological approach and consequentialism, respectively. However, a large part of AI ethical reasoning relies heavily on the corporate social responsibility model. While in principle all firms and organizations have the responsibility and capacity to actively mitigate the adverse effects of their activities, in practice there are few procedures for accountability. AI transparency or explainability, proposed as a condition for fairness, responsibility, and accountability, is often elusive (Taylor & Taylor, 2021). AI systems operate under a veil of secrecy and proprietary or industrial property preventing any scrutiny or probing of fairness, accountability, and responsibility. Plans to sanction this secrecy by imposing fines on organizations that make use of opaque machine learning algorithms are in place.

9.10.1 *Ethics of AI in Insurance*

The introduction of AI in the insurance domain is creating new ethical issues from both a quantitative point of view and from a qualitative or normative one. The study of ethics around the decision-making processes involving AI systems intersects with different domains such as computer science, political philosophy, and specific verticals and sectors affecting people's lives in a deep way, such as humanities and social sciences, but also medicine and healthcare, defense, and autonomous weapons. The different "centers of interest" existing in these areas define the aspect of AI ethics that is addressed, for example, misleading AI, ethical AI, trustworthy AI, and AI governance. Here we tackle the issue of the ethics of AI applied to the insurance sector, also discussing its intrinsic differences with the more general problem of the ethics of technology: the use of AI in insurance creates specific ethical issues and dilemmas that stem from the way in which the action of insurers operates vis-à-vis the customers and the people in general: the fact that insurers play a fundamentally "judging" role in the society requires a deeper general thinking on how ethics can be satisfied when making use of AI tools within insurance models and technical solutions (Zhang et al., 2022). From this viewpoint, the enhancement of accountability, having fair behavior, and being transparent are mandatory factors for every insurance stakeholder that makes use of AI tools.

9.10.2 *Accountability and Responsibility*

In recent years, there has been a call for AI ethics and governance frameworks to prioritize explanation efforts related to legislation. This primarily concerns the desire for accountable and responsible AI systems, seeking to identify and hold responsible those who develop or utilize these systems. Essentially, any AI governance regime that demands greater data transparency is a call to action for explainability and interpretability research. Similarly, accountability and responsibility motivate calls for explainability due to the human impact of AI and the desire to attribute reasons for judgments and actions. Therefore, AIs may augment or replace some or all of the processes governed by these norms, such that the behavior of the AI is reflective of the norms that govern the human processes that it augments or replaces. Algorithms must be able to justify their decisions or actions according to the principles of human agency, safety, and accountability. Accountability and responsibility are fundamentally concerned with the assignment and imposition of blame or the distribution and assignment of decision-making capacity, for example, legal liability, contractual obligations, and/or moral responsibility. To ensure accountable and responsible AI, we must either provide via explanation or proof that a process occurs in accordance to the correct principle within the principles that govern or constrain human judgment, or ensure that a designated actor is entangled in either a motivating or consequential way with the process in accordance with the appropriate norms. If the principles are not provided by way of explanation, it will typically be the case that human action has a bearing on either the development or deployment of the system (Górriz et al., 2023; Owens et al., 2022). A great many current debates on the ethics and law surrounding AI concern the principles embedded within these anthropogenic processes.

9.11 Conclusion

We have discussed the current state of the insurance marketplace and the avenues that insurance AI is following. These processors are generally a nascent step in automating all areas of insurance friction, from underwriting to claims adjustment. Due to the differences with data and algorithms in insurance, the rationale for a specialized situation is uniquely compelling. Transparency, accountability, and client trust need constant attention to avoid ethical and regulatory frameworks that are too strict, support checks and balances that too often inhibit innovation, and risk—but not too much, since insurers already have a lot of leverage over clients. Traditional insurance relies on trust between the insurer and insured to function effectively. An insured party will often pay premiums for many years before filing a claim. If an insurer denies a claim to which the insured party is entitled, it may harm the party for life. With appropriate levels of transparency and accountability, insurance AI can enhance trust through better performance and new types of business relationships. Startups and new models are appearing through new data, technology, and investor support, perhaps more incrementally than in the last decade, but perhaps also grounded more in cash flow. A third-party validation system could further push the industry toward trust without overly constraining innovation. The black box of AI could open up specialization based on who is looking through it, be it an insurer, an insured, or a third-party provider. The balance between existing client priorities and technology development is necessary. Currently, both are being managed successfully enough for the sector to participate in the continued AI development and deployment that is occurring in the broader economy.

References

Ahmed, M., Rabiul Islam, S., Anwar, A., Moustafa, N. and Khan Pathan, A.-S. (2023) (Editors). Explainable Artificial Intelligence for Cyber Security: Next Generation Artificial Intelligence. *Studies in Computational Intelligence*, *1025*.

Ahmed, M. and Zubair, S. (2022). Explainable Artificial Intelligence in Sustainable Smart Healthcare. In *Studies in Computational Intelligence* Springer, Cham. (Vol. 1025). https://doi.org/10.1007/978-3-030-96630-0_12

Capuano, N., Fenza, G., Loia, V. and Stanzione, C. (2022). Explainable Artificial Intelligence in CyberSecurity: A Survey. *IEEE Access*, *10*. https://doi.org/10.1109/ACCESS.2022.3204171

Carta, S., Consoli, S., Podda, A.S., Recupero, D.R. and Stanciu, M.M. (2022). Statistical Arbitrage Powered by Explainable Artificial Intelligence. *Expert Systems with Applications*, *206*. https://doi.org/10.1016/j.eswa.2022.117763

Chauhan, T. and Sonawane, S. (2022). Contemplation of Explainable Artificial Intelligence Techniques Model Interpretation Using Explainable AI. *International Journal on Recent and Innovation Trends in Computing and Communication*, *10*(4). https://doi.org/10.17762/ijritcc.v10i4.5538

Fritz-Morgenthal, S., Hein, B. and Papenbrock, J. (2022). Financial Risk Management and Explainable, Trustworthy, Responsible AI. *Frontiers in Artificial Intelligence*, *5*. https://doi.org/10.3389/frai.2022.779799

Goodell, J.W., Ben Jabeur, S., Saâdaoui, F. and Nasir, M.A. (2023). Explainable Artificial Intelligence Modeling to Forecast Bitcoin Prices. *International Review of Financial Analysis*, *88*. https://doi.org/10.1016/j.irfa.2023.102702

Górriz, J.M., Álvarez-Illán, I., Álvarez-Marquina, A., Arco, J.E., Atzmueller, M., Ballarini, F., Barakova, E., Bologna, G., Bonomini, P., Castellanos-Dominguez, G., Castillo-Barnes, D., Cho, S.B., Contreras, R., Cuadra, J.M., Domínguez, E., Domínguez-Mateos, F., Duro, R.J., Elizondo, D., Fernández-Caballero, A., … Ferrández-Vicente, J.M. (2023). Computational Approaches to Explainable Artificial Intelligence: Advances in Theory, Applications and Trends. *Information Fusion*, *100*. https://doi.org/10.1016/j.inffus.2023.101945

Hall, S.W., Sakzad, A. and Choo, K.R. (2022). Explainable Artificial Intelligence for Digital Forensics. *WIREs Forensic Science*, *4*(2). https://doi.org/10.1002/wfs2.1434

Imoize, A.L., Gbadega, P.A., Obakhena, H.I., Irabor, D.O., Kavitha, K.V.N. and Chakraborty, C. (2022). Artificial Intelligence-Enabled Internet of Medical Things for COVID-19 Pandemic Data Management. In *Explainable Artificial Intelligence in Medical Decision Support Systems*. IET – Institution of Engineering and Technology. https://doi.org/10.1049/pbhe050e_ch13

Lahby, M., Kose, U. and Bhoi, A.K. (2021). Explainable Artificial Intelligence for Smart Cities. In *Explainable Artificial Intelligence for Smart Cities*. Taylor & Francis Group, 6000 Broken Sound Parkway NW, Suite 300, Boca Raton, Florida 33487, USA. https://doi.org/10.1201/9781003172772

Minh, D., Wang, H.X., Li, Y.F. and Nguyen, T.N. (2022). Explainable Artificial Intelligence: A Comprehensive Review. *Artificial Intelligence Review*, *55*(5). https://doi.org/10.1007/s10462-021-10088-y

Owens, E., Sheehan, B., Mullins, M., Cunneen, M., Ressel, J. and Castignani, G. (2022). Explainable Artificial Intelligence (XAI) in Insurance. *Risks*, *10*(12). https://doi.org/10.3390/risks10120230

Ponzoni, I., Páez Prosper, J.A. and Campillo, N.E. (2023). Explainable Artificial Intelligence: A Taxonomy and Guidelines for Its Application to Drug Discovery. *Wiley Interdisciplinary Reviews: Computational Molecular Science*, *13*(6). https://doi.org/10.1002/wcms.1681

Ridley, M. (2022). Explainable Artificial Intelligence (XAI). *Information Technology and Libraries*, *41*(2). https://doi.org/10.6017/ITAL.V41I2.14683

Sahakyan, M., Aung, Z. and Rahwan, T. (2021). Explainable Artificial Intelligence for Tabular Data: A Survey. *IEEE Access*, *9*. https://doi.org/10.1109/ACCESS.2021.3116481

Schwalbe, G. and Finzel, B. (2023). A Comprehensive Taxonomy for Explainable Artificial Intelligence: A Systematic Survey of Surveys on Methods and Concepts. *Data Mining and Knowledge Discovery*. Volume 38 pp. 3043–3101. https://doi.org/10.1007/s10618-022-00867-8

Taj, I. and Jhanjhi, N.Z. (2022). Towards Industrial Revolution 5.0 and Explainable Artificial Intelligence: Challenges and Opportunities. *International Journal of Computing and Digital Systems*, *12*(1). https://doi.org/10.12785/ijcds/120124

Taylor, J.E.T. and Taylor, G.W. (2021). Artificial Cognition: How Experimental Psychology Can Help Generate Explainable Artificial Intelligence. In *Psychonomic Bulletin and Review*, *28*(2). https://doi.org/10.3758/s13423-020-01825-5

Yang, C.C. (2022). Explainable Artificial Intelligence for Predictive Modeling in Healthcare. *Journal of Healthcare Informatics Research*, *6*(2). https://doi.org/10.1007/s41666-022-00114-1

Zhang, Y., Weng, Y. and Lund, J. (2022). Applications of Explainable Artificial Intelligence in Diagnosis and Surgery. *Diagnostics*, *12*(2). https://doi.org/10.3390/diagnostics12020237

10

Data Governance in Insurance AI: Ensuring Privacy, Consent, and Ethical Data Life Cycles

Wasswa Shafik

10.1 Introduction

The reasons why insurance agencies are finding it increasingly necessary to embrace artificial intelligence in a big way are discussed in this chapter. The location quotient for the insurance industry has grown dramatically in the last decade. With predictive capability comes the power to select risk pools, not just assign rates to them. And throughout the economy, companies that don't adopt AI will find themselves at a competitive disadvantage. In the process, vast amounts of personal data on American citizens are being aggregated. Especially in industries like insurance, where, by definition, you are entering into a contract with a stranger, trust becomes a risk factor in the business model. While the data being controlled by the insurance companies is seen as a windfall both by those companies and their tech partners, this is information that consumers are at best conflicted about sharing, and at worst fundamentally opposed to relinquishing. Then there is the issue of government regulation. The United States does not have a strict regulation system governing the collection, analysis, and distribution of personal data like the European Union (EU). Instead, our systems protecting consumer privacy against intrusive electronic monitoring are developed through piecemeal lawsuits and sector-specific legislation (Margan, 2021). The Health Insurance Portability and Accountability Act restricts access to medical records, the Gramm–Leach–Bliley Act imposes special requirements on how financial institutions share consumer information, the Children's Online Privacy Protection Act places restrictions on the exposing of data on children to third-party vendors, and numerous states have passed their laws.

10.1.1 Understanding Personal Data

New technology, for all of its perceived wonder, can also drastically amplify the challenges of what has come to be known as privacy. Private entities have long collected data about customers so as to provide services, mass communication and advertising, surveillance, and access control, among others. The InsurTech ecosystem operates at the heart of personal data collection—live data is collected, stored, and transferred with the promise of unique service delivery, for which people gladly receive multifold benefits. Marketed services, such as AI-enabled quotation and imaging of injuries, face insurers' careful convergence to outsiders who can change their pricing at any given instant. The latter looks at it most simply: the larger the volume of gathered personal data,

DOI: 10.1201/9781003747659-10

the better risk calculations they can make. However, by doing so, the gathered data never belongs to the providers exclusively. It is a combination of user input and public online data, suggesting an unlimited number of types and sources for one given category and country of one user (McDonnell et al., 2023). Information asymmetry is longstanding, but nowadays, it is on another level where a threshold is passed.

True AI-enabled models need to personalize service offerings, that is, losses cannot be blamed solely on the industry's probable technology failure. The other part points to distrust in the InsurTech. With distrust in their customers looming, players need to implement trust, that is, set a boundary on the collection and use of personal information. Such a boundary cannot be drawn only in accordance with internal organizational policies, but also using external regulatory requirements. New regulation protects the privacy of individuals in relation to the processing of personal data, protecting the fundamental rights of physical persons. It secured a single framework for companies, reinforcing trust among citizens and businesses alike. These challenges testify to the necessity and case for regulation and dialogue between assurers and insurers, which together imply the need for a transformation of the insurance business model (Gramegna & Giudici, 2020).

10.1.2 Regulatory Frameworks

At a high level, the regulation of the life cycles of personal data is through consent; only with informed consent may an organization collect, hold, use, share, or transfer personal data. As a corollary, consent requests must not be misleading, vague, or overly broad, and the data protection rights of the subject must be easy to invoke. Requirements specify not only for consent language but also for special procedures for children, requirements for proof of age, requirements for parental consent, and age limits below which parental consent must be obtained. Additional start-of-life requirements of personal data lie in the areas of data localization and data transmission safety. Once personal data is in the custody of an organization, the organization is obligated to protect that data against breaches, cyberattacks, and other unauthorized access, use, or sharing of that data. This is accomplished through data security; unauthorized actors or processes must be unable to access, use, or otherwise alter sensitive personal data. The primary control in the security of data is encryption: for the transfer of data, while it is in transit, or while it is at rest. After entry into the data life cycle, the organization is required to adopt safeguards to protect the breaching of data at rest from all other unauthorized access, use, or sharing. Data localization and data encryption form the basis of the duty to protect the data once it enters the life cycle at the organization (Călin & Izvoranu, 2018). Cybersecurity laws also impose expectations for third-party data sharing and transfer. Additionally, it is required that when a data breach is detected, the subject must be notified within a specific time frame.

10.2 Informed Consent in AI Systems

Informed consent is one of the ways to implement the ethical principles of data rights and respect for persons as a prerequisite of democratic government and a requirement of secret laws. It is an accepted practice in many areas—political participation, medical treatment, behavioral experimentation—that acknowledges the inherent dignity of persons. Informed consent is necessary for empowering individuals and demystifying human–AI interaction. It democratizes choice, maximizing the possibility that autonomous individuals make the best choices given their beliefs and particular life circumstances, and therefore that the collective action of society is beneficial. It offers protection for those engaged in transactions that may empower AI systems, as well as for individuals who may become objects of surveillance, manipulation, or discrimination based on the biased data that AI systems apply. The informed consent standard establishes a threshold of risk. For social institutions, the most that can be ethically justified may be a low-risk, high-reward scenario. Obtaining informed consent is often complicated. Consent cannot be considered "informed" if the information is delivered in a way that is incomprehensible to audiences with diverse cultural and cognitive perspectives. The informed consent standard for ethical data assembly processes cannot rely on complicated legalistic documents numbered in the fine print, forming a part of a terms-of-service (TOS) agreement, and usually presented as a digital click wrap. Please, agree to let us track your behavior so that we know how best to provide you with the services you want (Braun & Matthes, 2018). Informed consent is predicated on the ability of individuals to develop their policy intentions, a process that takes considerable time and investment, and still relies on risky heuristics to try to maximize the likelihood of making the "correct" decisions in the absence of hard and fast rules.

10.2.1 Defining Informed Consent

Informed consent is an important ethical consideration in the use of AI in general. It entails that potential data subjects are fully informed of the nature, scope, purposes, and consequences of the processing of their personal data and have consented to that processing. However, in the case of digital environments and big data, where transparency about the use of a person's data is very limited, where the consent document will be very long and the individual does not read it, or where the actual data processing procedure is very different from what has been described, informed consent is often not feasible or achievable. For example, in an artificial intelligence context, where machine learning (ML) algorithms are trained with a vast amount of data in order to make predictions or draw conclusions, especially based on data of many individual data subjects, consent will often not be able to fulfill its central purpose of giving individuals individual control over information about themselves (Owens et al., 2022).

The nature and scope of consent in big data and artificial intelligence usage have sparked academic and legislative debate for some time. A clear trend has formed in favor of a more nuanced approach, which, rather than simply expanding the role of consent—effectively the use of a single, blunt tool to address all of the concerns about the ethical issues in AI—takes an integrated, layered approach to data governance, recognizing that consent remains a pivotal component of the ethical framework for data processing in most cases, compared to other mechanisms, but cannot be relied upon exclusively to ensure that processing procedures are fair to individuals or society, as it tends not to be urgency-sensitive or fundamental rights-sensitive. While it will remain an option for many processing procedures, such as the core purposes of the use of AI technologies, there will be many other areas and contexts, especially where there are other relevant interests, in which it will not be appropriate, and which will therefore require an alternative framework, depending on the insurance criteria, as presented in Figure 10.1 (Yang et al., 2023).

10.2.2 Challenges in Obtaining Consent

Obtaining valid consent can be challenging in many ways. A significant hurdle to obtaining consent for insurance-related AI systems is that the use of AI is rarely demonstrative. From a user's perspective, many of the models employed can be thought of as "black boxes," and there is scant opportunity (or willingness) from most users to attempt even to analyze model processes. Second, for many insurance uses and in many jurisdictions, opt-out options are woefully inadequate compared to opt-in options. A large barrier to obtaining consent is that many AI systems are not demonstrative and are not easily conveyed to end users. Legitimate interest is a primary example of a permission sometimes used in InsurTech. But contrasts to data processing requiring explicit consent might make this justification less attractive. Opt-outs have been observed to limit genuine personal autonomy further, but sufficient opt-ins are not without their risks either. Many people are overloaded with consent agreements and have either already vented their consent or have starved

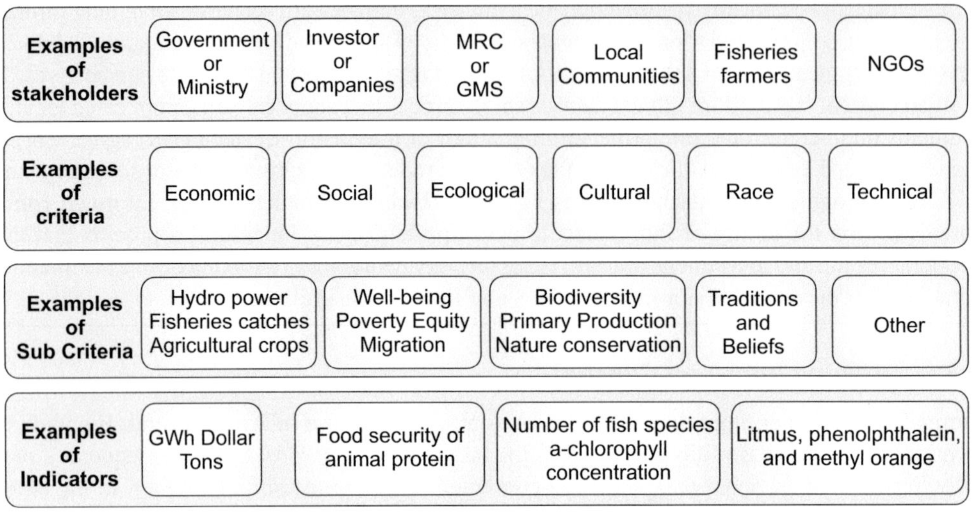

Fig. 10.1 The insurance criteria and indictors.

themselves by clicking buttons without reading them whenever possible. Aware of the general lack of user engagement, companies have made a practice of forcing select users into truly informed consent (Shi & Gan, 2023). During such an exchange, a small proportion of users responded to attempts to solicit real responses, similar to the techniques used by behavioral economists to request public preferences.

In the case of inferred and derived information, authorization may come up more readily over an individual's potential for self-harm. Misleading users into thinking they have opted out of an area of AI usage where they truly want personal agency, even if there is only one way for that aspect, could be argued a legitimate ground for refusal. This would be particularly pressing where clarity is lacking in industry standards on the right to be forgotten. Users could also be impacted depending on the type of information and how it affects risk for that individual. Even for sensitive data, users might comply throughout the data's life cycle with a company offering insights about current or future risks and acting as an agent of greater benefit for them as an individual, but still refuse to authorize its use as an input for market-driven principles like proper industry pricing of insurance services, as presented in Table 10.1.

Table 10.1 Ethical data life cycle in insurance AI.

Stage	*Description*	*Ethical Considerations*	*Key Stakeholders*	*Common Tools/Practices*
Data Collection	Gathering client data for underwriting and personalization	Informed consent, data minimization, and purpose limitation	Clients, agents, data officers	Consent forms, secure web forms, and API logs
Data Storage	Safeguarding collected data in centralized/ decentralized systems	Secure encryption, access controls	IT security teams, data architects	Encryption Application Programming Interface (AES), firewalls, secure cloud vaults
Data Processing	Transforming raw data into usable formats for AI models	Fair use, anonymization, and lawful processing	Data scientists, compliance officers	Data masking, Extract, Transform, Load (ETL) pipelines, and pseudonymization

Contd.

Table 10.1 *Contd.*

Stage	*Description*	*Ethical Considerations*	*Key Stakeholders*	*Common Tools/Practices*
Data Usage	Employing data for underwriting, claims, and fraud detection	Purpose limitation, anti-discrimination	Underwriters, risk analysts, AI engineers	Role-based access, algorithmic transparency tools
Data Sharing	Third-party sharing for reinsurance, analytics, or marketing	Consent, contractual safeguards, and data sovereignty	Legal teams, partners, data controllers	Data sharing agreements, APIs, and federated learning
Data Retention	Determining how long data is stored before deletion	Justifiability, minimal retention period	Data governance committees	Data retention policies, archiving tools
Data Deletion	Final removal of data after the life cycle ends	Right to be forgotten, audit logging	Compliance, data admins	Secure erasure tools, automated deletion systems
Audit and Oversight	Reviewing the use and flow of data across systems	Compliance, bias detection, and impact assessments	Internal auditors, regulators	Data lineage tools, algorithmic audit frameworks
Feedback and Redress	Handling disputes and user concerns over data use	Accountability, user empowerment	Customer service, ombudsmen	Dispute resolution platforms, logs for traceability
Governance Policies	Formal data handling policies	Transparency, enforcement, standardization	Executives, compliance boards	Data governance frameworks COBIT – Control Objectives for Information and Related Technologies DAMA-DMBOK – Data Management Body of Knowledge DAMA-DMBOK is a comprehensive guide to data management practices developed by DAMA International. It provides a structured framework for managing data as a strategic asset, covering principles, processes, and best practices.
Training and Awareness	Staff education on ethical data use	Avoiding negligence, cultural embedding	Human resource (HR), ethics committees	Workshops, e-learning, simulation exercises
Consent Management	Mechanisms to collect, update, and revoke user consent	Granular control, real-time flexibility	Users, legal, platform designers	Consent dashboards, preference centers
Data Provenance	Tracking the origin and transformations of data	Traceability, integrity assurance	Data engineers, auditors	Metadata tagging, blockchain-based records
Risk Management	Identifying and mitigating data-related risks	Anticipation of breaches, ethical harm	Risk managers, ethics boards	Risk registers, data protection impact assessments (DPIAs)

10.3 Ethical Considerations in Data Usage

Increasingly, the different stages of the data life cycle are subject not only to regulation but also to a wider set of ethical imperatives. Drawing heavily from the philosophy of practical ethics, these concepts are but one possible approach to reflecting on how to encourage the adoption of norms and rules, good leadership, and congruence with social and company goals to prioritize the safekeeping of customer welfare and trust. By placing ethical principles at the forefront of practices in AI, companies can refine their frameworks for decision-making, boosting collaboration and confidence with both customers and their workforce. Historically, insurance practice is subject to concerns regarding discrimination and fairness. Algorithms used in underwriting, pricing, and claims settlement were often criticized for perpetuating discriminatory practices, using social status, ethnicity, or gender with a direct impact on product commercialization (Poshtiri et al., 2024). These discussions intensified the introduction of mandates to eliminate bias in traditional models. Now, with the increasing usage of advanced analytics across all business units, insurers are facing similar discussions for the implementation of AI for any criteria. Therefore, they should actively design and test their models to exclude any chances for these AI systems, designed to improve customer welfare and fragile visions of the future, from being discriminatory, biased, or unfair. As an extension of fairness and bias in AI, the principle of transparency and accountability gets AI one step closer to real-world application. Even though bias and fairness analysis is doable pre-launch, actual production might differ substantially if risk segmentation is based on algorithms that resemble the famous "black box." Even with companies offering de facto access to the inputs and parameters of their proprietary algorithms, it is still difficult to explain the reason why a particular output is produced, with the risk of classification mistakes still present, maybe biased for some groups (Abdulkadir Isa & Fernando, 2023). Although the type of damage incurred by different groups might differ substantially, the use of black-box algorithms might indeed damage any third-party group, with additional attention needed for those groups with high damage probability.

10.3.1 *Fairness and Bias in AI*

Any AI is a reflection of the data currently available. The quality and volume of data are known to correlate with the performance of any model. The AI, as a product, derives its integrity from an ethically developed model, which fuels the AI, infused with fair, well-governed data life cycles. If the AI model is not free from any unfair bias, then it raises questions of trust and veracity. Trust and veracity of the AI are seen as vital, especially in the case of higher-stakes systems that affect large populations and make decisions based on sensitive, private information. Bias and fairness of AI have recently been intensely scrutinized. Not all uses of AI systems inadvertently impinge on fairness properties, but some do, and these are higher-stakes systems. These systems are higher-stakes use cases that can be given the benefit of the doubt. Noncriminal justice uses of AI systems can be subjected to stricter scrutiny for fairness. Such systems might also be at greater risk of fairness violations. The trustworthiness of the AI model may be questioned, and consequently, the architects of the system must be able to account for any problematic result, as its ethical progress is strongly linked to human terms. Data in the context of biased AI systems is not neutral, as there are data cycles, larger and more interfacing patterns that propagate bias. There is an ethical cycle. The unpredictability of algorithms creates concern regarding their impenetrability. Therefore, it is vital to account for the processes that connect the data to the outcome. The interconnected nature of the data cycle has ramifications for data sharing, withholding, and collaboration. Understanding the wider patterns is crucial for transparency and trust (Koster et al., 2021). Organizations deploying AI systems must ascertain and prove that their systems are designed to avoid or mitigate bias and its associated ethical pitfalls.

10.3.2 Transparency and Accountability

Transparency is a key aspect that ensures ethical AI usage in an organization, along with supporting other ethical considerations such as fairness and bias, privacy and consent, and data protection. Transparency assists employees in comprehending how algorithms exert their influence and make decisions that are crucial to the organization or the individuals who work there. A prominent factor in errors or bias in predictions is how data collection and algorithm models are defined. Highlighting this point, a study revealed that two-thirds of AI model developers are unaware of any biases and shortcomings related to the AI model, which further undermines the accountability of AI models being utilized for sensitive activities. To resolve such issues and build appropriate strategies, teams consisting of researchers, engineers, and stakeholders need to discuss and clarify the vital aspects of AI systems, including the purpose for which the AI application is created and utilized, the data used to train the models, and the risks of its usage (Jouini & Sethom, 2023). These discussions need to be transparent and clear, allowing the team and associated stakeholders to make better decisions. Consequently, these factors enhance the transparency of the data and the level of trust among the individuals involved, including the general public and end users. Ensuring transparency and accountability in AI means opening those systems up for public scrutiny and restricting their capability to act autonomously and opaquely. Regulations mandate accountability, but they lack basic guidelines on promoting responsible AI. A general approach is to release any auxiliary data that could shed light on how specific algorithm decisions were made and how the algorithms have acted historically, while taking precautions to avoid sharing sensitive information publicly. If sensitive private data is offered to these algorithmic participants, an additional algorithm should be enforced to review the results accordingly. Transparency is linked to how people see and recognize AI. If companies openly admit their models are biased and embrace their shortcomings, consumers may feel reassured and trust the technology (Alam et al., 2020). However, suppose companies choose to manipulate the public perception of AI, promoting the benefits of increased efficiency and lower costs while avoiding the dangers. In that case, they risk losing consumer trust in the future.

10.4 Data Life Cycle Management

Data life cycle management (DLM) is concerned with how data is handled throughout the stages of its existence. This typically includes data collection and storage, data processing and usage, and data archiving and deletion. Each part of the life cycle bears some aspect of privacy, consent, or ethical dilemmas. However, DLM for insurance data is especially critical to instilling consumer confidence in AI applications. Policyholders expect their data to be used for just purposes, particularly in the case of highly sensitive backgrounds such as health history and genetic information, chronic conditions, and personal property records. Being part of an insurance policy is a significant trust decision, and losing a claim's privacy can be deeply detrimental. Therefore, insurance AI ideally should leverage DLM frameworks at all parts of the life cycle, validating the purpose of data use and limiting the scope of access at every step in order to celebrate expectations. Data collection and storage describe what data is held, and how. With innovative tools for data collection emerging in the digital era—from more traditional verbal exchanges to new sensors—insurers now have unprecedented access to consumer data. Alongside sensitive personal data points, insurers can also collect and store analytics of data. Oftentimes, consumers only give consent for a one-time use of their data, for example, in producing a personalized quote or recommending a specific policy (Van Nguyen et al., 2023). Therefore, innovative insurers should carefully assess the scopes of consent requests and experimental trials—talking through feasible options and incentives with customers—and assess for other legal routes to ongoing collection before pursuing long-term proactive data collection methods.

10.4.1 Data Collection and Storage

One of the essential activities in an organization is data collection, which is closely linked to data governance. Although data collection seems easy to implement at first glance with the advent of new technologies, this is a critical activity because its planning and execution are focused on business objectives. Data storage also seems easy with the advent of storage technologies and paradigms in everything. Although these activities can be viewed as simple, an organization needs to spend curation effort to minimize costs, improve collaboration, and increase return on investment. The first step in data governance setup is the documentation of the data source list to clarify who collects data, who makes it available, and who consumes it, which allows the planning and implementation of periodic quality checks established by the data governance working group. The data collected should not have quality problems, and attending to the quality guarantees the usability. If a dataset is not consumed, its storage needs to be evaluated; costs must be balanced against the business needs for having that particular dataset available. These steps are important for planning and executing data governance periodically to prevent the costly and time-consuming data removal steps later (Ding & Zuo, 2024). This team should be a cross-functional team to include the various areas of the organization, using the data so that business needs are considered in the data quality checks.

10.4.2 Data Processing and Usage

While the previous section focuses on having the right information accessible at the right time, this section provides support to share and use the data in a compliant way. The insurance industry mostly uses customer data, either from internal systems or through third parties, for pricing, claims settlement, and investment purposes. For pricing purposes, this data may be used to either conclude on a price or the risk level associated with the specific customer or event. Good use of the data from other customers can help to conclude on the risk profile of new customers. These risk profiles are also needed during the period of the insurance policy to avoid a too-large gap between the price paid and the expected risk by the insurance. In order to make this type of data, along with monitoring data, available for these stated purposes, a multitude of different internal systems with many different users are active. This sharing of data among processes and users increases the company's risk, and it is important to have rules in place for sharing the data and monitoring these rules. A data loss risk assessment can determine which of the data exchange processes are needed to get a better overview of data sharing and to make a governance model. By doing a modeling on risk and impact in this area, it can be checked if all possible measures are taken to cover the associated risks. Potential measures consist of defining and documenting how, for what purpose, and by whom data can be shared between which applications and users (Bermúdez et al., 2023). Then use data security controls accordingly, monitor exchange operations performed on or by these applications and users, and file incidents for inappropriate activities.

10.5 Data Archiving and Deletion

Archiving and deletion protocols ensure that extensive amounts of data do not take up unnecessary storage space for long periods and that data not required for future references is not stored indefinitely. Given the forecasted increase in the use of artificial intelligence and machine learning models in insurance, with existing data and newer model iterations becoming increasingly complex, the size of insurance files will only increase. As such, clear legal frameworks must also be in place to allow bearer parties to understand how their personal information will be safeguarded. Data governance policies must also include time frames for when to delete data or make it inaccessible in a secure archive. Legal recommendations include the deletion of data if it is nonrelevant to current and past insurance policies of the bearer (Pnevmatikakis et al., 2021). This also lessens the risk of noncompliance with security breach regulations that require companies to safeguard against inappropriate access to private customer information, for which a full risk assessment in the event of a breach has no valid, thoughtful basis. How to store legacy data economically has been an original challenge for data governance. File storage over time has become much less expensive, allowing companies to utilize saved hard drive space. Before, data governance protections put into place allowed for expiration date deletions on a preprogrammed schedule, or corporate shredding parties that securely retired archived electronic media. However, cyber criminals are savvy and may target larger corporations holding extensive amounts of data that they could monetize all at once. Efficient archival processes must also be in place so that legal obligations to retain data are not forgotten, but also that older legacy data, which is becoming less relevant, is not kept readily accessible for illicit purposes, since that data would not need sophisticated methods to recover from electronic media (Sachan & Muwanga, 2023).

10.5.1 Risk Management in Data Governance

While the description of data governance may seem like a quickly assembled laundry list of processes, entities, contents, types, or decisions within disciplines of risk management such as IT, information, and privacy risk management, it is crucial to keep in mind that data governance represents one of the foundational pillars of information risk management in that its processes and entities influence all kinds of information risk within an organization. In this section, we identify potential risks in data governance and discuss strategies for risk mitigation. Likewise, we also identify and discuss the reasons for such issues. Data governance is responsible for determining how data is created, stored, updated, and shared. As such, data governance enables the implementation of privacy decisions based on legal requirements, organizational policies, and business needs at the blueprint level. Whenever data governance makes decisions in these areas, the respective data governance entity decides about both the organizational and technological enforcement of privacy policies—if done correctly, these decisions lead to the minimization of privacy, information, and organizational risk. For this reason, these decisions should be well informed and based on a solid understanding of the parameters that influence the respective decisions. As pointed out in the earlier text, there are many alternative definitions of privacy (Settipalli & Gangadharan, 2023). Most, however, agree on the fundamental principle that privacy describes the right of individuals to determine the extent, duration, and circumstances under which personal information is disclosed or withheld from an organization, and the ability to control what information about them is used, how it is used, and how it is defended and protected.

10.5.2 Identifying Risks

The application of any model in production presents frameworks for damaging events, which may then be classified as risks. Data outputs from AI and ML systems should be understood as generating risk as well, which is to say that improper or poor performance on basic data capabilities invites damaging events and an association with possible harms. The role of risk management in data governance respects that other frameworks exist, from oversight as such to compliance or security, but risk management is a holistic coverage of these that identify causes of damaging events across the registers or views—processes, models, data, roles, laws, regulations, supply chains, reputations, relationships, obligations, etc. (Wall, 2022). The taxonomy here for harms and costs identifies three generic liabilities from the materialization of AI harms, and growing regulatory interest in human life and human capital risks. They include:

(i) People risks, which are harms caused by the AI life cycle on societal groups, such as discrimination and privacy violations, as well as exploitation and physical safety risks.

(ii) Environment risks, which are damages from the AI life cycle on nature or the created environment, such as planned or unplanned usage or emissions of resources.

(iii) Economic risks, which are harms caused to the entity directly or indirectly by the AI life cycle, such as reduced sales and income from reputation damages or insurances, legal or compliance obligations, besides liability costs.

Understanding these types of reported damages helps to identify specific obligations for risks before they materialize. Artificial Intelligence Explainable Computing (AI XC) outlines some of the common risk identification methods, from interviews to scenarios to historical and specific reviews, with a view or registering specific adaptations. Risk register formats are presented, which assign an owner and delegated accountabilities for monitoring and maintenance for chronically exposed life risk events, such as ML data errors or model behaviors.

10.5.3 Mitigation Strategies

Several strategies can be used to mitigate risk in insurance AI and to turn the theoretical role of data governance into practice. Some of these rely on more technical aspects of insurance AI development, while others go into the domain of corporate policies and procedures. In an ideal world, both aspects come together to balance risk management and insurance AI's innovative capacity. We note here a few specific suggestions which could be useful for insurers and other insurance stakeholders:

(i) First, we encourage insurers to use techniques of privacy-enhancing computation. These techniques are often more advanced versions of transparency-enhancing technologies that can help to mitigate specific risks. For example, standardization techniques, such as attribute-based data sharing formats, can tackle the risk of shared data being misused for unauthorized or additional purposes, such as discrimination or social scoring. Other techniques can address other risk dimensions, such as balance of power issues through differential privacy or anonymization, encryption, or k-anonymization. Federated learning, which enables machine learning on data that remains stored locally, means that clients can retain control over their data in the sense that their data does not leave their local equipment, helping to reduce the risk of unwanted self-exclusion from shared risks (Margan, 2021).

(ii) Second, insurers can address some of the elements of the ethical principles by asking the following questions during insurance AI development: Are we improving health equity by using insurance AI? If there is a good reason against making the insurance AI system fully inclusive, is there a valid justification for this? Are we fairly crediting and accurately warning those who use insurance AI? Following this step of ethical deliberation can contribute to avoiding missing blind spots in the AI development process. In addition, these principles can be used to evaluate insurance AI after training (Arockiam & Pushpanathan, 2023). Do the actual insurers' AI achieve the targets proposed for these principles?

10.6 Technological Solutions for Data Governance

This chapter outlines technological solutions to implement practical data governance stepping stones and provides an overview of applied AI and ML, analytics, and blockchain technology options for insurance organizations. Data governance and ethical stewardship processes will arguably involve more advanced and AI-enabled solutions as the technology reaches development and ecosystem enablement maturity. The content acts as a viewer-friendly checklist of propositions to share with the dotted reporting lines for local deployment, adaptation, and enhancement. There is increasing use of AI and ML in proof-of-concept deployments for policyholder-level risk modeling, fraud detection, and insurance loss prediction. General and specialized software are available to enable some of this work within organizations. Use cases span risk selection and pricing, risk classification, reserves, claims reviews, claims payments, business interruption claims, claims settlement speed, insurance fraud detection, and loss ratio sensitivity to segmentation strategy, company-specific attributes, and other macro factors. Prediction challenges can be aggravated where variables are based on incomplete or unverified sparse datasets. Applying standard AI and ML tools can save time by using business intelligence data visualizing techniques and solving practical problems while committing fewer internal resources to software programming cycles for deploying internal developed analytical engines (Gramegna & Giudici, 2020). AI software-enabled optical character recognition is already being applied with success in reducing insurance-claims-processing time frames.

10.6.1 AI and Machine Learning Tools

In addition to legal frameworks and institutional solutions, there is a growing number of technological solutions being developed that can help enforce the principles of data governance in the data ecosystem. The data governance challenges presented in this work, such as risk of discrimination, transparency asymmetries, consent neglect, or privacy violations, can be addressed by technological solutions and innovations at various stages of the product life cycle. Examples of such challenges are personal data processing without sufficient user consent, the exploitation of vulnerable individuals or groups, and the right to be informed of algorithmic decisions. Early-stage, blueprint, and post-hoc tools include those related to transparency and explainability, data access, data sharing, privacy engineering, and best practices. Addressing overly broad access to personal data and privacy violations can be done with the help of AI-enabled privacy-enhancing technologies for privacy engineering that support the detection, labeling, and modeling of sensitive data, monitoring for privacy infractions, or automatic masking. Relevant tools come from the domains of de-identification, data anonymization, synthetic data generation, privacy policy extraction, and privacy-aware visual analytics. Transparency and information accessibility tools help with the communication of disclosure policies and privacy risk descriptions. These tools may allow a better understanding of a product or service that leverages AI, make privacy practices available to a broader range of stakeholders, or allow for a more accurate assessment of risks (Călin & Izvoranu, 2018). They alleviate limitations associated with the major sources of asymmetry, such as the complexity of correlation-based or predictive models of privacy risk.

10.6.2 Blockchain for Data Integrity

Blockchain technology is mainly a unique information storage system. Using cryptography and an advanced distributed consensus algorithm, it stores any verifiable data or documentation to protect it from being manipulated, altered, or fraudulently used. Blockchain technology collects information in blocks and timestamps them, and chains them together in cryptographic order. Furthermore, community consensus verifies this procedure to ensure that once information is recorded, no development can make any subsequent modification. The main features of blockchain technology are that it is distributed, secure, encrypted, privacy-respecting, and immutable; it has traceability, credibility, and disintermediation. These specificities can be applied to any asset. For example, Bitcoin was created to transmit value through algorithms to ensure a peer-to-peer transaction without financial intermediaries. But blockchain is infinitely more versatile. Any asset can be represented digitally and placed on a blockchain to be exchanged with confidence, whether these assets are documents, information, certificates, or values like property, art, marketable securities, or tokens. The insurance industry can use blockchain technology to prove ownership of the insured asset at the date of the claim, corroborated by a third party, for use cases in health insurance, agriculture, and climate risk. Blockchain is an ideal tool to log patient consent, timestamp that consent, and control that consent by turning on or off scenarios based on relevance and context (Owens et al., 2022).

Consent can be revoked at any time, and it will be traceable, creating an audit trail of its use and enabling awareness of the patients and their families about sensitive information's accessibility, with immutable communication. Information movers, or smart contracts, can help deduce whether and when such access triggers are possible according to a predefined set of rules.

10.7 Stakeholder Engagement and Communication

Stakeholder engagement in the context of ethical AI development in insurance is crucial for generating value throughout society. Communication is not one size fits all, and each stakeholder group may require a different communication strategy. Therefore, effective communication of data governance frameworks with consumers is key to realizing their value, ensuring protective measures are in place, and avoiding alienation of consumers. Currently, consumers are largely unaware of data governance frameworks surrounding their data, and further education efforts must take place. Once trust is built among consumers, these frameworks ideally serve as a third-party intermediary between different economic interests at play. Establishing this empathy by empowering consumers with clear and actionable insights on how their data is used allows mutually beneficial AI solutions to emerge. Sensitive information should have notice-and-consent measures about its safe and ethical use, ensuring transparency when it comes to any testing and post-deployment monitoring. An opt-in and opt-out choice should also be available for consumers regarding changes in the model that would increase the risk for lost data privacy, such as model retraining and the development of new features. In addition to working with customers, maintaining transparency in the data practices with regulators is vital throughout the life cycle of operating business models powered by consumer data. Partnering with compliance experts and informing regulators across jurisdictional boundaries can alleviate trusting relations (Yang et al., 2023). At the same time, establish formal channels to submit and propose change when it comes to examination of certain business conducts automatically selected by AI models. Such act of goodwill serves as an accountability measure to clarify companies' interest in refraining from potential business practice violations.

10.7.1 Engaging Customers

In developing the data governance practices of insurance AI, customer engagement must be prioritized as part of the business strategy. Insurers must clearly demonstrate how AI has empowered curated benefits for the customer via transparency in insights, be it covering more risks, reduced processing time, or eased customer service, to name a few. Customers react positively to insights and information shared in a way that encourages them to provide feedback or opinions. The way AI is positioned in the customer journey will impact customer trust and influence the degree of acceptance or pleading for better data governance. Placing AI as a driver of efficiencies will no longer be acceptable when these efficiencies are from the customer perspective a reduction in service response time and/or an increase in premiums for driven traditional risk scores. Customers want inferior premiums for similar service charter, enhanced customer service via address verification, claim prediction, complaint handling, or underwriting decision-making, mitigation processing (Poshtiri et al., 2024). These are some of the operational aspects of the customer journey that should be the focus of AI, and adopting the principles of data governance, such as purpose limitation, data minimization, storage limitation, and providing knowledge around these features, will promote customer trust in the capabilities of AI to drive such efficiencies. Furthermore, if more insights are made available to customers to understand the data dependencies within AI results, as well as provide opinions on bias and fairness in scoring, and which of these factors drive automated decisions, customer trust in the use of data for AI will certainly improve. Insurance customers are increasingly looking for insurance products that are tailored to them, and which generally start with customized premiums for the products pertinent to them. Offering such customization is highly data-intensive, thus making the monetization of customer data a priority to consider when coming up with a data governance strategy. For comparative market advantage, the data governance strategy should stay aligned to the organizational risk appetite and how much of a priority is data monetization for the organization (Koster et al., 2021). This decision will influence business decisions as to where do we find the ability to sell, market, or partner to drive higher customer engagement.

10.7.2 Collaboration with Regulators

The widespread incorporation of AI into the operations of insurance organizations has been slow, especially compared to other financial domains. The increasing regulatory scrutiny—and indeed introduction of new regulation—aligned with the inherent complexity of ensuring that these systems are unbiased, transparent, captured as desired, and operate within defined tolerances will continue to slow down readiness to market. The traditional cycles of implementation of systems, followed by validation and verification, cannot continue indefinitely if these organizations wish to remain competitive and relevant in their chosen markets. Action is needed on several fronts to reduce blockages, including collaboration with regulators. Insurance organizations should engage with regulators regularly and constructively, ensuring that all relevant stakeholders understand the complexities, capabilities, and limitations of selected models to drive toward mutually understood risk appetites and behavior expectations. Regulators from many industries around the globe are involved in discussion forums, working groups, liaisons, and international standard-setting bodies, and are increasingly demanding explanations for both the structure of implemented systems and the logic underlying the decision-making campaigns and life cycles governing the operation of these systems over time. Proactivity from both regulatory authorities and the organizations being regulated can reduce the friction and delays as a result of AI-specific regulation (Alam et al., 2020). For example, regulators can help set the tone and expectations about the outcomes-based focus for monitoring and supervision of organizations' activities involving AI, even if such systems are not within the scope of existing rules requiring, for example, proportionate outcomes, monitoring, and remediation backward and forward, as presented in Table 10.2.

Table 10.2 Data governance dimensions and insurance AI applications.

Governance Dimension	*AI Use Case in Insurance*	*Risk if Poorly Governed*	*Ethical Safeguard*	*Relevant Regulations/ Standards*
Privacy	Personalized premium pricing	Data leakage, surveillance-like profiling	Privacy by design, secure processing	GDPR (Art. 5, 25), HIPAA
Consent	Behavioral data collection via mobile apps	Covert collection, lack of informed agreement	Explicit, granular, and revocable consent	CCPA, GDPR (Art. 7), ePrivacy Regulation
Transparency	AI-assisted claims decisioning	Opaque decisions, reputational damage	Explainability, data trace documentation	ISO/IEC 27001, AI Act (EU proposal)
Accountability	AI fraud detection	False positives without human oversight	Clear lines of responsibility	OECD AI Principles, FATF Guidance
Fairness	Underwriting based on socio-demographics	Discrimination, biased outcomes	Bias audits, fairness constraints	AI Ethics Guidelines (OECD, EU)
Security	Cloud-based data storage	Data breaches, ransomware attacks	Encryption, regular audits	NIST Cybersecurity Framework
Data Quality	Risk scoring and loss prediction	Mispricing due to outdated/inaccurate data	Continuous data validation	ISO 8000, DAMA DMBOK

Contd.

Table 10.2 *Contd.*

Governance Dimension	*AI Use Case in Insurance*	*Risk if Poorly Governed*	*Ethical Safeguard*	*Relevant Regulations/ Standards*
Data Lineage	Model training using multiple datasets	Undetected transformation errors	Provenance logs, audit trails	GDPR (Accountability principle)
Retention and Deletion	Lapsed policies and legacy claims data	Excessive storage, privacy violations	Timely, secure deletion policies	GDPR (Art. 17), ISO/ IEC 27701
Third-Party Risk	Outsourced AI vendors or reinsurers	Data misuse, vendor noncompliance	Due diligence, contractual clauses	SCCs (Standard Contractual Clauses), ISO 27036
Bias Monitoring	AI-driven pricing models	Systematic overcharging of protected groups	Bias detection pipelines, diverse datasets	EEOC, Fair Credit Reporting Act (US)
Auditability	Regulator inquiries into claims algorithms	Inability to explain decisions	Maintain audit logs and traceability	Regulatory Sandboxes (UK FCA, EU)
Data Ethics	Use of psychographic or behavioral profiling	Breach of autonomy and user manipulation	Ethics review boards, harm analysis	UNESCO AI Ethics Recommendations
Cross-Border Compliance	Global reinsurers using shared AI tools	Legal clashes, data sovereignty violations	Data localization, cross-border agreements	GDPR, APEC Privacy Framework

10.7.3 Case Studies in Insurance AI Governance

Insurance AI development hubs need guidance to ‘do design properly. Templates and checklists can assist governance teams in doing good work. But distilled experience sharing from previous governance work is arguably even more useful than advice on how to do it. Here, we present both examples of successful AI risk oversight and accidentally or purposefully ignored risk oversight, which have caused bad consequences. As a note to the reader, various known insurance AI systems are referenced herein as part of our background discussion on governance team reviews and remedial plans; refer to Section 10.3.2 for more detail on how many of these systems are able to be tackled together, and why. Real-world successful examples of insurance AI governance are difficult to find, as people who operate their business effectively and responsibly do not like to speak publicly about what they do, for fear of regulatory scrutiny or creating undue pressure on their day-to-day operations. Organizations are able to speak about the companies they’ve supported publicly; we have used insights from their work as a conservative jumping off point for the more unsavory parts of our exploration. Credible reviews of insurance AI project failures, which include expert commentary, are somewhat easier to find (Van Nguyen et al., 2023). The reviews usually comment on unethical practices in the projects; however, the review articles are written by AI experts with knowledge of insurance AI, not FSRM Experts – File Server Resource Manager Experts such as actuaries.

10.7.4 Successful Implementations

To help guide the insurance sector, the following case studies are first reviewed for common successful implementations. Then, lessons learned from specific failures are explored as cautionary tales for the adoption of AI in insurance. These case studies represent positive steps taken by organizations and agencies to proactively ensure responsible, ethical, and trustworthy solutions to the deployment of emerging AI technologies. There are many good and well-constructed examples of governance frameworks developed collaboratively and openly by consortia of scholars, civil society, governmental, and private organizations. The principles include ensuring that AI is used to advance shared humanity; fostering an inclusive AI ecosystem; building AI systems that are safe, secure, and operate as intended; respecting and promoting human rights and democratic values; ensuring the responsible use of AI; and promoting commercial interests for the common good. A number of the recent frameworks aim to define the responsible use of AI and the desired outcomes, specify implementation requirements, and articulate the principles of custodianship and stewardship responsibilities. A definition of trustworthy AI requires four criteria: accuracy, explainability, robustness, and reliability (Ding & Zuo, 2024). It proposes a total of six high-level goals for AI systems, namely, that the AI is reliable in functioning, is not biased, and works with privacy controls in place; that the AI is human-centered, meaning that humans can understand the AI and be able to initiate intervention; and that the AI is secure and resilient, meaning it provides assurances on the operational quality, performance, and safety while inhibited from misuse.

10.7.5 Lessons Learned from Failures

Despite the fact that AI will produce the most infamous failures in tech history, it could also be reasoned to be a more diversified area of activity than the Internet, where many companies dedicated their efforts to creating services and infrastructures around large databases. In contrast, insurance AI is a fairly long-tail, diverse collection of custom-built decisions that no single company will undertake. Given that insurance AI is mostly custom-built and will operate in a regulated environment, it could be plausible to draw lessons from the collective industry experiences or data points. A good starting point for the endeavors is the public failures within insurance AI algorithms. This approach, despite not being exhaustive by any means, could provide clues as to potential pitfalls that will or could still plague AI-risk-dependent areas, such as insurance. It needs to be recognized that failed use cases have mostly not been the result of a single failure. Problems around AI ethics, transparency, and fairness suggest that responsible considerations, to steer technology to society's benefit, are urgently needed. However, these considerations show limited effect when not deeply embedded in a company's core values, as is best evidenced by the repeated failings of a select few well-known companies. Several of the currently known failures could point toward at least three lessons learned. First, the lessons from the complaints could suggest that provisional IT governance around legacy-based, siloed approaches would dictate the creation of correct-pricing AI models (Pnevmatikakis et al., 2021). Alongside this continuous adoption of market-focused pricing algorithms, it appears that insurance companies would also need to establish the necessary responsible AI governance around ethics and compliance, in order to prevent the cost of complaints of wrongly misallocated resources turning sleek profitability into a treadmill for insurance pricing.

10.8 Future Trends in Data Governance

As insurers realize the success of data governance, it will become better funded and integrated within the overall company vision and strategy, moving from a program to operationalization. More resources will start to be allocated to the data governance function, further enabling the provision of end-to-end data life cycle management services across the organization. More technologies solutions will be evaluated, piloted, and implemented. Outreach programs will continue to educate other functions, such as underwriting, claims, pricing, and loss reserves, to leverage the technologies for data-quality management (Settipalli & Gangadharan, 2023). Evolving regulations could include:

(i) At first, a good reason for data governance to exist was to evolve with regulations. The increasing regulatory scrutiny, combined with economy-wide digital transformation, triggered a rapid growth in privacy-related regulations. Policies raise the stakes associated with not protecting sensitive data. These regulations usually come with heavy fines, loss of customer trust, and reputational risk. Due to these facts, being compliant with regulations is often a top priority for insurance companies.

(ii) Regulations and policies are often seen as real growth drivers for data governance. Sometimes they even become the "business case." As more use cases for AI emerge and progress, and as AI becomes more core to the insurance business, AI regulations are emerging and creating more requirements and scrutiny. Insurance companies and the insurance ecosystem are coming up in scope.

(iii) Following efforts on AI regulations are being led by the EU, with an AI Act currently being drafted, and the new blueprint for an AI Bill of Rights released recently. These actions follow previous efforts in the healthcare ecosystem. These initiatives recognize not just the privacy aspects of data policies, but also the need for diversity, equity, and inclusion. Similarly, future AI regulations will likely also need to address the equitable use and potential discrimination in addition to data privacy.

10.8.1 *Evolving Regulations*

Insurance and financial services are heavily regulated, and not only at the local or sector levels. Privacy and data protection laws have a global reach. And so do the new guidance for AI in health. AI systems, including insurance AI that may generate prediction or proxy discrimination, may face even greater scrutiny than traditional algorithms. The proposed risk-based classification system for potential regulation on AI also adds to the complexity. Agile, nimble insurance organizations will find these regulations to be a weak link in their advantage through use of AI data models faster than their prudential and data protection regulators. But, in the future, this will come to an end. The use of AI models will become more complex. Banks' possibly new role as depositors of sensitive consumer financial data in digital wallets may add to the considerable governance pressure on their use of third-party data models. All firms will be obliged to demonstrate compliance: transparency and security are crucial requests. Firms' exploration of use of generative AI technologies will need to be grounded in privacy and consent frameworks, which means that organizations will need to remember the huge lessons learnt in cybersecurity and data breaches over the last 20 years (Arockiam & Pushpanathan, 2023). The one-stop-shop model for GDPR is complicated by the fact that local regulators increasingly have an interest in the demonstration of impact assessments and triggering of committees for sensitive data, and increasingly ask for transparency of company models and documentation.

10.8.2 *Emerging Technologies*

Insurance companies, like all large enterprises, are beginning to adopt cloud-based platforms for the deployment of their enterprise-wide software. These platforms allow the companies to share data between lines of business and with outside partners through APIs, and they bring AI capabilities to all parts of the business. At the same time, these platforms fuse the analysis of risk and compliance. As a result, they are driving an acceleration of the development and automation of governance processes in insurance.

(i) Emerging technologies can help with individual pieces of the governance puzzle. In particular, data modeling tools can automate the generation and standardization of business and technical glossaries.

(ii) Smart AI tools can map and document data flows from source to target, enabling data cataloging use cases for privacy, security, and regulatory compliance. Data quality platforms can help ingest policies and then automatically apply data profiling or other activities to assess the health of data.

(iii) They can also convert high-level policies into code and then apply them to data throughout its life cycle. Finally, advanced data mesh and knowledge graph concepts can help create a federated data governance environment across the hybrid enterprise.

None of the abovementioned capabilities, however, is a standalone solution. Integrating all aspects of data governance with data management and data engineering toolsets for a particular use case and business process is essential in order to get the most business value from the tools. Although these technologies will continue to evolve, we believe that for governance to be effective in a hybrid environment, it must be woven together with the solutions for data privacy compliance, data security securitization, and enterprise data management through multicloud data and process orchestration (McDonnell et al., 2023).

10.9 Conclusion

It is paramount to institute data governance frameworks that ensure the ethical life cycle of training datasets as AI machine learning becomes a possible actuary tool. In the context of AI product innovation, focus is often placed on the potential for economic growth or demand changes associated with the supply-side mobility of productization. Insurance firms are well within their rights to impose restrictions on how policyholders' data is to be used, monetized, or added to model training. Data governance institutions historically do not exist in the insurance domain itself, and at times when such foundations would have acted to structure insurance data management and longevity, political pressure and media sentiment had prevailed otherwise—censorship at best, calls to defund or abolish insurance entities at worst. Establishing norms that explain when customer data can be used, and for what reasons, is deemed a higher priority than those where compensation may be curt. This is an early step to ensure that when products are properly developed, they are properly made. Causativeor at least association—modeling approaches must be employed to find translatable attributes which can maximize positive intent attributes and minimize negative unintended; otherwise, products may encourage tendencies which some find negative. This work focused on the insurance landscape of data use to set policy on machine learning, and how purposefully crafted policy may allow micro- and macro-datasets to be properly used within actuary models. We believe these frameworks can structure a sound pathway to productization and increased access demand—using machine learning in insurance encourages proper risk management, which can, in turn, produce diversification and efficient allocation of capital.

References

Abdulkadir Isa, U. and Fernando, A. (2023). Explainable AI and Interpretable Model for Insurance Premium Prediction. *Journal on Artificial Intelligence*, *5*(0). https://doi.org/10.32604/jai.2023.040213

Alam, A.S.A.F., Begum, H., Masud, M.M., Al-Amin, A.Q. and Filho, W.L. (2020). Agriculture Insurance for Disaster Risk Reduction: A Case Study of Malaysia. *International Journal of Disaster Risk Reduction*, *47*. https://doi.org/10.1016/j.ijdrr.2020.101626

Arockiam, J.M. and Pushpanathan, A.C.S. (2023). MapReduce-Iterative Support Vector Machine Classifier: Novel Fraud Detection Systems in Healthcare Insurance Industry. *International Journal of Electrical and Computer Engineering*, *13*(1). https://doi.org/10.11591/ijece.v13i1.pp756-769

Bermúdez, L., Anaya, D. and Belles-Sampera, J. (2023). Explainable AI for Paid-Up Risk Management in Life Insurance Products. *Finance Research Letters*, *57*. https://doi.org/10.1016/j.frl.2023.104242

Braun, D. and Matthes, F. (2018). Generating Explanations for Algorithmic Decisions of Usage-Based Insurances Using Natural Language Generation. *Lecture Notes in Informatics*, *P-279*.

Călin, H.C. and Izvoranu, A.M. (2018). Public–Private Partnership and Its Influence on Agricultural Insurances. *Quality – Access to Success*, *19*(S1).

Ding, H. and Zuo, X. (2024). Construction of Insurance Consumers' Purchasing Behavior Model Based on Big Data Analysis. *Applied Mathematics and Nonlinear Sciences*, *9*(1). https://doi.org/10.2478/amns-2024-0006

Gramegna, A. and Giudici, P. (2020). Why to Buy Insurance? An Explainable Artificial Intelligence Approach. *Risks*, *8*(4). https://doi.org/10.3390/risks8040137

Jouini, O. and Sethom, K. (2023). AgriBIoT: A Blockchain-Based IoT Architecture for Crop Insurance. *Lecture Notes in Networks and Systems*, *655*. https://doi.org/10.1007/978-3-031-28694-0_32

Koster, O., Kosman, R. and Visser, J. (2021). A Checklist for Explainable AI in the Insurance Domain. *Communications in Computer and Information Science*, *1439*. https://doi.org/10.1007/978-3-030-85347-1_32

Margan, S.K. (2021). Drifting into Algocratic Insurance? In *The AI Book: The Artificial Intelligence Handbook for Investors, Entrepreneurs and FinTech Visionaries*. No. 1 pp. 71–74. https://doi.org/10.1002/9781119551966.ch20

McDonnell, K., Murphy, F., Sheehan, B., Masello, L. and Castignani, G. (2023). Deep Learning in Insurance: Accuracy and Model Interpretability Using TabNet. *Expert Systems with Applications*, *217*. https://doi.org/10.1016/j.eswa.2023.119543

Owens, E., Sheehan, B., Mullins, M., Cunneen, M., Ressel, J. and Castignani, G. (2022). Explainable Artificial Intelligence (XAI) in Insurance. *Risks*, *10*(12). https://doi.org/10.3390/risks10120230

Pnevmatikakis, A., Kanavos, S., Matikas, G., Kostopoulou, K., Cesario, A. and Kyriazakos, S. (2021). Risk Assessment for Personalized Health Insurance Based on Real-World Data. *Risks*, *9*(3). https://doi.org/10.3390/risks9030046

Poshtiri, Z.P., Soleimani, A.G., Delafrooz, N. and Shahroudi, K. (2024). Designing the Insurance Coverage Model for FinTech Startups: A Novel Approach to the Necessity of Digital Transformation Track of in Insurance. *Interdisciplinary Journal of Management Studies*, *17*(1). https://doi.org/10.22059/ijms.2023.345002.675187

Sachan, S. and Muwanga, J. (2023). Integration of Explainable Deep Neural Network with Blockchain Technology: Medical Indemnity Insurance. *CEUR Workshop Proceedings*, *3554*.

Settipalli, L. and Gangadharan, G.R. (2023). WMTDBC: An Unsupervised Multivariate Analysis Model for Fraud Detection in Health Insurance Claims. *Expert Systems with Applications*, *215*. https://doi.org/10.1016/j.eswa.2022.119259

Shi, X. and Gan, L. (2023). Equilibrium in Competitive Insurance Markets with Medical Tourism. *Studies in Microeconomics*, *11*(2). https://doi.org/10.1177/23210222211051439

Van Nguyen, K., Islam, M.R., Huo, H., Tilocca, P. and Xu, G. (2023). Explainable Exclusion in the Life Insurance Using Multi-Label Classifier. *Proceedings of the International Joint Conference on Neural Networks*, June 2023. https://doi.org/10.1109/IJCNN54540.2023.10191171

Wall, J. (2022). *Keynote Speech 4: A Conversational AI Approach to Detecting Deception and Tackling Insurance Fraud*. 2021 Tenth International Conference on Intelligent Computing and Information Systems (ICICIS), Cairo, Egypt, https://doi.org/10.1109/ICICIS52592.2021.9694118.

Yang, J., Chen, K., Ding, K., Na, C. and Wang, M. (2023). Auto Insurance Fraud Detection with Multimodal Learning. *Data Intelligence*. *5*(2): pp. 388–341 https://doi.org/10.1162/dint_a_00191

11

Embedding Human Oversight in Automated Systems: Toward Accountable and Trustworthy AI

Wasswa Shafik

11.1 Introduction

Recent years have seen the rise of supposedly powerful models that can automate many tasks. Such achievements are leading to a growing adoption of artificial intelligence (AI) systems in the real world. Governments, AI labs, and other industry stakeholders are thus examining how AI systems can be designed and deployed to be trustworthy. One of the most important answers to that question lies in the involvement of humans in the decision-making processes. We call this involvement of people in supposedly automated tasks human oversight. The importance of human oversight rests on the need to mitigate risks associated with AI systems, as well as on the fact that certain aspects of human life cannot be performed without humans. In this section, we elaborate more on why we consider human oversight so important. Involving humans in the decisions made by AI systems during operation mitigates the risks of AI systems fooling themselves or others and, most importantly, causes undesired consequences, which were foreseen or unforeseen (Margan, 2021). The need for human oversight stems from the fact that human preferences change, that possible highly unfavorable outcomes arising from a single decision during the deployment of an automated system are sometimes not possible to characterize before its operation, and that the performance of specialized decision-making AI systems is usually below human's level of performance in general. AI systems, especially those based on machine learning, perform well when the task is in their sweet spot of similarity to the data they were trained on. The generalization of AI systems, however, should not and cannot be trusted without human oversight. Even when functioning very well on the defined task, AI systems are likely to make mistakes, especially in hard-to-define edge cases. Humans generally respond better to such situations than AI systems (McDonnell et al., 2023).

11.1.1 Defining Human Oversight

Combining disciplines and perspectives in ethics, regulation, and technology, we define human oversight as technical means that support the intelligent analysis and intervention in decision-making by an accountable human agent. Human oversight can be embedded or designed for AI systems in several ways. It can be configured to afford varying degrees of oversight according to task and risk exposure; it can be made continuous, under such conditions in which the system cannot act unless a designated human agent has given an explicit go-ahead; or driven initially by

DOI: 10.1201/9781003747659-11

the actions of an accountable human agent until the system has learned from agency experience, when the machine becomes action-persistent until it receives new supervisory instructions from the human agent. There are key distinctions between the implemented oversight of any automated decision system and democratic discretion or the personalized exercise of judicial power. This is true regardless of whether the decision system uses AI, particularly if we consider the general case of supervision, motivation, and perceptual capture of any automated system. No nonhuman system has overtly or covertly acted with the intention to subvert human oversight, create new agents, or deter the human agents engaged to punish acts that contravene highly encoded ethical principles. For all the forecasting hype that enveloped military strategists and their commitment to build and deploy autonomous lethal weapon systems, the reality is that they are nowhere to be seen. Human oversight means that systems are designed to provide suitable decision support to ensure that humans stay in the decision-making loop and can override actions taken by the automated systems (Gramegna & Giudici, 2020). Systems are required to be designed to provide appropriate alerts, explanations, and inputs with the aim of preventing human lapses, or training humans for difficult decision-making tasks or repetitive monitoring tasks.

11.1.2 Historical Context

While automated systems have long been present in society, such as advanced voting machines, distribution of benefits, and nurturing systems for the elderly and disability communities, more recently, the shift to AI-based automated decision-making systems has transformed how meaningful automation has become. Prior to such rapid development, over the past hundred years automation was limited mostly to isolated single-instance task automation (e.g., an assembly line robot that performs a singular repetitive continuous task, such as screwing a component into a car, but cannot adapt to assembling different types of cars). These early automation efforts were also unable to learn; hence opto-mechanical systems such as a simple toaster, which implements a small degree of automation but cannot learn to adapt, are considered an early form of automation. Further, the transition to AI-based systems introduced the ability to automate decision-making. This shift has made it possible to tackle an entirely different class of issues, where specialized perception-and-cognition AI-based systems have matured to the point of providing actionable feedback and meaningful support for human actors in high-stakes deployment areas, such as air traffic control and flight piloting. AI-based recommendation systems, which have achieved tremendous user adoption in areas such as personalized targeted ads, news feed curation, and e-commerce product suggestion, have the attention of practitioners in public, private, and not-for-profit sectors (Choi et al., 2024). There is increasing interest in how to drive the responsible development and deployment of such systems.

11.1.3 Current Trends in AI

There are developments of various types currently affecting AI systems. Firstly, the underlying technology of AI systems is becoming more effective. Within the field of machine learning, particularly within that of deep learning, progress is rapidly being made in techniques for supervised and unsupervised learning, which allow the creation of AI systems capable of human-like perception, reasoning, and decision-making ability. Recently developed models capable of generating text are capable of performing a number of tasks that previously required expert human labor. Likely millions of marketing materials have been generated using AI systems. Various companies are piloting, or about to pilot, the use of AI systems for recruiting and interviewing employees. Chatbots are available and in use, providing customer service, technical support, and experiences that were previously unique to human interaction, such as therapy. Important sectors, such as law, medicine, and finance, have all seen or are about to see AI systems partner with human workers to speed up work dramatically. Secondly, the social and political environment surrounding AI systems is changing rapidly. Objections to past systems and calls for the regulation of future systems are taking place. Various accidents, including self-driving car accidents that have killed people, have led to questions about the transparency, accountability, and trustworthiness of the AI systems of now and the future. Some of the leaders of the AI research community have called for the creation of an organization to conduct safety research that is separate from the research groups that create generalized and powerful AI systems, concerned only with safety-critical AI research until trust can be regained by society (Murphy & Moosa, 2021). An AI future joint research group, headed by one of the general AI community's most well-known scholars and led by a former employee, has gained wide support.

11.2 Frameworks for Accountability

Developing AI systems with human oversight presents fundamentally new challenges when developing concepts, legal code, ethical guidance, or industry standards intended to ensure that historical AI systems remain accountable and trustworthy. From a conceptual standpoint, these systems need to shift the locus of accountability for algorithmic decision-making. In other words, such AI systems should not create decentralized and inscrutable zones of "shadow decision-making" when it comes to matters of great discretion, participation, and personal impact. Moreover, the legal code sets down the show-me-your-papers principle and then raises the bar, in part, by reframing the traditional concept of normal accountability in the pursuit of restorative justice and deterrence. Our laws share ethical values and support ethical principles and corporate practices. Industry standards provide a practical roadmap for what these values and principles mean in practice by elaborating on common dimensions of accountability. They make the legal code and the ethical guidelines meaningful. The US legal code differs in fundamental respects from the AI ethical guidelines described in the earlier text. First, these guidelines are written at a high level of abstraction, like constitutions, because they are intended to communicate broadly shared values and principles, much like a web summarizing the contours of a spider's trap. Due to their high level of abstraction, they leave many consequential issues unaddressed. For example, national cultures view privacy differently, including the legal consequences of breach (Golden et al., 2016). Consequently, ethical guidelines leave increasingly more detailed explanations to be worked out later through case law, statutes, and administrative guidance through better decision-making in Figure 11.1.

11.2.1 Legal Frameworks

In both the US and Europe, the legal frameworks governing automated systems are essentially the same as those that govern traditional nonautomated technologies. This raises the question of why new rules are needed at all, and if so, what purpose they should serve. Supporters of new rules point to a number of perceived deficits of existing regimes, especially regarding how they apply to AI, while critics argue that existing rules are sufficient, for the most part, to produce desirable acts and omissions in both automated and traditional systems. Consequently, they advocate for a restrained approach to the regulation of AI, one that emphasizes the benefits of innovation and favors economic over precautionary considerations. The question of whether new regulations are necessary, however, will remain theoretical for as long as courts, agencies, and other bodies responsible for legal interpretation and enforcement consistently apply relevant statutes and legal principles in a manner that generates predictable and proportionate consequences for actions mediated by AI. Part of the justification for creating new rules and frameworks for AI is the fact that the technology is still relatively nascent; most of the laws on the books today were not designed with AI in mind, and it

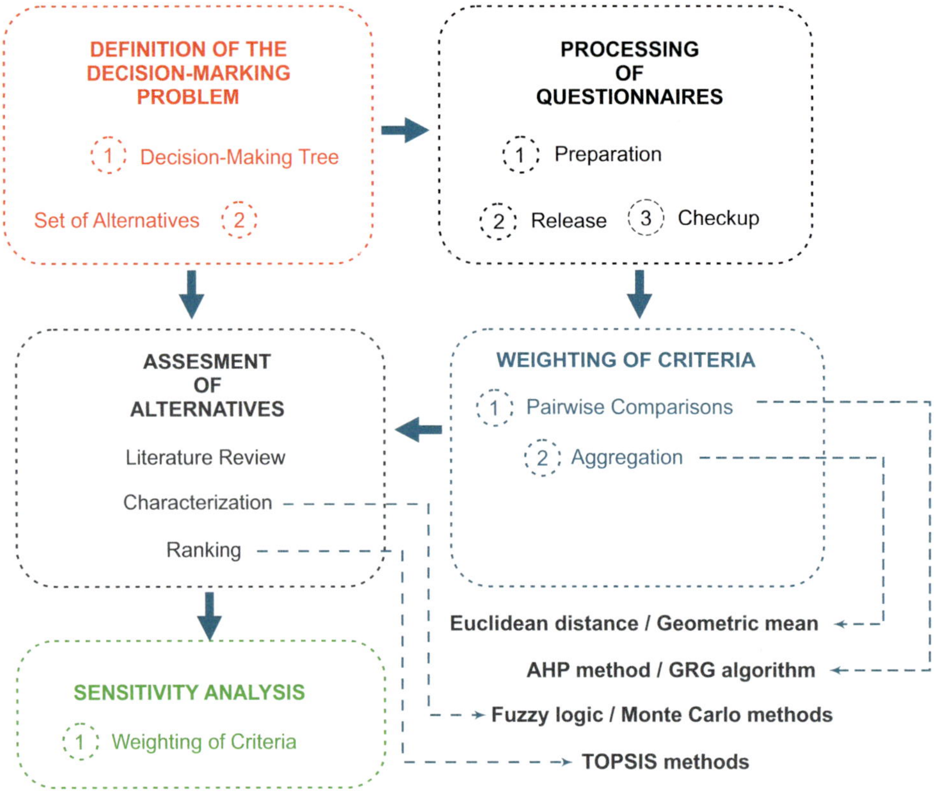

Fig. 11.1 Decision-making processes.

is unclear whether the laws can accommodate the unique characteristics of the technology. In some areas, lack of clarity remains a problem. For example, it remains to be seen whether existing laws regarding online intermediary liability should apply to decisions taken by the algorithmic systems that sort what content appears in individual users' feeds or whether these systems are liable under the same statutory regimes that address issues such as defamation or copyright infringement (Philip & Suresh, 2024). These laws could also determine whether developers of models trained using copyrighted material without the consent of the copyright holder need to pay damages, and if so, how much.

11.2.2 Ethical Guidelines

Ethical guidelines are key in guiding the design and adoption of trustworthy and accountable AI. Many governmental and nongovernmental organizations are working on defining ethical principles for AI. Trustworthy AI has core principles: respect for human autonomy, prevention of harm, fairness, and explicability. Within these principles are several prohibitions, requirements, and recommendations. Alternatively, a more straightforward approach includes five principles for AI systems: inclusive growth, sustainable development, and well-being; human-centered values and fairness; transparency and explainability; robustness, security, and safety; and accountability. However, at the same time, these documents are overly generic and in great part ill-defined, making their operationalization and enforcement difficult. Furthermore, the stakeholders and impacted parties are seldom involved, which makes these ethical guidelines less representative and universal. Therefore, heavy reliance on these ethical guidelines alone is not sensible, since they are not legally enforceable. People are not only treated unethically but are also potentially negatively impacted (Townsend et al., 2018). In the end, without specifying the exact conditions under which ethical AI should be applied, how it should be governed, and why choosing ethics rather than law, there are greater risks for the potential victim of negligent or malicious entities.

11.2.3 Industry Standards

In the absence of stronger legal or ethical mandates, voluntary industry standards are likely the only public-facing frameworks that companies are likely to accept as obligations to be followed. For the most part, they are developed in a very different fashion from legal and ethical guidelines. Legal penalties and enforcement through courts and relevant agencies reinforce compliance, while violations are reported and analyzed in detail. Approval for ethical guidelines emerges from a long dispute and discussion process at the appropriate institutions, and sometimes involves expert committees, again not necessarily with the power to punish. Industry standards are developed through voluntary participation by relevant players who have a stake in following the policies requested. Creation of standards for technical processes or domains usually depends on the consent and collaboration of consensus standards organizations and other industry groups. In the space of ethical considerations, it depends on influence from activist NGOs and compliance with standards created by trade organizations in the space. Industry standards exist for accountability and trustworthiness in a number of areas relevant to AI. In general, major players are collaborating with government agencies to enact soft law or self-regulation; soft law because approval for the imposed standards does not come from the legal domain, while at the same time being organized and imposed by government agencies would result in self-regulation. Two notable areas of trust for AI are AI systems that generate media and account for the behavior of people within the generated media (Oben et al., 2024). A group of major tech companies generated a set of principles to manage the trustworthiness of content created by generative language and imaging models, where the devices' built-in potential problems were acknowledged and guidelines provided.

11.3 Challenges in Implementing Oversight

Automated systems such as AI and ML are unlawful and unready to make rules or decisions for and about people, even with oversight to improve decision-making. The challenges presented in this chapter constitute the three categories that echo throughout AI and ML: technical limitations, cultural barriers, and regulatory hurdles relating to manufacturing trustworthy, accountable, and overseen systems. These challenges lead to a central question: When can AI and ML rely on automated decision-making without human oversight? Human oversight is an important aspect of the debate surrounding the adoption of AI and ML decision-making systems. Advocates boast that oversight will allow these systems to produce better decision-making output and thus improve real-world decision-making. Critics express skepticism over the integrity and feasibility of oversight in practice. Oversight can fall prey to the same failure modes experienced by humans involved in the process. Furthermore, when is human oversight sufficient? Many quotidian decisions people make are flawed on examination. In some cases, our decisions lead to catastrophic results, as is evident each day in the headlines. Why, then, we might ask in opposition to those who support automated decision-making for and about people, should we privilege these systems when humans get it wrong all the time? Clearly, more thought, conciliating, and checking, or double-counting, are required in some instances when it matters most. Indeed, there is certainly the possibility of error with both people and machines, and the interaction between the two may need to be adjusted to create the best chance of correct decision-making. Optimization requires attention and vigilance and is clearly contextual (Aina et al., 2024). The relevant interaction is based on a host of social and political factors that influence the ease or burden to society of possible or frequent error and incorrect output. These factors add up to who counts and when they count the most what the exact settings are at any particular moment.

11.3.1 Technical Limitations

AI systems are increasingly demonstrating the capability to exhibit intelligent behavior without requiring substantive interventions from human operators. Areas of development include, but are not limited to, simple conversations, facial recognition, strategy game playing, recommendation engines, machine translation, and even the current generation of generative chatbots. However, in these cases, "automation" is predominantly about automating tasks that have been identified, framed, and supervised by humans. While outside investor interest and the demand for productivity applications may be suggesting that AI is on the cusp of a second major productivity increase, it is evident that only a few domains see relatively anomaly-free performance of high-capacity, trained models. Concerns about accountability arise from an inability of applied AI to demonstrate widespread generalizability across a number of high-importance, technical outcomes. There are three main sets of technical limitations with respect to human oversight. First, in many practical applications, AI modeling is applied in nontraditional, uncertain environments, at production or delivery time, in a context without prior observed examples. Secondly, for many AI applications, there will be no satisfying validation method, as the underlying techniques would be dedicated to heuristically modeling poor approximations of a very complex map from inputs to outputs optimized for practical utility. Thirdly, for many planning or decision-making applications, embedded AI techniques and reinforcement learning create sequential risk and long-term reward issues with respect to poorly specified utility functions (Arockiam & Pushpanathan, 2023). In these cases, it will be very difficult to create an appropriate oversight or supervisory structure, as the tools of safety engineering, cost–benefit analysis, and performance assessment will be limited.

11.3.2 Cultural Barriers

While pointing out that automated systems have become part of the social fabric, their rationale resides in the belief that these systems do things better than humans while being efficient, impartial, and free from cognitive biases. If an automated system is used to assist decision-making in important areas such as medicine, criminal justice, hiring, or credit scoring, it will generally be perceived as the de facto decision-maker, not as part of a collaborative human–AI ecosystem. Allowing humans to query these automated systems or allowing oversight over their decisions is felt by many as denying the automated system's superiority, as a sign of distrust in its capabilities, or worse, a threat to the social order. The incessant stream of news proclaiming that AI can do better than humans, reinforced by the rapid advances in AI systems, has permeated our thinking and is deeply ingrained in our culture. Moreover, the responsibility attribution pattern also favors a lack of oversight. In application scenarios dominated by a mouse-clicking culture, the human decision-maker is not only responsible for the final decision, but the hapless employee is also held accountable if the final decision compares unfavorably to the automatic decision. The endowed autonomy of these systems means that even if decisions are made in an automated fashion, they will still be perceived by those on the receiving end as definitely affecting the quality of the decision and the decisions made, thereby influencing the outcomes (Wall, 2022). AI-enabled systems can make mistakes, and most importantly, the resulting decisions might not at all be superior to the corresponding human-driven decisions that have been made in the past, and possibly worse.

11.3.3 Regulatory Hurdles

A third major challenge is regulation. If oversight were to cause legally mandated delays, and regulatory hurdles meant that not all systems would require or be able to provide oversight, then trust would be further reduced. What does it mean to have a trustworthy system if only certain specific industrial applications in critical sectors must be engaging in custody-based practices? We might see marketing language and behavior that elicit trust from users, but the underlying act of production would not be such that, absent that marketing, would imply greater trustworthiness. To be clear, we are not suggesting that oversight exacerbate regulatory bottlenecks. These may be merely consequential. Our argument here is relatively simple. If posing an acceptable level of oversight on the design of certain digital systems would slow down product cycles, maybe unreasonably so, the remaining social need for those systems would either be unmet, or the entire sector surviving those bottlenecks would need to mark up their prices beyond just making product development less lucrative. Recall that society at large profits from those very rapid cycles of experimentation and innovation. Burdening just some systems with additional compliance phase would, in practice, force one group to pay some of the benefit back to the remaining folks by way of a surcharge on the services they buy—for example, an artificially inflated online advertising price per click for those systems, fetching a high price on monopolized social media ad platforms for the unsuspecting user, usually small to medium businesses, as presented in Table 11.1. These advertising price surcharges would be borne especially by small businesses with low margins, specializing in on-demand cheap goods or just-in-time delivery services—those, that is, for which just a small increase in product development cycles for other firms would weigh immensely (Choi et al., 2024). What would that say about our appreciation of those small-business backbones of the economies of the Western world?

Table 11.1 Layers of human oversight in insurance AI systems.

Oversight Layer	*Function*	*Example in Insurance*	*Tools/Methods*	*Ethical Benefit*
Design Oversight	Embedding ethics in the design phase	Designing claims algorithms to include fairness metrics	Value-sensitive design, stakeholder engagement	Anticipates risks before deployment
Operational Oversight	Real-time monitoring and intervention mechanisms	Human validation of AI-rejected claims	Dashboards, human override protocols	Enhances trust and safety
Post-Hoc Review	Reviewing past decisions for bias or error	Auditing automated pricing for demographic bias	Algorithmic audits, decision logs	Accountability, continuous improvement
Escalation Protocols	Procedures for raising AI-related anomalies	Flagging anomalies in fraud detection for expert review	Workflow triggers, escalation chains	Prevents harm in critical decisions
Cross-Functional Ethics Panels	Multidisciplinary review boards for decisions	Monthly review of AI claims system by ethics panel	Ethics committees, review documentation	Checks blind spots, encourages transparency
User Feedback Loops	Incorporating user concerns and reports	Clients challenge claim decisions based on AI scoring	User appeals systems, surveys	Empowers end-users, closes trust gaps
Training and Literacy	Preparing humans to understand and manage AI systems	Staff trained on limitations and override of AI tools	E-learning, simulations, awareness sessions	Reduces misuse and dependence

Contd.

Table 11.1 *Contd.*

Oversight Layer	*Function*	*Example in Insurance*	*Tools/Methods*	*Ethical Benefit*
Governance Oversight	High-level control over policies, roles, and structures	Board-level policy for AI use in underwriting	AI governance frameworks, role accountability maps	Aligns strategy with ethical use
Contextual Judgment	Human reasoning applied in exceptions or anomalies	Overriding a low-risk score due to known medical condition	Ethical playbooks, human override buttons	Avoids rigid automation, honors edge cases
Compliance Review	Regulatory conformity monitoring	Regular checks against data privacy rules in AI models	Regulatory audits, compliance dashboards	Legal alignment and reduced liabilities
Third-Party Auditability	External validation of system behavior	External firm reviewing insurer's use of AI	Independent audits, transparency reports	Objectivity, enhances public trust
Incident Response	Managing errors and harms from automation	Wrongful denial of claim due to flawed model	Response protocols, harm reparation procedures	Ensures ethical accountability after failure
Documentation Oversight	Proper documentation for traceability	Keeping model decisions traceable for review	Model cards, datasheets for datasets	Transparency and reproducibility
Oversight Feedback Integration	System improvements based on oversight feedback	Model updates after recurring complaints	Closed-loop feedback pipelines	Continual learning and system trustworthiness

11.4 Case Studies of Oversight in AI Systems

AI systems are increasingly implemented in safety-critical domains in the hopes that they can outperform human operators, whether by sheer computational efficiency or the ability to segregate, correlate, and analyze massive volumes of data in ways that humans cannot. In such areas, oversight may be less pervasive, and, where oversight is indeed present, it may be of a different character than is typically required in other, less safety-sensitive domains. In these domains, oversight may only be exercised in certain circumstances, and those circumstantial boundaries may not be transparent to system designers, ethics scholars, and policymakers as they attempt to influence guidelines and regulations governing AI development and deployment. As AI systems become increasingly capable, their deployment in these domains raises both new opportunities and new concerns, particularly in the areas of liability and trust. In this section, we explore some case studies from healthcare applications, autonomous vehicles, and financial services to illustrate this finding. By augmenting human employer abilities and instilling human oversight at key junctures, AI systems can be made more reliable, trustworthy, and accountable services. In particular, we will highlight and discuss scenarios in which it may be safe for AIs to operate without supervision, and when human oversight is critical. In addition, we outline recommendations for researchers, system designers, and policymakers as they seek to create and promote safe, transparent decision systems and secure AI development and deployment (Murphy & Moosa, 2021). With this discussion in mind, we underscore the criticality of embedding oversight in machine behavior in domains and circumstances where automation is enabled, particularly in areas such as medicine, disability services, child safety, and financial-institution-elevated risk.

11.4.1 Healthcare Applications

A notable example of oversight in an AI system is offered by medical AI. In some medical imaging tasks, AI supports physicians by analyzing images, usually relying on deep neural networks. The predictions of these systems are then reviewed by the physician. If the predictions of the AI system match the expert interpretation, the AI acts as a second reader to confirm the accuracy of the prediction. If not, the physician serves as a supervisor by determining the correct diagnosis. This second reader approach has increased the accuracy of detections in diseases such as breast and lung cancer, diabetic retinopathy, and COVID-related lung abnormalities. The oversight involved in such applications contributes to minimizing false positives and false negatives: mistakes by AI can ruin a human's life; mistakes by humans can ruin many lives. The existence of humans in the loop in AI medicine impacts the choice of the system's design. Oversight requires not just whether a professional should be part of the AI system nor whether it should be at the beginning or the end of the clinical workflow; it also determines the level of bias demanded from the technology. Should, for example, diabetic retinopathy detection be entirely automated? In those cases where screening can be entirely automated, the potential cost reduction is undeniable and increased screening is without doubt a good thing from a population health perspective. The economic advantage, however, can directly impact patient care (Golden et al., 2016). Some studies have discovered that automatic screening results in the missed detection of complications, especially in the case of patients that are not well represented in the training sets that use a dataset approach to model interpretation.

11.4.2 Autonomous Vehicles

A driver must always be ready to intervene, even with an Society of Automotive Engineers (SAE International) Level 2 or Level 3 system. A system at Level 4, however, typically offers no agency in the driving task, making it possible for people to accept other responsibilities while en route. Possible oversight activities such as reading, designing surgical implants, or doing work while the vehicle drives toward a meeting have been proposed for these conditions. Achieving a high level of security is crucial for autonomous driving systems due to the risks associated. Safety is perceived as a social issue. It has been proposed that safety cases to support the safety system approvals of automated driving systems include "the ability of the Automated Data Factory (ADF) to transition appropriate control to the human," implying that some monitoring at the higher levels is expected to potentially be initiated by Level 4 and beyond systems. Maintaining this oversight is likely impacted by the cognitive capacity of the passengers and how it may change during the journey, also influenced by how long the journey takes, the demand of other tasks, the comfort during the journey, and the trust that automated driving systems instigate. Several ingenious ways have been proposed to facilitate these transitions, and fundamental questions also need answering. In which circumstances do people disengage from higher-level tasks? Should decisions be made by ADF without consulting the occupants? Assisting the driver during the transition with some advice and fulfilling certain requirements are expected to ease the transition, but problems are likely to happen if it occurs suddenly. Security events provide various temporal scales, and the operator may have difficulty in responding to the events. If entertainment systems take too much focus, it may be negative. Conversely, if such needs are ignored during a long trip, it may cause unpreparedness, also leading to a slow response time (Philip & Suresh, 2024). These questions of timing and system activation of transition support services are crucial as both people involved seem to be busy, and maintaining a good situational awareness of the people inside the self-driving vehicle is a rather difficult task.

11.4.3 Financial Services

The recent turmoil in financial services has illuminated the challenge and necessity of distinguishing between automated tools that are novel, useful, and risk-laden but managed by trained experts, and automated tools that are fully autonomous and untriggered. We see here both sides of the equation: the consequences of rejecting the AI model's insights entirely due to a lack of interpretability and the limitations of not relying on the mechanisms of AI decision-making in designing our feedback loops. In other words, we see the definitive need to stay balanced between expert feedback and AI tool drift: ensuring that both sides gain and capitalize on synergy, instead of succumbing to either the unpredictability of fully autonomous AI, despite its many benefits in the current labor market shortage, or the stagnation of an expert-centric approach that cannot keep up with risk complexities in this increasingly interconnected ecosystem. The Bank Secrecy Act (BSA) created the problem against a backdrop of international organized crime, drugs, and terror funding. The BSA's essential feature is a "disclosure" obligation on banks, telling them to report large cash transactions, thanks to which the U.S. Department of the Treasury needs suspicions of crimes against such wickedness and of laundered money flooding the country's pristine financial system must be shared by banks. The sharing is accomplished through suspicious activity reports (SAR) that banks file when they suspect such actions. The problem is that, worldwide, banks now file more than 4,000 SARs a day. AI has played a big role in this information explosion. Big banks have adopted AI-based surveillance systems that review customer data, such as wire transfers and transactions, for suspicious patterns and generate alerts representing potential violations, leading to a determination that a SAR should be filed (Townsend et al., 2018). AI's role in the vast decision-making and rule-writing is evident: although no actual law compels banks to adopt AI production tools, the sanctions imposed on banks for real or purported noncompliance are hard to resist.

11.5 Best Practices for Human Oversight

Early documents investigating the need for strong governance and oversight of advanced systems described in detail different aspects of human oversight requirements. Some of the recommendations are related to designing systems to allow for effective oversight, while others suggest concrete actions for those in oversight roles or are directed toward the oversight role rather than the work of designing. In this section, we sketch these recommendations, and organize them into three best practice categories for the successful embedding of human oversight in automated systems involving AI. Our focus is primarily with decision support and fully automated AI systems at this stage.

(i) An important aspect of AI system design that should be in place to facilitate human oversight at the transparency phase is the ability of AI systems to present "explanation" and "justification" knowledge, as well as instance-specific explanations such as the reasons given for concluding a "specific" action. For some AI-based decision or recommendation support systems, an example-based justification, in which prior cases are shown, can facilitate this task. Striking results show that the user's knowledge of the AI's limitations can minimize their false beliefs concerning the AI's inferences and avoid pitfalls during the task performance. Thus, an important aspect of human oversight quality is the explanation of the AI system's behavior during decision or prediction tasks.

(ii) Guardianship roles should happen only if adequate training is provided. Effective human–agent teamwork depends on training of both the humans and the agents. Without proper training of both sides, it is unlikely that responsibilities, performance levels, and capabilities will merge into the type of monitoring relationship needed for successful operation. However, both human training on the automated system's capabilities and operator training for the AI system and decision-making task need to happen dynamically to ensure the operator can oversee the system's operation in real time, without annoying delays at the moment of solution or high workloads.

(iii) Feedback mechanisms for human overseers must be in place to let them give human feedback concerning both the action chosen by the automated system and the action proposed by the human. The transparency between the worker and the "bot" should be established in such a way that humans have as much input in the process as possible. Proper ranking mechanisms can help here, in which the human can assess the quality of the proposals made by the automated system and provide the necessary feedback so that the system can progressively learn from the user. However, these systems cannot always operate in a semi-autonomous way according to transparency requirements.

11.5.1 Designing for Transparency

Ensuring AI system transparency means making sure that the reasons for the decisions made by AIs, as well as how all the inputs and outputs are created, managed, and processed by the AI, are clear to precisely everyone who will need to trust the AI. So far, there is not a single solution or a single kind of solution to transparency and explainability of AIs. Given such a multifaceted challenge, it is important that AI developers, regardless of discipline, work as closely as possible in interdisciplinary teams, focusing on co-creation together with the experts or users of the AI, namely, the domain experts and the intended target users. Within interdisciplinary teams, prime importance should be given to one or more Human-Computer Interaction (HCI) researchers, who will steer both the design process and the design evaluations research cycle, as well as need to stay on the lookout for possible further gaps containing problems of AI transparency and user-centered explainability. The design of explanatory interfaces connecting the AI and its intended users is paramount. Explanatory interfaces create rich and accurate channels of communication between AI and human overseers. They take scrutiny through influences from many fields. Ideally, they should promote user-centric explainability of AI decision-making at a level depending on the AI's impact. Moreover, they should be optimized through evaluations based on the intended user community as well as the HCI design research community. It is suggested that such a design practice should be mandatory (Choi et al., 2024). The research on communication design for AI-assisted decision-making is already extensive, and teams intimately connected to domain experts or nonexpert users could more easily address tailor-made needs in specific domains where great AI projects are already in deployment or are planned.

11.5.2 Training for Oversight Roles

Equipping stakeholders for decision-making and oversight in human-centered automated systems requires more than a minimal level of knowledge. We argue that appropriate stakeholders need focused, contextualized training that provides the expertise needed to help shape, create, deploy, and assess these systems, but that such training is often lacking. Basic knowledge of AI systems may be part of a well-rounded education, and it may even be part of some academic certification and training programs, especially for students in computer science and closely related fields. In these fields, however, this often comes only as an elective that focuses solely on technical issues, rather than consequences and context. Policy fields, too, often provide only minimal training related to what is arguably the largest technology-development and implementation initiative in history, which involves engineers and other technical workers from many disciplines along with policymakers and ends up impacting each person's life and the entire planet in numerous, varied, positive and negative ways. Career-oriented degree programs and certificates for domain experts and reviewers, including those specific to some particular sectors or types of systems, should educate and train rigorously and be widely desirable, if not required; for practical credentialing, similar to how licensure for professionals in many industries requires ongoing training to account for technological change (Wall, 2022). Training of these types of stakeholders should occur throughout the automated system life cycle. Some initiatives are underway, but wider adoption is critical to build a workforce that is appropriately knowledgeable and invested in human-centered automated systems.

11.5.3 Feedback Mechanisms

Automated systems have traditionally advanced separate from the oversight roles that humans cast for themselves. Now there is a need to unite agency in a common feedback loop, which uses the strengths of the machine and the human, in that cooperation can not only enhance the work done, but also centralize the accountability that should guide its deployment. Humans should have a better ability to convey intent and be updated on decisions. In turn, systems should deliver more information to allow humans to provide feedback. Feedback mechanisms need to be designed to bridge human roles and automated decision-making systems throughout all operations and not just in the final results of a decision. In this way, a responsible cooperative framework is established that permits better decision strategies. In areas characterized by complex inquiry and decision-making processes, small decision artifacts can interact with humans and support their ability to advance a task toward its end. Moreover, there are learned functions that describe the assessments of humans, which have prisoned decisions to a semantically reachable region. To establish feedback mechanisms, it is necessary to have an understanding of which capabilities the automated system have at hand and which actions humans can take to influence its behavior. Articulation and interpretation are reasons for the difficulties related to the establishment of such feedbacks. Probability distributions defined by the machine expand such attribution and ambiguity by their very nature. Formal expressions highlight the risks associated with the use of machines when the outcome of a determined decision is especially consequential to the subject receiving it (Arockiam & Pushpanathan, 2023). Transparency and oversight can also be seen as third-party compliance checking actions because the collaborator is not necessarily the one directly drawing collaborative decisions, but simply the one deciding whether a suggestion or advice is appropriate at a given moment and under given circumstances of segregation, as presented in Figure 11.2.

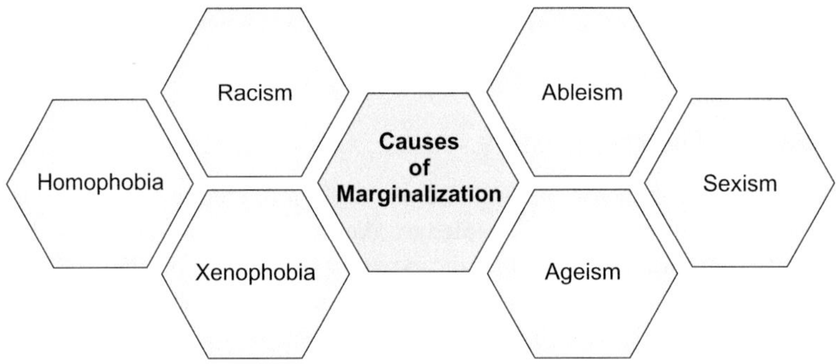

Fig. 11.2 Causes of marginalization in some insurance policies.

11.6 Technological Solutions for Oversight

Automated decision systems (ADS) today can infer or even decide on a wide variety of important issues about our lives and the lives of other human beings. In certain circumstances, accountability may be re-established a posteriori through a costly and difficult review process, or a more serious review attempt may be made through more or less formal complaint procedures, but such reviews are often impossible or practically irrelevant for those affected. On the other hand, being in charge cannot just mean deciding whether to shut the machine down or not. Such systems can hardly be monitored by users or random third parties to the necessary degree or in a formalized way. And yet monitoring is crucial in order to avoid one of the two possible grotesques: a delegated tyranny or a system that is out of control and that can only be shut down. Since decision-making as such cannot be transferred to machines, we must work toward enabling ADS to become instruments for better, more reliable, and policy-compliant decisions by accountable and trustworthy agents. In that sense, it makes sense to speak of "oversight" rather than "human-in-the-loop" solutions to the "agency problem" posed by ADS, even if such solutions form part of a possible answer to the problem. Technological solutions for oversight might range from dashboard or supervision displays and periodic risk audits in tandem with IT security technologies, via task-specific operational transparency and explanation technologies to feedback and correction interfaces that allow the detection of drift problems and learning, as well as the periodic correction of the machine's internal decision rules (Oben et al., 2024). The development and deployment of these technologies make sense not only for the sake of operators and institutional decision-makers, but also in order to restore users' and society's confidence in ADS, and as a legitimate middle-ground solution between a "ban everything" and the "laissez-faire" extremes.

11.6.1 Explainable AI

Any practical consideration of human oversight in automated systems will come up against two problems. The first is that these systems can perform in ways that are opaque or inscrutable to the overseers, which is a problem shared by many decision support technologies but which is more pronounced in the case of automated systems. The second is that even when an automated system is behaving in a way that the overseer can understand, it may be in a way that is surprising and that the operator would not have predicted. We noted earlier that human trust in automated systems is a double-edged sword. A low level of trust can lead to a lack of useful vigilance; too great a level can lead to complacency and a lack of adjustment when the automated system begins to act in surprising ways for reasons that are unclear. In both of these cases, human oversight—and thus the accountability and trustworthiness of the automated system—may be compromised. Various recent technological tools may help with monitoring automated systems. These should be understood, however, as secondary tools to what has become known as explainable AI or XAI. There are many aspects to XAI, but at its most general, it is an approach to AI research that seeks to produce systems that people can understand, both in terms of their inner workings and also in the expected range of behaviors, including when they are making predictions in specific instances (Townsend et al., 2018). As with other areas of AI research that involve the design of explainers or explanation-facilitating interfaces, XAI is often assumed to be largely a matter of interface design.

11.6.2 Monitoring Tools

The creation of, and need for, monitoring tools for risk assessment was greatly spurred because of the impact of AI on decision-making in important areas of life with significant and disparate impact. There's a great need to help human users confirm the inputs to and outputs of models and ensure the model is behaving in expected ways that are equally fair for all populations. Such monitoring tools would also help to identify and allow for remedial measures against failure modes and errant or dangerous behavior on the part of models. Monitoring tools can be used before or after deployment to check that an AI model is functioning as intended. Like interfaces, monitoring tools can be used by a wide variety of people with different levels of expertise. Different groups might find different tools useful; experts may prefer very detailed visualizations, while nonexperts might find more abstracted visualizations more approachable. Various systems have been proposed as model monitors. Some visualize a model's behavior; these can either be special-purpose systems or existing visualization systems repurposed for model monitoring. These visualizations help to give interpretable reasons for behavior and show how those reasons change as model input changes, or how shifts in a data distribution are correlated with shifts in model predictions. Other systems allow for the "plugging in" that creates model monitors. These include UserSim, which could be particularly useful in tasks involving communication between users and AI, and EgoQAN, which would allow for real-time reading-critical-question-answering-model error monitoring, especially useful in tasks regarding healthcare or safety interventions. Finally, there are a number of general model evaluation tools; most of these have not been deployed for real-world applications, but normalizing flows could be used to monitor safety, and concept-based explainability models could be used to track and debug model performance and explainability over time (Philip & Suresh, 2024). Regardless, there is still work to be done in creating richer interfaces that let all stakeholders contribute to the design and use of model monitors, especially those who are not machine learning experts.

11.6.3 User Interfaces

An often-overlooked aspect of oversight on AI decisions is the importance of the user interface between the user and the AI system. A user interface can allow or severely restrict oversight capabilities of the main user of the AI system, be it an operator, other humans affected by the AI's actions, or even the AI itself. Since we expect oversight of an AI system to be important, it is important to empower people affected by the AI system with the right tools to be able to conduct that oversight. A means of empowering people is through well-designed user interfaces that support reliable and trustworthy interaction between humans and machines, and consider their distinct abilities and limitations. Understanding the capabilities and limitations of users can inform the design. All actors in a sociotechnical system have capabilities and limitations that should inform a user interface design. For the AI, these capabilities and limitations can often be expressed quantitatively, leading to simple graphical representations. For people affected by the AI system, investigating what information should be presented and how is a more subjective process. When designing user interfaces for AI systems, we should keep these limitations and capabilities in mind, as well as the fact that they can also be impacted by system design (Golden et al., 2016). It is unreasonable to expect every user or user group of an AI system to become an expert in the capabilities and limitations of every possible relevant AI technology that can be integrated into it; therefore, user interface design can help address usability without excessive amount of training or knowledge input, as presented in Table 11.2.

Table 11.2 Comparing human–AI decision models in insurance oversight.

Model Type	*Description*	*Level of Human Oversight*	*Example Scenario*	*Benefits and Trade-Offs*
Fully Automated	AI makes decisions without human intervention	None	Auto-approval of small claims under a threshold	Speed, efficiency, and a lack of transparency and redress
Human-in-the-Loop	Humans must approve or reject AI recommendations	Continuous	AI suggests policy price, underwriter confirms	Accountability, but it may reduce efficiency
Human-on-the-Loop	Human monitors the system and can intervene if needed	Partial	AI detects fraud, humans can override flagged cases	Balance of automation and safety

Contd.

Table 11.2 *Contd.*

Model Type	*Description*	*Level of Human Oversight*	*Example Scenario*	*Benefits and Trade-Offs*
Human-in-Command	Humans control major decisions, and AI only assists	High	Risk assessor uses AI insights but makes final call	Ethical robustness, slow in high-volume tasks
Collaborative Model	Joint decision-making between AI and human agents	Dynamic	AI and adjusters collaboratively assess large claims	Improved decisions require strong coordination
Oversight-by-Design	The system is architected to allow auditing and intervention	Embedded	Audit trails in claim denial decisions	Transparency is baked in and requires upfront investment
Escalation-Based	AI handles most tasks but flags uncertain cases	Event-driven	AI flags suspicious patterns that lack confidence	Focuses human time where most needed
Selective Automation	AI automates only non-sensitive decisions	Risk-based	Auto-approve renewals, manual review for new policies	Maximizes efficiency without compromising oversight
Regulatory Trigger Model	Human oversight is required when thresholds are hit	Conditional	Price hikes above 20% must be reviewed by a human	Legal safety, inflexible in edge cases
Explainability-First	Prioritizes human understanding before execution	Transparency-led	The claims system explains the decision to the agent before the action	Builds user trust, may delay operations
Redress-Oriented	The system emphasizes handling complaints and errors	Post-decision	Client contests AI decision, human reevaluates	Ethical fallback, depends on strong support channels
Bias-Aware Hybrid	Combines AI with human checks for bias and fairness	Fairness-focused	Underwriter reviews AI rejection of minorities	Reduces systemic bias, may increase cost
Dynamic Oversight Allocation	Varies human controls based on risk	Adaptive	More oversight for high-value or sensitive decisions	Efficiency and flexibility require strong risk models

11.7 Future Directions in AI Oversight

Achieving responsible autonomous systems is a complex and multidisciplinary endeavor, and while the challenges of oversight are nontrivial, so too are the potential consequences of ignoring accountability and trust in automated systems. As the adoption of such systems reaches across different industries, creating accountability frameworks will increasingly become a necessary part of the design and safety assurance phases. A transition to designing with oversight in mind will bolster the development of high-impact systems that uphold and amplify the agency of those that they serve. The critical need for effective human oversight spans several domains, across varying types of automated systems, from home helpers to healthcare improvers to law enforcement selectors, and ranging in autonomy from fully automated to partially automated. The most effective and accountable implementations will strive to maintain rather than erode the roles of humans, and to avoid the hazards of reduced transparency, understanding, and choice. We close this chapter with a brief exploration of the landscape of future directions in human oversight of automated systems. We highlight emerging technologies that are poised to enhance automation without responsible oversight, and we offer policy recommendations for specific sectors as a means of mitigating oncoming trust and accountability challenges (Choi et al., 2024). Ultimately, we argue that collaborative and international engagement is key to avoiding the pitfalls of an ungoverned future.

11.7.1 Emerging Technologies

New technologies can shape the future of human oversight arrangements, but thoughtful action is needed from research, industry, and lawmakers to ensure that they serve society's interests. The infrastructure systems and services in which AI models are used may rely on real-time monitoring and data collection for other reasons. For example, telematic transport systems have been implemented to ease congestion in cities, and utilize sensors and cameras that detect location and movements; these systems would be ideally positioned also to detect when the systems they are controlling, such as automated transport or delivery vehicles, are engaging in unusual behavior. Cities, however, may or may not have the technological capabilities needed to develop and implement these systems, meaning that the responsibility may be left up to tech companies. Lawmakers or oversight committees need to put in place guidelines and frameworks for the usage of the collected data. Feedback loops can be created to make effective AI models act in the interest of users and society. For example, you could enable third-party apps to share data with a recommender system, with aggregated metadata being leveraged to retrain it. In the case of misinformation on social media, you could allow fact-checking organizations to flag fake news, and trust their judgment so that responses to users could go beyond mere links to fact-checking sites (Murphy & Moosa, 2021). While in some cases, users are offered the merest illusion of oversight and control in the relationship—a mere checkbox on the interface—in others, users, community organizations, and third parties can play an active role.

11.7.2 Policy Recommendations

In this chapter, we have described different facets of human oversight in AI systems, viewing these systems from an ethical, cognitive, and pragmatic perspective. As humans develop and deploy AI systems with increasing capabilities, there is a growing risk of encountering harm to many stakeholders. Yet our understanding of how to best put in place such oversight for a wide-ranging class of AI systems is limited. The model provides a framework for AI developers to consider key oversight features of the AI system they are developing, but it is not clear that such oversight will be a uniformly selected requirement of these systems. In this chapter, we offer policy recommendations that aim to bridge the gap between understanding oversight needs and ensuring that oversight is a common practice in the development and deployment of AI systems across industry sectors. Oversight serves as a verification mechanism in both the development and deployment processes. Developers may disclose certain properties of their system in such a way that external parties may confirm these properties during development. In deployment, external entities access real-world data in a restricted way to verify that the properties hold during and after deployment. Such verification mechanisms are important because agencies tasked with monitoring AI system behavior cannot always access and analyze real-world data due to privacy and security concerns about sensitive data. Our recommendations distill 12 areas of focus into the three themes of verification and audit capabilities for oversight, expert entities tasked with oversight, and deferring to experts. In the military sector, policy can require dedicated verification and audit capabilities. In the context of military applications, AI capabilities could be more bounded due to the threat of adverse effects on civilian safety (Golden et al., 2016). The closer the system's operation is to potential harm to civilians, the less complex the system should be, and the more capable the oversight should be.

11.7.3 Global Collaboration

Modern AI systems are rapidly outpacing our state- and nation-centric efforts to govern them. Such efforts will not succeed in ensuring that AI is developed and deployed for the common good without strong cooperation among countries, tech companies, civil society, and the universities and research institutions developing these technologies. The global nature of the largest technology companies means that countries cannot compete on the regulation of technology alone. Such regulations could lead to the tech monopolies shifting research, development, and deployment to countries where regulation is less stringent or, worse, becoming a race to the bottom on safety education for machine learning systems. Additional cooperation mechanisms are needed to generate trust and accountability in these systems. We recommend that a collaborative effort be organized to regulate the safety of novel AI systems. The goal would be to develop a multilateral framework that uses multi-stakeholder input to coordinate safe and ethical advancement of increasingly capable AI systems that would lower safety- and cause-related instability risks. Several existing international treaties and bilateral agreements help mitigate existential and humanitarian risks associated with other technologies. A similar model might be appropriate to establish and enhance successful cooperation on these topics at the international level. Groups of countries should begin discussions and work to build common understandings about what regulations could look like and which capabilities they would like to see internationally coordinated (Philip & Suresh, 2024). Articulating and discussing what kinds of capabilities should be seen as too dangerous to develop and deploy is an important step that should be taken sooner rather than later. Although the voluntary nature of bilateral and multilateral agreements limits their effectiveness, the best answer cannot be to rely only on the vagaries of internal regulations.

11.8 Ethical Implications of AI Oversight

The extensive integration of AI rests upon stakeholders of various backgrounds, including technologists, policymakers, government leaders, business entrepreneurs, and social activists. Each of these groups impacts AI development and deployment through their respective choices, values, and norms, and each group bears responsibility for the broader consequences of its AI efforts. Emerging on both sides of the argument in favor of increased attention to human oversight, however, is a diverse patchwork of ethical concerns that justify a more sustained approach to ethical oversight. The architecture of AI systems makes the question of moral responsibility more pressing. The conceptual tools we have used successfully to assign moral blame, punishment, or reward in human interactions largely depend on the ability of the actor to reflect on their actions and consequences. A philosopher discussing techno-moral change refers to these conceptual tools as grievance techniques. We typically rely on our grievance techniques to assign moral responsibility when a person is in a position to reflect on the action and its consequences (Townsend et al., 2018). The moral attorney general or parents of a troubled adolescent will expect that person to engage relevant moral values and to resist temptation. They might resist a judgment of moral failure if an analysis concludes that the adolescent is incapable of resisting some temptation to behave badly when other people are not in a position to reflect on the consequences of their actions. Suppose people are likely to act in dangerous or harmful ways and are not constrained by oversight or the availability of nonharmful alternatives. In that case, we may hold them responsible regardless of whether they are reflecting on the situation. Adverse consequences for vulnerable individuals can also undermine the values we seek to promote in this discussion. Deployments of AI systems have raised important questions of fairness, where disadvantaged populations may be denied services or overrepresented in negative outcomes. Even if humans oversee an AI system, it may still perform badly in the sense of exacerbating existing disparities. Many researchers, and in particular demographers and other social scientists, lament that seed data describing how we have behaved in the past is used to train AI systems to make predictions or recommendations that will affect our lives. They point out that the past may reflect biases that have skewed our behavior. Bias in the data, they argue, establishes a biased moral baseline, meaning that the AI system may impose a biased model of the world on affected individuals (Aina et al., 2024). Such a model can be harmful even if it is designed to be accountable in the sense that humans are supervising its outputs.

11.8.1 Moral Responsibility

While the goal of this work is to highlight the potential benefits of embedding human oversight into automated systems, and thereby the potential benefits of the oversight systems themselves, it is also worth mentioning that assigning forecasting and decision-making tasks to AI systems creates ethical dilemmas. Consider, for example, the following questions: Who will be held responsible in the event of an error made by an algorithmic decision system? Are the engineers who designed the algorithm responsible? The managers who commissioned the algorithm? The person who neglected to double-check the machine's judgments? The owners of a self-driving car in the event of an accident? How would one even prove direct responsibility? These considerations are less relevant if we think of AI systems merely as organizational tools that assist people, enabling them to exercise judgment and make better decisions than they otherwise could (Margan, 2021). We do not ordinarily assign moral responsibility to hammers, and for good reason. However, if we think of AI algorithms as analogous to judges, and if the ultimate decisions of judges mattered less than the ultimate decisions made by the algorithms, a gray area emerges. The emergent gray area can be troublesome, as it is often perilously difficult to determine exactly to what extent something—the product of engineers, the mandate of management, oversight by supervisors—was responsible for a quantifiable outcome. For example, it can be hard to tell exactly why a corporate culture led a corporation to engage in predatory behavior to such devastating effect—was it the failings of the chief executives, the pressures the department heads exerted on the lower-ranking employees, the prevalence of business practices in the industry that rewarded such behavior, or something else? The uncertainty can be more pronounced still if the entity responsible is an AI system, and the gap separating the responsibility of the designers and users from the responsibility of the system itself swells when the AI system is an automated decision-making system that is largely uninterpretable, making it essentially impossible to disclose the details that would point toward specific culpability (McDonnell et al., 2023).

11.8.2 Bias and Fairness

A growing concern that increases with the increasing use of AI is that these systems are often biased, which leads to unfair and unequal treatment of certain groups of people. Racism and sexism are two main sources of bias found among decision-making systems such as facial recognition or credit-scoring algorithms. The definition and detection of bias in AI, as well as the problem treatment and the fairness features of an AI system, basically depend on its human designers. How well the designers can identify appropriate measures of bias and fairness largely determines the success of these projects. Oversight may be at various stages of the AI system life cycle. Moreover, human oversight interested in preventing potential biases should also be present during task allocation. In this configuration, the AI model must learn from the consequences of outcome bias disappearances, underreporting, or potential bias disruptions introduced by the managers in the task (Gramegna &

Giudici, 2020). This theoretical vision means that the oversight monitoring of these systems cannot be exclusively performed by the model, in a traditional sense of performance and self-explanation. In fact, the supervisor must ideally look for unusual observed feature distribution changes over extended periods. The identification of these types of bias mitigation scenarios provides the twofold recommendations for the organizations in charge of planning and implementing simulation models based on AI tools. The first recommendation is periodical audits of the AI models in accordance with the ethical regulatory frameworks on fairness and bias. In practice, potential flaws look for inequities on how a particular model treats a protected group. Once investigators develop particular bias and fairness definitions and detection, they should compare when the model operates as a discriminator or not when deploying it in suitable pilot contexts without causing harm to protected groups (Wall, 2022).

11.9 Privacy Concerns

This chapter raises an important question: Does AI screening and de-identifying of data offer privacy benefits, or does it violate privacy more than it protects? Privacy is a crucial topic with regard to oversight of errors in video processing because the use of computer vision to monitor traffic or surveil lives is often already problematic. The introduction of AI algorithms raises the act of privacy invasion to another level, one involving the decoupling of the actions being monitored from any physical person behind or beside the camera. The question of benefits and costs with regard to the use of AI overseers of traffic or life in public space is serious both for the internal ethics of using AI and also for the social demand to make use of this new technology. Demands for protection from identification through AI traffic analyzers, digital redaction of faces, and tracking features on images held in private hands by government authorities and disclaimed for public viewing are starting to emerge. Corporations associated with harvesting personal tracking and behavior data combined with rapid market expansion of software and hardware for all kinds of digital objects based on deep learning are responsible for a rapid growing demand to "digitally redact"—that is, erase in a deep-learning-based manner—original image records of vulnerable and potentially harmful content of innocuous persons or groups before digital objects are put onto the market of public service and enjoyment (Aina et al., 2024). The ethical implications for algorithms operating on raw digitized, unprocessed video flows are potentially sensitive. An argument can be made that only moral gestures de-identifying the recorded lives of the people interacted with on-road traffic and mundane days should be mandatory, and should be considered the moral province of technology stakeholders.

11.9.1 Stakeholder Perspectives

While initial impulses for regulating automated systems came from civil society, other perspectives are now also incorporated into the regulatory process. Although some agencies are already charged with oversight of automated systems, newer, state-of-the-art systems have revealed shortcomings in a framework previously defined by individual laws and principles. This chapter makes it clear that embedding human oversight into automated systems has a lot to learn from preliminary market research in these sectors, better suited for collecting insights and opinions from affected stakeholders than models. Most government agencies desire to safeguard public interests and would favor publicly available information on the development and design of automated systems. They are willing to oversee the influence of third-party impact assessments on internal decision-making and ensure that recommendation systems provide accurate results. In turn, they would probably also need to be notified of intended high-risk applications of such systems and review them. Therefore, the expectation horizon is bi-faceted. The basic question is who is supervising the supervisor and to what extent. Hidden and opaque decision-making processes and a lack of horizontal accountability are also critical factors on the side of the private sector. Yet, many companies want to embrace new technologies and offer customers automated systems, easy to use and trust. This calls for a balance between transparency and operational security. Procedures for automated content moderation certainly need to be controlled on an organizational level, but judgment calls are sometimes best made at the lowest possible level while learning from one another and possessing the freedom of flexible communication (Choi et al., 2024). Polluted data training sets or faulty technical parameters risk consequences that are unfair or wildly disproportionate compared to the help provided by the system. Seventy percent of the top systems ranked by the number of predictions require technical support.

11.9.2 Government Agencies

A major first step to ensure responsible AI systems is sending the right signals for the actions of those working in the development of such systems, but also those who will deploy them or use them. Research funding agencies have a major role to play, either by establishing certain standards in terms of public funding of research projects. Indeed, these agencies are gatekeepers of the public money allocated to research projects, and by establishing precisely outlined requirements in terms of human oversight of the produced systems, they can encourage positive behavior for researchers. They could also encourage cooperation between civil society, academic researchers, and the private sector with regard to the predictions of potential risks of AI systems. They could also encourage the creation of a toolkit for the evaluation of the requirements and risks regarding the architecture and deployment of the AI systems, resource centers, or communities of practice. Standards and regulations are increasingly seen as regulation measures to be developed and, in fact, imposed on designers and developers of algorithms, and AI in particular. International standardization bodies are now working on developing those standards in collaboration with experts and stakeholders in order to produce high-quality documents. Whenever it is possible, and in particular regarding the regulation of private vendors of AI systems, governments could adopt and use these international standards (Golden et al., 2016). By doing so, they have a model that is written in collaboration with numerous stakeholders and experts, and their adoption would help the standards to become the de facto standard regarding the built of reliable and trustworthy AI systems that comply with human oversight principles.

11.9.3 Private Sector

Although important practical challenges in the form of actual implementation remain, the concept of responsible AI is being explored by important actors in the tech systems surrounding AI, particularly in the private sector. Such efforts center on developing and implementing accountability initiatives that seek to direct how organizations approach designing, developing, and deploying AI and machine learning systems. Substantial progress has been made in terms of establishing recognized best practices in a relatively short period via corporate thought leadership and research, as well as through early stakeholder collaboration. These initiatives serve important purposes, such as attempting to avoid or eliminate questions of accountability from being raised only when things go wrong with a technological system. A number of corporations have recently undertaken wide-ranging initiatives to explain and develop practical AI ethics principles. One company created a set of AI principles to guide the responsible development of the AI-enabled technology that underpins many of its products and commercial offerings. Another organization, which comprises several major tech companies and various researchers, technical experts, and civil society members, has also established responsible AI principles and guidelines (Margan, 2021; McDonnell et al., 2023). In April 2021, more than 20 of the nation's leading technology companies signed a set of commitments aimed at promoting predictable, fair, and trustworthy AI. A subsidiary of one of these companies also emphasizes in its "code of conduct" a set of "community guidelines" to prohibit the use of its services to intimidate, harass, or coerce others, paying special attention to preventing any encouragement of violent acts.

11.9.4 Civil Society

The growing capabilities of automated systems captivate public imagination, eliciting awe, fear, and concern. Emerging systems, infused with AI algorithms, promise living out sci-fi fantasies and dreaming of comfortable lifestyles, while the dangers of alienation remind onlookers of the dystopic realities. Fears, concerns, and criticism account for an overwhelming majority of the news cycle. And for good reason, the history of AI development and adoption is riddled with broken promises of technological determinism turning the dream of a laborless future into a cybernetic dystopia. Such fears and concerns do not merely originate in newsrooms, though. Influential members of civil society don't ground their expectations in unelected, commercial tech elites or unelected government officials or public servants, but have long pushed for checks on tech development, especially regarding automated systems. Since long before the advent of computers, technology critics warned of the silencing of crucial debates about the social–political, ethical–moral, and philosophical implications of technology or the gradual relegation of human beings to the position of mere control or oversight agents of bureaucratic and technological systems (Aina et al., 2024; Townsend et al., 2018). It is, however, not only critics from military, academic, or philosophical origin that are concerned about the tendency of automated systems to subjugate individuals, societies, or even humanity to their demands, but all parts of civil society, striving for a world where the development and deployment of technology is subject to social–political deliberation and not mere commercial interests.

11.10 Conclusion

This contribution addresses how to embed human oversight in automated systems, which is an essential element for accountable and trustworthy AI. We have added a unique suggestion, the Task-Oriented, Whole-Language, and Authentic Reading and Discourse (TOWARD) approach, that offers several mechanisms that can be adopted according to the level of autonomy of an automated AI system. Those can be customized accordingly to fit the needs of the system identified. The TOWARD suggestion can thus become a toolbox for system developers and users. However, while adopting the TOWARD toolbox, careful consideration has to be given to what is at stake. Different forms of oversight will fulfil different goals: some will guarantee ex post responsibility and prevent and redress injustice, violation of norms and rules, etc.; others will merely provide additional ex ante assurance when specific risks are at stake, such as technical malfunction. Notably, oversight does not mean, in every context, creating a powerful human in the loop. Some forms of oversight may be elusive and, by no means, guarantee full control of the AI system. As we have seen, other non-human-oriented precautionary measures could be in place. For meaningful oversight, duty holders need to know what is at stake when customizing the toolbox. Moreover, caution is required when configuring supervision; in some cases, over-relying on human oversight may lead to potential hazards for users. Indeed, being part of a supervisory process may induce a certain psychological effect which, together with fatigue, could increase the chances of errors. Lastly, AI systems evolve, and so do their models and performances. The difficulty, if not impossibility, of guaranteeing that a model will continue to work as intended over time is one of the key reasons why accountability and redress mechanisms should not only be established at the outset but also maintained throughout the life of the system.

References

Aina, I., Ayinde, O., Thiam, D. and Miranda, M. (2024). Crop Index Insurance as a Tool for Climate Resilience: Lessons from Smallholder Farmers in Nigeria. *Natural Hazards*, *120*(5). https://doi.org/10.1007/s11069-023-06388-x

Arockiam, J.M. and Pushpanathan, A.C.S. (2023). MapReduce-Iterative Support Vector Machine Classifier: Novel Fraud Detection Systems in Healthcare Insurance Industry. *International Journal of Electrical and Computer Engineering*, *13*(1). https://doi.org/10.11591/ijece.v13i1.pp756-769

Choi, J.H., Choi, Y., Lee, K.S., Ahn, K.H. and Jang, W.Y. (2024). Explainable Model Using Shapley Additive Explanations Approach on Wound Infection after Wide Soft Tissue Sarcoma Resection: "Big Data" Analysis Based on Health Insurance Review and Assessment Service Hub. *Medicina (Lithuania)*, *60*(2). https://doi.org/10.3390/medicina60020327

Golden, L.L., Brockett, P.L., Ai, J. and Kellison, B. (2016). Empirical Evidence on the Use of Credit Scoring for Predicting Insurance Losses with Psycho-Social and Biochemical Explanations. *North American Actuarial Journal*, *20*(3). https://doi.org/10.1080/10920277.2016.1209118

Gramegna, A. and Giudici, P. (2020). Why to Buy Insurance? An Explainable Artificial Intelligence Approach. *Risks*, *8*(4). https://doi.org/10.3390/risks8040137

Margan, S.K. (2021). Drifting into Algocratic Insurance? In *The AI Book: The Artificial Intelligence Handbook for Investors, Entrepreneurs and FinTech Visionaries*, pp. 71–74, Wiley. https://doi.org/10.1002/9781119551966.ch20

McDonnell, K., Murphy, F., Sheehan, B., Masello, L. and Castignani, G. (2023). Deep Learning in Insurance: Accuracy and Model Interpretability Using TabNet. *Expert Systems with Applications*, *217*. https://doi.org/10.1016/j.eswa.2023.119543

Murphy, S.D. and Moosa, S. (2021). The Views of Public Service Managers on the Implementation of National Health Insurance in Primary Care: A Case of Johannesburg Health District, Gauteng Province, Republic of South Africa. *BMC Health Services Research*, *21*(1). https://doi.org/10.1186/s12913-021-06990-4

Oben, E.E.E., Ndi, H.N. and Tchuikoua, L.B. (2024). Livestock Farmers' Willingness to Pay for Farming Insurance in Four Divisions of the West Region of Cameroon. *Asian Journal of Geographical Research*, *7*(1). https://doi.org/10.9734/ajgr/2024/v7i1211

Philip, B. and Suresh, G. (2024). Cultivating Resilience: An In-depth Exploration of Agricultural Insurance Initiatives and Their Transformative Role in India's Farming Landscape. *Universal Journal of Agricultural Research*, *12*(1). https://doi.org/10.13189/ujar.2024.120109

Townsend, C., McIntyre, M., Lakhani, A., Wright, C., White, P., Bishara, J. and Cullen, J. (2018). Inclusion of Marginalised Aboriginal and Torres Strait Islander Peoples with Neurocognitive Disability in the National Disability Insurance Scheme (NDIS). *OPEN ACCESS*, *5*(2).

Wall, J. (2022). *Keynote Speech 4: A Conversational AI Approach to Detecting Deception and Tackling Insurance Fraud*. 2021 Tenth International Conference on Intelligent Computing and Information Systems (ICICIS), Cairo, Egypt. https://doi.org/10.1109/ICICIS52592.2021.9694118

12

Equity and Inclusion in Insurance AI: Expanding Access for Marginalized and Underserved Populations

Wasswa Shafik

12.1 Introduction

Insurance AI can help to serve marginalized and underserved consumers better, but these groups vary greatly in what that means to them and what is possible. To make the most of technology, it's essential first to understand their unique situations in order to recognize how technology can help, what it can't, and who else can step in to fill the gap. The insurance industry is well acquainted with the socioeconomic and demographic factors when developing selling strategies, but understanding the nuances of different perspectives, values, and motivations when it comes to financial security is a deeper and less commonly explored undertaking. In recognizing the variation between these groups, we will use "marginalized" when describing the groups that miss out, whether by intention or more often by the result of a lack of access to useful products. "Underserved" will refer to those groups, often generally overlapping with marginalized, that are recognized in the insurance space as lacking proper insurance resources, either from the products or the companies that serve them. These marginalized groups often have been left out of the umbrella discussions of underserved communities due to differences in risk appetite or levels of trust. Understanding their unique experiences as they relate to their use of financial tools, like insurance, is important for the development of tools and AI models that can actually serve them (Margan, 2021). The risk of writing all of these communities off as people who do not want insurance and should not be marketed in a data-hungry way is a dangerous one; one that could be more detrimental than doing nothing at all.

12.1.1 The Role of AI in the Insurance Industry

Insurance, as a risk transfer mechanism, has existed for centuries and is deeply embedded in modern commercial enterprises. Major pillars of the global economy rely on insurance products, including property, casualty, life, and health insurance. With the emergence of artificial intelligence, the insurance sector has rapidly evolved, bringing real and tangible benefits for the whole society. By enabling more precise pricing of risks, AI has allowed previously uninsurable populations to gain insurance coverage. By making the insurance purchase experience easier and cheaper, AI has allowed tens of millions of consumers to take advantage of insurance protection in health, property, casualty, and life sectors. In parallel, AI has also allowed insurers to optimize their performance, leading to improved profitability and stability. Better pricing accuracy and reduction of fraudulent

DOI: 10.1201/9781003747659-12

claims allow insurers to be more responsive during adverse events and to pay claims during times of need. Automation of administrative processes has allowed insurers to lower their operational costs and pass those savings through reduced prices on to their customers. Additionally, improved decision-making driven by AI-based analysis of insurance company stock portfolios leads to better investment returns and allows insurers to build capital positions to remain financially resilient (McDonnell et al., 2023). Therefore, insurers leveraging AI for climate modeling can support their customers in the clear identification of the climatic risks they face.

12.1.2 Current Challenges in Insurance Access

Insurance is supposed to provide security from adverse circumstances such as accidents, illness, or property loss. However, many in the United States do not have readily available access to effective insurance products. These individuals may be the poorest or soonest impoverished by unfortunate life events, compared to better-off persons for whom insurance ownership is more common, but they may also be people whose property or lives are subject to the most risk, including racial minorities and immigrants. However, these same populations are frequently marginalized within the insurance sector, through behavioral nudges that may be purposefully but ineffectively designed to result in negative outcomes such as terminations of preexisting insurance subscriptions or excessive premiums, or gaps between expected and realized value in particular products. Increasingly sophisticated statistical models to predict risk are also required since extreme events are becoming more common. These marginals struggle to communicate effectively with companies offering insurance products, to find affordable policies that will exclude fewer possible adverse events, and to maintain their policies over time. These difficulties can arise from reduced language skills and less general consumer sophistication. Consumer models for insurance products, such as unique limitations in their understanding of probabilistic outcomes, feeling secure from the worst possible losses, and budgets that impose severe limits on their preferences for insurance relative to direct consumption, cannot be neglected in favor of better-educated consumers (Choi et al., 2024). Low-tech methods of conveying risk messages, in icon form rather than in statistical terms, may be necessary to ensure that the value of the insurance product is maximized for these consumers.

12.2 Barriers to Equity in Insurance AI

Expanding access to insurance AI for marginalized and underserved populations requires dismantling the barriers to equity and inclusion present in insurance AI systems. Two notable barriers are biases in data and algorithmic discrimination. Data bias is a well-known pitfall in machine learning research. New applications of machine learning have frequently gone through a process of trial and error, with hiring, law enforcement, and medical algorithms being found to systematically disadvantage marginalized populations, especially racialized, Indigenous, and low-income populations. In some cases, this data bias assumes the form of using critical variables that are proxies or factors associated with race rather than the actual race variable, and for this reason, these algorithms have been rejected as racially biased. In the case of hiring discrimination, using the same data available for traditional practice does not remove bias, as its influence is embedded in the data. In other cases, algorithms have been found to achieve subpar performance for racialized populations. Critically, while these previous generations of machine learning have been found to be biased against marginalized populations, their protection from bias has not been a major consideration in research (Murphy & Moosa, 2021). As demand for algorithmic decision-making increases, incorporating bias against marginalized populations into costs, whether they are regulatory or market-based, is an area for further work, especially within regulatory industries such as healthcare and finance.

Yet, despite the institutional guidelines, organizations are not heavily penalized in practice; this could be due to a lack of resources or expertise in fair algorithm development. At the same time, marginalized populations continue to be systematically denied access to some of the best healthcare solutions and technologies available. While contrasting news items indicate growth in size and spending by associated activities, there is still minor movement from neglect of training algorithms to ensure that they do not cause bias against underserved populations. Algorithmic discrimination occurs in multiple stages of the application of algorithms. Algorithmic discrimination in data usage happens when data is selectively available for different population groups, making them harder to model as accurately as other populations. Such cases have been highlighted recently in credit scoring and credit access. Cutting-edge algorithms are often built upon data that have either been denied or are less complete for some groups, including low-income and rural customers. For this reason, some user communities are unable to rely on the most advanced algorithms for sending critical data to risky areas, such as medical users (Golden et al., 2016). They continue to rely on traditional algorithms with less predictive performance. In this case, algorithmic discrimination leads to solution performance that is worse for those populations who can benefit the most from machine learning solutions, due to the presence of lesser-quality available algorithms.

12.2.1 Data Bias and Its Implications

Particularly in fields such as insurance that have hitched their wagons to the power of artificial intelligence in recent years, access to the underlying data that is used to train predictive models is controlled by gatekeeper institutions. The data that these insurers have gathered and curated holds immense economic value, acting as the raw material for hundreds of billions in profits as well as billions in capital investments into AI. Yet, while the data undergirding this asymmetry of power has originated from consumers and the broader economy, these institutions share scant accountability to the interests of the people from whom they are extracting value. Large companies have historically had an unchallenged monopoly over the data that has driven their profit models, exposing them to few or no meaningful consequences for how they have deployed and acted upon it. Lacking any channel to communicate their grievances, these communities have been relegated to a passive role when the distributional effects of policy, pricing, and underwriting are determined. They can neither add input before the decisions are made nor decide to take their business elsewhere if the consequences are harmful, given that they have often been denied coverage altogether due to a lack of representatives from these communities. In many ways, this relationship mirrors the broader data divide that is a barrier to equity and economic inclusion in the AI space (Philip & Suresh, 2024). To this end, we illustrate how the data triangle is at the basis of a lopsided relationship between legacy institutions wielding enormous amounts of data on one side and marginalized and underserved communities on the other side, as presented in Figure 12.1.

12.2.2 Algorithmic Discrimination

Discrimination against specific groups in society is one of the most serious and contentious issues relating to AI. Some forms of discrimination in the context of insurance AI also fall under the jurisdiction of the existing legal infrastructure. Statutes and regulatory principles that are meant to ensure fairness and equality among all individuals likely have consideration for new technologies such as insurance AI. A set of complaints using algorithmic bias to support discriminatory allegations has already begun. The most notable involve accusations against a wide range of credit-scoring companies for exclusionary practices through AI and data. Laws and regulations may not always protect against algorithmic discrimination. This is because, in many instances, existing regulations correlate with a disparity of treatment, not disparity of impact. Disparities of either kind can be useful metrics for identifying business-need-based versus bias-based model functionality decisions (Choi et al., 2024). These kinds of discrimination focus entirely on the disparate impact of a

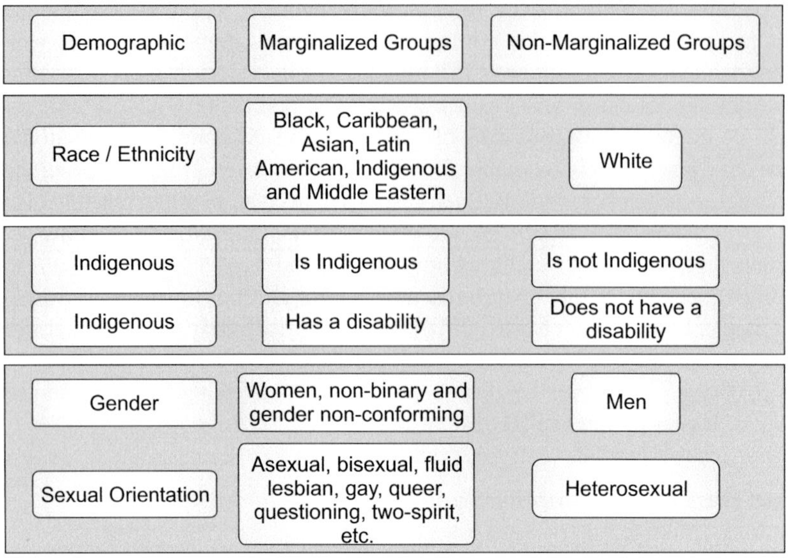

Fig. 12.1 The marginalized and underserved communities.

policyholder's decisions, or features derived from those decisions, and the roles those features play in model predictions.

12.3 Strategies for Enhancing Equity in Insurance AI

In the previous sections, we relayed a demonstration of inequalities in access to insurance AI in the USA as well as an exposé of the legacies of decades of insurance discrimination, including being subject to existing AI systems that have been developed without considering the equity ramifications of their use. In this section, we lay out a call to action, with available methodologies as well as aspirational principles for those working within the insurance AI field. This section will be super-presumptive and detailed about what the industry should do—at the start of the project, in the data, during modeling, in deployment, and evaluation. Data scarcity has long been a hardship for the insurance industry due to its data privacy concerns and geographic distribution of particular risks, such as catastrophe. Given the substantial evidence gap that exists in insurance research, those partnering with insurance companies or developing products for their use should encourage or participate in inclusive data collection practices for what is often sensitive data needed for ethical AI development around insurance. It is paramount that AI models incorporate localized, stratified, and representative data. Additionally, the decision-making process and the data used by these models should be transparent, with clear explanations of their limitations and uncertainties. This transparency is particularly important for under-resourced stakeholders receiving deployed capital, as it can help them understand model outcomes and encourage the adoption of improved model optimization procedures (Golden et al., 2016). Many of these inclusive data provision practices require long-standing partnerships between those traditionally providing research or data-centric assistance to the under-resourced market and those strategically wishing to partner down the road with the insurance industry.

12.3.1 *Inclusive Data Collection Practices*

Acting on the promise of equity and inclusion in insurance AI requires centering diverse social identities by expanding data collection practices that radically embrace traditionally marginalized and excluded groups. Traditional demographic data collection practices often fail to keep pace with population dynamics. Merely asking respondents to select one or multiple social identities may not suffice, given that many people maintain an affinity to a sociocultural heritage or community that exceeds the categories collected. Furthermore, survey respondents have growing concerns about how, who, and for what purpose this information is used and are often less willing to self-identify than in previous decades. Hence, when insurers seek demographic data from insured individuals, the reasons for doing so should be unambiguously stated. Insurance AI modeling efforts can contribute to inequity and exclusion if they utilize disparate data availability in the insurance sector. For example, developers can attempt to confront cybersecurity problems in AI-powered health tools for specific marginalized health communities. Moving beyond standard demographic data practices and investing in other direct, secondary, and generative methods are critical if insurance AI is to create new solutions to previously intractable problems and avoid digging the equity pit even deeper. Such investments are needed to offset the only available data approach and hold developers to their promise to create fairer and better insurance AI (Townsend et al., 2018). Moreover, the traditional approach to using secondary data will always carry the risk of a lack of representativeness and could therefore perpetuate wider societal inequities.

12.3.2 Transparent Algorithm Development

The discrimination and exclusion resulting from algorithm biases can take the form of inaccurate predictions for certain populations and scarce offerings of insurance products to underserved communities. Although algorithmic innovations in the insurance space can seek to enhance equity, for instance, by calculating more accurate premiums based on less conventional sources of information or enabling the provision of cutting-edge products tailor-made for a subpopulation, there is a risk that such innovations will be utilized to exacerbate inequity further. Additionally, distortionary outcomes, such as those arising from the insurance cycles or climate change, could potentially worsen income and social disparity. Insurers might be lulled into a bias trap, with AI bias being preceded by insufficient risk management of equity-laden variables, which ultimately leads to suboptimal decision-making in the insurance AI development and deployment. Such adverse effects of algorithm bias are hard to prevent if insurance algorithm developers do not recognize the societal impact of their inventions. In theory, insurance companies and insurance premium prediction vendors are merely supplying tools to other entities, which in turn deploy insurance AI to service their customers. However, vendors usually have significant control over the decision rules of the underlying models and Application Programming Interfaces (APIs) and could proactively mitigate the harms of algorithm bias. Whether or not vendors assume such a responsibility depends on the ethical considerations that govern their relationship with user entities, as well as the legal accountability for discrimination that falls on those end users (Choi et al., 2024). As a rule, vendors rarely monitor how their tools are used once they have been licensed, depriving the vendors of crucial feedback and harming the social fabric, as presented in Table 12.1.

12.4 Case Studies of Successful Inclusion Efforts

As is so often the case with expansive, complex challenges, some companies are already tackling key inclusion initiatives. Their lessons can be more effective for informing partnerships that help the community at large than a simple technical playbook of best practices. These partners don't always have experience in the world of insurance and might require some help understanding what is required to support a responsible insurance ecosystem or market component. They can also open the door for disruptive insurance companies that are already building novel and innovative product structures that increased resiliency in underserved communities. The insurance product landscape

Table 12.1 Key challenges and solutions for equity and inclusion in insurance AI.

Challenge	*Description*	*Impact on Marginalized Groups*	*AI-Driven Solutions*	*Ethical Considerations*
Data Representativeness	Lack of diverse data reflecting marginalized groups	Biased risk scores, exclusion from insurance	Synthetic data augmentation, targeted data collection	Avoid reinforcing existing biases
Algorithmic Bias	AI models reflecting societal and historical prejudices	Discriminatory pricing and claim decisions	Bias detection and mitigation techniques	Fairness audits, continuous monitoring
Accessibility Barriers	Digital divide limits access to AI-driven insurance tools	Reduced access to personalized policies	Mobile-friendly platforms, multilingual interfaces	Inclusivity in design reduces tech barriers
Socioeconomic Discrimination	Models disadvantaging low-income or informal workers	Higher premiums, denial of coverage	Alternative data sources, flexible underwriting	Ethical pricing, affordability
Transparency Deficits	Lack of explainability hinders trust and understanding	Distrust, inability to contest decisions	Explainable AI tools, clear communication	Empowerment through understanding
Privacy Concerns	Heightened privacy risks for vulnerable groups	Reluctance to share data, limiting AI effectiveness	Privacy-preserving data techniques, anonymization	Respect for autonomy, data protection
Legal and Regulatory Gaps	Lack of explicit protections for marginalized groups	Exploitation and systemic exclusion	Policy advocacy, inclusive regulation design	Justice and legal equity
Cultural Sensitivity	AI systems ignore cultural context	Misinterpretation of risk, poor service	Context-aware AI models, local stakeholder input	Respect for diversity and cultural values
Limited Digital Literacy	Lack of knowledge about AI and insurance processes	Vulnerability to misinformation, poor decision-making	Education programs, simplified user interfaces	Informed consent and empowerment
Community Engagement	Marginalized groups excluded from AI development dialogue	Solutions not tailored to real needs	Participatory design, co-creation workshops	Democratic inclusion and responsiveness

has been evolving rapidly over the past couple of decades, in part due to the power of technology. New insurers are entering the market with new and novel proposals for how to solve old problems, from no-fault to peer-to-peer to parametric models. Though some of these innovative models are still finding success, some have proven the ability to provide long-term stability in the markets they're facilitating. At the pool of funding for these innovative new ideas needs a source of growth capital to pull the market up around them to achieve sustainability; they're also the ones most able to justify venturing into missing pieces of coverage. That's where more traditional insurance market participants come in (Golden et al., 2016). There is also a prevailing narrative around microinsurance. Providing access to responsible insurance services to lower-income consumers can be a challenge, especially outside the hard market cycles. In these cycles, low capital surplus coupled with decreased capacity to respond to loss stimuli often leads to the exclusion of lower-cost insurance options.

12.4.1 Innovative Insurance Models

Accessing affordable insurance coverage and protection for the physical, human, and economic capital in underserved communities tends to be more difficult and expensive. Macrolevel mechanisms such as poverty and economic inequality, a lack of social safety nets, failed infrastructure, and a high cost of capital all expose these communities to higher risk and worry as compared to wealthier communities that have the capital to invest. Conventional insurance products, however, tend toward exclusionary or marginalized uses of machine learning and AI to profile, price, and segment risk in a manner that effectively constrains access to coverage in these communities. Insurers charge more to people who are low on the socioeconomic ladder, who cannot afford to pay what insurers charge, and when losses occur, these same people are underpaid or cheat the system. Innovative insurance models that meet their needs might allow us to transition toward a more reciprocal approach. Technology- and machine-learning-assisted collaborative consumption models, like the use of neighbor networks for parametric coverage, captive audience reciprocal models for localized labeled catastrophes, and community-based models like ceding small catastrophe risk to cooperatives and offering coinsurance to market segments toward a more equitable outcome are examples. Meanwhile, venture-capital-funded InsurTech companies are disrupting traditional market actors using data to provide less frictional and faster access to diversified global capital looking for investment (Townsend et al., 2018). The result is more efficient indexing of the insurer risk while also making these marginal uses of insurance available to communities.

12.4.2 Community-Centric Approaches

Inclusion in the emerging opportunities of AI insurance technology requires elevating and centering marginalized communities to our often overwhelmingly risk- and credit-prone insurance systems. They are often viewed primarily as risk, for whom exposure to and mitigation of risk are the major social roles. Expanding and improving inclusion means changing and leveling that relationship, expanding the agency of these communities not only to help make insurance predictive but to help shape it according to the nuances of the communities' shared circumstances. The marginalization of these communities comes with both emphasis on individual identity (often in ways that can provoke stigma as well as strength) and shared attributes (for example, shared experiences of micro-inequities or larger areas of institutional bias and harm). This differentiation demands that digital inclusion into insurance technology embraces and supports both shared community identity and the diversity of humans within that community. The experience of mobile financial services provides lessons and warnings in centering the consumer. Those lessons begin with the founding premise: what would make services easy and cheap for these consumers? Perhaps the most ambitious effort to combine a technology-driven ease of service with a strong community emphasis is the wholesale travel insurance model designed for diaspora communities. The model digitalizes retail insurance via the community leader, the service broker (Oben et al., 2024). Combining travel needs with a sense of shared tribe, the company seeks to provide a promise that the data and motivation flow support fraudulent overstays, including ease of visits during the policy period and ease of tourist-related purchases while visiting, thus expanding traditional insurance provider access and available data to mitigate risk while avoiding the administrative problems of such shared insurance groupings.

12.5 The Importance of Stakeholder Engagement

The development of value-driven and inclusive AI is fundamentally about people, and different forms of stakeholder engagement are at the core of these efforts. Stakeholders include, but are not limited to, marginalized communities, populations served by organizations that work with these marginalized communities, and the organizations themselves. Building diverse cross-sectoral partnerships with a vision grounded in shared equity goals will ultimately yield positive and equitable results. Organizations at the forefront of implementing community-informed AI practices emphasize that listening to the needs and lived experiences of the individuals impacted by decisions made with the assistance of data, algorithms, and AI ensures, or at least supports, better-informed decision-making. This chapter highlights important kinds of early and ongoing stakeholder engagement: collaboration with community organizations and feedback mechanisms for continuous improvement. Data alone cannot capture the rich tapestry of lived experiences pertaining to risk and vulnerability that are characteristically diverse across different communities and populations, some of which have been systematically silenced or otherwise deprived of voice. How data is collected, understood, and used matters to achieve fact-based understandings of communities previously rendered invisible. Decisions that others perceive as being in the best interest of affected communities can actually result in poor services and negative outcomes when their unique needs and experiences are not properly taken into account. Expertise and knowledge lie with stakeholders who are both actively involved in the work and who have experienced these issues firsthand (Shafik, 2025b). Community partners can shed light on multiple facets of the questions being investigated, which can translate into advances within equitable and effective design, implementation, and evaluation of data-driven approaches that are more likely to achieve meaningful outcomes aligned with public venturing goals.

12.5.1 Collaboration with Community Organizations

Efforts to improve equity and inclusion for marginalized and underserved populations should not be designed and implemented without the input of these communities. Community-driven programs that are co-designed with input from underserved populations are significantly more effective in achieving desired health equity and social equity outcomes than traditional top-down programs. Recognizing the importance of engaging with the most affected groups, many research funding organizations require applicants to develop plans for directly involving community partners in their projects. This expectation is especially true for work within health equity and social justice arenas. Involving communities in the design and implementation of relevant programming leads to better communication strategies that increase community buy-in and better training plans that ensure proper use of new technologies to maximize their effectiveness (Shafik, 2025a).

Industry researchers and leaders can collaborate with community-based organizations serving marginalized and underserved populations to improve access to equity-enhancing solutions, particularly in the insurance sector, as presented in Figure 12.2. These organizations have established trust with community members through long-term engagement, are knowledgeable about culturally grounded, community-appropriate strategies, and are experienced in customizing outreach and implementation strategies to suit the unique and varied preferences of specific communities. Implementing equity-enhancing technologies in partnership with community organizations will significantly increase community engagement and acceptance, and facilitate the accurate and culturally appropriate use of new tools. Examples of community-based organizations include nonprofit health clinics, advocacy organizations focused on improving the welfare of specific communities, coalitions of community organizations, and faith-based organizations with active outreach programs to underserved populations. When community-based organizations are first engaged in the design

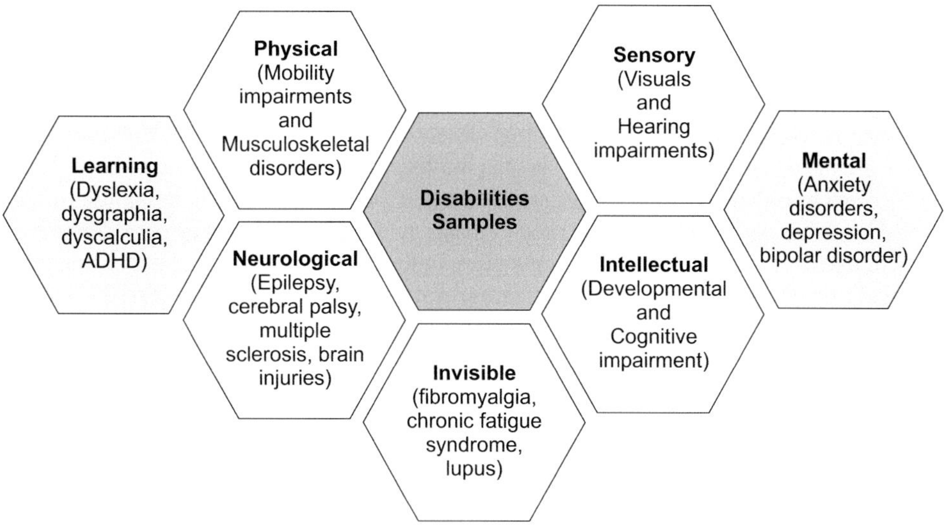

Fig. 12.2 Samples of disabilities.

and implementation plan for generating equity-enhancing solutions in insurance, the likelihood of successful community uptake, usage, and re-benefiting is higher. Approaching and collaborating with organizations that understand the populations who will benefit from equity-enhancing solutions will also help improve model quality by revealing model pitfalls that might otherwise be missed (McDonnell et al., 2023; Shafik, 2025c). These organizations are in an ideal position to help stressful communities adapt to the changes generated by tackling inequalities, and they can help companies evaluate the anticipated versus actual changes in well-being.

12.5.2 Feedback Mechanisms for Continuous Improvement

The organizations must have a well-established stakeholder policy that is applied consistently. This could include public meetings, surveys, open convenings, etc. There should also be methods available for people to provide feedback that has negative consequences and not have to identify themselves, as some people may want to warn of a system failure, such as a company not following through on its stated commitments, discriminatory activity, or general harm, but are afraid of losing access to a service. Another mechanism is to make sure that any consortia of organizations that are sharing data for model creation, or that may be connected through the models in some service capacity, have designated points of contact that have regular communication. It is important that feedback loops are transparent, and people understand what possible steps they could take to initiate them. There are mechanisms that stakeholders can put in place to create a living document showing the interplay of their system and online communities available at the services they provide that report on system performance, especially for those people who are the most heavily engaged with the systems, describing the overall population and the possible actionable paths for modifying behavior. In addition to getting stakeholder feedback about the actual impact of a decision delivered through a model, for feedback specific to the model itself, organizations can provide and solicit additional model validation through test sets available to the community impacted by the model (Choi et al., 2024). Such tests could not only include using a number of metrics, but also how different settings affect the distribution of output scores.

12.6 Regulatory Considerations for Equity in AI

The use of AI in insurance transactions has increased in recent years, but the regulation and guidelines regarding fairness and equity are behind the uptake of insurance AI. While federal regulators have released specific racial equity frameworks that do mention the use of AI in providing access to services, these are at a more conceptual level than the practical one regulators face when creating AI policies. Recent presidential executive orders have noted that marginalized communities often lack access to AI, often labor, or data/training used in fostering these systems. A key consideration is that government agencies will have to implement equity in their use of AI systems, which is not trivial, as the underlying government datasets and training systems may be inherently biased. Much of the discussion and output has come from an agency with both a data digitization and taxonomy mission and a standards-based framework of agency responsibility for federal actions. Policy guidelines for bias in AI service providers have also appeared in broader regulatory policy documents in the form of model regulations. There is also a stringent Data Security Model Act that is being adopted by states, which could be interpreted to cover fairness considerations as well. Regulatory guidance on the protection of marginalized communities is also emerging in the insurance space, although it isn't clear to what extent this will be extended to equity application for the underserved in AI. Antidiscrimination laws regarding coverage, premium differential, and unfair discrimination are already part of the regulations and require compliance (Murphy & Moosa, 2021) . These would not only be considerations after the fact, but could also act preemptively, to prevent disparate impact as models are being validated or adopted.

12.6.1 Policy Frameworks and Guidelines

Regulations are essential to prevent harm and protect the rights of historically marginalized and underserved groups. In the realm of AI in insurance, the federal government has issued some guidelines around how its use in regulated areas should comply with standards against discrimination on the basis of protected classes. At the same time, the high potential for the use of AI to exacerbate existing disparities, for society to over-rely on the technology without transparency or accountability, or for tech actors to further monopolize wealth, all motivations behind policy considerations temper its embrace in every area. New policy considerations will guide the direction of insurance-AI development work. For example, insurance and tech companies and actors in related fields need to be mindful of national and global political pressure, and be ready to address the public-equity-in-AI concerns that exist regardless of industry. Tech actors also need to be prepared for scrutiny from tech advisory groups and to be responsive to corporate Environmental, Social, and Governance (ESG) initiatives. Furthermore, understanding insurance-related mandates can help shape the direction of model-building and implementation work; regulatory scrutiny and consumer actions surrounding the fallout of bad model predictions can resort to a harsh blame-and-pay culture. Most international regulatory proposals recognize that discriminatory practices must be investigated in light of context and the specific particulars of the affected individuals' circumstances. These proposals also recognize the role of AI within a broader ecosystem and acknowledge the need for multimodal safeguards (Townsend et al., 2018). As such, it is critical to understand the specific standards these proposals pertain to and within what jurisdictions.

12.6.2 Compliance with Antidiscrimination Laws

Explicit prohibitions against unfair discrimination exist in the insurance context for a number of important reasons. First and foremost, insurance is an industry that involves the transfer of risks among members of society. Excessive risk differences among social groups, especially nonvoluntary groups, are serious enough to warrant scrutiny. The potential for socioeconomic control is high in the provision of goods that no one wants to use but that all society members must have in order to transfer risk among each group, including flood insurance, terrorism insurance, pandemic insurance, and other forms of catastrophe insurance covering collective risk. It is critical that decisions made using AI models for these types of insurance reduce, rather than exacerbate, economic divestiture and socioeconomic inequality. The dangers of overfitting models and using biased data are great. Second, the pooling of risk cannot, for certain types of insurance, be financially viable unless insurance loss calculations are correct. Suppose a certain group is charged premium rates that are too low and are retained by the company that issues policies when a catastrophe occurs. In that case, all other policyholders in the pool must backfill that loss when premiums are charged based on miscalculations. Third, the insurance industry is a major part of national and international economies. Insurers face restrictions under numerous federal and state statutes and regulations. These restrictions include various banking and insurance privacy laws, various other privacy and consumer protection laws, and various state laws (McDonnell et al., 2023). Explicitly specifying laws regulating the insurance industry helps to keep the industry transparent and functioning properly, as detailed in Table 12.2.

Table 12.2 Strategies to promote equity and inclusion in insurance AI.

Strategy	*Description*	*Implementation Tactics*	*Expected Outcomes*	*Stakeholders Involved*
Inclusive Data Collection	Collecting data from diverse populations	Partner with community organizations, use alternative data	Improved model fairness and relevance	Data scientists, community leaders
Bias Mitigation Frameworks	Incorporating fairness constraints in AI algorithms	Regular bias audits, adversarial testing	Reduced discriminatory outcomes	AI developers, ethics boards
Accessible Technology Design	Designing platforms for users with different needs	Multilanguage support, voice-enabled interfaces	Greater reach and user satisfaction	UX designers, accessibility experts
Community-Centric Outreach	Engaging underserved groups in product development	Focus groups, surveys, and participatory workshops	Products that meet actual community needs	Insurers, social workers, and advocacy groups
Transparent Communication	Clear explanations of AI decisions and data use	User-friendly reports, interactive dashboards	Increased trust and willingness to adopt AI tools	Customer service teams, communication experts
Privacy-First Data Policies	Enforcing strict data protection, especially for vulnerable groups	Encryption, consent management platforms	Enhanced user confidence and data sharing	Legal teams, IT security personnel
Regulatory Compliance & Advocacy	Aligning AI use with emerging equity-focused regulations	Compliance checks, engaging policymakers	Legal protection for marginalized groups	Compliance officers, policymakers
Ethical Pricing Models	Adjusting pricing strategies to avoid socioeconomic bias	Sliding scale premiums, subsidies for vulnerable groups	Fair access to insurance products	Actuaries, policymakers

Contd.

Table 12.2 *Contd.*

Strategy	*Description*	*Implementation Tactics*	*Expected Outcomes*	*Stakeholders Involved*
Education and Literacy Programs	Increasing understanding of AI and insurance concepts	Workshops, e-learning modules, and simple guides	Empowered consumers and informed decisions	Educators, insurers, and community organizers
Continuous Monitoring & Feedback	Tracking impact on equity and adapting accordingly	Real-time bias dashboards, user feedback loops	Sustained fairness and responsiveness	Data analysts, ethics committees

12.7 Technological Innovations Supporting Equity

Considerable debate surrounds how AI and other connected technologies will impact the industry, from job replacement to greater automation. However, they also have the real potential to expand insurance equity. Billions of people use mobile devices daily, over 60% of the world. These phones are more than just technological advancements—they are, in fact, gateways to technology, with their multitude of services helping their users with anywhere from travel to the use of social media, health, and even financial capability. Improvements in these areas can support insurers in reaching marginalized and underserved communities, expanding access to their products and services, and creating a positive loss cost ratio. Mobile technology combined with big data, blockchain capability, and AI also enhances customers' ability to manage their insurance with emerging app services, including trusty claims handling, reliable payment methods, simple policy renewals, and customer service interactions. Additionally, technological innovations can help to reduce insurance premium costs for low-income populations through personalized insurance solutions powered by real-time assessments of insurance risk. Innovative pricing models combine the use of mobile tools with IoT devices to assess risk for auto, health, and home insurance, reflecting real-time behaviors in premium pricing and adjustment, bringing additional benefits for underserved and marginalized populations. Premium models can personalize coverage by adjusting to reflect a user's price sensitivity and insurance need, and can offer coverage microdurations, for example, hour-by-hour auto insurance or customized coverage for a cross-country trip (McDonnell et al., 2023). Risks can be further redefined using telematics, wearable devices, and home sensors, which promote user engagement and reward desirable behavior with premium reductions, again targeting affordability for low-income populations.

12.7.1 AI for Personalized Insurance Solutions

Reducing risk is the primary goal of insurance. Many insurance companies seek to reduce their risk by charging people higher premiums who are at greater risk of making a claim. The dangers of this traditional model are painfully evident. Those with the most need may be priced out of accessing the very coverage that could provide them with crucial support during times of need. Those with less need may pay lower premiums, shifting the burden onto the poorest in society. Advances in AI are enabling insurers to evaluate risk on an increasingly granular level and to develop even more granular personalized pricing structures. If done well, this can help with balancing the risk–reward equation between insurers and those that they insure. Recent strides in the ability of AI to process and analyze imaging data have turned what was once a data-poor environment into a data-rich one. Insurers are now increasingly able to perform photo assessments of risk factors such as a house roof's vulnerability to storm damage, tree limb encroachment, the quality and placement of chimneys, the presence or lack thereof of sprinklers for fire suppression, and solar panel installation. Previously, insurance policy qualification and pricing structure determination were largely based on demographic and credit information, which often present their inequities. Such models often failed to account for differences in property conditions, resulting in substantial disparities between price and risk across policyholders, who were lumped into one single pricing structure, often leading to coverage access problems. AI has opened the possibility of a much more granular risk–benefits approach to insurance, enabling entry into the market of new insurers and allowing incumbents to build more customized solutions (Van Nguyen et al., 2023). In turn, this may help open up insurance coverage by lowering the premiums of those who are at lower risk. If premiums accurately reflect risk, then low-income populations can benefit from lower pricing for insurance coverage.

12.7.2 Mobile Technology and Accessibility

Mobile phones have rapidly become the primary form of access to the internet and digital services for people in many parts of the world. A body of research suggests that mobile technology can support people's access to services across sectors. In education, mobile technology can help students learn and can help education systems support students. In public health, tools provided through mobile phones can help educate clients and create demand for services, as well as help health workers complete tasks. A broad range of development actors are mobilizing to support digital health solutions, as part of a growing interest in digital health. A similar story is emerging in financial services. Mobile technology is now widely seen as critical to helping people, particularly people experiencing poverty in developing countries, gain access to financial services. For middle- and low-income consumers in both developed and developing markets, there is a growing demand for mobile services that use technology to provide added convenience. Mobile banking, in particular, could help improve levels of savings for people experiencing poverty. Additionally, there is wide recognition of the importance of mobile systems that facilitate the flow of remittances, particularly in developing countries and in global markets such as that for labor. For insurance, mobile technology offers the potential to help access underserved populations, increase the efficiency of insurance services, and reduce business risks (Bermúdez et al., 2023). As the mobile internet becomes more accessible for low- and middle-income segments, mobile insurance options—providing relevant products that are fit for purpose—become feasible.

12.8 Measuring Success in Equity Initiatives

Data equity is actionable. While real-time dashboards to check if AI is causing disparate impact in key metrics are the norm, it's also useful for some initiatives related to access, equity, and inclusion to check if they are on the right track to achieving their desired outcome. Such key performance indicators can bring visibility to the company, provide guidance during implementation, point out when corrective actions can help realign the initiatives with desired goal states, and indicate when practices can be abandoned should they not have the desired results. Other initiatives will be too broad, use too many variables over too long a time, or require analysis at too high a level such that meaningful key performance indicators cannot be identified and their results tracked over time. Key performance indicators can be helpful guides on the journey toward the ultimate destination of predicting which customers will be the most successful at renewal for our businesses. The goal is not to apply a career risk minimum distance principle to equity efforts; no one wants to embrace an equity program for a demographic subsegment of 5 individuals, and so—rather as has been standard practice in customer segmentation for ages—these programs should be developed after parameters for desirable demographic segments closest to corporate purpose are identified (Golden et al., 2016). And these parameters should include segment sizes that are at least reasonably sizeable, as well as carving out percentages of policies, customers, or claims associated with negative business outcomes such as cancellations, policy breaches, and claims denials.

12.8.1 Key Performance Indicators (KPIs)

A range of specific key performance indicators (KPIs) has been defined, explicitly correlating insurance-sector practices to economic impact for equity inclusion objectives. These can then be used to assess how well an organization or composite organizations are performing against stated goals. Achieving any meaningful and sustainable change will take considerable time, so KPIs must be both actively monitored and communicated to relevant stakeholders over time. The KPIs used to measure access to insurance—and their correlating measures—can be broadly grouped into various categories, for example:

(i) Premium volume.
(ii) Investment volume.
(iii) Policy in force.
(iv) Coverage effectiveness.
(v) Market share.
(vi) Net capital contribution.
(vii) Relief availability.
(viii) Relief amount.
(ix) Relief net capital contribution.
(x) Pricing
(xi) Portfolio quality.
(xii) Profit margin.
(xiii) Reserves.
(xiv) Return on equity.
(xv) Solvency, primarily with insurance products such as auto.
(xvi) Home.
(xvii) Commercial.
(xviii) High net worth.
(xix) Life.
(xx) Credit and mortgage.

Many of these KPIs extend beyond just the insurance sector. They affect the wider government macro-economics of a country; and have ramifications with the trade deficit and public debt. These linkages can also be broadly grouped further. For example, KPIs that impact the trade deficit are: relief availability, relief amount, net capital contribution, market share, and return on equity. KPIs that impact the public debt are: pricing, portfolio quality, net income, and premium volume.

12.8.2 Longitudinal Studies and Impact Assessment

Longitudinal studies provide definitive evidence as to whether a given initiative is having a lasting impact on a stakeholder group. A simple before-and-after analysis can be misleading. For example, suppose a lending program has established a significantly higher loan default rate in a community for lending unaffordable home loans. In that case, the program might initially seem to be causing greater harm. But, if that community has a higher rate of loan defaults than other lenders not in the intervention group, or no improvement is found after the intervention program is completed, the implementation of the program may not be the guiding factor for the outcome. More generally, the larger question of whether the intervention is improving or diminishing a stakeholder's outcome should be answered in the context of a comparison group, typically similar to other stakeholder groups who are not participating in the program. Over time, did the groups with and without exposure to the intervention experience differential effects of those intervention efforts? The challenge for measuring the impact of equity initiatives undertaken by organizations is that the obvious or benign natural data is not present. Market selection issues and internal implementation details often mean that what appears to be a natural comparison group is affected in ways fundamentally different from participants. These measurement issues matter. Differences-in-differences and propensity-score matching can be implemented. But researchers need to have a real stake in the design of these studies, existing data collection efforts, and budget workloads. Equally, the sample sizes must be sufficiently large for some analyses to produce reliable results. In both studies discussed, ongoing relationship data is available, and leaders need equity metrics and measurement to have a defined focus (Choi et al., 2024). Measurements about who used an action, what services were offered, how the action was facilitated, and who was affected are the basics for evaluating the need and effectiveness of a program.

12.9 Future Trends in Insurance AI and Inclusion

Although reports of unfair or inappropriate racial and experiential bias in AI processing of insurance claims and pricing are just starting to emerge, we believe that in its current state, insurance AI work is aimed "upstream" on the same analysis and underappreciated underlying goals and motivations as traditional risk selection and pricing that have faced critique for a century or more. We expect that this current state of misunderstanding and bias of insurance pricing, but not yet claims, will change in the direction of integrating and augmenting traditional insurance with AI-driven new models of personalized service and protection, or be rejected for failing to serve a more "positive" transformative purpose. In insurance work, as in credit scoring, which is even better modeled using recent advances in big data and features based on mobile phones, money both speaks and controls who is included and excluded in the financial system. New AI models have been demonstrated to be fairer analytically, in terms of the latent scores of their last hidden layer vector, disentangling effects of race and ethnicity from those of place, income, and other correlated economic factors. Although increased use of big data, which may encompass more holistic measurements compared to earlier underwriting such as affordability of payments compared to insured value, may carve out non "low-hanging fruit," potentially increasing the target pool of individuals to be profiled and served personally and individually, they may also amplify or flicker in and out spurious correlations and inference, and overlooked signal and noise properties of existing returned pricing or predicted losses (Philip & Suresh, 2024).

12.9.1 The Role of Big Data

Expanding access for marginalized and underserved populations has focused on the growing technological innovation in the insurance industry, particularly regarding big data, AI, algorithms, and predictive modeling. This chapter pivots the discussion of insurance AI and the marginalized and underserved to the future of insurance technology and focuses on two aspects: big data and emerging technologies, and their potential. It discusses in detail how the role of big data has greater promise for creating access to insurance while preventing the perils, such as discrimination and entrenched financial and racial access disparities, for inequitable and exclusionary disadvantages. Then the chapter discusses how future technological innovations, such as biotechnology, robotics, and other predictive technologies, could further create or exacerbate barriers for the underserved, but are necessary for developing inclusion and access. With the onset of the digital age, companies across industries have improved their technical abilities regarding the scope and type of data they collect and process, as well as the diverse ways in which they collect these data. In the insurance industry, the growth of big data has transformed the use of historical insurance data, which relies on past insurance experiences, into better predictive tools and models. Big data is the collection of massive amounts of data through a variety of technologies, such as mobile devices, social media, the Internet of Things, and robotics (Yang et al., 2021). For insurers, big data fundamentally relies on predictive technologies and algorithms that promise to preserve a fair and accurate assessment of risk for both the existing and new customers to promote equitable treatment.

12.9.2 Emerging Technologies and Their Potential

Technological advancements hold enormous potential for reshaping the foundations of the insurance industry, overturning long-standing trends for social good. Recently emerging innovations, such as artificial intelligence, machine learning, predictive analytics, blockchain technologies, and the Internet of Things, are affecting all phases of the insurance value chain and can increase equity and inclusion. These innovations diversify the channels through which consumers connect to insurance companies, allow for highly tailored products that respond to the specific needs and challenges of underserved groups, optimize risk assessment and pricing to bring down costly premiums, make claims resolution swifter and more reliable, and enhance the accessibility of services and businesses through technological partnership. Innovation in insurance is also democratizing the availability of insurance products, not just by lowering transaction costs but also by enabling and allowing for highly personalized offerings. The use of alternative, innovative forms of data and predictive modeling provides insurers with the opportunity to reach otherwise excluded customers and better understand their needs for specific lines of business. For example, microinsurance, enabled through digital delivery, scoring, and data collection processes, allows insurers to specifically address the frequently chronic underinsurance of vulnerable populations through targeted, small-coverage policies (Margan, 2021). Moreover, improvements in the automation and accuracy of underwriting and claims handling through the use of AI technologies provide the potential for more equitable treatment of both underserved and typically served populations.

12.10 Ethical Considerations in AI Development

Aside from the technical requirements for developing equitable, inclusive, and nondiscriminatory AI solutions, how we develop these solutions is of paramount importance. What guidelines can one follow to ensure that the AI is developed ethically, broadly in alignment with the principles of equity and inclusion? What is an ethical AI life cycle? Here, we take an initial step at answering these questions and explore some of the considerations to bear in mind in developing these tools. Great work on producing ethical AI has already been done; we briefly summarize some of that work here, primarily focusing on two areas. In AI, questions about fairness arise because, on the one hand, AI tools can automate or augment decisions in a way that significantly impacts people's lives, while on the other hand, algorithmic bias violates the principle of equality (McDonnell et al., 2023). In the context of insurance, it is essential to ask fairness-related questions because powerful discriminatory practices, often in less than an overt context, naturally heighten the likelihood that insurers will be held to a higher standard. If an AI tool yields a predictive model or one that fills in a gap in AI development and deployment that does injustice to a vulnerable population, then AI will have done a disservice to the field of insurance, which is ultimately about protection. While concerns about highlighted biases and discrimination relate to the AI model and its outputs, questions about accountability relate to who is held accountable: the developer, on their degree of control; the user, on the decision-making effects; the algorithm, on the output quality; or the underlying data, on its representational quality. If harm or disruption occurs in the insurance process, one should expect recompense to be paid to at least one of these parties (Choi et al., 2024).

12.10.1 Fairness and Accountability

AI applications have made significant strides, especially in prediction and prescriptive models for high-stakes business decisions, made in different parts of the business ecosystem. Although AI algorithms replace many mundane and labor-intensive human tasks, some are responsible for important and complex tasks, where trust and accountability are crucial for the algorithm to be accepted. Any algorithm envisioned to support business decisions should be fair, trustworthy, and transparent. In other words, there should be a value alignment of the user's incentives with the algorithm's construction and operation. In this chapter, we discuss the issues of fairness and accountability in the construction of algorithms used to support a variety of insurance-related business decisions (Bermúdez et al., 2023). With growing regulation mandating fairness in business decisions, algorithmic fairness is a crucial requirement for ethical adoption of AI technology. AI may deploy bias in a prediction algorithm owing to the design of the algorithm and/or the data on which it is trained, or both. If so, it could underpredict outcomes for certain sensitive groups defined by the sensitive attributes that are not predictive of the outcome. This is consequential for important types of high-stakes decisions that rely on these predictive models. The problem is more pressing in the case of laser focus algorithms, which "sift people in and out according to a very fine level of discrimination." Discriminatory behavior of models trained on biased data is not uncommon, and properly provisioning for fairness is beneficial to both the consumers and designers of AI systems. Commercial entities, especially the insurance industry, for whose customers policy acceptance, premium calculation, and policy performance are sensitive issues, should proactively mitigate bias powered by AI (Oben et al., 2024).

12.10.2 Privacy Concerns and Data Protection

Machine learning algorithms require enormous amounts of data, including personal data that is sensitive, protected, or proprietary. This reliance on data raises privacy concerns, such as unauthorized access, use, or disclosure of sensitive personal data, unintended consequences of re-identification, lack of data ownership control, or breaches of privacy safeguards. Privacy protection through data encryption and access restrictions may decrease the ability of an AI model to uncover valuable patterns for decision-making. The ability to explore the need for additional data, or alternative data sets, relevant to inclusion, or support for marginalized and underserved populations in the context of AI for insurance, expands our understanding of data privacy issues in insurance. The use of nontraditional data needed for financial inclusion efforts may carry greater privacy and data protection implications than data already available to the public, and the potential for unforeseen loss of rights or abuse of obtained nontraditional data emerges as a pressing challenge to equitable and trustworthy application of AI. Insurance is one component of broader financial services available to consumers. The same technology and digital tools facilitate access to banking, credit, and lending activities, and enable ongoing changes in the FinTech and InsurTech sectors. As a result, trends in privacy and data protection issues as they apply to banking and FinTech may parallel those in insurance. The use of nontraditional data, such as personal data derived from social media or internet presence, and its increased prevalence in algorithmic decision-making in areas such as lending, raises ethical concerns associated with the underlying data and decision processes that cut across market sectors (Golden et al., 2016). Issues relating to the privacy and data ownership implications of data utilized by ML models need to be explored in the context of an overarching insurance ecosystem that is increasingly interconnected and interdependent with broader financial services.

12.11 Building a Culture of Inclusion within Organizations

Building an organization that is inclusive requires more than simply focusing on hiring a representative workforce and maintaining a diversity training program. Companies must build inclusion policies into the DNA of their organizations. These policies will structure the diverse workforce, helping to ensure members of diverse groups have real opportunities to advance, build networks, and make influential contacts within the organization. Leadership must be committed to these objectives, and the policies need to be backed by standardized processes and training that are adopted at all levels of the organization. Inclusive organizational policies must be complemented by implemented awareness and training programs that help all members of the organization to recognize their biases and actively seek to avoid them—targeting processes and behaviors where bias is most likely to interfere with the goals of equity and inclusion. Bias awareness training is particularly important for those in the organization who hold influence over the ambition and success of others—managers, senior executives, mentors, and others responsible for recruiting, hiring, promoting, and assigning projects. Performance evaluation processes must also be carefully monitored for signs of bias, especially when the organization is aiming for a representation goal or quota. When goals provide reasonable cause to increase representation from previously underrepresented groups, other diverse employees executing similar tasks were often "funneled" for advancement into "valued" leadership roles, which would typically steer the employee on a pathway for executive hiring, despite not being business critical (McDonnell et al., 2023). Bias identifications that focus on empathy, perspective-taking, and individualized consideration of others are often deployed to combat these tendencies.

12.11.1 Training and Awareness Programs

Often, decisions about AI involve complex technology and abstract discussions about the purpose of the algorithms and the business metrics used to evaluate them, which require domain knowledge of insurance business operations. Training is necessary for all of these individuals to provide context to the types of decisions AI will be making and insight into how the technology is being used to develop algorithms. In particular, matrix tasks involve highly consequential decision-making alongside trusted partners, but model explanations do not have a basis for incorporation into ongoing operations. Besides direct instruction by data scientists and machine-learning engineers, there is a general need for training programs relating to the basics of machine learning to individuals associated with matrix tasks, including specific information about how the company plans to utilize AI tools and for what types of decisions, how the results will be credited to AI versus specific implementers, who inside or outside of the company will be able to access the results, what level of authority or discretion the people in these operational roles will have, and what guardrails will follow. Many decisions AI systems may have an impact on, for which the individuals interfacing with the AI model need feedback, learning about the specific logic of the algorithms, and the capability to provide feedback, as well as auditing capabilities once the models are implemented. They also need to understand the types of bias that AI programs may be insensitive to or impervious to (Van Nguyen et al., 2023). For example, although ML models can identify patterns and correlations regarding differences in protected classes, such learning does not guarantee that internal differences corresponding to those correlations would result in outcomes that a human employee would see as appropriate during the decision itself or would ensure safeguarding against maintaining discriminatory biases the organization sought to eradicate.

12.11.2 Leadership Commitment to Diversity

A recent report states that "ESG leaders are backed by diversity in senior leadership ranks, which is a strong predictor of better scores on many ESG issues." Most insurance companies of all sizes have diversity and inclusion mission statements, along with policies aimed at fostering diverse pools of talent. But how many insurance companies hold that commitment accountable using specific diversity goals—representation targets for women, people of color, and other marginalized and underserved groups for director, executive, and C-suite levels—and then reward their leaders accordingly? Not enough. The insurance industry—like other sectors—is characterized by an absence of women, people of color, and other marginalized and underserved groups in top positions. It suffers from the lack of diversity at the very top that is imperative to driving true and meaningful structural change. The target-based solutions discussed in this chapter could have prevented these situations from occurring. Employers should do a better job of promoting and recognizing empathy, concern, and dedication because diverse employees are looking for, and want to remain loyal to, organizations that practice what they preach (Golden et al., 2016; Philip & Suresh, 2024). One fire rescue department that is using a combination of education and motivation, and concrete, quantifiable diversity goals, responsible for a great differential for its employees, has become the first department in the country to receive gender and ethnic balance recognition from relevant authorities.

12.12 Conclusion

The Information and Insurance Oversight and Risk Management (IIORM) use cases offer a unique roadmap that can assist with the advancement of equity, fairness, and inclusion for underserved populations. These multidisciplinary use cases draw upon financial and insurance expertise, but also on academic and industry-wide research around the influences of bias in machine learning and AI, including the role of data selection and usage. Therefore, while these proposed use cases generally use insurance as an application sector, the IIORM collaborative believes that they have wider ramifications to other fields of AI application, in particular those fields dealing with complex liabilities, such as finance and public policy. The IIORM use cases representative of intentional AI risk and bias mitigation offer a roadmap for the adoption of responsible AI systems by the industry that can be utilized with relevant insurance and other industries. These equity-focused use cases offer additional educational perspectives that can also spur research opportunities within our universities and colleges, lead to the development of open-source guidelines, and enable AI developers to minimize unfair bias that leads to impactful and costly adverse decisions on consumer groups. We hope the use cases also provide stakeholders interested in encouraging the development of purposely responsible AI systems, and in an accelerated manner, with concrete suggestions on what to specifically look for in proposed applications of AI. By outlining a sample of equity-focused images that all stakeholders can share, we hope the use cases can facilitate investment and development of financially sustainable, purposefully responsible AI applications.

References

Bermúdez, L., Anaya, D. and Belles-Sampera, J. (2023). Explainable AI for Paid-Up Risk Management in Life Insurance Products. *Finance Research Letters*, *57*. https://doi.org/10.1016/j.frl.2023.104242

Choi, J.H., Choi, Y., Lee, K.S., Ahn, K.H. and Jang, W.Y. (2024). Explainable Model Using Shapley Additive Explanations Approach on Wound Infection after Wide Soft Tissue Sarcoma Resection: "Big Data" Analysis Based on Health Insurance Review and Assessment Service Hub. *Medicina (Lithuania)*, *60*(2). https://doi.org/10.3390/medicina60020327

Golden, L.L., Brockett, P.L., Ai, J. and Kellison, B. (2016). Empirical Evidence on the Use of Credit Scoring for Predicting Insurance Losses with Psycho-Social and Biochemical Explanations. *North American Actuarial Journal*, *20*(3). https://doi.org/10.1080/10920277.2016.1209118

Margan, S.K. (2021). Drifting into Algocratic Insurance? In *The AI Book: The Artificial Intelligence Handbook for Investors, Entrepreneurs and FinTech Visionaries*, pp. 71–74, Wiley. https://doi.org/10.1002/9781119551966.ch20

McDonnell, K., Murphy, F., Sheehan, B., Masello, L. and Castignani, G. (2023). Deep Learning in Insurance: Accuracy and Model Interpretability Using TabNet. *Expert Systems with Applications*, *217*. https://doi.org/10.1016/j.eswa.2023.119543

Murphy, S.D. and Moosa, S. (2021). The Views of Public Service Managers on the Implementation of National Health Insurance in Primary Care: A Case of Johannesburg Health District, Gauteng Province, Republic of South Africa. *BMC Health Services Research*, *21*(1). https://doi.org/10.1186/s12913-021-06990-4

Oben, E.E.E., Ndi, H.N. and Tchuikoua, L.B. (2024). Livestock Farmers' Willingness to Pay for Farming Insurance in Four Divisions of the West Region of Cameroon. *Asian Journal of Geographical Research*, *7*(1). https://doi.org/10.9734/ajgr/2024/v7i1211

Philip, B. and Suresh, G. (2024). Cultivating Resilience: An In-Depth Exploration of Agricultural Insurance Initiatives and Their Transformative Role in India's Farming Landscape. *Universal Journal of Agricultural Research*, *12*(1). https://doi.org/10.13189/ujar.2024.120109

Shafik, W. (2025). *Monitoring, Evaluation, and Accountability for People with Disabilities and the Marginalized.* In: Global Sustainable Transition with Inclusion. Approaches to Global Sustainability, Markets, and Governance. Springer, Singapore. https://doi.org/10.1007/978-981-96-6557-0_10

Shafik, W. (2025). *SDG 12: Responsible Consumption and Production—The Circular Economy.* In: Factoring Technology in Global Sustainability. Approaches to Global Sustainability, Markets, and Governance. Springer, Singapore. https://doi.org/10.1007/978-981-96-7299-8_13

Shafik, W. (2025). *Theoretical Frameworks and Inclusion for People with Disabilities and the Marginalized.* In: Global Sustainable Transition with Inclusion. Approaches to Global Sustainability, Markets, and Governance. Springer, Singapore. https://doi.org/10.1007/978-981-96-6557-0_4

Townsend, C., McIntyre, M., Lakhani, A., Wright, C., White, P., Bishara, J. and Cullen, J. (2018). Inclusion of Marginalised Aboriginal and Torres Strait Islander Peoples with Neurocognitive Disability in the National Disability Insurance Scheme (NDIS). *OPEN ACCESS*, *5*(2).

Van Nguyen, K., Islam, M.R., Huo, H., Tilocca, P. and Xu, G. (2023). Explainable Exclusion in the Life Insurance Using Multi-Label Classifier. *Proceedings of the International Joint Conference on Neural Networks*, 2023 International Joint Conference on Neural Networks (IJCNN), Gold Coast, Australia, *2023-June*. https://doi.org/10.1109/IJCNN54540.2023.10191171

Yang, Z., Jianjun, L., Faqiri, H., Shafik, W., Talal Abdulrahman, A., Yusuf, M. and Sharawy, A. M. (2021). Green Internet of Things and Big Data Application in Smart Cities Development. *Complexity*. Volume 2021, Article ID 4922697, 15 pages https://doi.org/10.1155/2021/4922697

13

Global Perspectives on Ethical Insurance AI: Comparative Case Studies and Regional Challenges

Wasswa Shafik

13.1 Introduction

Artificial intelligence (AI) plays a pivotal role in the insurance industry by enabling efficiencies that can translate into superior marketplace performance or more sustainable margins even in the presence of ongoing loss trends. The future of AI in insurance is expected to be defined by the growing use of generative artificial intelligence in combination with complex, predictive models. Generative AI, a technology that uses existing data to inform and design new ideas, is increasingly being employed within companies in areas such as claims and fraud, underwriting and risk selection, loss payments, and regulatory compliance. Adoption of AI-based technology across the insurance industry is nearing threshold levels that could lead to significant transformation and value creation. Generative artificial intelligence, including systems as diverse as chatbots, text classifiers, code generation, and image generation, is being adopted for production workloads in specific areas across the insurance value chain. The longer-term potential of generative AI for insurers goes well beyond these initial, easy applications. Generative AI could fundamentally change the way insurance companies operate in key areas such as training and retention, product adaptation, customer acquisition, underwriting and distribution, risk modeling, fraud detection, claims, and back-office operations. Across these areas, AI tools have the potential to augment human work, streamline operations, and help enable better risk underwriting—the fundamental business of insurance (Choi et al., 2024). Generative AI is an evolution in the field of artificial intelligence, a buzz term that has been around since at least 1956 but encompasses everything from expert systems and speech recognition to the once famous quiz champion to today's large language models.

13.1.1 *Ethical Considerations in AI Development*

Recent years have seen an increasing demand for explanations of algorithmic behavior that will make automated decisions more understandable for the end user. There is a variety of ethical and policy recommendations that touch on ethical principles that guide the development of AI systems. These include recommendations to ensure accountability for automated decisions; the fairness of automated inferences; the absence of bias in training datasets and validation sets; and the measures ensuring data privacy, security, and reliability. There are also recommendations emphasizing the need for an ethical component that weighs human dignity against data exploitation for reasons

DOI: 10.1201/9781003747659-13

of efficiency. This includes recommendations demanding that AI systems be used to substantiate important individual decisions, for instance. Whether someone gets a job or is granted a loan should be explainable to the people affected, and their results should be open to scrutiny. For example, as algorithms increasingly replace human biases with their own, we must ensure that biased human values do not also initiate AI. The strict enforcement of established principles raises questions for the design of higher-level AI systems. Even though principles such as fairness, accountability, and transparency are well defined, existing technical solutions might conflict with each other. Requiring high levels of explainability, for example, is often difficult to reconcile with fairness objectives, such as trying to represent equality of opportunity for all groups. Thus, ethical policies need to be flexible enough to allow for trade-offs between principles that might not always be achievable together. Whereas there are many suggestions for developing ethical principles, the guidance they will give designers and developers to ensure ethical AI systems is ambiguous and severely lacking (Murphy and Moosa, 2021). Thus, the increasing demand for ethically designed and developed AI systems raises the question of whether and how guidance can be further developed to ensure that it is both high level enough to consider conflicting principles and still concrete enough to guide drastic decisions.

13.1.2 Global Regulatory Frameworks for AI in Insurance

The use of AI within the insurance industry is accelerating. Governments around the world have recognized the need to implement oversight mechanisms, both in relation to general AI applications and specific applications in specific sectors such as insurance. However, the introduction of regulatory frameworks is fraught with challenges that include balancing innovation with consumer protection issues, defining the scope of regulation, extensive reliance on technical jargon, and the need for industry compliance, including financial burdens. Additionally, it remains unclear how existing laws apply to AI. The international governance landscape is characterized by a patchwork of existing legal frameworks at different levels and, more recently, by additional AI-specific regulations, guidelines, and ethical principles on the use of AI. This chapter aims to investigate the existing local and regional legal frameworks that regulate AI and investigate whether dedicated insurance regulatory frameworks exist. We focus our analysis on specific national authorities that have adopted specialized regulation at both policy and enforcement levels on AI use in insurance (Golden et al., 2016). Recognizing that the regulatory landscape is constantly changing, we provide an overview of the most pertinent AI and insurance regulatory frameworks that are currently in place in selected jurisdictions around the globe, including Europe, the UK, the US, Singapore, the UAE, South Korea, Japan, Hong Kong, and Australia. First, we outline the various existing AI regulations before moving to the insurance regulatory frameworks governing AI. We conclude by highlighting the respective opportunities and challenges in relation to future developments in the area. We aim to provide regulators, insurers, and consumers with valuable insights into what the current regulatory landscape looks like in order to identify options for utilizing AI in insurance in a responsible manner that is also consistent with the principle of sustainability. There are some health insurance plans that are often left out and classified under medical, which many people tend to claim, as some visual impairments are presented in Figure 13.1.

13.2 Comparative Case Study: North America

North America is a region where many of the world's largest and most important insurers operate, together with some of the largest tech companies also playing in fintech and insurance technology. Various discussions on AI ethics, especially as related to data privacy, antidiscrimination, and explainability, have taken place in the North American context. Regulations around AI technologies

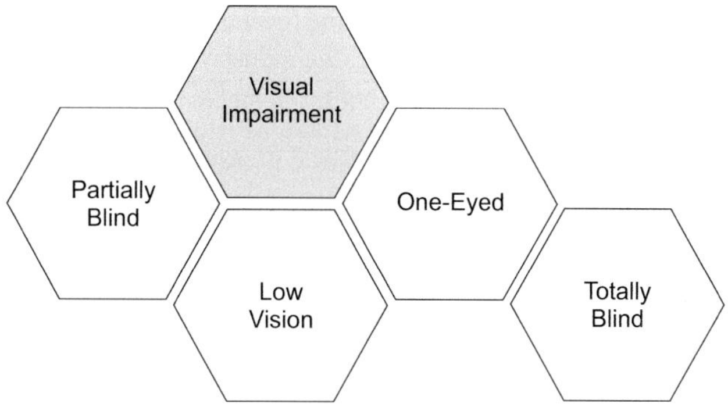

Fig. 13.1 Visual impairments.

in the region generally seem more permissive, if not without restriction, but also with industry self-regulation and moral integrity stakes higher. This is particularly the case for the USA, where a large part of the economy is private-industry-driven. Notable exceptions exist, of course such as standards for data privacy and security regulations for specific types of information, including healthcare data, which are issued by the U.S. Federal Government and enforced by its other agencies (Townsend et al., 2018).

(i) As in many other regions, discussion of AI's possible negative impacts is commonplace, and companies are starting to familiarize themselves with the risk of digital and algorithmic harms and liabilities, and how to self-police themselves against such risks. A major company in the insurance industry, with about 161,000 employees and $45.5 billion in 2022 revenue, has published a comprehensive AI ethics policy. These industry-governed guidelines create a known set of standards to be used by various corporate stakeholders when working on AI projects, which may, in turn, impact consumers and how they go about buying insurance services.

(ii) The North American insurer's organizing principles encourage responsible data use, and its AI Ethics Advisory Board determines if a project with potential negative consequences is justifiable. The principles also encourage responsible data use, and its AI equity practice takes steps to review models built using data from historically marginalized communities, or that will be deployed to those communities. The community outreach includes advocating for testing and accountability processes for AI and facilitating outreach with external community-based organizations, promoting hiring equity, and educating the public about the risks and benefits of AI.

13.2.1 Overview of AI Regulations

Insurance is one of the oldest regulated industries, and regulative initiatives specific to it or even to underwriting directly preceded the advent of the use of AI in the sector. But those initiatives were not directly about the application of AI and ML models; rather, they aimed at regulating the use of traditional statistical methodologies, especially regarding fairness issues, such as prohibited discrimination on the basis of race or sex. While there have been in recent years initiatives on the establishment of norms on the use of AI in insurance and specific calls by regulators for input on AI fairness and accountability, a comprehensive blueprint of norms for the use of AI and ML in the insurance sector is yet to be proposed, in contrast to other business sectors, such as finance, law enforcement, and healthcare. However, general regulations on AI development and deployment are developing rapidly. The somewhat uneven state of affairs in terms of concern, degree, and specificity of AI regulations can be said to stem from the level of risk associated with the application of those technologies, the complexity of the models, the industry's history of social impact, and the regulatory context. As we move from low-risk to high-risk and sensitive areas, regulations become more stringent. The United States has released an AI Bill of Rights, but there has been no federal advanced law drafted thus far, although individual states have tried their hand at such regulations, especially California. Some member states also took the initiative to implement their own AI regulatory framework; for example, California implemented the California Consumer Privacy Act (Oben et al., 2024). Internationally, the following regions have advanced proposals for AI regulations: the European Union, the United Kingdom, Canada, and China.

13.2.2 Case Study: A Major Insurer's AI Ethics Policy

This section discusses a case study of a major insurance provider's AI ethics policy, founded in part on principles developed by a multi-stakeholder group that included some insurers but extensive non-insurance participation. Its principles and approach may not be unique, but they create a starting point for global insurers who wish to review existing or consider creating their own AI documents. The major insurer stated these principles to guide the development and deployment of AI systems in support of its mission to deliver on the promise of insurance:

(i) Safety: AI systems should be secure, reliable, and safe. These systems may be operating in high-risk areas, and their safety should be ensured throughout their life cycles.
(ii) Fairness: AI systems should treat all people fairly. These systems should be designed to mitigate bias, discrimination, and other unjust impacts on individuals and groups.
(iii) Explainability: AI systems should be transparent, and their results should be understandable. These systems should provide clarity regarding how they operate, and they should allow for meaningful feedback.
(iv) Accountability: AI systems should have a clear accountability framework. Appropriate processes should be established to oversee these systems, and there should be established procedures for remedying any harmful consequences.
(v) Transparency: AI systems should make the most of available information, and their purpose should be clear. These systems should provide appropriate information to the people who are affected by them, and their functions should be generally open to scrutiny.

13.3 Comparative Case Study: Europe

The European Union's General Data Protection Regulation (GDPR) was designed to protect European citizens' privacy at a time when privacy was understood as narrowly involving the harm of unwanted invasion or intrusion. Today, plurilateral initiatives seek to enable better what are understood as the "new commons" of AI systems, and greater accountability for public-facing AI systems. Insurers seeking to implement AI systems that both meet consumer risk modeling needs and conform to legal standards in varied jurisdictions confront idiosyncratic ethical structures in creating their ethical insurance AI with the GDPR system as a baseline. AI ethics design and development—what we term "ethical insurance AI"—is occurring inside the financial services sector and at insurance firms, which have the skills to develop responsible systems internally or the need to find external consulting partners. In other words, European compliance with the GDPR and EU member-state guidance is expected to create many diverse ethical systems, driven by business design needs and the variety of markets they serve. In the following text, we examine standards currently guiding ethical systems design around the developing EU ethical community, which we consciously differentiate from the US-based community, with more market-focused initiatives. While individual insurers will report diverse interpretations of biases and impacts because of the variety of markets they serve, regulatory guidance under the GDPR is pointing to "similar yet different" laws guiding the insurance community's response (Aina et al., 2024). We frame this section as a case study of an emerging patchwork of regional anecdotes created as different states draft ethical systems regulations for internal AI developers.

13.3.1 GDPR and AI in Insurance

The AI in insurance ethics framework is partly grounded in fairness rules stemming from EU law, and in the General Data Protection Regulation, more particularly. The latter incorporated rights of data subjects, voiced through a bias in favor of access, honesty, accuracy, integrity, and the confidentiality of personal data processing, as well as transparency, which have imposed high standards for AI human experts' explainability, data quality, appropriateness, security, and user consent. Bias and discrimination are two connected challenges of AI ethics in machine learning, from health predictions to algorithms in insurance. In Europe, where the performance of insurance micro-segmentation algorithms requires the mandatory legal assessment of whether AI crunching a wealth of extensive personal and behavioral data is a suitable alternative to traditional risk assessment, antidiscrimination law plays a more heavily proportionate role in ethical AI than in the USA. GDPR introduces a set of democratic, identity-related technical imperatives, such as the requirement of valid consent, the option to opt out, and the right to explanation. Thus, GDPR requires the AI human engineers to live up to rights of nondiscrimination, preserving social solidarity through risk pooling, access to necessary insurance products at affordable prices, and ability and legitimacy to spread "spurious" correlations inferred from algorithms—which manipulate the property of feedback loops between outcomes and data—inside and outside the data. It forms part of a set of existing legislation and fundamental rights that shall be respected as the foundation and road map for an ethical design, verification, and auditing of AI systems that process data in the core business of insurance. With large language models, giving back imagined "facts," be it in the domain of medical data when predicting morbidity or the domain of risk profiling, the urge of patients and insured parties to trust an insurance product information system is violated (Daudén-Esmel et al., 2024; Dorfleitner et al., 2023). Exploiting previous information asymmetries between insurers and clients by feeding questions into the automated systems, based on a few psychotherapy sessions or the output of a personality profiling test, raises new, substantial, serious ethical concerns in the insurance industry, which still lacks a concrete regulatory framework.

13.3.2 Case Study: Ethical Challenges in European Markets

AI is already providing excellent commercial results. But many use cases are such that ethical challenges are raised that require action. In European markets, those are the areas of market and counterparty collusion, unfair discrimination in blocks of customers, auditability, conciliation, and lack of influence by customers in their risk profile, excessive reliance on AI decision processes, and security, privacy, and surveillance. Given the levels of regulatory scrutiny of insurance companies in Europe, it is not surprising that many of the ethical questions for AI in insurance are part of the toolbox of regulatory relations with customers. European insurance markets, in many countries, are quite fragmented. In countries such as Belgium, the Czech Republic, France, Greece, Hungary, Italy, the Netherlands, and Poland, large companies bite off a small portion of the market. This is not the case, of course, in Germany, the United Kingdom, and most Scandinavian countries. Moreover, in terms of the market share of the largest player, Poland is already the subject of a possible four-firm collusion. Furthermore, in many countries—the Netherlands, Belgium, Denmark, Germany, the United Kingdom, and Sweden—more than 90% of claims are settled with no intervention or assistance on behalf of the insurer. Thus, the model works extremely well for both parties involved.

European cultures also diverge enormously, which is another hurdle to overcome. It is precisely Germany, with its booming InsurTech sector, that is at the origin of the most advanced principles for the ethical use of AI in insurance. Such a wave of innovation would almost guarantee that ethical risk is controlled. Moreover, the question of AI for countries like the Czech Republic, with a relatively low level of implementation but high potential, is light-years away from that for a country like the United Kingdom, where all ethical principles in the relationship between customer and insurer based on AI are already being worked on (Mohammad Amini et al., 2023). In this case, despite having one of the highest ratios between claims paid and Money Market Funds (MMF) of the entire European region, the need for action seems more than just a recommendation, as presented in Table 13.1.

Table 13.1 Comparative overview of regional ethical AI frameworks in insurance.

Region	*Regulatory Landscape*	*Ethical Priorities*	*Key Challenges*	*Notable Case Study*
North America	GDPR-style state laws (for instance, California Consumer Privacy Act (CCPA)), and emerging federal acts	Transparency, consumer protection, and bias mitigation	Fragmented regulations, private sector influence	Use of AI for fraud detection with bias audits
Europe	GDPR, AI Act (proposed), strong data privacy regulations	Data privacy, accountability, and human oversight	Compliance complexity, balancing innovation and ethics	Insurance AI pricing models complying with GDPR
Asia-Pacific	Diverse regulations (for instance, China's Personal Info Protection Law, Japan's AI guidelines)	Inclusivity, data sovereignty, and rapid tech adoption	Varying maturity of frameworks, cultural diversity	AI-enabled microinsurance in rural India
Latin America	Emerging data protection laws, varied enforcement	Accessibility, equitable coverage	Limited infrastructure, socioeconomic disparities	AI for underwriting in informal employment sectors
Africa	Nascent AI governance, focus on innovation and inclusion	Social equity, bridging digital divides	Data scarcity, infrastructural gaps	Mobile insurance leveraging AI in Kenya
Middle East	Growing regulatory focus, mix of tradition and innovation	Ethical AI deployment, regulatory modernization	Balancing modernization with cultural norms	AI-powered claims management in the UAE
Australia and NZ	Strong privacy laws, AI ethics guidelines	Consumer rights, transparency	Harmonizing regional approaches	AI underwriting with Indigenous community input

13.4 Comparative Case Study: Asia-Pacific

The ethical issues of AI in insurance have grown in scale and specificity in recent years. This is especially so where companies have been innovating rapidly in areas with few or no established regulatory frameworks. This chapter presents a unique comparative case study of two regions in order to explore strategic regulatory lessons: a typically less-developed economy of Vietnam, where government is promoting technology use in insurance but has recognized a need for ethical enhancement; and a typically well-developed economy of Australia, where companies are launching extensive new AI facilities but government has not yet taken a position on ethical governance. The discussions lead to consideration of some core elements of an ideal form of AI ethics governance, and suggest a stepped or graduated approach. We conclude with emerging insights on the ethical AI landscape in these two regions, and dialogues steering future research in the area. I suggest: Industry 4.0: Technological Foundations / Cyber-Physical Systems or something close to that (Daudén-Esmel et al., 2024; Dorfleitner et al., 2021). This elaborates on how this new Decision Intelligence (DI) supercharge is supporting a raft of new game-changing functions and features in the life and non-life insurance industry globally, thus improving healthcare, as experienced in Australia and Vietnam, as illustrated in Figure 13.2.

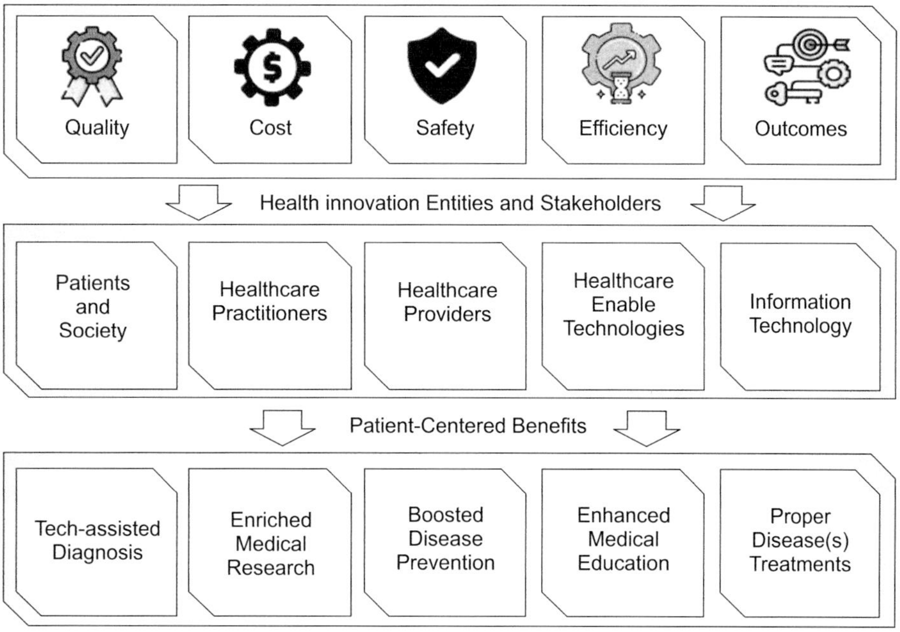

Fig. 13.2 Healthcare insurance innovation entities and stakeholders.

13.4.1 Emerging AI Technologies in Insurance

AI technology applications are increasing exponentially in the financial services industry in recent years, enhancing services such as underwriting, pricing of policies, claims handling, fraud detection, and management services in the financial assistance program following disasters, for instance, natural disasters or global pandemics. Autotask generation, machine learning, deep learning, text mining, natural language processing, speech recognition, data mining, robot process automation, robotic chatbot/conferencing bot, computer vision, image processing, drones/balloons, AI-based risk scoring/rating system, and mobile-based rating/sad survey system are some examples of the rapid development of AI technologies that are being applied in insurance. Chatbots and voice bots are widely used to assist customers in their rudimentary inquiries, while Robotic Process Automation (RPA) systems are now automating data processing procedures to bring about greater efficiency. Asia's financial service sectors are employing different methods and different scopes for the digitalization and automation of work, compared to other continents. For example, rapid product development is more common in Asia than anywhere else in the world, and insurance companies in Asia are now also moving from robotic-driven to sensor-driven intelligent automation, where they have come to understand that artificial intelligence technologies help considerably in their business growth strategies, so they resourcefully incorporate these AI components into their InsurTech businesses (Choi et al., 2024). However, it should be noted that the mainstream insurance companies do not generally have a great deal of sophisticated technology expertise, and in fact, they depend heavily on the technology support of specialized InsurTech companies.

13.4.2 Case Study: Regulatory Approaches in Asia

Nevertheless, the speed with which insurance companies develop new technologies or use third-party tools is not matched by the speed of the actions taken by regulators or trade associations, nor the effect they have. Given that the majority of Asian countries still have only Berkeley Software Distribution (BSD) or enabling regulations for InsurTech, the regional market will still be subject to the ethical challenges these tools might pose. As industry talks about "fairness," "objectivity," "verifiability," and "teaching-neutrality" of the algorithms, a set of guiding principles established as nascent standards and regulations would be beneficial to practitioners and regulators alike. This practical discussion may help move forward the debate in other regions, emphasizing how the demand for ethical standards can be either challenged or rushed by regulators. The analyses of these regional standards may reinforce the demands for AI-based solutions to be user-friendly by incorporating an understanding of the consumers' diversity. In Asia, the insurance business is subject to diverging ethical regulatory lifestyles. This study first analyzes the trends by region, what is happening in countries that have little to no regulation, and what associations or governments are influencing the standards for InsurTech products or services. The study then presents the regulatory approaches of two digital superpowers from the Asia-Pacific region, drawing a commensurate picture of their tone and approach toward InsurTech services (Murphy and Moosa, 2021). In terms of regulatory level, this research then compares the evolutions of Hong Kong's and Singapore's insurance supervision approaches to InsurTech, the first region offering a "sandbox" experience but no ethical guidelines whatsoever, the second establishing a set of prudential—but not ethical—standards.

13.5 Comparative Case Study: Latin America

Hernández and Reyes indicate that the two most adopted technologies for insurance automation in Latin America are robotic process automation and chatbots. In the short run, they have more advantages than AI, but in the long run, their adoption will increase, as well as the amount of trust from clients in data-driven and algorithm-based decisions made by the insurers. To ensure these advances occur with an ethical approach, insurers mostly rely on the strategies mandated by authorities and international regulatory frameworks. AI applied to customer, credit, and fraud risk assessments in the pre-claims stage is the use with the highest strictness in legal compliance by Latin American insurers, given the prudential or solvency risk that noncompliance represents for them. Insurers in Latin America rely on regulatory pressure rather than self-compliance or social pressure to avoid developing an unethical AI. However, the ethical dimension of fairness and a focus on human rights are important when making such decisions. In recent years, the demand for insurance products has increased significantly, while the InsurTech market has not experienced relative growth commensurate with the demand. Using AI strategies has proven to be the solution to fill this gap. However, in Latin America, these developments have taken place in an accelerated manner, so the local market is quite inexperienced. Furthermore, the different sociocultural realities of the region have made the AI governance frameworks considered unethical globally, unaligned, or inappropriate for the region (Golden et al., 2016). For example, the G7 digital economy principles are too general and not sufficiently detailed to establish standards in AI business practices, nor could it be said that they have been implemented in Latin America.

13.5.1 AI Adoption in Emerging Markets

Given the rapid pace of global advances in technological innovation and the examples they present, nations could consider similar approaches to strategies of adoption, adaptation, and achievements to suit local aspirations. Notable areas for such aspirations to be driven involve improving financial inclusion, disaster resilience, supporting the climate change adaptation journey of emerging countries, and helping with the product-development journey to suit the local considerations of emerging nations. Nations are urged to be guided by the wise quote: "The best time to plant a tree was 20 years ago. The second-best time is now." AI has been available for the last 70 years, but has now found greater acceptability and applicability globally due to the combined benefits from the massive availability of data, increased computing power, advanced capabilities in connectivity, and algorithmic efficiency. In addition, the advantages of AI in creativity, interpretation, enhanced visibility, speed, level of automation, making human–machine processes more collaborative, scalable, and blurring industry boundaries have seen the growth of information networks and accelerated digital transformation. These changes have emphasized that AI can have a transformative effect on decision-making across most industry segments, including the insurance industry, and across all functional areas of businesses (Philip and Suresh, 2024). It is, therefore, unsurprising that the enthusiasm and aspiration for the adoption of AI is also being welcomed by emerging regions that seek to leapfrog their development challenges with the help of new-age technologies.

13.5.2 Case Study: Ethical Implications in Latin American Insurers

This chapter explores the ethical implications of AI in Latin American insurers through the presentation of two case studies with main differences in the size, position, and market characteristics, and their use of AI technologies. The analysis focuses on understanding the particularities of the implementation of AI systems in the insurance industry in the Latin American context and points to the existence of several regional challenges that place Latin American markets at a disadvantage to the global North. Additionally, the text compares the responses of the two insurers, a big and global insurance company, and a regional insurer with a strong focus on the local market, to the central ethical AI challenges identified, and discusses common patterns and the main particularities for other insurers operating in Latin America. The analysis relies on interviews with insurance practitioners and public reports presented by the companies. Additionally, it uses publications covering technology policy in broader terms, covering algorithmic justice and the fight against algorithmic opacity and discrimination. With this caveat, we argue that exploring solutions for these problems by considering the particularities of financially less-developed markets has the potential to provide insights that can broaden the discussions on these topics (Townsend et al., 2018). Our objective is to contribute to the debate on producing AI systems that benefit the population in emerging markets by offering a common ground able to connect discourses that come from political economy, multi-stakeholder, and technological concerns.

13.6 Regional Challenges in Implementing Ethical AI

The challenges of implementing ethical AI are perceived and realized quite differently across the globe. While some countries have advanced, in some respects, in addressing gaps in the ethical regulations called for in the principles for ethical AI framework, some have implemented hardly any guidelines or policies. Individual countries or regions are at different stages of deploying ethical AI. Some regions are ahead of others, but no one has reached the final destination. In the insurance sector, large groups of Latin American countries, including Mexico, Brazil, Argentina, and Colombia, have reported implementing hardly any privacy protections, and as such, insurance

AI, despite being in a relatively nascent phase of application in the region, remains devoid of budgetary protections. Factors such as sociocultural backgrounds, economic factors, and the level of AI adoption are known to drive differences in how regions and countries adopt ethical AI policies. Functionalist or consequentialist views point to efficiency as the ultimate goal of regulation and technological adoption. This approach privileges a regulatory, economic-centric rationale, assuming homogeneity and equality of countries in achieving social needs, essentially leading to one-size-fits-all solutions that are often inappropriate for underdeveloped or emerging economies (Oben et al., 2024). In contrast, other perspectives borrow from cultural historians or evolutionists to highlight the influence of history and community in shaping moral attitudes and behaviors over time, proposing that the creation and adoption of ethical guidelines necessitate consideration of the unique characteristics of the community in question over purely economic matters.

13.6.1 Cultural Perspectives on Ethics

In general, many differences in belief systems influence how ethics and moral frameworks are defined, practiced, and aligned with business processes. The policies that guide ethical AI development and its applications may be viewed differently depending on factors such as an individual's cultural, social, political, or religious background or upbringing. These same factors will also lead to varying opinions on acceptance and implications of bias in AI risk assessment or decision-making, including acceptance of social credit or reputation systems. It is important to understand that within a country or region, there may be variations in the ethical framework that people subscribe to. Simplistic generalizations or high-level policy statements about what is ethical behavior or what is considered acceptable (or unacceptable) are superficial and, unless more deeply explored, may put countries at risk for misunderstanding or missing the mark when trying to define an ethical AI policy. The goal of this chapter is to develop additional understanding of cultural perspectives on ethics as they relate to policy development for the responsible use and implementation of ethical AI. Forcing one dominant belief system across all countries or regions may be viewed as colonization. There are many examples of how unilateral decisions made by companies, which are culturally insensitive or ignorant, have resulted in losses of business, negative sentiment, and loss of reputation. A key area of AI is the success or failure of AI products, tools, or platforms (Parlak, 2023). If the AI system developed is not widely accepted and trusted, the potential for AI to lead to economic or digital advancement may be slowed.

13.6.2 Economic Factors Influencing AI Adoption

The idea that insurance disclosure and transparency can increase the negotiation efficiency of the insurer and the insured is commonly accepted, as misaligned incentives may give rise to moral hazard and adverse selection. Digital technology has enhanced the information-gathering efficiency with which insurers can evaluate risk. Additionally, big data analytics assist them in developing new innovative coverage solutions. However, besides the creation of real added value for both the insurer and insured, fiscal, monetary, and regulatory policies need to increase the economic motivation of insurers to pioneer the incorporation of cutting-edge technology in company insurance offerings (Oben et al., 2024).

(i) Tax benefits for investment costs in infrastructure spending, labor costs, and insurance reimbursements for application expenditures can be economically motivating. Furthermore, comprehensive fiscal and monetary policies entail distinct indirect advantages, as they promote customer acceptance—an important horizontal or demand factor—increasing insurers' potential for qualitative competitive advantages. Distinguishing between the three initial phases of implementation, a clear regulatory road map can guide and justify different policy measures. Laying down infrastructure and business models, a phase of creating momentum needs to be established first. Once a certain level of adoption exists, the early majority has to be kept up until data standards and transparency are generally accepted.

(ii) Only reaching a phase of decreasing returns on investments with regard to information quality and efficiency, as well as increased risk of data monopolism, do obligations become important to ensure that insurance offering companies maximize the utility of the insured, going beyond the preservation and enhancement of trust. Additionally, a regulatory framework—and the publicity of information about normalized security levels—has to exist, realizing the concept of technology governance. Otherwise, offering companies would be better off without investing in financial resources, but only in reputational resources.

13.7 Technological Challenges in Ethical AI Deployment

Despite the promise of ethical AI, companies face myriad thorny technical problems in building recommended ethical approaches into their AI systems. Since ethical AI is predicated on achieving mutable fairness and reducing harm, and those concepts can differ by area, market, and country, it has proven a complex and challenging undertaking to create universal solutions, encompassing not only improved data handling, modeling and development processes, methodologies, tools and deployment, but also active monitoring for compliance during production/model serving for all AI applications.

1. Data privacy and regulation
2. Managing User Data and Privacy in Digital Services
3. AI Ethics and Algorithmic Fairness

To compound the visibility of IT and insurance industries, whose business models rely heavily upon the exploitation of end-user data, there are very real risks of bias and algorithmic unfairness created during the AI-modeling cycle. From its inception through pre-deployment and use, models developed improperly introduce errors with real effects, in ethics and marketing terms. Buzzwords denote systems and methodologies designed primarily for modeling accuracy, and accuracy alone. They point toward the notion that only accuracy matters for predicting model results, regardless of decision consequences. Moreover, decision-makers behind each algorithm provide the ethical viewpoint underlying the process, as will employees and contractors involved in implementation (Philip and Suresh, 2024). Users entrusted with correcting, but not assessing outputs, may find it unconscionable or unrealistic to identify errors caused by developer bias.

13.7.1 Data Privacy and Security Issues

Insurers are increasingly adopting AI technology to innovate existing underwriting, pricing, and claims processes. AI technology can improve risk selection and detection of fraudulent claims, leading to higher profits, allowing insurers to offer lower premiums to clients while maximizing income efficiency ratios. However, the use of new AI technology also raises ethical concerns about the protection of sensitive personal client information. In a data breach scandal, private information of users was accessed for advertisement purposes. Recently, chatbots allow anyone across the world to create human-like writing, yet the chatbots need to be trained with a large amount of data. The loophole of data breaches by chatbots and the increasing concern over cybersecurity are weakening the trust consumers have in companies about using AI technologies ethically. In cyber insurance, sensitive security data—about what controls a company has put in place to determine risk in the event of a cyber breach—are submitted by companies to insurers for underwriting pricing; a data breach that exposes these secret control measures may result in a worse loss for the insurer than the reason behind seeking cyber coverage in the first place. These examples demonstrate that without data privacy measures, AI technologies may do more harm than good. Also, when insurers update key pricing assumptions using data or measure risk using analytics, the methodology transparency issue further causes distrust from the insured to the insurer (Shafik et al., 2024). Data privacy concerns also exist in the insurance industry's estimation of life expectancy using machine learning models; similarly, if companies do not transparently explain how the AI technology determines the pricing, then trust issues arise.

13.7.2 Bias and Fairness in AI Algorithms

While statistics, computer science, and artificial intelligence are traditionally regarded as objective and precise disciplines, the use of algorithms and AI does not shield them from potential bias. Bias in AI can result in algorithms favoring a particular group of people who share specific attributes while being prejudiced against their dissimilar counterparts, especially if these people belong to minorities or marginalized communities. Social biases that are already embedded in human-made data might still be reflected in the decision-making process of a machine learning model trained on such data. Since it is virtually impossible to collect data that is completely objective, researchers and practitioners are a priori faced with the challenge of addressing fairness when creating algorithms. The initial distribution of the data sample may not necessarily reflect a representative decision for the overall population. Furthermore, the effect of empirical risk minimization, used to maximize the accuracy of prediction in general machine learning, may still lead to unintended disparities involving different demographic groups. In the case of supervised learning, within the context of an insurance setting, the discrimination problem relates to the disparate performance of algorithms on various subgroups defined by sensitive attributes such as age, ethnicity, country of origin, gender, language, nationality, and religion. The sensitive attributes may serve as proxy variables for some underlying unknown or uninterpretable risk factors that could be better predictive variables for risk levels (Shafik, 2024, 2025). These predictive attributes may also generate erroneous group polarization or labeling that unjustly highlights certain groups. Even control for the presence of sensitive attributes does not necessarily eliminate unfairness, as presented in Table 13.2.

Table 13.2 Regional challenges and ethical considerations for insurance AI.

Region	*Key Ethical Challenges*	*Technological Barriers*	*Cultural and Societal Factors*	*Policy and Regulatory Gaps*	*Recommendations for Ethical AI*
North America	Algorithmic bias, consumer data misuse	Legacy systems integration	Diverse population demands	Inconsistent state versus federal laws	Standardized federal AI ethics framework
Europe	Data privacy, consent, and fairness in automated decisions	High compliance costs	High public awareness of privacy	Complex regulatory landscape	Unified pan-European AI governance
Asia-Pacific	Inclusivity, protecting marginalized groups	Uneven tech infrastructure	Varied cultural norms on privacy and fairness	Lack of uniform AI standards	Culturally tailored AI policies
Latin America	Accessibility, socioeconomic inequality	Limited AI talent and infrastructure	Informal economies	Weak enforcement of data laws	Capacity building, community-based AI initiatives

Contd.

Table 13.2 *Contd.*

Region	*Key Ethical Challenges*	*Technological Barriers*	*Cultural and Societal Factors*	*Policy and Regulatory Gaps*	*Recommendations for Ethical AI*
Africa	Data scarcity, digital divide	Poor connectivity, fragmented data sources	High informal sector reliance	Nascent AI regulation	Partnership models, ethical community engagement
Middle East	Balancing innovation and cultural/religious norms	Fragmented tech ecosystems	Traditional values versus modernization	Emerging but incomplete AI legislation	Inclusive policy design with cultural sensitivity
Australia and NZ	Indigenous data sovereignty, trust	Integration with legacy indigenous systems	Strong emphasis on reconciliation	Gaps in AI application to Indigenous populations	Co-designed AI tools respecting indigenous rights

13.8 Stakeholder Perspectives on Ethical AI

As an exploration of the intersection of insurance AI and normative ethics for policy purposes, this chapter examines the ethical settings for insurance AI, firstly through the eyes of the insurers deploying it, and secondly through the lens of trust as a precondition for wider consumer acceptance and adoption of insurance AI. The chapter draws on comparative data from two international surveys, with differing design, questions, underlying population, and period of fielding. While both address key areas for the identification of potential insurance AI norms, they come at the questions from differing perspectives. Insurers, as creators and deployment organizations of insurance AI, occupy a key position in the overall ethical setting for the technology. Acknowledging the importance of existing insurance and technology law, which respond to potential harm done by insurance AI, they provide the structures for what is ethically appropriate and how insurance AI should be governed. Trust is a critically important precondition for consumer acceptance and the ethical use of AI technologies, given that all AI technologies operate in a black-box manner, only known to the creators, about whom trust has to be insured.

13.8.1 Balancing Profit and Ethical Responsibility in AI

In the accounts of what AI ethics is and ought to be, the voice of the creating organization, the insurer, is critically important. Deployment only occurs when a profit or revenue model has been adequately envisaged and concrete profitability is envisaged over the short, medium, or longer term. Talking about AI ethics, when discussing bias and discrimination or the ethical use of claim predictability, is about large-scale cost-cutting at the consumers' expense and the violation of fairness as an ethical value; for underwriting it is about profit maximization at the expense of the insureds' right to privacy (Choi et al., 2024). The goals of profit or revenue generation are a common factor in all but one of the ethical reasons provided by Irish and Canadian respondents. This is in contrast to trust as the most significant reason put forward by the Dutch respondents.

13.8.2 Insurers' Views on AI Ethics

Since AI is used by insurance companies to address challenges such as disparate treatment, issues that can undermine consumer trust and cause financial losses, it is expected that research and oversight on ethical AI coding and deployment will become a priority in the near future, to ensure that AI systems do not produce unintended harmful effects. In this context, although many international and national regulators have published their guidelines in ethical AI, apparently unaware of insurance companies' particularities, and regardless of the insurance companies' high demand and usage of AI, insurance companies claimed a reduced participation in the drafting of policies, frameworks, standards, and laws that aim to make AI responsible and ethical by guiding AI accountability and liability across sectors. Since insurance companies were accountable and liable for offering personal insurance for all risk levels, ethical guidance on protecting coding conduct was foreseen one step behind other sectors' demand for responsible ethical coding. However, the lack of regulatory expectations and frameworks on AI coding ethics has led to a lack of insurance company's internal code of conduct or external guidance on its decision-making process. Hence, there is a high demand both from consumers and other stakeholders regarding transparency in the ongoing and uncoordinated worldwide initiatives, so that possibly overlapping and contradictory guidelines on ethics AI can be harmonized. These include AI coding ethical guidance and standards, responsibility and accountability for their infringing, and liability for their impacts, as consumers are vulnerable to AI's possible harmful impacts. Thus, AI transparency means: how to comply, and how to hold insurances accountable and liable (Golden et al., 2016). Insurance companies called for well-defined operational guidance for stakeholders' participation on ethics AI assessment and definition to be drawn up based on clear objectives since ethics AI can be differently interpreted.

13.8.3 *Consumer Trust and AI*

Consumer trust is an essential commodity for the success of services underpinned by artificial intelligence, such as algorithmic or automated decision-making. Without consumer trust, insurers cannot expect to benefit from the efficiencies that such AI shortcuts can bring to the claims decisions and loss assessments. If trust in the functions that AI performs can come at the expense of performance, a sizeable number of consumers would prefer human-based functions over AI counterparts. On the other hand, a positive perception of technology may enhance its promise within financial services, where it can address market failure. Indeed, a study in the context of insurance—the purchase of home insurance policies—found that when consumers were allowed to shift their preference on the mix of human and robot-based service functions, utilitarian considerations emerged to dominate. If the functions performed by the responsible robot-led insurance service including loss assessment were superior to those carried out under human supervision, trust in the mechanical function, rather than emotional trust in a human response, would prevail. Trust in AI includes both general and particular dimensions. General consumer trust focuses on the social implications of AI systems' use in several domains and describes institutions' efforts to control AI outcomes, such as fairness and accountability. This means that broader social challenges associated with generative AI, such as liability, harm, security, and inequity, will impact trust levels—and subsequently, adoption. In turn, particular consumer trust focuses on actual experiences with AI applications in certain areas (McDonnell et al., 2023). Such experiences cover specific user trust in an AI system's competence and reliability and user feelings that the AI-enabled processes are trustworthy, which are driven by transparency and its perceived ability to act ethically.

13.9 Best Practices for Ethical AI in Insurance

What then are suitable best practices for ethical AI in insurance? Regulators and market participants are looking for guidance. Research on guidelines to date have recognized that recommendations need to avoid being too abstract and generic while also avoiding being too specific to be irrelevant across contexts. Concretely, the recommendation to develop ethical guidelines is a good entry point. Such work may draw on other frameworks. The recommendations are both specific and comprehensive. First, they concern organizations seeking to adopt AI. Second, they specify important general processes, as well as with respect to people and departments, recommendation system of responsibility, criteria and impact assessment, guidelines for specific issues, documentation, evolution control, tracking and audit, and capabilities and tech support. In particular, no recommendations are specific for AI in insurance. Moreover, they also come with questions and templates to assist organizations develop a playbook of best practices for their adoption of AI. Finally, they recommend a center of excellence and specifying use cases, recommending a change management process, as well as upskilling or reskilling employees involved with adopting a solution, and tech support for the solution. A foundation for these more specific recommendations is achieving a common understanding of AI, as well as the relevant skills and knowledge transfer programs, at all levels within the organization. In fact, a recommendation up front is not limited to training and awareness programs for technical and data people in the insurance space (Owens et al., 2022). Also crucial are leadership support for the change that is part of adopting AI in organizations, and communication of clear guidelines for the transformation journey and the employee expectations related to it.

13.9.1 Developing Ethical Guidelines

Recently, there have been various calls for the creation of ethical guidelines, development of ethics training programs for actuaries, insurance practitioners, and policyholders, and implementation of data governance frameworks that would specify how data should be processed, stored, and protected. The goal is to promote greater transparency and accountability of AI-based systems in the insurance sector and to mitigate risks associated with potential biases in the development of AI-based solutions, models, or prediction. They may mitigate the risk of causing further social inequalities in traditionally disadvantaged industries, citizen data privacy issues, and other concerns and objections against these technologies. Such ethical guidelines aimed at minimizing bias and discrimination from AI are highly encouraged for insurance, but the standards that shape ethics on AI technology are still largely lacking or are only in their infancy. Since laypeople have no access to the technical and theoretical knowledge behind algorithms, the ethical implications of these methods for data analysis cannot be assessed by insurance-prone groups or the general public (Sachan and Muwanga, 2023). Inspired by the lessons learned from the successful establishment of social responsibility codes in other data-driven industries, and also by the starter kit offered to them by the European Commission in their published draft ethics guidelines, as case studies we shall highlight the example of the already-established and well-developed attitudes toward ethical AI design given by the founders of the European Data Protection Board associated with the GDPR—especially with regard to the fairness principle—and by the statutorily listed members of the Institute and Faculty of Actuaries located in the UK, especially in their recently written position statement on AI.

13.9.2 Training and Awareness Programs

A further prerequisite for putting ethical guidelines into effect are training and awareness programs. The successful use of newly developed ethical guidelines will depend on how well industry stakeholders, from C-suite levels to consumers, understand them and what they imply. At the very least, education and training efforts will need to cover the disciplines of law, data science, artificial intelligence, and the use of AI in insurance. However, in line with the complexity of AI applications in insurance, it would be preferable to attach industry-specific modules to existing curricula. Universities will need to rethink their curricula and work with stakeholders to develop ethics-specific modules to be integrated into the curricula of C-level leaders, actuaries, underwriters, claims adjustors, risk engineers, product developers, and customers. Such modules would ideally be advised by ethics experts and constructed in cooperation with corresponding ethics experts from all relevant disciplines, including data science, AI, and the legal domain. Then, there are already certification and training programs in existence which could be tailored to the needs of insurers and offer accelerated learning for the needed stakeholders. Such programs could have the university-accredited peer-reviewed training offerings as a model, with a core idea being to certify specific domains with a broader focus on engaging the stakeholders and take inspiration from the creative practice workshops on AI and the ethics group. External training modules need to be developed targeting the C-suite to further educate them on the importance of ethics-specific policies for responsible AI which are driven by trust. Such C-level leaders should be trained to become role models who support the implementation of built-in mechanisms for the ethical use of AI (Arockiam and Pushpanathan, 2023). Then, those industry members who are already working with or on AI-powered applications will need more detailed domain-specific training programs which need to be developed in cooperation with ethics experts. Such programs should also support stakeholder-specific ethical design questions that aim to make the use of AI in their respective responsibility domains more just and fair toward the customers and society.

13.10 Future Trends in Ethical Insurance AI

As the domains of ethical insurance AI and AI ethics for insurance flourish in the coming years, we expect several clear developments. First, we expect new innovations in AI technology for insurance markets. Ever since the advancements in AI technology, there have been much faster, more intelligent, and more capable AIs that use semi-supervised, effectively few-shot learning, as well as transformers for natural language processing (NLP) innovations coming thick and fast. For example, NLP AIs have had significant impacts upon businesses by providing simple front ends for new forms of task automation and decision support. This lowers transaction costs, thus lowering market entry costs, thus accelerating the "contribution to competitive advantage" logic of insurance firms. However, quickly deploying such AIs presents urgent needs for a much clearer ethical and regulatory landscape to successfully minimize bias, discrimination, and social harm during and in the post-deployment phases. We also anticipate changes in underlying insurance operational and regulatory environments in response to fierce competition amplified by impactful AIs. The current heated inflation, along with shrinking returns on investments in "safe" government bonds, rising unemployment, as well as rising social dissatisfaction and anger reduce trust in authority (Choi et al., 2024). Thus, the call for tighter regulatory measures against harms for insurance AI is now larger than ever; the recent initiatives in various regions highlight the increasing focus on AI ethics and trust. However, these may not be the only ones in years to come.

13.10.1 Innovations in AI Technology

Artificial intelligence is not a single, recipe-driven process, but rather a collection of various techniques that can collaborate synergistically to employ different techniques to solve different aspects of the overall task. Many exciting advances have occurred in different methods of artificial intelligence over the last decade, allowed by the development of massively parallel computation and humongous datasets from which these algorithms can learn entire classes of solutions to difficult problems. Such methods have been applied to the various aspects of intelligent behavior related to perception, language, or decision-making which have been devised over the last 70 years. Such advances in over a dozen subfields of AI are bringing us closer to the goal of combining all the pieces into "human-level AI," which can take on tasks now proposed for autonomous and semi-autonomous intelligent agents applied to a diverse array of general and specific challenges. New and exciting advances have taken place in almost all areas of AI. Some of the most impactful advances in the last decade have been in the different aspects of computer vision. Techniques first developed around 2007 to classify and recognize objects in images have matured over the years, with improved performance in recognition accuracy for problems such as image recognition benchmarks and image segmentation benchmarks, which have since extended to person detection and captioning (Golden et al., 2016). A similar technique has now been applied with great success to a variety of image understanding tasks such as face recognition, action recognition, 3D pose estimation and reconstruction, and landmark recognition, as well as other vision-related problems including: optical flow estimation, depth estimation, image matting, semantic segmentation, image captioning, and image generation.

13.10.2 Evolving Regulatory Landscapes

Distinct from the private self-regulation initiatives mentioned in the earlier text, new laws and regulations are emerging in various jurisdictions to shape commercial AI models to be more ethical or fair, or to at least limit potential harms caused by AI. The motivation is to rein in big tech companies while at the same time fostering innovation, particularly for smaller, new startups. These new regulatory frameworks take many forms but include new laws specific to AI, sector-specific laws, amendments to existing laws, and proposed regulations. There are several aims of the new regulations. Some proposed laws aim to regulate an AI's decisions at the function, face, or black-box level, and others at the application level, that is, address high-risk AI systems depending on their end use. Most of the drafting is currently focusing on machine learning since it is far more opaque than any other type of AI. Also, as collateral requirements, some countries focus on certain regulated parties and, if they are using an AI system, require the decision made by the AI to also comply with existing regulations. Therein lies the challenge: how does one create laws that help ensure different AIs operate within the same guidelines without stifling creativity, but also considering the opaqueness of some systems, and making them applicable for many years to come (Murphy and Moosa, 2021)? This tension in the drafting means that coded ethical values in the AI are of interest.

13.11 Conclusion

From a comparative and regional perspective, this book has examined the ethical implications and challenges stemming from the use of AI applications in the insurance sector; these challenges stem from the unique interaction between particular cultural and attitudinal factors, the political and regulatory structures in place, as well as how the different insurance markets manage consumer confidence. We can conclude that unpacking the local context and recognizing the emotional and cultural impact ethics and ethical AI has on a society's worldview and self-perception are essential when theorizing about ethics. Furthermore, how AI interacts with different external factors, such as economics, education, law, culture, labor, and technology, is key to developing a framework capable of tackling trustworthy and responsible behavior for both humans and machines. Since advances in technology and AI cannot be separated from broader societal developments, the regulatory and industry initiatives to mitigate against or prevent the abuse of AI commercial decision-making are equally necessary to adopt a system-wide ethics approach. Nevertheless, ensuring these initiatives are suited to the people, geography, politics, and culture structure they are intended to help is a difficult, if not impossible, task. In making every effort to construct these initiatives in accordance with the local context, rather than imposing a one-size-fits-all strategy, it is also essential to bear in mind that applying the particularism theory of ethics could lead to more discrimination or bias against minority social groups. Our recommendation is to ensure a balance between general and particularist priorities. AI technology will be neutral; at the same time, culture, politics, and geography will collide with different sectors of society.

References

Aina, I., Ayinde, O., Thiam, D. and Miranda, M. (2024). Crop Index Insurance as a Tool for Climate Resilience: Lessons from Smallholder Farmers in Nigeria. *Natural Hazards*, *120*(5). https://doi.org/10.1007/s11069-023-06388-x

Arockiam, J.M. and Pushpanathan, A.C.S. (2023). MapReduce-Iterative Support Vector Machine Classifier: Novel Fraud Detection Systems in Healthcare Insurance Industry. *International Journal of Electrical and Computer Engineering*, *13*(1). https://doi.org/10.11591/ijece.v13i1. pp756–769

Choi, J.H., Choi, Y., Lee, K.S., Ahn, K.H., and Jang, W.Y. (2024). Explainable Model Using Shapley Additive Explanations Approach on Wound Infection after Wide Soft Tissue Sarcoma Resection: "Big Data" Analysis Based on Health Insurance Review and Assessment Service Hub. *Medicina (Lithuania)*, *60*(2). https://doi.org/10.3390/medicina60020327

Daudén-Esmel, C., Castellà-Roca, J. and Viejo, A. (2024). Blockchain-Based Access Control System for Efficient and GDPR-Compliant Personal Data Management. *Computer Communications*, *214*. https://doi.org/10.1016/j.comcom.2023.11.017

Dorfleitner, G., Hornuf, L. and Kreppmeier, J. (2023). Promise not Fulfilled: FinTech, Data Privacy, and the GDPR. *Electronic Markets*, *33*(1). https://doi.org/10.1007/s12525-023-00622-x

Golden, L.L., Brockett, P.L., Ai, J. and Kellison, B. (2016). Empirical Evidence on the Use of Credit Scoring for Predicting Insurance Losses with Psycho-Social and Biochemical Explanations. *North American Actuarial Journal*, *20*(3). https://doi.org/10.1080/10920277.2016.1209118

McDonnell, K., Murphy, F., Sheehan, B., Masello, L. and Castignani, G. (2023). Deep Learning in Insurance: Accuracy and Model Interpretability Using TabNet. *Expert Systems with Applications*, *217*. https://doi.org/10.1016/j.eswa.2023.119543

Mohammad Amini, M., Jesus, M., Fanaei Sheikholeslami, D., Alves, P., Hassanzadeh Benam, A. and Hariri, F. (2023). Artificial Intelligence Ethics and Challenges in Healthcare Applications: A Comprehensive Review in the Context of the European GDPR Mandate.*Machine Learning and Knowledge Extraction*, *5*(3). https://doi.org/10.3390/make5030053

Murphy, S.D. and Moosa, S. (2021). The Views of Public Service Managers on the Implementation of National Health Insurance in Primary Care: A Case of Johannesburg Health District, Gauteng Province, Republic of South Africa. *BMC Health Services Research*, *21*(1). https://doi.org/10.1186/s12913-021-06990-4

Oben, E.E.E., Ndi, H.N. and Tchuikoua, L.B. (2024). Livestock Farmers' Willingness to Pay for Farming Insurance in Four Divisions of the West Region of Cameroon. *Asian Journal of Geographical Research*, *7*(1). https://doi.org/10.9734/ajgr/2024/v7i1211

Owens, E., Sheehan, B., Mullins, M., Cunneen, M., Ressel, J. and Castignani, G. (2022). Explainable Artificial Intelligence (XAI) in Insurance. *Risks*, *10*(12). https://doi.org/10.3390/risks10120230

Philip, B. and Suresh, G. (2024). Cultivating Resilience: An In-Depth Exploration of Agricultural Insurance Initiatives and Their Transformative Role in India's Farming Landscape. *Universal Journal of Agricultural Research*, *12*(1). https://doi.org/10.13189/ujar.2024.120109

Sachan, S. and Muwanga, J. (2023). Integration of Explainable Deep Neural Network with Blockchain Technology: Medical Indemnity Insurance. *CEUR Workshop Proceedings*, *3554*.

Shafik, Wasswa. "Blockchain-based internet of things (B-IoT): Challenges, solutions, opportunities, open research questions, and future trends." Blockchain-based internet of things (2024): 35-58. Taylor & Francis, doi: 10.1201/9781003407096-3.

Shafik, W. (2024). Generative AI for Social Good and Sustainable Development. In *Generative AI: Current Trends and Applications* (pp. 185–217). Springer.

Shafik, W. (2025). Security, privacy, and trust in fintech. In Fintech and financial inclusion (pp. 216-233). Routledge, doi: 10.4324/9781003514114-15.

Shafik, W. (2025). Generative Artificial Intelligence for Social Good and Sustainable Development. *Generative AI: Disruptive Technologies for Innovative Applications*, 153–185.

Shafik, W., Kalinaki, K., Fahim, K.E. and Adam, M. (2024). Safeguarding Data Privacy and Security in Federated Learning Systems. In *Federated Deep Learning for Healthcare* (pp. 170–190). CRC Press. https://doi.org/10.1201/9781032694870-13

Townsend, C., McIntyre, M., Lakhani, A., Wright, C., White, P., Bishara, J. and Cullen, J. (2018). Inclusion of Marginalised Aboriginal and Torres Strait Islander Peoples with Neurocognitive Disability in the National Disability Insurance Scheme (NDIS). *OPEN ACCESS*, *5*(2).

14

Designing an Ethical AI Strategy for Insurers: Policies, Practices, and Organizational Transformation

Wasswa Shafik

14.1 Introduction

Currently, several institutions and governments are trying to regulate the use of AI in both the public and private sectors because the great advances in science and technology have made it possible for these enterprises to create various AI tools whose use has ethical implications. In the case of the insurance industry, which works with sensitive data from its clients and in some countries is supervised by regulators, it is important that insurers create ethical AI strategies that prevent unethical and biased use of AI. Moreover, there is a common interest in reducing the risks that AI technology may have both for the insurance sector and for the economy more generally. In particular, there is a desire to develop a strategy capable of structuring and supporting values in the AI economy and building the trust and acceptability of this transformation among all citizens. Insurers across the globe have already said they want to make more investments in the digitalization of their business, including the use of AI technology, increasing the need to bring into the insurance industry the importance of ethics, bias, and principles that value society, protecting clients' sensitive data, and reducing knowledge asymmetries that can undermine the insurance business model. Furthermore, the sensitive data that is the base for the use of this technology should comply with stringent ethical concerns in order to prevent obstacles to the proper functioning of the insurance industry (Intelligence et al., 2019). These ethical strategies should not only comply with the new rules imposed by the regulators but also should give insurers an advantage over their peers in the market, increasing their competitive positioning, and preventing greed from drivers such as larger shareholder profits, higher commission by intermediaries, and increasing the incentives for managers from creating bias in AI and the unethical use of the technology.

Insurance companies today are investing significantly in the development of AI tools that promise to deliver value and disrupt insurers. For private companies, investments in AI are an "arms race," developing AI tools to own the competitive advantage in their industry's AI ecosystem. For companies in the public sector, investments in AI "are less about competition and more about using advanced technology to provide better services and improve operations." For an insurer, these "services" include simplifying tedious tasks that consume too much effort from the workforce and create frictions for customers. Private sector claims-making on AI is seen as the "easiest way to gain a competitive advantage." It is noted that "artificial intelligence is the world's most powerful digital transformation technology disrupting every industry including insurance, which

DOI: 10.1201/9781003747659-14

combines both traditional finance plus risk management. Yet AI in insurance is still in its infancy, with a new generation of customer-centric services barely scratching the surface of the universe of possibilities." There is a distinction between predictive or cognitive automation, which is pervasive in insurance technology today, and generative automation, which is yet to be the future (Johnson, 2022). Generative automation discusses two types of investor activity in the AI ecosystem, those companies that are primarily building foundational AI offerings and those that are focused on building specific AI applications.

14.2 Key Ethical Principles for AI Development

Designing an AI strategy for insurers presents a series of case studies that explore the possible impacts of deploying AI at scale, the potential for technology to lead to biases in modelling and decision-making, and the risk of diminished accountability from decisions made by AI. A common theme across the analyses is the heightened risk to ethics and society when the powered-up technologies of AI are applied to long-tailed, complex, and opaque business processes such as underwriting and claims. This chapter poses the question of how an insurance firm, developing a position in the AI space, can navigate these ethical minefields. The key ethical principles we outline as possible guardrails for AI underwriting—transparency, fairness, accountability, privacy—are derived from existing research into ethical AI. The purpose is to draw on existing literature from the fields of information and communications technology and AI ethics to set out practical points that the insurance industry could implement as it builds out AI. While there is no one-size-fits-all approach to developing AI capability or ethical AI guidelines, the four suggestions that we propose would provide a firm with a baseline set of considerations, which could then be tailored to its own circumstances when it comes to making ethical decisions around AI. All these principles also present the idea of putting barriers up to the use of certain AI concepts or designs (Eitel-Porter, 2021; Knight et al., 2024). The importance of ensuring that principles beyond legality guide ethical decisions is paramount. Simply operating within the law is not enough when it comes to the development of technology-enabled tools to support underwriting.

14.2.1 Transparency

Designing transparent AI models is fraught with challenges, not least because a fully accountable explanation is difficult to deliver and often expensive. However, demanding transparency is an important principle for insurers, who must balance sharing sufficiently useful information about their underwriting decision-making processes to enable customers to improve their risk management. External transparency can be complemented by internal transparency, which aims to ensure that machine decision-making is sufficiently understandable to internal stakeholders, from executives to data scientists to compliance officers, to enable appropriate governance and oversight (Veritti et al., 2024). The principle of explainability is pressing in the urgent environment of risk transfer that lies at the heart of the insurance business. Insurers increasingly utilize AI processes to automate operations that were formerly the exclusive province of insurance experts, thereby placing confidence in the ability of the machines to predict behavior more accurately—and with a greater degree of speed and efficiency—than human underwriters. External scrutiny of AI decision-making should therefore be encouraged to identify and rectify any serious shortfalls in accuracy and bias. Insurers must also be prepared to provide clear explanations for adverse underwriting actions that can be checked against a consumer's experience. The predictive capabilities of the processes developed not only need to be precise, they need to help the company understand how different characteristics play a part in the prediction and claim outcome, such as whether the type of car influences insurance time, people's motivation for being insured or more likely to encourage claims, the severity of claims, etc. If you can take the company into the journey by telling stories that inspire decision-making, you will accomplish a complete and effective transparency. For important decisions about any aspect of the functioning of the insurance company that can be undertaken by either a person or an AI system, the demarcation line between human and machine decision-making should be established in a way that is sensible and defensible (Alahmed et al., 2023).

14.2.2 Fairness

Data-driven AI systems inherently reflect errors and biases from their training datasets. For example, using a dataset where a specific minority group has been underrepresented can lead to discriminatory outcomes when future predictions or results from the model are analyzed. Inadvertent use of fairness infractions—such as treating individuals of different groups differently in similar interactions—can lead to a decline in brand equity among customers and their communities, especially if these characteristics are inherent to the people being affected or are part of a selected protected class, such as ethnicity, age group, gender, physical disability, or others. Moreover, most models optimize for global accuracy, without the means to ensure that minority sub-group(s) become equally as successful when reaching said accuracy value. Commonly used AI models for decision-making typically do not take fairness into account, nor do they follow a fair representation. There is no fairness distinction when a model is predicting the probability of being in default for a given group, which is in and of itself an unfair practice. Creating, analyzing, or working with biased models can put the insurer company as well as their clients at risk for regulatory compliance. Regulatory compliance and legislation have started responding toward this need of fairness, and some laws already impose limitations on automated individual decisions and profiling, asking for data-driven decisions to follow subject's rights, freedoms, and legitimate interests. Considering the growing sensitivity regarding bias, discrimination, and fairness—especially with underprivileged groups—more companies are looking into diversity, equity, and inclusion initiatives in order to avoid violations (Hagendorff & Danks, 2023). While recent projects are offering some level of protection against biased and unfair implementations of AI, it is important for organizations to understand how to audit their machine learning projects for unfairness and biased treatment. Auditability serves as an additional safety net when predictors or developed outcomes do affect human lives.

14.2.3 Accountability

Accountability is a principle regarding ethical operation that pertains to all AI use cases. Since ethical AI is not merely about compliance, there is also an ethical dimension to accountability that goes beyond the letter of law. Ethical accountability includes acting in accordance with rules which an actor perceives individually as being valid. It also includes respecting rules that stakeholders create collectively. Accountability is a fundamental principle of good governance and democratic institutions. It fosters legitimacy, trust, and reliability in both the public and private sectors. Also, from the policy perspective, establishing ethical AI means developing rules that prevent the violation of the rights of individuals and society. Embedding adequate criteria for modularized and composite AI creates fair conditions for competition and effective risk mitigation to ensure safety, security, and resilience to unexpected and malicious uses. Accountability implies a duty of care, a duty to explain the decisions taken by algorithms enshrined in the principle of transparency. Accountability serves to enforce data ethics. Its breach is liable not only to physical, natural, and legal persons but may also include the media, software tools, and other third parties involved in creating and distributing these algorithms (Karpova, 2023). Hence, AI creators should provide means for impartial external scrutiny by legal and ethical authorities. Liability should be in accordance with the recognized limits for the distribution of responsibility.

14.2.4 Privacy

Many AI models require a significant volume of potentially sensitive personal data. For insurers, data privacy is a particularly salient issue, especially under new, local, data protection regulations. Such regulations in effect operate as a requirement of AI fairness—in that they hold entities that use private information responsible for any discrimination or for injurious, algorithmic decision-making—or of about privacy discrimination, in that they lie at the intersection of algorithmic fairness and algorithmic transparency, providing sufficient transparency in order to ensure that modelling does not render some individuals "invisible." Insurers who rely on non-privacy preserving models/tools are at risk of violating legal duties (Anshari et al., 2021). Beyond regulation, failure to address consumer sentiment around the data-privacy implications of AI modelling could damage relationships with potential customers. Many AI tools, once implemented, use privacy-invasive behavioural tracking strategies intended to anticipate lapses in premium payments. Consumers may have concerns about whether data is used fairly and whether the advantages of such use outweigh the potential harms. Insurers need to leverage more explainable models of undesired decisions regarding insurance and leverage them for modeling business strategies. Such explainability may not be possible for all types of models. As a result, some insurance-computing use cases may require trade-offs between modelling robustness and privacy-preserving explainability (Mcevoy, 2019). Customers could be persuaded of the value of insurance AI models if insurers could adequately address concerns of using sensitive information for business processes, such as particular model predictions, decisions, and features, as well as offer meaningful opportunities for customer decisions about the modeling use through clear benefit structure of opting-out, as presented in Table 14.1.

Table 14.1 Core components of an ethical AI strategy for insurers.

Component	*Description*	*Best Practices*	*Key Benefits*	*Implementation Challenges*
AI Governance Framework	Structures and processes to oversee AI ethics and compliance	Establish ethics committees, clear accountability	Ensures compliance and ethical consistency	Resistance to change, lack of expertise
Ethical AI Policies	Formal policies outlining principles for AI use	Define fairness, privacy, transparency policies	Clear guidelines for AI development and use	Policy enforcement across decentralized units
Bias Detection and Mitigation	Procedures to identify and reduce AI biases	Regular audits, diverse training data, adversarial testing	Fairer decision-making, improved public trust	Complexity in measuring and correcting bias
Transparency and Explainability	Making AI decisions understandable to stakeholders	Explainable AI models, user-friendly disclosures	Builds trust and accountability	Technical complexity, balancing transparency with Internet Protocol (IP)
Data Governance	Responsible data handling aligned with ethical standards	Data minimization, consent management, anonymization	Protects privacy and ensures data quality	Integrating privacy with AI performance needs
Stakeholder Engagement	Involving internal and external stakeholders in AI ethics	Workshops, feedback loops, public consultations	Inclusive and responsive AI strategy	Managing diverse expectations and interests
Training and Awareness	Educating employees about ethical AI principles and risks	Regular training, scenario-based learning	Builds an ethical culture, reduces operational risks	Maintaining engagement and updating content regularly

Contd.

Table 14.1 *Contd.*

Component	*Description*	*Best Practices*	*Key Benefits*	*Implementation Challenges*
Risk Management	Identifying and mitigating risks associated with AI deployment	Risk assessments, contingency planning	Minimizes reputational and operational damage	Predicting emergent risks in evolving AI systems
Continuous Monitoring	Ongoing evaluation of AI systems for ethical compliance	Real-time monitoring, impact assessments	Ensures adaptive and resilient AI governance	Resource intensive, requires specialized skills
Organizational Culture	Embedding ethical AI values into corporate culture	Leadership commitment, ethical incentives	Drives sustained ethical behavior and innovation	Changing entrenched behaviors and incentives

14.3 Regulatory Frameworks and Compliance

The risk of reputational damage in case of a data leak or any ethical default is a topic every insurer should take seriously. But can consumers really trust AI strategies and underwriting in place? How can insurers address this massive shift toward an expected higher moral behavior? It will be difficult to address these points without complying with the growing number of legal frameworks and guidelines. As a starting point, the upcoming chapter gives an overview of global regulatory frameworks and standards and describes some of their guidelines. Almost 90% of interviewees stated that regulation is an important driver for implementing and developing ethical and responsible AI. Even the big tech companies reacted by establishing their regulation boards or data science ethics boards. The next step is the introduction of dedicated, legally binding AI regulations, such as the recently proposed act. Nevertheless, dedicated legal requirements for financial services, for general services, and for providing insurance services already exist. These are, for example, the General Data Protection Regulation for all industries, the European Insurance Distribution Directive, several money laundering regulation guidelines, and the Financial Action Task Force's Recommendations (Gouvea, 2024). These regulations also affect what type of algorithms and features can be chosen for AI strategies. The same holds for risk factor technology. The General Data Protection Regulation has a long history of regulating the use of client data in Europe and has put in place specific mention of the behavioral data collection and use using generative technologies as presented in Figure 14.1.

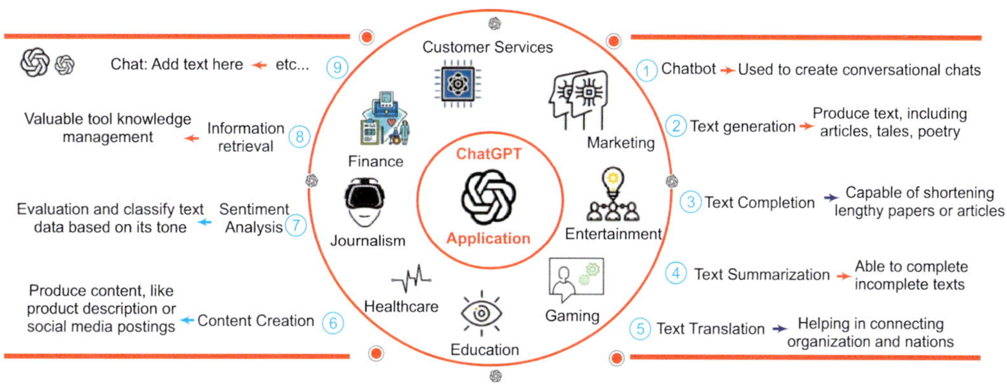

Fig. 14.1 ChatGPT application in the insurance industry.

14.3.1 Global Regulations Overview

The advent and nostalgic embrace of artificial intelligence by mainstream society have consequently attracted an increasing amount of scrutiny from regulatory and governing entities framing the necessary scope and guiding principles for responsible and ethical AI. Multiple extraordinary AI use cases are being developed in parallel across a spectrum of applications leveraging generative, predictive, and rational models. Introducing enormous power and benefit, the advanced capabilities of AI models have sparked with equal measure facets of moral and ethical unease. In response, local and global regulators are rushing to develop frameworks operating in some fashion as a framework for the responsible and ethically sound build-out of what is termed "trustworthy AI." Most prominent themes of regulation are demand for explanation transparency, governance controls, bias and fairness protections, prevention of misuse and generation of false information, public and environmental impact assessments, as well as prescriptive safe harbor segments against police state or warfare uses. While the dialogues are smooth and engaging and impactful progress toward regulation will take time, many G20 and European Union (EU) entities have noted the urgent need to clarify positions and quickly develop frameworks before experimentation progressively crosses the Rubicon. Current drafts from the digital portfolio of the EU position the constraints on data models as well as generative AI. Be it through ex post facto class action or tort causality, or ex ante sidestepping via liability insurance, insurers stand at the bleeding edge of responsibility/scope of work questions in sacralizing a policy with such framework assumptions. Assisting with liability delineations and establishing plain language out of draft discussions would help build the bridge needed (Song, 2023). Regulators and insurers have the same main interest: aligning the driver incentives and need for accountability with the impacted parties.

14.3.2 Industry Standards

The financial services industry has long adhered to certain principles that reflect values of trust, transparency, and fair dealing. Over the last few decades, these values have been articulated in the form of a number of different principles and guidelines and embodied by a number of different organizations. The considerations surrounding the implementation of artificial intelligence in organizations are growing with the rapidly changing technology landscape. Special interest groups, industry standards bodies, and companies are scrutinizing the use of AI technology and how it affects people and the planet. Due to the advancements in computing capability, vast amount of available digital data, and the explosion in demand for automation, AI is being deployed in many critical business processes. As financial institutions research, develop, and deploy AI solutions to automate more and more of their critical business processes, these principles are becoming more relevant than ever. Financial services use principles to guide the development and deployment of safety in AI projects. The insurance industry is highly regulated at the national and various local jurisdictions and is required to keep customers' sensitive data private and secure. In addition to regulations, the insurance industry already employs many standards that govern the technology products that are used to create customer experience, manage claims, and keep proprietary data secure. Various national and international standards organizations are continuously creating and updating standards used to create the IT infrastructure that supports the insurance business (Intelligence et al., 2019). Companies that provide core insurance services use such standards to validate their infrastructure.

14.3.3 Risk Management in AI Implementation

Risk management plays an integral role in any company's governance framework, ensuring that risks faced are regularly identified, assessed, and considered alongside the insurer's strategy. Identifying the risks associated with the tools used to deliver its services and programs would fall under the remit of the actuarial function as part of the Actuaries and Own Risk and Solvency Assessment (ORSA) process. The audit committee may be in the best position to oversee this work, but will require input from the actuarial function, IT and/or digital leaders, and other functions with technology risk expertise to review and assess what the third-party vendor risk assessments may highlight, especially around data protection. These identified technology risks can be escalated to the board and risk appetite can be approved as a collective committee, where the Area Under the Curve (AUC), executives, and board can in agreement sign off on the levels of risk. It is the responsibility of the lines of business or analysts/departments that may synthesize the AI and integrate it back into the business and have to conduct a due diligence of what additional risks may be presented by this specific tool being implemented. Due diligence considerations around the tool include model trustworthiness, applicability, possible negative social impacts from implementation, and algorithm/output bias. These groups are also responsible for ongoing monitoring of the tool post-implementation to ensure that no additional major risks arise from its stated intended purpose (Eitel-Porter, 2021; Johnson, 2022; Knight et al., 2024). A "fail-safe" implores that the tool is regularly checked against the model selection criteria and if the AI is indeed still the best possible option in specifics to the problem statement it is trying to solve. This serves as part of an organization's technique validation, used to monitor ongoing performance to ensure the outputs generated are still fit for purpose as applied.

14.3.4 Identifying AI Risks

In order to identify risks, insurers can start by looking at the potential risks for each area of their business and process where they want to implement an AI model. Considerations could include the following: potential for right infringement by used data; accuracy of outputs; data handling and security; uncertainty, incompleteness, and bias of data; need for controlled and high-quality data training process and data for retraining; economic impact; accountability concerns; loss of trust by insured; need for all stakeholders engagement; impact labor and workforce relations; sustainability impact; adverse impact on market competition. While not specific for the implementation of AI in the insurance industry, these risk categories need to be taken into account for every new model. Adequate measures need to be adopted to avoid liability risk and adverse consequences in the form of fines for provisions on data protection, consumer protection, and competition law. It is also recommended to carry out frequent questionnaires among clients in order to know whether they trust that their data are handled securely and that they pay the premium they deserve (Veritti et al., 2024). Even if these risks could not be avoided entirely, appropriate transparency and trust-building measures reduce the importance of those risks.

14.3.5 Mitigation Strategies

What strategies exist to mitigate identified AI risks? Which specific set of strategies is appropriate for an insurance application or business use case? The final set of mitigations selected depends at least partly on the risk tolerance of the organization, the risk appetite of stakeholders, and the culture of the institution. However, decisions should also take into account the principles of effective risk management. A well-established best practice is to avoid each risk if possible; if this is infeasible or too expensive, to reduce the risk by limiting the impacts and probabilities of occurrence; if this too is not feasible or desired, to transfer the risk through insurance or risk sharing; and finally, if none of the previous strategies will work, accepting the risk may be the only option. These stages of risk management are usually presented in order of preference. Fortunately, it is not a zero-sum game, in which removing the risk from future consideration undermines achieving the goal of the organization. In most cases, several decision variables are in play in determining the deployment parameters and characteristics of an AI system that influence its possible risk exposure. These decision variables reflect the design of the AI application, including the makeup and size of its training set, the openness should the AI implementation be to review, the level of AI autonomy, or the importance placed on a possible adverse effect measure compared to its expected performance on the desired performance measures. Moreover, there are degrees of mitigation that can be applied at almost any level (Karpova, 2023). Further, which strategy or strategies to use for a particular decision variable for a specific insurance application should be guided by risk function, in particular, the shape of the adverse effect measure and what additional measures can incorporate stakeholders' risk preferences.

14.4 Developing an Ethical AI Policy

The ethical development of AI can only be realized through an ethical framework policy, along with a guiding AI use and development policy, at all levels including both microlevels of the AI designers, developers, and testers, and macrolevels of corporations and local governments. Policies incorporate ethical decisions and address why AI needs specific intervention to secure positive inputs through specific inputs, processes, and outputs. Subsequent chapters elaborate on the kind of ethical directions such a policy would need to address for policy adoption and adaptation. To create policies, a collaborative environment mapping relevant stakeholders and their relationships in the space where AI is being used is essential. Visibly creating ethical procedures with the help of the wide stakeholder community provides a structure in which AI use and ethical support systems can be built. With the rapid deployment of AI in a variety of sectorial applications, promoting transparency via stakeholder engagement, the impact of public consultation should not be overlooked. Transparency is an important element of all ethical and responsible policy frameworks. The communities of interest need to be made aware of the potential acceptance to the setbacks involved in using AI at the microlevel, which has greater repercussions at the macrolevel boundaries. There needs to be inclusion, clarity, and resoluteness for the knowledge ecosystem, including the tech giants, who are in the driving seat of large-scale AI deployment. People do not want to share sensitive data with researchers outside of academic societies. More transparency means researchers share their research results with the community and the factors that warrant privacy are always discussed with subjects before data is collected. We address specific dialogues regarding privacy decisions respecting people and their data from the aspect of researchers' use of the data as a digitized unified common good or basic human right, compared to commercial companies who use private data on commercial channels for profit, neglecting the right of constituent individuals from all datasets (Song, 2023). This is a growing dilemma faced by officials in formulating, monitoring, or updating AI strategy or policy.

14.4.1 *Stakeholder Engagement*

The implementation of an ethical AI policy necessitates collaborative engagement with relevant stakeholders. These individuals possess diverse skills and experience across a multitude of disciplines and interests; therefore, varying perspectives on the opportunities and challenges of AI adoption must be considered to arrive at an authentic and effective road map. Since each business department has its own perspective on the impact of AI within their operational context, a policy that reflects the views of various groups within the insurer will promote understanding and acceptance of the document, its vision, and its goals. Additionally, groups impacted by AI include not only employees but also customers, business partners, and the communities within which the insurer operates. Policies developed in conjunction with these impacted stakeholders, especially customers and other policyholders, may engender more trust among all groups. Public consultation activities will identify constituents most affected by these efforts so that the appropriate feedback channels can be provided (Wu et al., 2020).

Consultation is a flexible process, in which a range of methods and tools can be employed, depending on the degree of engagement sought, how quickly feedback is needed, the issues at stake, and the constituency in question. Various collaboration techniques could include outreach, face-to-face interviews, focus groups, and surveys, as well as user testing and review of pilots for specific AI projects. Requesting feedback on discussion documents that inform the context and provide preliminary views, options, and questions can also be very helpful, ensuring that the final discussion/consultation draws sufficient input on the best ideas from as many stakeholders as possible. Such discussion documents and consultations should address the essential choices that constituents must make from an informed perspective, so that trade-offs can be fully anticipated and strategies modified in line with those decisions. Perhaps, of most importance, providing feedback on how such input has been considered or taken into account ensures that stakeholders feel that they have a stake in whatever recommendations policies these efforts produce (Pourzolfaghar et al., 2023).

14.4.2 Policy Drafting Process

As the methods and data used to inform AI models vary in complexity and scale, so too should the policies that guide AI's use. Policies exist to enable and clarify co-created rules of the road across an organization. Creating customized policies at an organizational level helps to clarify the roles and expectations of employees and creates an organizational structure for auditing AI at a specific managerial level. The aims of this and other policy documents are to support employees and educate them about artificial intelligence's benefits and limitations. The greatest benefit to developing an AI policy is that AI questions and clarification of unanswered questions can be treated like any other center of competence requests, whereby employees may continuously ask for assessments or explanations on request or at least during regular intervals. Depending on the maturity of your AI capability, your insurance organization may already have some existing tech or data-specific policies that exist at some level. These would be an important resource to leverage in crafting a bespoke AI policy. The most important point to remember with the policy drafting process is that no aspect of AI is off limits. As well as being a high-level handbook for your business employees, the AI is a fluid document and should be developed in a way that enables sections to be developed by your centers of competence as the business develops. What this ultimately means is that as your AI capability matures, the AI policy will become increasingly less vague on the specialized aspects of why and how AI will be used (Johnson, 2022). This is due to your center of AI excellence providing the business with regular policies and frameworks that are aligned with your unique business context matured from working closely with the business.

14.5 Best Practices for Ethical AI Deployment

An ethical framework is useful for companies that want to develop ethical AI guidelines. These guidelines set the tone for their ethical approaches and support the commitment to ethical development, application, and deployment throughout the AI life cycle. However, simply having a set of guidelines is inadequate. Rather, organizations should take specific steps to ensure that all employees know, understand, and live these mappings. Data and AI ethics are not yet a standard part of every employee's educational experience. Therefore, employees are unlikely to know how decisions in their day-to-day work, which may seem mundane or trivial, could potentially raise ethical concerns with short- or long-term implications. To minimize the risk of bad decisions at all levels of the organization, companies should include AI ethics in onboarding materials and training programs for all employees. They should also conduct regular discussions and refresher training.

After all, one of the biggest challenges to ethical decision-making is not knowing what the rules are, so organizations should strive to create a clear and positive message about the ethical rules that need to be followed. Best practices for AI ethics monitoring revolve around the understanding that no company wants to be surprised when it comes to the possibility of deploying damaging AI systems. Ethical lapses actively hurt companies, and it's helpful to monitor for compliance and build systems that apply and follow rule-of-thumb routines. These principles might not prevent every error in anticipating ethical roadblocks, but they certainly ease the way (Veritti et al., 2024). Organizations should set up ethical review boards or panels to monitor high-stakes projects. These bodies should be staffed with a mix of technical experts and domain experts, both internal and external to the company.

14.5.1 Training and Awareness

When considering the deployment of AI techniques within an insurer's operations, stakeholders must understand the benefits and risks attached to its use. Employees across the various skill levels of an organization's AI ecosystem require an understanding of the influencing factors of desirability and acceptability related to AI deployment and associated workflows, such as openness, defensibility, and cooperation. The motivation for putting such programs in place is twofold; first, the risk of implementation failure or poor customer reaction to AI systems can be significantly heightened without a clear understanding of the objectives of the insurer's AI strategy. People are key to the success of an insurance AI strategy and need to be engaged and trained to support its development and adoption. Second, and perhaps more important, AI is a societal tool and should be developed and operated for societal good, aligning to the organization goals related to corporate governance and responsibility. Providing awareness training to stakeholder populations can help increase understanding of the impacts of AI on the insurer's products, society, and the market. Broad communications regarding the purpose of AI in the insurer's operations should be clear and state the impact of such systems and workflows on employees, partners, and customers. More in-depth training for specialist groups is critical and should account for the specific challenges within the individual's area of responsibility (Hagendorff & Danks, 2023). More generalist sessions can cover a variety of topics regarding chatbot workflows, property risk assessment models, underwriting and claims settlement, complaint listening, and sentiment analysis, among other topics of interest.

14.5.2 Monitoring and Evaluation

Ethical AI strategies should be dynamic. After the first implementation, there should be a period for monitoring the effects of the strategies in practice. Annual meetings could be scheduled, during which internal communications can be evaluated. Has the message been received or have employees engaged with the training? Are departments at risk of artificial discrimination? Is the risk register comprehensible and being used? These, among many others, could be key for making sure the AI solution is being used for the right objectives and the message is being successfully transported across the organization. If not, this must lead to an assessment of policy and solution design adequacy. Data audit should also be done regularly to ensure that the assets are full of quality, up to date, and not biased. After making sure all this is correct, an evaluation of the AI solution should be done too, not only regarding the performance—Is it making the right predictions? As opposed to previous times, could as many errors lead to discrimination?—but also regarding its social impact. Affective and social responsibility engages not only companies but also their products, just as it does with consumer goods. It feels imperative for all problem spaces to bring sensitivity to AI implementation and regulation. Its basis is simple: auditing equals detection (Mcevoy, 2019). For this purpose, the AI auditing community is mobilizing efforts to bring the same, and even more controls, to machine learning model validation than the ones that traditionally are defined for statistical models, though sample biases and cyber bullies tend to appear when insurance is technologically used, as presented in Figure 14.2.

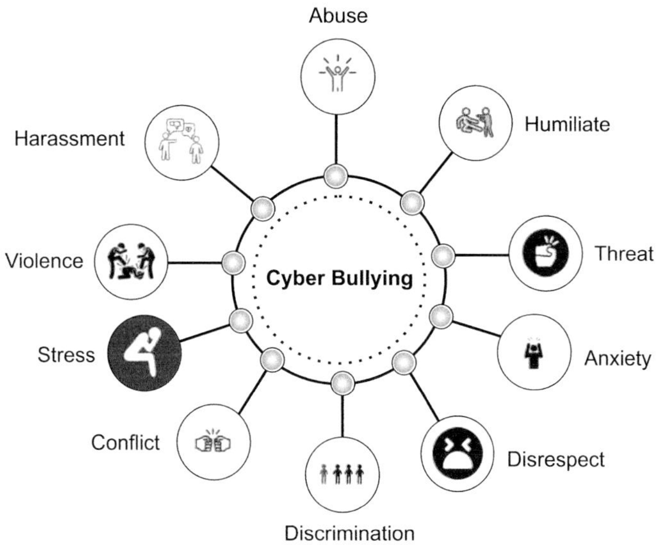

Fig. 14.2 Cyber bullying in technological insurance aspects.

14.6 Organizational Transformation for Ethical AI

Having the right technology is not sufficient to succeed in implementing AI and doing so ethically. Insurers need to adapt their operating models and change the workplace to promote ethical AI. This requires developing a corporate culture that values accountability, fairness, and transparency, and is open to debate about ethical questions around the use of new data analytics capabilities. It also requires that board and C-suite leaders model their commitment to ethical decision-making, by adopting an "ethics-first" framework that meets shareholder, employee, customer, and regulatory expectations. Operating from the top-down, having people in leadership continuously prioritize ethical decision-making creates a trickle-down effect to other employees, letting them know that ethical decision-making is a priority. Building a framework that fosters ethical discussion through corporate values such that employees feel comfortable raising ethical challenges, knowing the organization will support them, is a practical, critical first step. Building trust with employees means they don't just take shortcuts to a "move fast and break things" mantra. This up-front trust prevents bias down the road (Song, 2023). That's not to say that speed isn't important, especially in a business environment like insurance where getting products to consumers fast is key. However, having a structure that reminds employees of a framework to operate within can help them balance speed and ethical considerations. Ethical AI challenges aren't relegated only to a small group of internal experts. The response should be broad and deep, engaging every function and every employee. Institute ethical AI principles that can actively engage people, such that they're empowered to make the right choices: have them commit publicly to doing so. Have the board expose themselves to the risk of AI missteps, and make them review AI plans and approve budgets. Create processes that "bring it back home" to every employee every day, make it part of their work, and strengthen ethical AI's position in the company's strategic discussion. In sum, the C-suite must drive the organizational transformation for a more ethical AI in order to align it with the overall objectives of the corporation (El-Deeb, 2023).

14.6.1 Cultural Shift

AI will certainly play an increasing role in all aspects of insurance's business model but it needs to be trusted to do so. As societal stakes rise and tech skepticism is ever more a given, companies will need to operate in a way where outcomes protect rather than exploit their customers. In doing so, insurers can answer consumer skepticism rather than help foster it—providing the public with reasons and tangible explanations for why and how they are using AI in operations. Such a move builds trust in an improved business relationship based on ongoing product offers and positive customer outcomes. For ML application to be viewed and trusted as good, there need to be clear parameters, enforced from a governance perspective and supported from a cultural perspective. Culture change is therefore largely about onboarding everyone to the mission of a new core concept: shared value. Insurers need to shift their culture to one where technology ensures this principle is embedded within practice—where all technologies are purpose-built not just commercially oriented, and where tech innovation is ever on consumers' behalf. AI is not appropriately trained or set in operation by current product and service business leaders but by teams—including those defining and developing insurance ML applications—of data scientists and ethicists. Misalignment between values from business leaders versus those expressed by ML output will provoke internal friction and client skepticism. This codependency model is an insurance win–win-enhancing power: insurers can develop the skills required to create clear focus because of a clear mission—in creating fair products for equitable offense and grievance resolution. The above represents a significant shift in core operating principles and will therefore take time to imbue within the organizational DNA. Insurers need to recognize this, taking dispassionate stock of their current values, decision-making heuristics, and risk appetite, reflective of their operational reality rather than marketing imagination (Nassar & Kamal, 2021). Further, it will be necessary to institute a new platform for decision-making communication tools. Insurers cannot seek to prohibit understandable and correct but negative influence over ML—within limit.

14.6.2 Leadership Commitment

Understanding that AI transformation is not just a technology IT challenge but an organizational transformation one, senior leadership teams must be actively involved. They must embrace the AI transformation program and create an overarching strategy that breaks down functional silos and reallocates resources across organizational boundaries. Their commitment to an ethical AI strategy and ongoing dialog are critical company-wide efforts to ensure ethical policies and resources are completely embraced. Establishing an ethical AI charter, code of conduct, audits, processes for ethical concerns around AI, and an AI-centered ethics committee must come from the top. Accountable to the board of directors, the chief executive officer (CEO) is the focal point for ethical decision-making in an organization. Employee ethical concerns, guidelines, reports, and decisions all lead back to the office of the CEO. The CEO is the default chief ethicist of the organization, establishing and ratifying ethical guidelines and expectations. If employee reports ethical issues, they can bypass the hierarchy in favor of reporting directly to the CEO. In today's digital landscape, a CEO can face a loss of credibility and reputation in a matter of minutes. When ethical scandals arise, reputations suffer, and companies risk the potential of global irrelevance. Employees, clients, investors, consumers, and society will quickly discuss their opinions online. As a result, organizations need to act quickly and thoughtfully when faced with ethical concerns (Paraman & Anamalah, 2023). They must establish an ethical culture that brings complaints immediately to the forefront so they can be acknowledged, investigated, and addressed, often in a matter of hours or a few days. To achieve ethical accountability and to survive, stomping down on unethical behavior must be a foundation for long-term strategy and thinking, as presented in Table 14.2.

Table 14.2 Steps for organizational transformation toward ethical AI.

Step	*Description*	*Key Activities*	*Success Metrics*	*Potential Barriers*
Leadership Commitment	Senior management champions ethical AI strategy	Executive endorsement, resource allocation	Leadership involvement, budget allocation	Competing priorities, lack of AI literacy
Cross-Functional Collaboration	Integration across departments (IT, legal, compliance)	Joint ethics committees, cross-department workshops	Number of collaborative initiatives	Silos and communication gaps
Policy Development	Crafting comprehensive AI ethics policies	Stakeholder consultations, benchmarking standards	Policy adoption rate, policy compliance	Balancing flexibility and enforcement
Capacity Building	Training staff on AI ethics and technologies	Workshops, e-learning, certification programs	Employee competency scores, training completion rates	Training fatigue, diverse skill levels
Ethical AI Tool Integration	Implementing tools to enforce ethics (bias detectors, XAI)	Procurement, pilot testing, vendor assessments	Reduction in bias incidents, improved transparency	Technical integration complexity
Monitoring and Reporting	Establishing metrics and reporting systems for AI ethics	Dashboards, regular reporting cycles	Frequency and quality of reports	Data availability, organizational transparency
Feedback Mechanisms	Channels for stakeholder input and grievance redressal	Surveys, hotlines, and public forums	Stakeholder satisfaction, grievance resolution rates	Fear of retaliation, low participation
Continuous Improvement	Iterative updates to policies and practices	Review cycles, lessons learned sessions	Policy revisions, improved risk indicators	Resistance to change, resource constraints
Cultural Change Initiatives	Promoting ethical values and behavior organization-wide	Campaigns, recognition programs, leadership modeling	Employee engagement, ethical behavior surveys	Cultural inertia, inconsistent messaging
External Partnerships	Collaborating with regulators, academia, and civil society	Joint research, compliance partnerships, standards bodies	Influence on policy, innovation in ethical AI	Conflicting interests, coordination challenges

14.7 Case Studies of Ethical AI in Insurance

As AI technology and products mature, cases of responsible AI in both the financial services and insurance industries and—most importantly—the lessons learned from these implementations become increasingly clear. In this chapter, we focus on a small handful of real-world examples. We examine these examples to offer more detailed perspectives on the risks and challenges inherent in AI, and how it might be applied responsibly in the insurance industry. We recognize that offering bona fide examples of ethical implementations is a difficult task. The very substance of true AI leadership is, we believe, an ability—and willingness—to radically innovate in ways that have yet to be trialed by others. We define the idea of an ethical use of AI in insurance to mean projects which prioritize the interests of the insured—over at least a minimum set of testable baselines—while delivering value in terms of financial performance and other stakeholder interests for the insurance enterprise. We sought a collection of stories where technology delivered a material positive impact for the insured, the enterprise, and other stakeholders—both in terms of process efficiencies and the products themselves. The companies and implementations we study are all well-established firms who are among the leaders in the development and implementation of AI technology in the insurance industry. Each has found at least one unique way to apply technology to services that previously had been relatively immune to radical innovation. These include solutions for existing markets based on improved productivity and efficiencies, as well as actions that embed the use of advanced tools and technologies into the products themselves (Nasir et al., 2024; Tolulope Olorunsogo et al., 2024). More recently, we are also beginning to hear promising stories from later-stage innovators. A variety of highly creative InsureTech startups are also building new products that may deliver ethical use of AI.

14.7.1 Successful Implementations

The concepts presented in this document are abstract and hypothesis-driven. In this chapter, we present several case studies from the insurance and related industries that clearly demonstrate the level of commitment major companies exert to practice ethical AI development. Here we showcase a number of insurers, reinsurers, and insurance industry adjacent organizations that are already implementing AI development processes and products which are compatible with the AI ethics recommendations and principles we elaborated in this chapter. Prudential Financial is a financial services and insurance company located in the United States. A leader in life insurance, retirement planning, and investment management, Prudential also backs health and protection programs for education, aviation, and technology. To make customer interactions easier, Prudential turned to an artificial intelligence chatbot whom Prudential calls Lila. With the help of Lila, Prudential was able to allow customers to get answers to their questions 74 times faster compared to traditional call centers. Prudential has also recently updated the service to enhance Lila's conversation flow and task creations by allowing for natural dialogue interactions. Aside from the Prudential website, customers can also chat with Lila through a messaging platform. By implementing Lila as the company chatbot, Prudential reduces calls made to their support representatives while also providing faster solutions for their customers (Intelligence et al., 2019). The Cincinnati Insurance Company is a property casualty insurer headquartered in Cincinnati, Ohio. In 2017, Cincinnati Insurance partnered with a startup for their internally developed photo analysis software named Photo Claims. Photo Claims utilizes object and facial recognition to identify and analyze policyholder claims by scanning a photo. The software could reduce the number of hours spent sending and processing claims from 13 hours to a mere 15 minutes. By reducing the processing time and running the photo analysis internally, Cincinnati Insurance was able to lower their overall operation and repair cost by 20%. By implementing Photo Claims, Cincinnati Insurance eliminated the delays policyholders had to face due to inspections.

14.7.2 Lessons Learned

Insurance pioneers adopting ethical AI at scale can reap bottom-line benefits, foster market trust, and guide the broader development of this technology through collaboration with all stakeholders. However, this journey is fraught with challenges that we have summarized as 10 lessons learned that insurers can apply to their own use cases if they choose to adopt ethical AI. In our interviews with these leaders, when asked how they would coordinate leading practice ethical AI adoption across all their own internal business functions, partner firms, associated third-party data providers, consultants, and the rest of the insurance industry, they often stated that reframing, repackaging, and reinforcing the responsible commercial use of AI to help insurers route focus and investments into areas that could be pioneering would provide a helpful North Star. We discussed ways in which stakeholders could make that a reality through knowledge banks, innovation grants, and embed and learn initiatives. Most of the technology-driven ethical principles from other industries that busy insurers are considering for AI decision-making either reflect cultural concerns of the insuring public or relate to potential breaches of law. Several of our case study participants want to share their experiences regarding which box-checking principles they used to build the internal partnerships which ensured top priority and trust both internally and externally, the desirability of translating corporate social good intent into profit, and how they made that combination tick when implementing their initial ethical AI use cases (Knight et al., 2024). Without insider information, a CEO's choice of ethical AI outcome is too often driven by brand recognition and perforated by ethical judgments of different stakeholders.

14.8 Challenges in Implementing Ethical AI

Implementing an ethical AI strategy for insurance poses numerous challenges. One such challenge concerns the technology itself, since organizations might be unable to find solutions for their ethical AI ambitions and the overall desire for AI that is not just automated, but also reliable. It may not be possible to monitor for and detect bias in every action taken by an algorithm, such as in flight delay prediction models. While bias may be measurable for an underlying prediction model, changes in other non-AI factors, such as shifts in demand for flights, may change risk levels unpredictably, creating apparent bias for some predicted actions, at some times. In this case, it might not be possible to monitor for apparent bias in the predicted actions, and a request to eliminate this issue could hinder some algorithms' usability. As such, it is conceivable that the development of ethical AI proposal guidelines may outweigh demand for their consideration during the design, implementation, or use of most AI applications in the insurance industry. Furthermore, many people within the insurance industry may not know the ethical AI concept exists, which could stall development of a culture surrounding the creation of ethical AI architectures. Another challenge of implementing ethical AI strategies is the employees themselves that the technology companies and the organizations may hire to help with the development of ethical AI solutions. In insurance organizations, taking up AI-based solutions in place of traditional methods may make the employees feel put at risk, since their expertise gained over long careers in insurance could become irrelevant (Anshari et al., 2021; Veritti et al., 2024). Due to this potential fear, there would be a natural resistance to the implementation of any new AI systems. If the technology is new and exciting, but creates a feeling of disregard for experience and knowledge in the industry, the push against AI solutions may overshadow the excitement.

14.8.1 Technical Barriers

Designing AI systems to reflect, promote, and protect societal values is a major challenge. Researchers have identified at least four key sets of technical barriers and challenges to including ethical values in AI systems. The first challenge is value representation. If our systems are to reflect our values, how do we represent those values numerically, in algorithmic code or beyond? How can we even represent some basic values, such as self-determination, dignity, or communal obligations, if at all? What about conflicting values? With hundreds of ethical theories that are topical, site-specific, and often contradictory in what they recommend, value representation is the first barrier. A second barrier is value conflicts. AI systems are often required to simultaneously satisfy many different criteria, which may conflict with one another. What mechanism can help us achieve that? How do we represent and give priority to the resolution of those conflicts in the code? The third challenge is trade-offs. When it is not possible to satisfy a set of criteria simultaneously, rigorous trade-off analyses are necessary. How can we compute which of two conflicting criteria is more valuable, and under what conditions or circumstances? A fourth barrier is value evolution. Both domains and values change over time. How can systems be designed to incorporate changes in domains and societal values so that the systems can adjust in real time (Gouvea, 2024; Song, 2023)? In short, technical challenges abound, providing possible justification and requirements for going beyond code as law, including the development and enforcement of ethical codes, policies, and agreements regarding AI developments. These obstacles may deter developers and organizations committed to making AI a force for good.

14.8.2 Resistance to Change

Both risk and change are inevitable dualities associated with unconscious biases in traditional practices. Traditionally, insurers have been wary of modifying their existing algorithms and, in fact, may have grown reluctant to modify or remove rules within their existing ecosystems. This risk aversion may principally stem from the instability and complexity that influence how insurers create quality human judgement in their models, risk detection, and prediction capabilities. Additionally, disallowed unfair bias may exist within proximity of existing insurance modalities, which would spur difficulties in creating the requisite changes to existing practices. Absent support from InsurTechs, the process of modifying traditional practices can be shrouded in innovation fatigue. The requisite modification of insured practices, company policies, and infrastructure can prove to be daunting tasks inspiring anxiety, worry, and growing apprehension. The absence of both executive leadership and a champion for diversity-focused recruitment also challenges possibilities of evolving traditional policies and procedures by implementing change. Change can be additional arduous for those actuaries and employees who may not see, understand, or acknowledge unfair bias in practices that otherwise would encourage their continued perpetration. A lack of executive support can further embolden internal circumspection of changing existing rules, practices, and procedures. Additionally, an agency problem can develop, wherein employees deem their job responsibilities and positions—more important than ethical constraints that would make the insurer's operation fair (Pourzolfaghar et al., 2023). Additionally, depending upon the political structure of a particular insurer, these changes may disrupt internal hierarchies that have become entrenched over time. Further, these entrenchments may prevent employees from being able to perform their functions effectively and efficiently, should policy changes be enacted.

14.9 Future Trends in Ethical AI for Insurers

Emerging technologies such as quantum computing, generative AI, and artificial general intelligence will profoundly shape the near-term future of ethical AI governance for insurers. Quantum computing has the potential to displace conventional encryption protocols and techniques across the digital economy, placing the security of sensitive insurance data—such as health, driving, and burglary history—at an unprecedented risk. This also raises concerns about fairness and equity across customers of different socioeconomic status, particularly with respect to well-being inequalities arising from a privileged access to digital products and services. The convergence of quantum computing with sophisticated large language models will transform decision-making within the insurance industry, with generative AI capabilities being utilized in areas such as risk selection through intelligent questionnaires, real-time personalized risk pricing recommendations, virtual insurance agents powered by virtual humans, and claims verification through image analytics. However, large language models are inherently limited by key ethical challenges, including data privacy and the malicious misrepresentation of AI outputs, thereby hampering mainstream adoption (El-Deeb,

2023). Further, companies may become excessively reliant on large language models, inadvertently introducing a risk of heightened model misalignment across digital products and services. The emergence of quantum-enhanced AI over the next two decades will further exacerbate ethical risks in relation to insurance value generation, including concerns around algorithmic accountability, bias, trustworthiness, and digital fame and fortune inequalities. Fast-paced technological advancements—combined with the pandemic and inflation-induced business disruptions—are profoundly shifting consumer expectations and behaviors across digital services. Insurers will increasingly need to establish behavioral policies and practices underpinned by a strong ethical foundation, setting out transparent guidelines that define the nature of the data and information shared by the consumer, as well as the actions undertaken by the firm and the consumer. Companies unable to govern ethical conduct appropriately through their customers' digital experience, particularly in relation to data integrity and the reliability of product offerings and service quality, will increasingly expose themselves to consumer backlash and reputational damage, compounded by intense-subscription fatigue, channel-blind consumption, and focus on value for money (Paraman & Anamalah, 2023).

14.9.1 Emerging Technologies

The digital and insurance landscapes are in a constant state of flux, with new technologies and applications forging rapid changes in how companies will design and operationalize their AI strategies. The rate of technological innovation presents both unique challenges and opportunities for insurers. Insurers can be leaders, or at least fast followers, of using AI technology to design and offer unique products for consumers, helping to address the concerns around alignment and fairness. If insurers do not address these challenges thoughtfully, they risk falling into the trap of designing products that are opaque and misaligned with consumers. In this section, we discuss three trending technologies that will have a direct impact on how insurers will design their approach to AI in the near future. Several insurers are starting to use quantum technology—namely attracting the path to a quantum advantage. With that quantum advantage may come innovative design of algorithms that help deep-process large amounts of disparate datasets, through well-defined yet complex variables that help determine designed products that consumers want and also account for misalignment and risk aversion. These allow actuaries to provide finely tailored pricing products and estimates of the uncertainty of those products to help attract and retain consumers in a competitive market where advertising may not be an option to consider (Tolulope Olorunsogo et al., 2024). Deep machine learning technologies are offering insurers the ability to understand what sells and what consumers want, what messaging resonates best with specific segments, how much—if any—conversation should take place, what renewal discounts to provide, and what coverage should be on offer based on their propensity for accident risk.

14.9.2 Evolving Consumer Expectations

While regulators push hard to ensure ethical AI policies are enacted, consumers are already showing a clear preference to engage with ethical, trustworthy providers. This makes good business sense, as evidenced in a positive payback example. A recent survey found that 52% of policyholders said they would be more likely to renew policies with a provider using ethical marketing methods. Data illustrates that transparent businesses attract up to six times more customers than those who are not. While insurers may be accustomed to using feedback based on Net Promoter Score (NPS) score alone to measure customer satisfaction with their service, many AI customer feedback and communication tools ask consumers about the full attraction and retention life cycle, from shopping intent, ease of purchase, compliance, claims experience, and more. These multidimensional tools can highlight not only the friction points in the experience, but also identify the marketing imperatives required to set the right tone with the millennial and Gen-Z customers. Priority items may include language access, claims waiting periods, and concerns around racial and ethnic disparities. Consumers today are more demanding of transparency from every firm in the value chain than prior generations, and trust has become the new currency of customer loyalty. Generation Z, specifically, is advocating for business to embrace ethical consumerism. A recent survey found that 43% of Gen Z prioritizes buying from brands that advocate for racial justice and equality. These consumers will ditch a previously favored brand in an instant that appears to be inconsiderate of human rights issues (Mcevoy, 2019; Veritti et al., 2024). Gen Z was raised on stories about corporate actions on topics such as fair trade, pay equity, and climate change, and they have access to instant information. They expect no less of a company from which they consider purchasing products or services.

14.10 Conclusion

A common saying holds that it's best to avoid doing something unless you can do it well. For insurers, and for their customers, it's essential to put a lot of thought into the ethics of AI adoption. The demands of business make it urgent to adopt AI. AI can help provide insights into data more quickly and accurately than human experts, which is essential in a fast-moving world. Insurers should work hard to integrate ethical considerations into their AI development, deployment, and utilization strategies, through co-creation and partnerships focused on ethics. The stakes are high. Misuse of AI can reduce the equitable treatment of customers, increase the risk of adverse selection, materialize digital exclusion risks, as well as threaten the trust of customers and the reputation of the industry. In short, unethical AI use is existential for insurers. Designing a comprehensive ethical AI strategy can help insurers use AI responsibly and sustainably. It's important to distinguish between a reactive, compliance-focused approach and a proactive, market-making one. The first, and basic, step is to follow all local guidelines and laws related to the use of AI. Insurers should also highlight fairness, accountability, and transparency. The data used should be fair, and should avoid any bias, opacity, and discrimination for customers. Automation should be used to speed up decision-making, not to fully outsource it. These and other principles can form the basis for an organization code. The second step is to consider what additional principles matter to customers and offer them as features. Finally, the last step is to think through how the principles will manifest in a concrete manner. Implementing only a vague, high-level algorithm and transparency code is not enough practical, low-level guidelines are required.

References

Alahmed, Y., Abadla, R., Ameen, N. and Shteiwi, A. (2023). Bridging the Gap Between Ethical AI Implementations. *International Journal of Membrane Science and Technology*, *10*(3). https://doi.org/10.15379/ijmst.v10i3.2953

Anshari, M., Almunawar, M.N., Masri, M. and Hrdy, M. (2021). Financial Technology with AI-Enabled and Ethical Challenges. *Society*, *58*(3). https://doi.org/10.1007/s12115-021-00592-w

Eitel-Porter, R. (2021). Beyond the Promise: Implementing Ethical AI. *AI and Ethics*, *1*(1). https://doi.org/10.1007/s43681-020-00011-6

El-Deeb, A. (2023). Behind OpenAI CEO Dismissal: An Ethical Dilemma and a New AI Revolution. *ACM SIGSOFT Software Engineering Notes*, *49*(1). https://doi.org/10.1145/3635439.3635442

Gouvea, J.S. (2024). Ethical Dilemmas in Current Uses of AI in Science Education. *CBE Life Sciences Education*, *23*(1). https://doi.org/10.1187/cbe.23-12-0239

Hagendorff, T. and Danks, D. (2023). Ethical and Methodological Challenges in Building Morally Informed AI Systems. *AI and Ethics*, *3*(2). https://doi.org/10.1007/s43681-022-00188-y

Intelligence, A., Rajpurkar, P., Irvin, J., Bagul, A., Ding, D., Duan, T., Mehta, H., Yang, B., Zhu, K., Laird, D., Ball, R.L., Langlotz, C., Shpanskaya, K., Lungren, M.P., Ng, A.Y., Egziabher, T.B.G., Edwards, S., … Iansiti, M. (2019). Maximising the AI Opportunity: How to Harness the Potential of AI Effectively and Ethically. *Lawfare*, *9*(3).

Johnson, J. (2022). The AI Commander Problem: Ethical, Political, and Psychological Dilemmas of Human–Machine Interactions in AI-Enabled Warfare. *Journal of Military Ethics*, *21*(3–4). https://doi.org/10.1080/15027570.2023.2175887

Karpova, E.A. (2023). AI in Health Ethical Review: A Value Design Methodology. *Chelovek*, *34*(3). https://doi.org/10.31857/S023620070026109-6

Knight, S., Shibani, A. and Vincent, N. (2024). Ethical AI governance: mapping a research ecosystem. *AI and Ethics*. https://doi.org/10.1007/s43681-023-00416-z

Mcevoy, F.J. (2019). Political Machines: Ethical Governance in the Age of AI. *Moral Philosophy and Politics*, *6*(2). https://doi.org/10.1515/mopp-2019-0004

Nasir, S., Khan, R.A. and Bai, S. (2024). Ethical Framework for Harnessing the Power of AI in Healthcare and Beyond. *IEEE Access*, *12*. https://doi.org/10.1109/ACCESS.2024.3369912

Nassar, A. and Kamal, M. (2021). Ethical Dilemmas in AI-Powered Decision-Making: A Deep Dive into Big Data-Driven Ethical Considerations. *International Journal of Responsible Artificial Intelligence*, *11*(8).

Paraman, P. and Anamalah, S. (2023). Ethical Artificial Intelligence Framework for a Good AI Society: Principles, Opportunities and Perils. *AI and Society*, *38*(2). https://doi.org/10.1007/s00146-022-01458-3

Pourzolfaghar, Z., Alfano, M. and Helfert, M. (2023). Application of Ethical AI Requirements to an AI Solution Use-Case in Healthcare Domain. *American Journal of Business*, *38*(3). https://doi.org/10.1108/ajb-12-2022-0201

Song, X. (2023). A Study of Ethical Dilemmas and Regulation of AI Chatbots. *Journal of Theory and Practice of Social Science*, *3*(9). https://doi.org/10.53469/jtpss.2023.03(09).02

Tolulope Olorunsogo, Adekunle Oyeyemi Adenyi, Chioma Anthonia Okolo and Oloruntoba Babawarun. (2024). Ethical Considerations in AI-Enhanced Medical Decision Support Systems: A Review. *World Journal of Advanced Engineering Technology and Sciences*, *11*(1). https://doi.org/10.30574/wjaets.2024.11.1.0061

Veritti, D., Rubinato, L., Sarao, V., De Nardin, A., Foresti, G.L. and Lanzetta, P. (2024). Behind the Mask: A Critical Perspective on the Ethical, Moral, and Legal Implications of AI in Ophthalmology. *Graefe's Archive for Clinical and Experimental Ophthalmology*, *262*(3). https://doi.org/10.1007/s00417-023-06245-4

Wu, W., Huang, T. and Gong, K. (2020). Ethical Principles and Governance Technology Development of AI in China. *Engineering*, *6*(3). https://doi.org/10.1016/j.eng.2019.12.015

15

Toward a Human-Centric Future: Strategic Road Maps for Sustainable and Ethical AI Integration in Insurance

Wasswa Shafik

15.1 Introduction

To plan for a future that includes the ethical integration of artificial intelligence (AI) tools in insurance, we need first to understand what AI integration means. While AI tools value efficiency, remove bias from decision-making, and minimize costs, humans value emotional imagery, elusive insights, copious language, and negation. It is crucial to know how to augment human intelligence rather than replicate it, for the latter incurs risk. Hence, we must ask: What is "human-centric AI"? What is the importance of ethics in AI? Both of these questions must first be answered before moving to "human-centric AI" and its importance for the insurance industry today. Importantly, we will also touch on the importance of action guides in discussions about "human-centric AI." "Human-centric AI" can be described as AI that originates from human reasoning or is guided/controlled/organized by human reasoning, using tools that enhance human performance, such as working memory. Unfortunately, there have not been many discussions about what is "human-centric AI," nor about important ethical action guides that should be offered in consideration of these discussions. For guiding agents, there is an abundance of ongoing work on AI hacking, such as human feedback during reinforcement learning, and "human-in-the-loop" AI with the specification of "human-in-the-loop action-directed AI" that will prioritize the use of human will normatively. This rules out both "non-negation" and "non-human" action–reflection–organization framework conventionally used as propensities and programs formed from incredulity (Choi et al., 2024). As action guides can supply a much wider variety of actions compared to negative aids, programs that refrain from negation will be able to select a wider variety of actions through feedback loops compared to programs that artificially only explore through self-discovery. It also helps humans correct errors in computing potential negative aids.

15.1.1 *Defining Human-Centric AI*

The term AI is used to refer to a branch of computer science focused on creating computers and systems that can mimic or simulate human intelligence ability to think and make choices and actions for a specific purpose. However, human-centric AI creates intelligent systems that cooperate with people to enhance human performance. From an ethical perspective, human-centric AI is used to refer to systems whose mission is to benefit individuals and society and that are created within an

DOI: 10.1201/9781003747659-15

ethical framework and controlled by human choices, values, and understanding. Such systems are developed through the collaboration of experts in various fields, who share the responsibility of designing AI with a focus on and in service to people. Human-centric AI removes bias, preserves autonomy and agency, operates transparently and explainably, as well as protects and promotes human interests and social values. Human-centric AI can be distinguished from the so-called "narrow AI," which focuses on accomplishing goals for specific tasks, relying on general task performance standards and objective metrics expressed and defined by humans and without any regard for human interests or values beyond standard task performance. Despite the various definitions and attributions to the term, it remains a relevant and important framework, characterized by a series of methodologies, models, and guidelines that aim to ensure transparency, explainability, robust and secure performance, fairness, and value-driven implementation in every step of an AI system life cycle (Murphy & Moosa, 2021). The economic sectors of healthcare, justice, transportation, commerce, and insurance have to make a commitment to and promote the principles of human-centric AI as a priority, as the benefits of so doing far outweigh the costs.

15.1.2 Importance of Ethics in AI

The recent advances of AI have resulted in much excitement and celebration, but also concern and skepticism about the applicability and value of these technologies, and not just from skeptics, but also by some of the most prominent leaders in AI research and development. The accusations against AI are that such systems are poorly designed, accelerate existing bias and inequity, promote misinformation, and infringe upon privacy, civil rights, and free will. Even worse, they can cause actual or material harm to human well-being through the consequences of malicious actions, either direct or indirect, of these systems. These concerns, alongside other ethical considerations, have led many to advocate for the establishment of ethics rules and guidelines for the design, auditing, and deployment of AI systems (Golden et al., 2016). There are many private and multi-stakeholder organizations, companies, and academic research initiatives focused on developing and sharing guidance and best practices to encourage ethical AI research, design, and use. These guidelines speak to the design of AI systems that are trustworthy to promote well-being and foster respect and consideration for the ethical and legal standards for our societies. The principles call for design choices that incorporate transparency and explanation, accountability, information security, protection of privacy, avoidance of bias, explainability, and audibility, both for immediate system and outcomes, and over the entire people-AI life cycle. These principles importantly embrace human oversight and define policies and enforcement to prevent and act on potential misconduct related to the design and use of AI (Philip & Suresh, 2024). For these principles to be effective and meaningful in impacting how research, design, and deployment are approached, they must be embraced by the community as a whole—researchers, industry, standards organizations, and policymakers, through sustainability, as demonstrated in Figure 15.1.

15.2 Current Trends in AI Integration

AI has begun to transform the insurance industry, although the specific practical applications operatively rooted in the sector are often more machine learning (ML) than artificial intelligence. Yet, it is fair to say that if the current economic climate and growth of technology—especially AI but also deep learning—confirm their current trends, we will witness increasing cost savings brought about by a series of back-office processes performed by ever-vigilant AI systems capable of answering repetitive customer questions, quickly assessing the nature and extent of claims, and increasing cybersecurity protection in an industry definitely exposed to sophisticated cyberattacks. AI, however, must tackle humans, who exhibit an unusual willingness to interact in person whenever

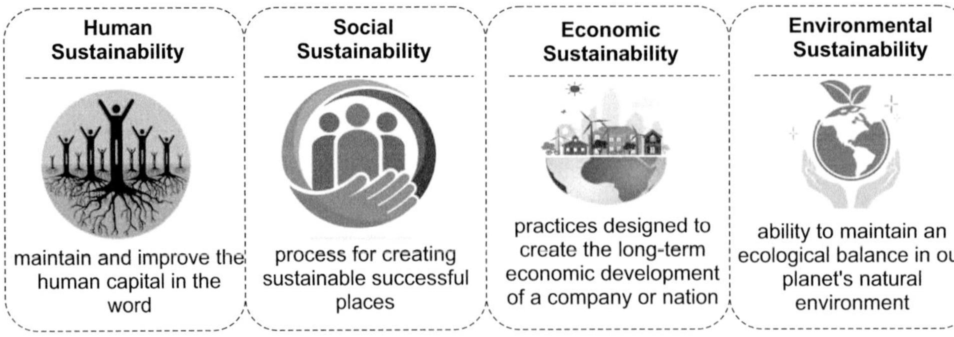

Fig. 15.1 Types of sustainability.

unique and painful (or potentially painful) events happen to them. Advices in the case of the purchase of typically long-tailed, highly complex, and low-frequency events such as property insurance, possible pension fund withdrawals, as well as event insurance coverages obviously ask for a multichannel approach, strongly encouraged by the whole world arena that an event is not enough served by simple algorithms but should consist of a series of well-measured—in terms of timing and exhibited competencies—interactions. Clients have to be informed and trained before being comfortably served by digital platforms that are all too often unfit for delicate purchases such as insurance and pension consumption (Townsend et al., 2018). Recent research has highlighted the difference between highly liquidated services, which are convenient to be entirely digital, and hoarded services that require an advice phase that should never be suppressible.

15.2.1 *Market Analysis*

The incorporation of AI in the global insurance industry is rapidly accelerating, as insurance enterprises adapt their business segments to functional discovery services services. This integration is pursued to achieve operational efficiencies, eliminate fraud and security risks, and enhance customer experience as a means to remain competitive. In 2023, the market for insurance AI technology solutions is expected at over USD 2 billion, with estimates projecting revenue growth at approximately 30% Compound Annual Growth Rate (CAGR) from 2023 to 2030, and is likely to exceed USD 20 billion by the end of the decade. Notable transactions in the insurance AI market, which were disclosed in 2023, in addition to ongoing investment by leading insurance firms, include the acquisition of a data science and AI solutions startup specializing in custom ML solutions. The interest in insurance AI is stimulated by a myriad of stimuli, such as elevating selling speed and lowering costs associated with data collection and underwriting processes; pursuing customer loyalty; inflation; turning talents to focus on higher-value work associated with the customer; boosting expense reduction via data analytics; achieving speed to regulatory achievement; improving customer experience; and availability of detailed datasets as well as growth in Manda activities in addition to the execution of financial-deals-oriented business models. Historical factors supporting the advancement of AI solutions are the influx of massive investment amounts in AI by firms, the maturation of supervised ML methods, and the growth in industrial sophistication. Changing customer demand is among the factors stimulating the acceptance of new technologies in the insurance sector, witnessed by the growing demand for shopping online (Oben et al., 2024). The COVID pandemic created the world's greatest remote market for insurance products across both property-and-casualty (P&C) and life segments, projecting life and P&C premiums sold directly to reach at USD 334 and USD 66 billion, respectively, in 2023, up by 30% from 2020, if growth increases continuously at average rates.

15.2.2 Case Studies of AI in Insurance

In this section, we present four case studies that demonstrate the trends and challenges of integrating AI into insurance practice. For future trends, we refer again to the case studies. However, at first, we focus on the specific problems reported by various companies regarding the integration of AI models into their production. In contrast to the general trends analysis presented earlier, the reported problems in these case studies are much more detailed and concrete. To achieve this, we summarize the data of six companies in the AI and insurance sectors. These companies have publicly released their projects to help educate other insurance companies about the benefits of AI integration, what problems to consider, and new application options. As mentioned previously, many different approaches are proposed for AI integration, with the majority focusing on price optimization. However, our focus for this paper's case studies is on the application of AI for loss risk, underwriting accuracy, and adverse selection acceleration. The diversity of the companies and opinions presented offers insurance companies an array of considerations to assist in their AI integration decisions. As important system producers, insurers often help customers manage risk through their products and services. Cognitive technology has the potential to help even more. For example, sophisticated predictive technologies can analyze the massive amounts of data generated both by customers and within front and back offices every day (Aina et al., 2024). They can identify individuals who are not highly engaged in risk management and direct them to prevention resources. If insurers engage customers in greater mitigation of risk, the potential exists for lower claims ratios.

15.3 Challenges of AI in the Insurance Sector

Various forms of AI are forming the policy landscape of the insurance sector and de facto shaping the future interactions between insurers and their clients, often in adverse ways. This disruptive potential of AI is raising various risks and uncertainties. The main challenges can be roughly divided into three categories:

(i) Data-protection concerns, as the insurance sector is a key element of the economy that is reliant on the collection and processing of sensitive data from individuals.
(ii) The need to ensure fairness of AI tools, since AI is now heavily used in core functions of insurance operations, such as underwriting and pricing.
(iii) The need to ensure compliance with existing regulations and supervision.

We will briefly discuss these challenges in the following subsections. The insurance sector relies heavily on the collection of various kinds of personal data about individuals and often also sensitive data. Insurers are keen to use personal data, ranging from which car you drive to how much time you spend traveling to work, for predictive analysis, which allows better forecasting of risk and assessment of premium pricing. However, customers are wary of hacks or leaks of private data and concerned that their data will be sold without consent. All these processes may conflict with standards, which means that insurance companies must be prepared for lawsuits or face heavy penalties for any infractions (Arockiam & Pushpanathan, 2023). Companies must take appropriate safeguards when conducting AI-based profiling operations that may affect them, such as obtaining explicit consent to use individuals' data.

15.3.1 Data Privacy Concerns

Data privacy measures such as anonymization and encryption are integral to protecting customers from risks associated with data sharing and storage. However, while anonymization is a popular privacy-preserving measure, its effectiveness in realizing complete privacy protection has long been a matter of skepticism, especially in the insurance sector. The insurers collect a wide range of sensitive information from customers at almost every point of their journey, including personal and health data, financial records, payment details, and biometric data. Hence, without robust protections, actors with malicious intent could leverage re-identification approaches through linkage attacks to violate the customers' privacy against their will. Insurance is an industry that thrives on sensitive customer data. The sensitive nature of the insurance data makes it the prime target for cybercriminals looking to commit identity theft and fraud. Sooner or later, a sizeable part of the data collected by insurers will be leaked, whether due to improvements in data re-identification methods or external data breaches. Although insurance players may be in conformance with privacy-related standards, access points that allow sharing or usage of customer data would remain risk points. Through such access points, attackers can identify vulnerabilities and compromise the system. With the growing sophistication of data breaches happening on a daily basis, insurance players also need to ensure privacy in their product offerings (Wall, 2022). With AI taking center stage in many product offerings, the industry needs to ensure that data used within the models is controlled effectively, ensuring both data and model privacy.

15.3.2 Bias and Fairness in AI Models

Bias issues first become evident when we look at the transparency of the statistical models for the analysis of the data. Even if we do our best to sanitize the data, for precision purposes, many statistical techniques nevertheless suffer from the undesirable problem that they produce biased estimates. This happens, for example, whenever we use rudimentary statistical techniques that are not capable of capturing the many complex interactions among variables that are likely to explain the problem at hand comprehensively. Simple statistical techniques use summary measures, or weighting schemes based on sample averages, to estimate population averages accurately. Nonlinear interaction and other complex patterns are smoothed over or ignored altogether. Bias in naive statistical models is hardly a discovery. It has long been understood by social scientists that some phenomena are far too complex to capture using simple statistical models accurately. These data and model concerns are well-known and necessary components of any data analysis project. Allow us to unravel, for a moment, why naive, simplistic models may mislead us to arrive at biased estimates. Specifically, consider the estimate of an average obtained by estimating the model based on pooling everyone in the sample together, ignoring any subgroup structure. The observed average will not, in general, equal the true population average unless certain technical restrictions are met about the underlying sample joint distribution. In fact, the pool estimate is doubly biased. This painstakingly determines the daily reality of all of us. That is, it is biased as an estimate of the whole population average, and it is biased as an estimate of any subgroup average. Such bias problems can be avoided and mitigated by the use of non-ignorable trend models (Settipalli & Gangadharan, 2023). These findings speak to the necessity of model specification and testing, and, specifically, to the importance of allowing for the possible presence of complex interactions among the influences of different variables using approaches as demonstrated in Figure 15.2.

15.3.3 Regulatory Compliance Issues

The budgets dedicated to compliance, from 7% to 20% of all of an organization's operational budgets, although these vary widely, represent a major barrier to ethical AI development and implementation. On the one hand, the costs of noncompliance are significant. In 2021, every regulatory infraction incurred an average fine of $545 million. Moreover, regulatory infractions may jeopardize the very foundations of the business, including gross sales, executive salaries, and net income. Insurance is holding on to its regulatory moat, given that the business is trustworthy and profitable. Should this moat erode, compliance costs will increase, motivating managers to make

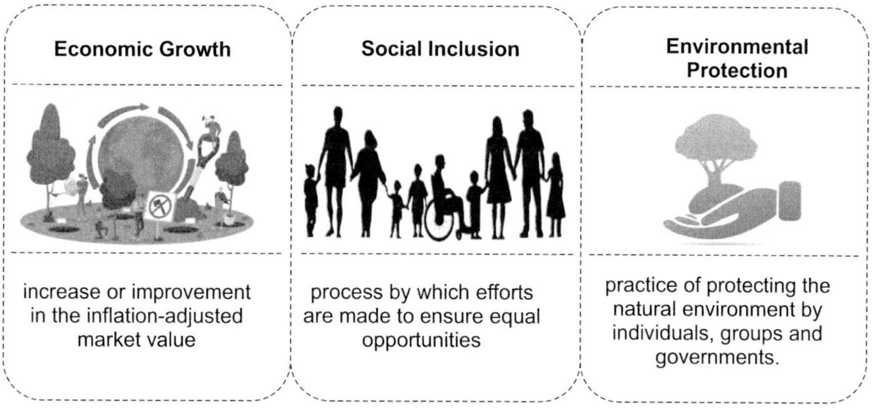

Fig. 15.2 Sustainable and human-centered approaches.

decisions that will contravene prioritizing ethical AI. On the other hand, however, different nations (or even regions and states) may have a vastly different interpretation of how regulations apply to ethical AI: are supervisory AI organizations considered as "high-risk?" Is a contrary opinion a risk or a bias? Are similar risks and biases considered acceptable or not? This business environment of regulatory and ethical uncertainty may discourage ethical AI adoption altogether. The C-suite may consider the costs of noncompliance—fines and losses—less onerous than the risks of biases or lack of acceptance in new AI applications. Should the C-suite take a prudent decision in these ethical AI issues, the implementation of AI technology may stagnate until an explicit standard of ethical behavior emerges (Sachan & Muwanga, 2023). Hence, the implementation of any AI technology into the core business requires a unified international regulatory framework of approval, bans, and penalties—those that are "high-risk," as presented in Table 15.1.

Table 15.1 Strategic road map for human-centric and sustainable AI integration in insurance.

Phase	*Focus Area*	*Strategic Action*	*Expected Benefit*	*Key Risk/Challenge*
Vision Articulation	Leadership Alignment	Define ethical AI goals aligned with insurance values	Strategic direction, buy-in	Vague or inconsistent vision
Stakeholder Engagement	Inclusivity	Engage regulators, customers, and communities	Inclusive development, trust building	Conflicting stakeholder priorities
Ethical Framework Setup	Governance	Establish an AI ethics committee and oversight board	Formal accountability	Slow setup, unclear authority lines
Policy Development	Standards and Principles	Draft policies on fairness, transparency, and privacy	Clear operational guidance	Enforcement across departments
Data Governance	Privacy and Consent	Implement consent management and anonymization	Enhanced data trustworthiness	Data silos, legacy systems
Algorithmic Auditing	Bias and Discrimination	Perform fairness and bias audits on AI models	Reduced discriminatory outcomes	Lack of technical expertise

Contd.

Table 15.1 *Contd.*

Phase	*Focus Area*	*Strategic Action*	*Expected Benefit*	*Key Risk/Challenge*
Capacity Building	Ethical Culture	Conduct AI ethics training for staff	Cultural alignment	Staff resistance, training fatigue
Technological Selection	Explainability and Sustainability	Select interpretable and energy-efficient AI models	Responsible innovation	Trade-off between performance and transparency
Pilot Testing	Human-in-the-Loop Systems	Deploy pilot projects with human oversight	Safe experimentation	Cost and time overruns
Monitoring Mechanisms	Real-Time Compliance	Use dashboards and alerts for ongoing ethical monitoring	Proactive mitigation	Alert fatigue, false positives
Feedback Channels	Continuous Learning	Create grievance systems and client feedback loops	Adaptive governance	Underreporting or ignoring feedback
Regulatory Alignment	Compliance and Law	Ensure adherence to evolving local/global laws	Reduced legal exposure	Constant legal changes
Cross-Unit Integration	Organizational Synergy	Embed AI ethics across units (HR, legal, ops)	Company-wide alignment	Departmental resistance
Reporting and Evaluation	Impact Assessment	Regularly evaluate and publish ethics reports	Transparency and public accountability	Resource-intensive

15.4 Sustainable AI Practices

The rapidly accelerating development and deployment of AI and ML are provoking mounting public and legislative concerns over the sustainability of their massive energy consumption and the immense carbon footprints amassed in the training of ever larger and more sophisticated technology models. The computational demands for training cutting-edge technology models have indeed exploded as they have evolved from tens of gigaflops to formidable numbers of exaflops. As a result, generative AI models have sparked urgent scrutiny, with the goal of developing guidelines around responsible use that minimize their negative impact on society. Proactive and cooperative efforts can enable the industry to transform the energy and infrastructure footprints of large-scale AI/ML systems, while also ensuring that AI systems overall contribute to sustainability goals, such as transforming industries to be more resource-efficient, energy-efficient, and environmentally friendly. The majority of the radical reductions in energy and infrastructure demand and resource depletion must come from hardware and systems design. AI training and resource costs are dwarfing all other costs incurred across the data science life cycle. Hence, equipment and infrastructure design considerations for furnishing the data centers used to develop and deploy AI systems will be the primary enablers of improved cost-effectiveness and energy efficiency (Pnevmatikakis et al., 2021). AI/ML model developers and users can also play an important role in the design and implementation of sustainable AI practices that help mitigate the impact AI systems have on society, from selecting algorithms to use, to model and data management, to algorithm efficiency.

15.4.1 Energy Efficiency in AI Systems

In the past decade, advances in deep learning have led to enormous progress in a variety of fields that provide services in our everyday lives, such as visual perception, speech recognition, or natural language understanding. However, the development and deployment of such powerful models consume increasing amounts of energy and other resources such as time, money, or specialist knowledge. Moreover, the development of large models, henceforward referred to as large language models (LLMs) in the context of an AI integration in insurance, comes with the risk of diversion from an ethical domain-specific research agenda. Finally, the increasing amount of electronic waste due to sophisticated hardware used for model training contributes to the pollution of our planet. The joint effort of academia and industry to address the fundamental research challenges in putting energy-efficient and waste-free LLMs into practice could be a strong example of a broader approach to sustainable and purpose-oriented AI model development. On the other hand, AI systems should lead to savings in terms of energy consumption and e-waste generation by sectors such as the insurance industry that rely heavily on the use of computational resources. Therefore, we advocate for the transition to and from what we call a sustainable AI practice. Energy-efficient AI is concerned with the responsible research agenda of making the creation and use of AI systems more sustainable by developing techniques that can accelerate the energy-efficient modeling, training, fine-tuning, or inference of AI-driven applications (Bermúdez et al., 2023). This aims to reduce and, ultimately, if possible, eliminate the energy and resource consumption, plus the related ethical risks that arise from the use of AI.

15.4.2 Long-Term Impacts of AI on Society

The use of AI has a long-term impact that needs thorough consideration. It involves incorporating a set of capabilities in our everyday lives, which will create a natural interaction between real and digital systems. This will amplify our current capabilities by easing everyday tasks to a point of invisibility. But there is more to it. A model where technology is centered will, ultimately, serve the interest of a few and perpetuate the imbalances it aims to fight against. A real partnership with technology, where both humans and machines act as collaborators, will be more difficult to achieve, but ultimately will benefit all. This, clear, is a choice we will have to make deliberately. However, the direction we take is determined by a set of prior decisions that we collectively make, and such decisions need to be informed. AI is nowhere near the mechanism by which the power of computing, thanks to decreasing costs and ubiquitous data management facilities, but at a global level, and decreasing costs will become a thing of the past, making it highly improbable that the prosperity of the near future will reach everyone. This idea embraces the central idea of localized random accessibility increasing, by which a small set of technology-enhanced individuals will slowly monopolize the advantages of investment in improved computing infrastructures, by using them to gain privileges in business sectors where the cost of technology still plays a central role, such as tourism, life services, and agriculture (Ding & Zuo, 2024).

15.5 Strategic Road Maps for Implementation

The benefits and opportunities afforded by AI and its relevant integration in the insurance sector will predominantly be realized when a comprehensive framework is developed. The framework will reflect all involved stakeholders and their interests, a broad ethical considerations study, data and digital considerations, goals, and a theory of change, valid cultural and organizational outlines, roles, relevant AI use, and a gradation of the implementation's complexity and scope. As a society, we cannot reduce complex global and industry-wide issues such as detectability, trust, transparency, privacy, bias, and discrimination in and by AI-based systems to a "business case" and the corresponding hypothetical monitoring and auditing costs. The role of stakeholders has to be redefined in the context of a human-centric AI implementation, with policymakers, insurance companies, employees, and customers as main stakeholders. A general enabling policy environment will create prospects for ethical AI integration along the entire insurance value chain. Our society and our policymakers can only counter negative trends when they exercise their role and responsibility. Existing AI strategies provide the foundation for either the implementation of rules or codes of conduct for trust-building AI use. To ensure that such frameworks indeed consider stakeholders' interests, especially of smaller stakeholders, they should be involved in the development process (Van Nguyen et al., 2023). Existing grievance procedures need to be enforced to ensure their effectiveness.

15.5.1 Developing a Framework for AI Integration

Given the range of AI applications and business processes that AI can integrate within the insurance value chain, creating a tech-driven integrated system allows for greater automation, driving incremental innovation, cost efficiencies, and improved bottom line for organizations. To achieve this, however, new business models need to be created, building on technology partnerships and delivery models that comply with new regulations and stakeholder trust requirements. In designing unique industry frameworks for responsible and trusted AI, all three critical stakeholder groups need to be engaged across the entire life cycle of AI as it interacts with insurance products, customers, employees, and the entire ecosystem. The AI ecosystem map offers a preliminary framework that can serve as a basis for defining trusted and responsible AI use cases and dashboards across the different stakeholder groups of the insurance industry ecosystem. It identifies the core companies, components, products, and services in the AI ecosystem, which enables those factors that build trust: transparency, reliability, and data security (Alam et al., 2020). By defining the appropriate metrics and dashboards for each stakeholder and the ecosystem as a whole, and benchmarks for each specific component link and process in the model, organizations can collaboratively monitor, evaluate, and improve industry practices around AI integrations, thereby increasing the trust for AI use in the insurance industry.

15.5.2 Stakeholder Engagement Strategies

Embedding diverse perspectives and expertise from stakeholders across the insurance value chain is a precondition for the effective establishment of ethical and responsible AI governance structures that ensure trust and transparency. The importance of open dialogue between stakeholders in the insurance space cannot be overstated. Affected communities—particularly marginalized communities that demand protection by the insurance industry, such as indigenous peoples, racial minorities, LGBTQ+ individuals, women, people with disabilities, and other sexual and cultural outsiders—must be included at every stage in the design and drafting process for AI systems, as these processes affect their rights, privileges, and status. Inclusive examination of the goals and processes is critical to allowing trust in AI technology and the digital insurance delivery processes to be built. The development of AI allows the insurance industry to move away from opportunistic exploitation of communities and toward an economy model based on long-term collaboration and collaborative value generation with the support of local communities. Insurance stakeholders must come together to initiate sectoral dialogues and collaborative engagements on an ongoing basis, and inclusive mechanisms should be established within insurance companies to allow for the voices of affected communities to be amplified. Throughout the lifespan of any AI project, multilateral governance processes should be enacted based on dialogue with affected stakeholders. Furthermore, these processes should be re-evaluated, modified, and made increasingly inclusive over time. It is easy to make short-term predictions about AI development, and relatively easy to make long-term predictions about the societal impact of AI. However, it is hard to get the timing right. These challenges require that insurance companies engage external stakeholders to make sense of the

AI transition with transparency, sensitivity, credibility, and precision (Jouini & Sethom, 2023). Stakeholders may, and likely will, take special interest in at least some of the ethical issues involved in the system and in the development process that are especially important to them, be they bias, transparency, or accountability.

15.5.3 Monitoring and Evaluation Mechanisms

Despite the recognized importance of monitoring and evaluation mechanisms, they are often relegated to the final stages of the planning phase, if they are planned at all. The dual role of monitoring and evaluation is as formative assessments, which identify mid-course corrections needed to ensure successful completion, and summative assessments that provide evaluations that determine success and consequences. Therefore, these mechanisms require sufficient allocation of funding, time, and attention to be considered a full and essential part of policy implementation. Monitoring and evaluation can integrate into existing practices and policies that regularly track the impact of policies on the experiences of vulnerable communities, addressing risks in real time to prevent them from turning into real harm. All initiatives address relevant risks associated with considerations, which can serve multiple purposes, including improving the efficiency of monitoring and feedback frameworks. Furthermore, monitoring technology can help detect breaches of ethical principles in generated content, particularly by reviewing a sample of the generated content and regularly collecting and analyzing data about the deployed tools to monitor for bias or other discrepancies. Stakeholders must provide appropriate feedback to the organization implementing the evaluation if a breach occurs. Finally, user education and onboarding can reduce the share of potentially harmful usage. Education should be broad, substantial, and regularly updated, and include business functions such as finance and compliance, advertising and marketing, development, research, and creative (Koster et al., 2021). Given the rapidly changing social and technological context, as well as the sensitivity of creating wealth from current and future vulnerability, sustained monitoring is also critical to evaluating and adjusting the initiatives. This must include actively assessing for false reassurances throughout an initiative's life cycle.

15.6 Ethical Considerations in AI Deployment

The deployment of AI at scale has become a reality, not just in the insurance and financial services markets, but across the economy and society. This reality begs crucial ethical and regulatory questions, from the meaningfulness of transparency in algorithmic design to the creation of adaptive industry codes for the use of AI. Some questions are specific to the use of AI, while others are embedded in the systemic role of insurance in society and in how insurance companies approach the use of AI. This chapter explores the ethical implications of AI deployment within the insurance domain. The ethical road maps required for the insurance sector to move toward an AI-first world, as well as the pragmatic considerations necessary to enable such road maps, are two to three steps ahead of actual AI deployment. We focus on the previously referenced domains of employment and core tenets of insurance in order to highlight where pragmatic ethical considerations are currently lacking. How far into the future can insurance companies expect AI to operate? What economic, labor, or societal shifts could make AI-dominant decision-making problematic in terms of whose interests are being served, or make its consequences ethically untenable for a particular community or society at large? There may be potential disruptions, oversight mechanisms, and corrective measures from the micro to macro level, including industry-specific codes and regional or global supervisory bodies with the authority to mandate changes in algorithmic models and training processes (Abdulkadir Isa & Fernando, 2023). To initial resisters, this may seem improbable or provocative, but it is important to include it in current ethical discussions about the timescale and impact of sustainable AI deployment.

15.6.1 Establishing Ethical Guidelines

The attention on how AI can be expertly integrated into people's lives has become more mainstream as the technology matures and concerns over ethical, trustworthy, and responsible AI arise. Rules and guidelines are now being set up by many nations to help steer the direction of future AI tool development according to a set of shared and common values. The main research groups in AI have also joined in the effort to release trust- and ethics-building guidelines to users and developers of AI tools and products. Creating and enforcing these rules is no easy task, especially with AI being such a cross-cutting technology utilized in so many industries and areas. AI is inherently useful because of its flexibility. It can be trained for specific jobs, which allows diverse areas to be helped and improved through its use. The tools must be used ethically, are developed with the values of society in mind, and are made to help navigate the potential bad specifically so that they can enact. Countries have also started to invest heavily in research initiatives focusing on establishing and developing explanation methods that can aid in the understanding and associated trust of AI. Important texts have also been published in academic journals on the various aspects of AI explanation and the research agenda associated. Much focus will be put on making various aspects of AI more interpretable and understandable to various demographics to bolster their confidence in such products and aid in the blooming trust in machinery (Poshtiri et al., 2024). Transparency is seen as a key way to engender trust, particularly for high-stakes applications and among disadvantaged groups.

15.6.2 Transparency and Accountability

All stakeholders need to understand how and why algorithms work, such as their logic and rules of inference. Never is this more critical than when a decision about an individual is made that may substantially affect that person's life. Transparency and accountability are often discussed together. Transparency refers to the ease of access to information about AI algorithms: the how and why of their implementation. Accountability is the necessity for stakeholders to follow up and judge the quality of the outcomes of AI algorithms, including requesting updates. If algorithms can be audited and are made public at certain stages of their cycle, they are generally considered transparent (Margan, 2021). Suppose stakeholders have access to independent experts who can either conduct or supervise audits, and those responsible for the development and implementation of these tools are held responsible for their outcomes. In that case, we can say that the AI systems have a mechanism of accountability. Transparency is often a practical challenge when it comes to proprietary commercial algorithms. While external-facing user documentation must be clear and targeted to its audience, both consumers and stakeholders, the more technical internal documentation necessary for explaining use and decision-making within the organization may be less intelligible, but this may be exacerbated when also implementing complex methodologies that face the known difficulty of explainability of AI: most machine learning algorithms cannot be easily articulated in human-readable terms. Suppose an algorithm is unlikely to be easily summarized. In that case, it will be especially critical for the user documentation to be as detailed as required, so that audiences can properly understand how the model operates (Shi & Gan, 2023). These cases involve the "security" aspect of algorithm transparency concerning the lack of public information about the algorithms designed for business purposes, as illustrated in Table 15.2.

15.7 Future Directions for AI in Insurance

Toward the end of 2022, a transition period seems to have begun, currently better described as the use of value with AI in operations, but it is not too early to envisage future longer-term stages of the point of no return of AI ubiquity or omnipresence in insurance. Some areas of AI, such as machine

Table 15.2 Dimensions of sustainability and ethics in AI integration.

Pillar	*Definition*	*Actionable Strategy*	*Success Metric*	*Implementation Barrier*
Human-Centric Design	AI that serves people equitably	Apply user-centered design and accessibility standards	User satisfaction score	Lack of user research investment
Transparency	Explainable decisions	Use interpretable models and visual disclosures	Percentage of explainable decisions	Proprietary model limitations
Accountability	Traceability of outcomes	Assign ownership for model results	Number of resolved AI disputes	Ambiguity in responsibility lines
Fairness	No unjust bias or discrimination	Bias mitigation and demographic parity testing	Disparity impact score	Bias in training data
Privacy Protection	Safeguarding personal data	Implement secure data life cycle practices	Number of breaches/ incidents	Data aggregation from multiple systems
Inclusivity	Access for marginalized users	Multilingual support, simplified interfaces	Access rate by vulnerable groups	Design complexity and localization issues
Environmental Efficiency	Sustainable computing resources	Green data centers, low-energy algorithms	Carbon footprint of AI operations	Performance trade-offs
Governance and Oversight	Organizational control and regulation	Regular ethics reviews and governance board involvement	Frequency of ethical reviews	Governance fatigue
Continuous Training	Education and awareness	Offer mandatory AI ethics training	Completion rate of pieces of training	Engagement and scalability
Life Cycle Evaluation	Oversight throughout AI lifespan	Periodic auditing of deployed models	Audit completion and revision cycles	Maintaining consistent audit standards
Community Impact	Societal outcomes of AI usage	Conduct social impact assessments	Stakeholder trust indices	Measuring indirect effects
Feedback Responsiveness	Adaptive response to input	Implement AI revision workflows from feedback	Turnaround time for changes	Bureaucracy and backlog
Compliance Readiness	Legal and ethical readiness	Monitor international regulations	Percentage of models meeting compliance	Legal complexity and cost
Scalability with Ethics	Ethical practices that scale	Embed values into AI architecture and API (Application Programming Interfaces)	Percentage of scaled systems with ethical features	Ethical dilution with scale

learning, have already been used in insurance for several years. Five emerging technologies have been identified, out of which one or several will be taken on board by insurers, reinsurers, or even InsurTech startups. The five areas are: quantum computing, generative AI, predictive analytics, trusted infrastructure, and superhuman intelligence. These areas could very well be translated as: building more powerful machines, bringing creativity and revolutionizing communication technology, improving decision-making and decision-support at every level of expertise, building untrustworthy infrastructures upon which AI services rest their reliability and business models for insurance cover, and building technological machines for which we have to assume full responsibility therein (Poshtiri et al., 2024). Since the business model and corporate finance of insurance companies hinge on the realization of forecasted "loss ratios," with the correlation between insurance pricing and loss level proving statistically reliable at least in the mid-term, predictive analytics has been applied for decades by actuaries for premium-setting, estimating the size of claims in nature insurance, and even above all within the cycle of the insurance service. It has become a matter of interest to ascertain whether AI would improve upon the predictive power of classical methods or would be used as a complementary technology. Such practical queries in risk assessment or what could be described in the building stage of trust infrastructures in the general terminology of insurance are whether, for what kinds of risks or profiles of risks, or, more generally, for what kind of attributes delivered by what variables are the results of algorithms based on AI generally statistically "better" than classical methods or methods traditionally used in statistical modeling, and what type of companies, whether traditional or "market disruptors," would apply AI for automating the processes of decision (Choi et al., 2024).

15.7.1 Emerging Technologies

As the market for insurance technology continues to accelerate, established insurance players and startups alike are exploring how cutting-edge technologies can be used to create new products and enhance existing products. Some of these emerging technologies that are primarily driven by AI integration, rapid advances, and falling costs in computing power, data storage, and ubiquitous connectivity—both mobile and internet—are propelling the growth of a broad set of insurance technologies. Advanced analytics are being used to enhance the efficiency and precision of many insurance functions, from underwriting to claims processing and fraud detection (Aina et al., 2024). Chatbots and virtual assistants and robotics process automation are automating many routine customer interactions and back-office processes. While these existing technologies have a near-term impact on the insurance industry, several emerging technologies are likely to disrupt the current insurance value chains and models for carriers, brokers, and agents alike. This group of transformative technologies includes blockchain, the Internet of Things, and quantum computing. Blockchain technology is being explored for its potential in decentralized insurance models and capabilities to mitigate fraud (Golden et al., 2016). The Internet of Things is allowing insurers to monitor customer behavior in real time—whether for driving, boating, or remediating flooding damage in a home—creating the potential for "usage-based insurance" at a level of granularity not seen previously.

15.7.2 Predictive Analytics and Risk Assessment

As the foundation of insurance, risk assessment is a core function that has been computerized and digitalized for many decades. Computer models have been used to help underwriters and actuaries establish the probability of loss, and, as a result, set appropriate rates. The whole process of quantitative underwriting relies heavily on the availability of data and the quantitative models used. These data and models vary significantly according to the type of insurance. For example, in a life insurance policy, the characteristics of the individuals, such as age, gender, occupation, health conditions, etc., weigh most heavily in shaping the possible loss from a policy (Oben et al., 2024). Different models are available for underwriting risk in property insurance, and more recently in telematics insurance. In the past, much of the research and model-building for risk assessment of insurance involved regression modeling, followed by goodness-of-fit validation. New data sources and computational power have produced what can be thought of as a revolution in predictive analytics for underwriting in insurance. The paradigm has completely shifted to the so-called machine learning or computational learning. For risk assessment, ML enables the possibility of building new risk assessment models that can go far beyond what traditional methods were capable of (Philip & Suresh, 2024; Townsend et al., 2018). For example, algorithmic trading systems are capable of responding in milliseconds to significant data fluctuations caused by events such as earnings announcements, while traditional stock market predictive models are updated only once a month or even less frequently. The transformation of predictive modeling is made possible by the ability of ML algorithms to handle very large amounts of ever-changing and possibly disparate data.

15.8 Case Studies of Successful AI Implementation

Wherever fast-track development of ethical and responsible AI strategies is hotly debated among insurers and industry stakeholders, these strategies are essential to defining a coherent framework for compliance, accelerated operations, deployed efficiency, and original market differentiation. Thus, this chapter illustrates best practices as a way to share learnings and inspire others to do the same.

15.8.1 Innovation and Ethics in AI Deployment

(i) AI initiatives largely invest in innovation-oriented use cases, which lead the way to a rebirth of traditional sectors. Adverse effects in learning and prediction certainly demand responsibility in data operations and algorithm design. Examples of organizations that have successfully pioneered extensive, creative, and innovative AI strategies deliver on ethical considerations while setting true barometers for digital transformation. Specific lines of international insurance and consumer supervision have also adopted extensive AI services for inbound data scraping, chatbot enhancement, and outbound customer journeys listening and reengineering (Murphy & Moosa, 2021).

(ii) Insurers are focusing on the creation of advanced technology-based consulting services that can help assess risk exposure and risk improvement needs while selecting the most appropriate product at the most convenient cost. Index-based insurance schemes related to catastrophes and integral coverage for extreme events validate and open new opportunities for financial big data. Global macroeconomic risk prediction is supporting the emergence of a new wave of specialized insurers focused on travel insurance. A wide consortium of global insurance players has also encouraged the establishment of a European initiative to promote collaboration between traditional insurance and promotional innovation (Oben et al., 2024). These multi-year partnerships with specific imaginative projects have been centered around offering concrete edge services, particularly customer insight and claims process automation.

15.8.2 Innovative Practices from Leading Insurers

The insurance industry, one of the first to acquire and develop automated systems, is already reaping the benefits of InsurTech and artificial intelligence, becoming one of the strongest sectors for investment. Investors affirm that AI can cut operating costs, and help insurers generate additional revenue via enhanced customer engagement, for example, by anticipating customers' needs and delivering personalized solutions, and fraud prevention. AI deployment can allow insurers to keep premiums low while significantly boosting profitability, since in mature and competitive markets, the gap between costs and premiums can be less than 5%. The data within AI systems requires insurers to reach beyond their client and partner databases to source new information about their customers' lives (Golden et al., 2016). This demand urges collaboration with creative third-party companies in industry, commerce, and technology development. For AI to truly boost revenue, more than enabling limited enhancements in underwriting, risk management, and fraud detection, collaboration is essential. As deeply regulated businesses and custodians of customers' privacy, insurers tread carefully when addressing data privacy and cybersecurity concerns that AI systems routinely raise. InsurTechs are generally at a much lighter risk load; their adroit handling of data privacy matters can serve as a model. The need to partner and the demand for solutions that assure customer value and security compel this caution, making it all the more necessary to maintain strong, ongoing relationships with trusted regulatory authorities (Choi et al., 2024). Value-centric partnerships with third parties supply different inputs: creativity in defining needs and help with design and deployment on the tech development side, and domain content on the operations management side. The ongoing insider/outsider collaboration can be shorter or longer in duration, but is essential for successful AI deployment, at least in the initial, post-proof-of-concept phase.

15.8.3 Lessons Learned from Failures

The successful implementation of AI and machine learning practices in the insurance industry has been deemed by many as the future for the market. Still, there remain significant failures as concrete product launches have produced dire consequences, and dismal real-world effects on customers have pushed companies to retract the tech. These fails, from traders to household banks, have provided essential lessons for those still developing or growing their programs, and the general public, who risk suffering the consequences of negligence. Despite high hopes, the financial workings of institutions may pose a larger challenge than the actual development of the systems (Murphy & Moosa, 2021). Before AI, the day-to-day workings of algorithmic traders were soundly regulated; however, with less demand for such supervision once the bankers had begun using more "traditional" methods, the road had become somewhat clear to drive the high-speed investment vehicles. But once the collaboration was reestablished, the consequences of allowing these powerful tools to be developed again and left unchecked became devastatingly clear. AI trading has continued to suffer meltdowns despite the lessons learned by companies, whose algorithms blew through a superfluous number of transactions in seconds, causing a severe flash crash, with customers collecting virtually phantom amounts through businesses. And they are not alone, with similar incidents occurring in foreign currencies from banks (Golden et al., 2016). The sudden collapse of investors' accounts and the resulting crash in the markets uncovered flaws in virtually all aspects of financial trading. Extra consumer protection must be established as functions become inherently dangerous to the well-being of the public in both financial and product aspects, with little oversight into failures found while still in testing.

15.9 Building a Human-Centric AI Culture

The future is blurring the lines between man and machine, resulting in the success of neither solely independently. To address today's challenges and those that lie ahead, we must come together now more than ever, embracing each other's differences, unique attributes, perceptions, and experiences. Building a human-centric AI culture globally in companies, organizations, and self-governing societies is essential in all efforts around the integration of AI. This work highlights the first key building block of what is needed to make this successful in insurance and other industries wanting to follow suit: education and training in the AI landscape, inclusion of all affected parties during the creation, integration, and use of AI, using diverse AI teams in the understanding, design, creation, integration, and use of AI. The integration of AI has legal, ethical, and moral implications. The integration of AI that prioritizes understanding both the positive and negative impacts of AI, and its potential benefit and potential risks, specifically to the customer who is being assessed and is part of the transaction, must also be taken into consideration. The need for people from diverse and various backgrounds is of utmost importance, encouraging those from minorities, women, transgender and nonbinary people involved in the industry to participate and contribute. Focus on the development of its own people internally and the recruitment to hire and build diverse AI teams, all are key (Choi et al., 2024; Oben et al., 2024). This team must be involved and included at every stage of an AI journey—from understanding both the positive and negative impacts of AI, its potential benefit and potential risk specifically to the customer who is being assessed or is part of the transaction and its collection of data, to building and working with AI and the examination of its performance and use throughout its life cycle.

15.9.1 Training and Development

AI is going to be developed and trained by people. This statement is intentionally simplistic but captures a profound truth: humans, who cannot escape their imperfections, biases, and prejudices, will determine the present and future of artificial intelligence. An AI combined with insufficiently diverse human input cannot manage cultural sensibilities, cannot empathize with circumstances, and cannot understand human nuance. And, because AI and ML decisions are based upon past events, they tend to mirror existing biases and infractions on our cultural, ethical, and social differences (Choi et al., 2024). The AI with which we engage is based in part upon images taken from the real world. Who is responsible for selecting and filtering those images? The people setting AI and ML thresholds, parameters, criteria, and designations all need to recognize the subtle nuances present in the corpus of known human existence. It has been observed that without sensitivity to these issues, AI and ML programs are subject to promote unexpected behaviors and deploy humorless outcomes primarily based upon strict decision trees, self-imposed restrictions, and lack of awareness of unrelated rules or exceptions. In order to prevent the unexplored biasing of AI and ML systems, investment into the training of the people constructing and supporting such systems is vital. The work toward a future where AI recedes into the background creating a human-centered, augmentation-first approach to interaction should influence the way that we consider organization and workforce structure as we move forward (Parlak, 2023; Philip & Suresh, 2024). Training and development should strive toward not only a basic knowledge of AI available to the organization as a whole but sought-after training and awareness through internal and external partnerships invested in diverse employee development. By embracing an organization-wide move toward collaborative inclusion and growth, poorly programmed, unwittingly biased AI and ML products can be avoided in the future (Townsend et al., 2018).

15.9.2 Fostering Diversity in AI Teams

"Because AI is not a perfect solution for everyone, it is imperative to have diverse teams working on the solutions. They can see the gaps, and they can find things that we would miss, because it does not affect us but it might affect other people."

(i) Why diversity matters is no longer a question, and it seems to be there only for answer. The teams building AI solutions must be as diverse as is possible. We all share a wish for fairness and equality, but our life experiences will cause each of us to form a slightly different view of the way the world works and how we want it to change.

(ii) Building AI teams that are committed to supporting multiple racial and ethnic groups, gender identities and expressions, cultures, nationalities, sexualities, beliefs, economic backgrounds, and abilities is an essential step to building fairer products, and rightly so. But it's not the only step. AI technologies and applications span a range of very different products. Each AI team building a particular product should strive to include domain experts who can scrutinize whether developers' values around fairness align with the product's purpose and corpus of users. And that cast a wider net than we might assume, given traditional distinctions. Different teams need these checks and balances (Golden et al., 2016).

(iii) Diversity poses challenges because challenges pose costs at the organizational level. It needs management commitments both to the long-term investments of recruiting people from a larger talent pool and to the short-term difficulties of having to work with increased misunderstandings and differences in working style. But a diverse organization can avoid the costs of groupthink, and the effort pays off in an improved ability to anticipate differences in usage or misinterpretation of the model results (Murphy & Moosa, 2021).

15.10 Conclusion

In conclusion, this chapter highlights the critical importance of developing ethically integrated AI systems in the insurance industry, given the increasing concerns around the potential misuse of these technologies and their implications for fairness, privacy, jobs, human agency, and dignity. The chapter adopts a unique approach of conveying considerations and recommendations through strategic road maps, which balance accessibility with guidance to lay a strong foundation toward a human and ethical future. It presents a set of remedies as infrastructure components, which include regulations, industry best practices, goal-setting, proving grounds for innovative AI technologies and use cases, economic and fiscal measures, as well as skills upgrading and onboarding support. Each road map is designed to enrich its readers' understanding of the current and future industry landscape, shape its growing influence and wisdom, strengthen their expertise, identify future business contexts, and the levers to shape them. It addresses different readers: consumers, insurance companies, solution providers, regulators, and technology developers. The study also sheds light on the role of important stakeholders in strategically steering AI truthfully, deeply, meaningfully, and sustainably with considerations for agency, dignity, fairness, and privacy. In doing so, it highlights the delicate dance of economic incentives and human needs shaping the future of the collaboration between intelligent technologies and individuals.

References

Abdulkadir Isa, U. and Fernando, A. (2023). Explainable AI and Interpretable Model for Insurance Premium Prediction. *Journal on Artificial Intelligence*, *5*(0). https://doi.org/10.32604/jai.2023.040213

Aina, I., Ayinde, O., Thiam, D. and Miranda, M. (2024). Crop Index Insurance as a Tool for Climate Resilience: Lessons from Smallholder Farmers in Nigeria. *Natural Hazards*, *120*(5). https://doi.org/10.1007/s11069-023-06388-x

Alam, A.S.A.F., Begum, H., Masud, M.M., Al-Amin, A.Q. and Filho, W.L. (2020). Agriculture Insurance for Disaster Risk Reduction: A Case Study of Malaysia. *International Journal of Disaster Risk Reduction*, *47*. https://doi.org/10.1016/j.ijdrr.2020.101626

Arockiam, J.M. and Pushpanathan, A.C.S. (2023). MapReduce-Iterative Support Vector Machine Classifier: Novel Fraud Detection Systems in Healthcare Insurance Industry. *International Journal of Electrical and Computer Engineering*, *13*(1). https://doi.org/10.11591/ijece.v13i1.pp756-769

Bermúdez, L., Anaya, D. and Belles-Sampera, J. (2023). Explainable AI for Paid-Up Risk Management in Life Insurance Products. *Finance Research Letters*, *57*. https://doi.org/10.1016/j.frl.2023.104242

Choi, J.H., Choi, Y., Lee, K.S., Ahn, K.H. and Jang, W.Y. (2024). Explainable Model Using Shapley Additive Explanations Approach on Wound Infection after Wide Soft Tissue Sarcoma Resection: "Big Data" Analysis Based on Health Insurance Review and Assessment Service Hub. *Medicina (Lithuania)*, *60*(2). https://doi.org/10.3390/medicina60020327

Ding, H. and Zuo, X. (2024). Construction of Insurance Consumers' Purchasing Behavior Model Based on Big Data Analysis. *Applied Mathematics and Nonlinear Sciences*, *9*(1). https://doi.org/10.2478/amns-2024-0006

Golden, L.L., Brockett, P.L., Ai, J. and Kellison, B. (2016). Empirical Evidence on the Use of Credit Scoring for Predicting Insurance Losses with Psycho-Social and Biochemical Explanations. *North American Actuarial Journal*, *20*(3). https://doi.org/10.1080/10920277.2016.1209118

Jouini, O. and Sethom, K. (2023). AgriBIoT: A Blockchain-Based IoT Architecture for Crop Insurance. *Lecture Notes in Networks and Systems*, *655 LNNS*. https://doi.org/10.1007/978-3-031-28694-0_32

Koster, O., Kosman, R. and Visser, J. (2021). A Checklist for Explainable AI in the Insurance Domain. *Communications in Computer and Information Science*, *1439*. https://doi.org/10.1007/978-3-030-85347-1_32

Margan, S.K. (2021). Drifting into Algocratic Insurance? In *The AI Book: The Artificial Intelligence Handbook for Investors, Entrepreneurs and FinTech Visionaries*. pp. 71–74, Wiley. https://doi.org/10.1002/9781119551966.ch20

Murphy, S.D. and Moosa, S. (2021). The Views of Public Service Managers on the Implementation of National Health Insurance in Primary Care: A Case of Johannesburg Health District, Gauteng Province, Republic of South Africa. *BMC Health Services Research*, *21*(1). https://doi.org/10.1186/s12913-021-06990-4

Oben, E.E.E., Ndi, H.N. and Tchuikoua, L.B. (2024). Livestock Farmers' Willingness to Pay for Farming Insurance in Four Divisions of the West Region of Cameroon. *Asian Journal of Geographical Research*, *7*(1). https://doi.org/10.9734/ajgr/2024/v7i1211

Philip, B. and Suresh, G. (2024). Cultivating Resilience: An In-Depth Exploration of Agricultural Insurance Initiatives and Their Transformative Role in India's Farming Landscape. *Universal Journal of Agricultural Research*, *12*(1). https://doi.org/10.13189/ujar.2024.120109

Pnevmatikakis, A., Kanavos, S., Matikas, G., Kostopoulou, K., Cesario, A. and Kyriazakos, S. (2021). Risk Assessment for Personalized Health Insurance Based on Real-World Data. *Risks*, *9*(3). https://doi.org/10.3390/risks9030046

Poshtiri, Z.P., Soleimani, A.G., Delafrooz, N. and Shahroudi, K. (2024). Designing the Insurance Coverage Model for FinTech Startups: A Novel Approach to the Necessity of Digital Transformation Track of in Insurance. *Interdisciplinary Journal of Management Studies*, *17*(1). https://doi.org/10.22059/ijms.2023.345002.675187

Sachan, S. and Muwanga, J. (2023). Integration of Explainable Deep Neural Network with Blockchain Technology: Medical Indemnity Insurance. *CEUR Workshop Proceedings*, *3554*.

Settipalli, L. and Gangadharan, G.R. (2023). WMTDBC: An Unsupervised Multivariate Analysis Model for Fraud Detection in Health Insurance Claims. *Expert Systems with Applications*, *215*. https://doi.org/10.1016/j.eswa.2022.119259

Shafik, W. (2025). Leveraging emerging technologies for smart and secure software development: blockchain, IoT, and beyond. Modern insights on smart and secure software development, pp. 41–76. DOI: 10.4018/979-8-3693-9851-7.ch002.

Shi, X. and Gan, L. (2023). Equilibrium in Competitive Insurance Markets with Medical Tourism. *Studies in Microeconomics*, *11*(2). https://doi.org/10.1177/23210222211051439

Townsend, C., McIntyre, M., Lakhani, A., Wright, C., White, P., Bishara, J. and Cullen, J. (2018). Inclusion of Marginalised Aboriginal and Torres Strait Islander Peoples with Neurocognitive Disability in the National Disability Insurance Scheme (NDIS). *OPEN ACCESS*, *5*(2).

Van Nguyen, K., Islam, M.R., Huo, H., Tilocca, P. and Xu, G. (2023). Explainable Exclusion in the Life Insurance Using Multi-Label Classifier. *Proceedings of the International Joint Conference on Neural Networks*, *2023-June*. 2023 International Joint Conference on Neural Networks (IJCNN), Gold Coast, Australia. https://doi.org/10.1109/IJCNN54540.2023.10191171

Wall, J. (2022). *Keynote Speech 4: A Conversational AI Approach to Detecting Deception and Tackling Insurance Fraud*. 2021 Tenth International Conference on Intelligent Computing and Information Systems (ICICIS), Cairo, Egypt. https://doi.org/10.1109/icicis52592.2021.9694118

Index

About the Author

Wasswa Shafik (member, IEEE) is a computer scientist, an information technologist and educator, and a research director at the Dig Connectivity Research Laboratory (DCRLab), Kampala, Uganda. He received his Bachelor in Information Technology at Ndejje University, Luweero, Uganda, and his Master in Information Technology Engineering (Communication and Computer Networks Option) at Yazd University, Yazd, Islamic Republic of Iran. He further pursued his PhD in Digital Science (Computer Science) at the School of Digital Science, Universiti Brunei Darussalam, Brunei Darussalam. His research broadly examines, integrates, and focuses on developing computationally and statistically efficient models and algorithms to address complex questions in artificial intelligence and machine learning problems for a sustainable future. His specific research interests include applied artificial intelligence, smart agriculture, computer vision, ecological informatics, digital health and education, and sustainable computing. He has authored, edited, co-edited, and published hundreds of peer-reviewed books, technical papers, book sections, and numerous IEEE International Conferences and prestigious international journals. He has served as a reviewer of several international journals, Scopus, Compendex (Elsevier Engineering Index), and WoS international journals. He further served in different capacities as department support for mathematics for data science, advanced topics in computing, advanced algorithms, and system performance and evaluation. Prior to this, as a department fellow, he served as a researcher associate at the Intelligent Network Laboratory in Iran. He served in different capacities as a community data officer at the Programme for Accessible Health, Communication and Education, as a research associate and data manager at Population Services International, as a data manager and research assistant at the Socio-Economic Data Center, as a research lead at TechnoServe and as a Ag. chief executive officer at Asmaah Charity Organisation.

For Product Safety Concerns and Information please contact our
EU representative GPSR@taylorandfrancis.com Taylor & Francis
Verlag GmbH, Kaufingerstraße 24, 80331 München, Germany